Defending the Public's Enemy

DEFENDING THE PUBLIC'S ENEMY

The Life and Legacy of Ramsey Clark

Lonnie T. Brown, Jr.

STANFORD UNIVERSITY PRESS | STANFORD, CALIFORNIA

STANFORD UNIVERSITY PRESS
Stanford, California

Printed in the United States of America on acid-free, archival-quality paper

Library of Congress Cataloging-in-Publication Data
Names: Brown, Lonnie T., Jr., author.
Title: Defending the public's enemy: the life and legacy of Ramsey Clark / Lonnie T. Brown, Jr.
Description: Stanford, California: Stanford University Press, 2019. | Includes bibliographical references and index.
Identifiers: LCCN 2018054675 (print) | LCCN 2018056419 (ebook) | ISBN 9781503609174 (e-book) | ISBN 9781503601390 (cloth : alk. paper)
Subjects: LCSH: Clark, Ramsey, 1927– | Lawyers—United States—Biography. | Attorneys general—United States—Biography. | LCGFT: Biographies.
Classification: LCC KF373.C562 (ebook) | LCC KF373.C562 B76 2019 (print) | DDC 340.092 [B] —dc23
LC record available athttps://lccn.loc.gov/2018054675

Cover design by Rob Ehle

Cover photograph: Courtesy LBJ Presidential Library

Text design by Kevin Barrett Kane

Typeset at Stanford University Press in 10/15 ITC Galliard Pro

To my grandfather, Dr. Alexis J. Richards, who inspired my professional path, and my mentor, Professor Donald J. Hall, who guided and kept me on this course.

"Speak out on behalf of the voiceless, and for the rights of all who are vulnerable."
Proverbs 31:8 (Common English Bible)

TABLE OF CONTENTS

PROLOGUE

IT WAS THE MORNING of November 8, 2008, and I was about to have my first formal meeting with Ramsey Clark concerning this book. As I waited anxiously for him in the lobby of his aging Greenwich Village apartment building, I pondered what he would be like when we finally met face to face. Although I am somewhat reluctant to admit it, this was actually not my first encounter with him. We had been in each other's company on two previous occasions, but both were memorably underwhelming.

In 1995, while interviewing for a teaching position at the University of Cincinnati College of Law, I was informed by my faculty host that in addition to a full day of interviews, I was also going to be treated to dinner and a lecture by none other than Ramsey Clark. Clearly, I was supposed to be impressed; however, I must embarrassingly disclose that I had no idea who he was. The name sounded familiar, but beyond that I had nothing. Everyone assumed that I knew the luminary with whom I had been invited to dine, and I was too self-conscious to tell them otherwise. They spoke of him as if he were some famous rock star or athlete, recognizable by a single name, like Elvis or Madonna or Prince. So, instead of outing my unhip ignorance, I clumsily feigned familiarity. A rather inauspicious beginning for his future biographer, huh? It gets worse, though.

The dinner was mind-numbing. I recall almost nothing about it except that I was seated at a circular table diagonally from Clark, he talked a lot, and the other dinner guests seemed totally engaged. I can't remember any of the topics discussed or even what I ate. I vaguely recollect that I struggled at first to follow the discussion in an effort to piece together who he was, but I quickly gave up and just tuned out. If anything, I was resentful of Clark for upstaging and monopolizing what was supposed to be my interview dinner. I don't think I spoke a single word besides placing my food and drink orders. To make matters worse, when we finished eating, I still had to sit through his lecture, which I found to be a rambling, sleep-inducing mess, literally. When I glanced over at my interview host, he was sound asleep—head back, mouth open. I figured, thankfully, this would be the first and last time that I would have to endure Ramsey Clark. I was wrong.

Our paths crossed again five years later at the University of Illinois College of Law during my second year there as an assistant professor. This time, I had a better idea of who he was, but only because I had taught a case in my civil procedure class in which he was sanctioned for having filed a frivolous lawsuit. The case was *Saltany v. Reagan*, as in President Ronald Reagan. Not surprisingly, Clark was not the president's lawyer. I will have much more to say about this case later. It is an important part of the journey.

My enhanced familiarity with Ramsey Clark did little to make this encounter any more meaningful than my first. He again delivered a lecture to the law school community, and notwithstanding my best efforts to pay close attention, it was no use. He quickly lost me with another meandering wreck of a speech. The question-and-answer session that followed was even more frustrating. I vividly recall him taking a rather straightforward inquiry from a student and transforming it into an opportunity for a ten-minute soliloquy on something that had nothing whatsoever to do with the question posed. I have since learned that he has a habit of doing this, even in casual conversation. I think it is unintentional, but I'm not altogether sure. Sometimes after a long, seemingly irrelevant verbal detour, he wanders back to the subject and reveals the pertinence of what had appeared to have been a tangent. He may have done that at Illinois, but, at this juncture in our relationship, I had neither the interest nor the patience to stick with him.

After Clark's lecture, there was a dinner in his honor, mercifully far less intimate than our previous one in Cincinnati—just about all of the faculty were in attendance. He said a few words to the gathering, and I do remember him being remarkably unassuming and gracious. I would not characterize him as overtly friendly, but he was definitely warm and genuine. I still did not understand why he seemed to be such a big deal to so many people, but this time I sensed something cool about him. My second meeting with Ramsey Clark created a bit of intrigue. Perhaps it would be worth learning more about him.

This was in 2000, and with each succeeding year, I dug deeper and deeper into his background, focusing principally on his tenure in the Department of Justice, but I also delved, at least superficially, into some of his controversial representations and causes. I began to notice that my students always got particularly energized when we covered *Saltany v. Reagan.* Then I realized that it was actually me who was energized. So maybe I was simply projecting my growing personal fascination with Lyndon Johnson's former attorney general. I really wanted to know why someone who seemed to have been a pillar of the establishment would sue a sitting president. I was curious, but not to the point of wanting to pour myself into what seemed like a side project. I was an untenured assistant professor after all. I did not have time to pursue intellectual titillation.

My perspective changed in 2005 when Ramsey Clark provided me with the incentive I needed to make his journey mine. In that year, he volunteered to be a part of the team of lawyers defending former Iraqi president Saddam Hussein in his high-profile trial on war crime charges. As I had learned through my general research, Clark was not shy about taking on puzzlingly controversial clients, but Saddam Hussein? Why on earth would a former U.S. attorney general willingly side with a man who was the number one enemy of the nation that he had ably and courageously served throughout the 1960s? I had to find out.

I spent almost two years researching and writing a law review article titled "Representing Saddam Hussein: The Importance of Being Ramsey Clark."[1] In doing so, I learned, surprisingly, that no one had, at that point, written a biography about him. I thought that was a travesty. The world needed to know and remember Ramsey Clark, and I decided that I would try to be the one to capture his legacy. Of course, I had no experience with such a project and had no idea where to start. Fortuitously, Professor

Stephen Gillers of New York University Law School, a prominent legal ethics scholar whom I admired and was casually acquainted with, contacted me about my article. As it turns out, he was a close friend of Clark. Professor Gillers had worked on his U.S. Senate campaigns and had been an associate at the New York law firm where Clark practiced during the early 1970s. He indicated that he liked my article, and I told him about my interest in writing a full biography. Gillers then suggested that I write Clark about this and send him a copy of the article.

I was less than enthusiastic about making contact with Ramsey Clark. Honestly, I was kind of hoping that he would never read my article, as parts were critical and questioning. Based upon what I had viewed online, it seemed that he was somewhat of a firebrand and clearly was not shy about filing lawsuits. Maybe he would come after me. After revisiting thoughts of my prior firsthand glimpses into Clark's pleasant, unassuming personality, however, I overcame my fears and sent him the article along with a letter that raised the subject of my writing a biography. I braced for the hit, but several weeks passed and nothing happened.

I had almost forgotten that I had sent the article when I received an unexpected voicemail message. It was warm, appreciative, and thoughtful. I remember him saying that I had done a lot of "heavy lifting" in researching and writing the piece. I found that to be an interesting choice of words, but I was not sure exactly what he meant. Was it simply a commentary on the length of the article—81 pages and 410 footnotes? Or was he referring to the effort I had expended to tell his whole story, not just a one-sided, distorted view? That is what he typically receives in media accounts. Few are willing to do the considerable work necessary to gain a greater understanding of him. I don't think he really cares. He ignores most of it. However, when someone goes the extra mile in assessing his story, he appreciates it.

I was nervous about calling him back, but I did so rather quickly, once I had excitedly told my wife about the message. Shockingly, he answered the phone himself. It was his home number, and he simply said hello. I asked to speak with Mr. Clark, and he said it was him. Since that moment on August 4, 2008, I have always addressed him as Mr. Clark. As we say in the South, "I guess that was just how I was raised." It is not proper to be on a first-name basis with someone of his seniority unless he says it's okay. He has never said, "Call me Ramsey." So, I haven't, at least not to his face.

That phone call—which turned out to be the first of many, many more— went very well. He could not have been nicer. I had so many questions that I wanted answered. Why had he prosecuted the Boston Five in the 1960s for conspiracy to aid and abet draft evasion? Why, on the other hand, had he never prosecuted Black Power originator Stokely Carmichael and black militant H. Rap Brown, chairman of the Student Nonviolent Coordinating Committee, for their antiwar and violence-inducing activities? What was his relationship like with his famous Supreme Court justice father? What did his father think of his son's post-government, controversial undertakings? So many questions, so little time. We were only able to scratch the surface, and I got my first up-close exposure to his rambling, discursive manner of speaking. One minute we were talking about Reverend William Sloane Coffin, Jr.—a member of the Boston Five—and the next thing I knew, he was telling me about his fondness for Chief Justice Earl Warren.

We did briefly discuss the possibility of my writing a book. Ever self-deprecating, Clark questioned my judgment in desiring to write a book about him but said he had no objection so long as I promised to "see the project through."[2] He acknowledged again my "heavy lifting" on the Saddam Hussein article, and complimented me, in a way, by stating that he had seen what I could do. Yet, he seemed a bit skeptical about whether I would persevere with what he knew would be a very challenging and time-consuming undertaking. Not knowing what he knew, I assured him that I would complete the book.

Now, eleven years later I realize why he raised the issue with me. He simply wanted to let me know what I was in for. There was a reason why, as of 2008, no one had written a definitive biography about this fascinating man. His life is a massive and extremely complicated subject. Others had apparently begun the work of telling his story; however, to that point, none had yet made it to the end.[3] At this juncture, it seemed that Ramsey Clark was warning me, perhaps preparing me for possible defeat. Naively undeterred, we agreed upon the mutually convenient date of November 8, 2008, for me to travel to New York for our first in-person meeting to commence my work in earnest. Well, actually our third meeting, but you already know about the other two. I guess the saying is true—the third time is the charm.

Fast-forward to November 8. The doorman at the apartment building told me to have a seat while he called "Mr. Clark" to inform him of my arrival. After making the quick call, he told me that Clark would be right down. I was nervous and a bit frightened. Even though we had had several very pleasant telephone conversations, I was still not sure about him. It was hard to get past all of the negative accounts that I had read online. As my wait got longer and longer, my fears increased. I began to think that maybe he was really some kind of rude prima donna, too full of himself to be punctual for a meeting with a lowly law professor. That seemed farfetched, of course, given what I had witnessed thus far. No need to be paranoid. Just wait.

He eventually exited the elevator and headed in my direction with sort of an old man's shuffle. I later learned that he has a bad foot and had previously broken his kneecap, requiring several surgeries. He looked frail, but still sturdy and tall as he approached, with a slight smile on his face and a warm gleam in his eyes. I stood to greet him, and we shook hands. He said "good to see you," but in a way that I had never heard before. When most people utter this phrase, it sounds like something you robotically say—like, "see you later" or "take it easy." The words aren't intended to convey a literal message. They are alternative ways of saying good-bye. And to me, "good to see you" was typically just another version of hello. Not when Ramsey Clark said it to me, however. He sounded like he really meant every word of what he was saying. Though we had chatted on the phone a few times, he had not actually seen me, or had no recollection of having seen me. Now, he truly was glad to see me in person, observe what I looked like, put a face to a name and a voice. In all of our telephone conversations, he invariably greets me with "good to hear you," and it always has the same sincere ring that "good to see you" had on the day of our "inaugural" meeting.

He gave me a long, firm handshake and apologized for keeping me waiting, explaining that he had to make his wife a latte before he left. I thought that was sweet and cool. I was way off-base with the prima donna speculation. We then left for our breakfast destination—the French Roast—and made small talk the whole way there. He wanted to make sure that we passed a mailbox as he had a letter that he needed to send. I noticed that it looked like official, work-related correspondence, but in his handwriting. Shouldn't he have an assistant that handles this sort of thing? Apparently not. No need to ask someone else to do something that he could just as easily do himself. Definitely not a prima donna.

As we walked, I could not help but focus upon Clark's attire. It was a bit chilly, and he wore a dark, waste-length jacket over a buttoned-down shirt, tucked into a pair of double-knit tan pants—straight out of the 1970s. He completed this ensemble with some hideous, black orthopedic shoes. Although he was neatly dressed, it was obvious that fashion was not of primary concern. His utter lack of pretention only increased my desire to learn more about him. Over a delicious breakfast of eggs Florentine and coffee, for which he insisted on paying, I began my meandering journey to understand the life and legacy of Ramsey Clark.

A PUZZLING JOURNEY

"[L]ife is full of turbulence and conflict, and I never try
to avoid either. In fact, I guess I seek them out because
that's where the chance to make a difference is."

Ramsey Clark[1]

THE SON OF conservative U.S. Supreme Court Justice Tom Clark, Ramsey
Clark rose to the highest reaches of government service as President Lyndon
Baines Johnson's attorney general before turning his back on the public
sector and embarking upon a journey that seems to have led him to what
many would characterize as the dark side. He went from representing the
United States and its citizens to defending and aligning himself with those
deemed enemies of not only America but oftentimes of the entire civilized
world, those so heinous that they are virtually universally condemned—Nazi
war criminals, brutal dictators, genocidal clergymen, and terrorist extremists.
Clark has not only provided legal counsel to individual clients in controversial
court proceedings, he also has acted as a private diplomat of sorts, speaking
out in defense of vilified regimes—such as, Iran, Libya, Iraq, North Korea,
and most recently, Syria—while concurrently blasting his own country and
pointing an accusatory finger at it for what Clark perceives as hypocritical
sanctimony. Who is America to judge? A nation that Clark is fond of describing as the greatest purveyor of violence in the world, using the famous
words from Dr. Martin Luther King, Jr.'s renowned antiwar speech delivered
on April 4, 1967, exactly one year before his assassination.[2]

How did Ramsey Clark go from admired government insider to staunch
defender of the public's enemy? That is the fascinating and complex question
of this book. It is a question that Clark himself has never really been forthcoming in answering. He simply maintains that he has not changed. "Although

I like to think I have grown through the years, I don't think my views have really changed. I fought for the same causes then as I do now."[3] To him, his life path has been fairly steady; he is the same person that he was as attorney general. If anything, society and the issues have changed, not him.

There may be some truth to his cryptic reasoning, but it alone is far too tidy an explanation for what has been perhaps the most enigmatic life of any public figure—ever. That may sound like an exaggeration, but it is not. Clark's life journey has been like that of a sophisticated yet shadowy Forrest Gump, surfacing in a jaw-dropping array of significant national and international events. Name virtually any controversial historical episode between 1961 and 2017, and the odds are that Ramsey Clark had some connection to it.

Desegregation of the University of Mississippi? Clark was there monitoring the combative admission of the school's first African American student, James Meredith. Watts race riots? He chaired a task force that examined the aftermath of the riots and authored a prescient report so honest that President Johnson refused to release it at the time. Civil Rights Acts of 1964 and 1968 and the Voting Rights Act of 1965? His involvement was instrumental to the drafting and passage of each of these landmark pieces of legislation. Assassination of Martin Luther King, Jr.? He was the first federal official on the scene and led the international manhunt for King's killer, James Earl Ray. Vietnam War? He controversially prosecuted high-profile antiwar activists Dr. Benjamin Spock and Reverend William Sloane Coffin, Jr., and he later paradoxically became a leading opponent himself of the war, even traveling to Hanoi to the shock and disgust of the American government and many citizens. Presidential campaign of 1968? He was the whipping boy for Richard Nixon's law-and-order platform, portraying Clark as a weak coddler of criminals and assuring Americans that they would have a new attorney general if he were elected.

Attica prison uprising? Clark along with famed attorney William Kunstler defended inmates charged with the assault and murder of a prison guard. Campaign finance reform? He ran for one of New York's U.S. Senate seats and almost won, even though he eschewed television commercials and refused to accept contributions in excess of $100. Iran hostage crisis? Clark was asked by President Jimmy Carter to assist in efforts to obtain the release of the hostages, and later acted independently of the American government in this regard, drawing a presidential rebuke and threats of prosecution for violating an executive travel ban. America's bombing of Libya? He vocally condemned this action and subsequently sued President Ronald Reagan and British Prime Minister Margaret Thatcher on behalf of civilians who were injured or lost loved ones in the bombing. Military confrontations with Iraq? Clark was at the epicenter, defending and providing aid to the Iraqi people, publicly accusing U.S. officials of genocide, and eventually serving as defense counsel to Saddam Hussein on war crime charges.

Amazingly, these are but a few examples. This list could go on for pages. It seems unimaginable that one man could have participated in so many sensational events in one lifetime, but Ramsey Clark did. And as the years passed, it became ever clearer that there was no issue too hot for him to touch, much to the dismay of even friends and former colleagues. For his choices of clients and causes, he has been called anti-American, a traitor, a communist, a fool, a kook, a dupe, a knee-jerk leftist, an anti-Semite, and a war criminal's best friend. These monikers for a man who spent eight loyal years in the Kennedy and Johnson Justice Departments, making a name for himself as a skilled administrator, a man of impeccable integrity and honesty, and a reliable and strident protector of the public good.

What in the world happened to Ramsey Clark? There are many theories.

Some contend that Clark just changed dramatically after his departure from the Justice Department. Journalist Josh Getlin postulates that "[s]omewhere along the way, the former attorney general . . . took a hard left and hasn't looked back."[4] Norman Podhoretz, former editor of *Commentary* magazine, is more direct and caustic in his assessment, summing up Ramsey Clark's post-DOJ form of radicalism as consisting of simply hating the United States and being willing to side with anyone who opposes it.[5] Columbia professor of sociology and journalism Todd Gitlin agrees: "Any tyrant or war criminal, as long as they're on the wrong side of the United States of America, [Clark] defends them. And not just in court; he seems to defend their point of view."[6]

A common thread in Clark's legal representations is that he seems to select clients who could aptly be characterized as enemies of the public, or at a minimum, enemies of the United States. Along these lines, one attorney sympathetic to many of the causes Clark supports damningly explained why in other areas she dramatically parts ways with him: "I perceive him as thinking that any enemy of the United States is a friend of his, and I think that leads him into representing people he should not."[7]

Although one of the most common critiques is that he is simply anti-American, Clark maintains that he loves his country so much that he is willing to oppose it in the interest of holding it accountable. To his mind, "If you really love your country, you work hard to make it right. . . . Anything else is an extreme act of disloyalty and an extreme failure of courage."[8] In other words, Clark considers himself a patriot, not a traitor. "A patriot should be first and most vigorous in criticizing and urging correction of his or her country's failures, omissions and wrongs."[9] The supreme wrong in Clark's view is our nation's failure to live up to its purported cherished ideals of democracy, freedom, and justice. His personal devotion to these tenets may very well be what drives him.

Clark has on a number of occasions expressed the view that America, as a monolithic whole, has become too obsessed with its military force and its wallet:

> America must liberate itself from its love of violence and its love of wealth—which are closely integrated. We are a plutocracy in the purest sense of the word—a government of wealth. . . . I completely reject violence. And yet, at the sacrifice of everything else, America spends hundreds of billions of dollars annually on violence. We really believe that might makes right, and that leads us to perpetual war.[10]

Clark's disdain and skepticism regarding American government officials is piercing. He believes that there is no level to which these individuals will not stoop. "Anything's possible as far as what they'll say; we know that. . . . They don't know as much as they claim to know, and they don't tell us what they really know. And they lie."[11] However, such harsh criticism of U.S. leaders by Clark is inequitable. He seems unable or unwilling to denounce his nation's opposition, its enemies. For example, during the Persian Gulf War, Clark heaped blame on the American government but would not similarly condemn Saddam Hussein for Iraq's invasion of Kuwait, only mildly conceding the wrongness of the invasion. He defended his one-sided appraisal by contending that "it's not only intellectually justifiable, but I think it's morally correct where there's a great danger attached to what you're talking about to address a single aspect of wrongful conduct, particularly when it's your own country. And if you don't, then you are used in the spreading of hatred."[12]

While there has undeniably been a fairly radical shift over the years by Ramsey Clark regarding both the content and passion behind his views, many fail to recall that he has always been a rather outspoken and polarizing figure. Some mistake his service within the Justice Department as signifying an embrace of the system. They forget or else fail to recognize that he was one of the most controversial attorneys general in our nation's history. Even as a government insider, Clark was viewed by contemporaries as being outside the mainstream, too liberal, too dogmatic, too committed to the plight of the oppressed. One commentator observed that Clark's "uninhibited idealism and fervent defenses of civil liberties earned him the nickname 'the Preacher.'"[13] John Tower, the Preacher's home state senator, believed such a predisposition actually rendered Clark "psychologically unsuited to the job of law enforcement."[14]

Along the same lines, Clark's compassionate treatment of black civil rights proponents, including radical fringe leaders of that movement—such as Stokely Carmichael, H. Rap Brown, and even the Black Panthers—inspired the wrath of President Johnson, FBI Director J. Edgar Hoover, and much of white middle- and working-class America. Calls for his ouster were common and popular. Holding Ramsey Clark up as the very symbol of what was wrong with America—not enough law and order—was integral to the 1968 presidential campaigns of Richard Nixon and George Wallace.[15] Even liberal Democratic nominee Hubert Humphrey found it necessary to distance himself from Clark, assuring the public that he too would have a new attorney general if elected.[16]

Following his departure from the Attorney General's Office, and clearly before as well, Clark evinced a deep-seated concern regarding the direction of America. In a 1970 interview following the publication of his bestselling book *Crime in America*, he said:

> I am—this sounds corny—concerned about this country. I have a hangup about that. I think we're in trouble, and I'm going to try to find ways to lend a hand. I'm concerned about racism, civil rights, civil liberties and freedom. I worry about the quality of life and international violence. I don't have anything else that really interests me, so I am going to try to lend a hand in those areas.[17]

Remarkably, this statement accurately captures what Ramsey Clark has done since 1961. He has thrust himself into the mix in relation to all of these issues; his interest has been steadfast, and he has certainly sought to lend a helping hand wherever he could. In his view, "[t]he measure of your quality as a public person, as a citizen, is the gap between what you do and what you say."[18] He has always wanted his country's expressed devotion to liberty, equality, and justice to match its conduct both at home and abroad. This is what inspires him. It is not hatred of America, but rather love that fuels his desire and efforts to hold his country accountable. Or at least that is what Clark tells himself.[19]

In many respects, Ramsey Clark's purported relationship with the United States can be analogized to that of a parent to a child. Most would agree that it is not true love for a parent to fawningly praise a child no matter how bratty or impolite the child is. Such parenting is likely engendered by guilt or fear of rejection, or a combination of the two. Or perhaps it's just born of pure laziness. True love is harder. Telling a child no or taking away cherished privileges in order to teach a life lesson is not comfortable; however, those who sincerely love their children and have their long-term best interests at heart are not reluctant to take such harsh and unpopular positions. And they are unconcerned with the conduct of other children, just as Ramsey Clark is loath to criticize other nations.

Granted, his treatment of the American government may, at times, approach what some might deem to be child abuse. Even loving parents who mean well can go too far on occasion. A "my country can do no wrong" attitude, though, probably goes too far in the opposite direction.[20] There is surely a happy middle ground, but that is not where Ramsey Clark has chosen to reside.

Some of Clark's acquaintances, rather than trying to explain what he does or why he does it, simply acknowledge that his transformational trajectory is somewhat inexplicable. His former law partner Melvin Wulf considers Clark to be a "total enigma," even though the two men worked together closely.[21] Wulf seems skeptical that anyone truly knows what motivates Clark, because he is "a bit impenetrable. He keeps his own counsel very, very closely."[22] Warren Christopher, Clark's deputy attorney general and later President Bill Clinton's secretary of state, was more circumspect in his assessment of Clark's perceived evolution. According to Christopher, "If there has been a change, it's Ramsey expressing deep things within his personality. But I wouldn't want to be a pop psychologist about this. I guess you'd just have to take a look at him from the very beginning."[23]

Clark's close friend Victor Navasky, former editor of *The Nation* magazine and manager of Clark's 1974 Senate campaign, believes that he is misunderstood and perhaps too forward-thinking for his era. Navasky views Clark as being "in the tradition of the great dissenters, Holmes, Black, and Brandeis, who say things that may turn out to be way ahead of their times, and were not appreciated in their own day."[24] Similarly, concerning Clark's many controversial representations, Navasky posits that he "really believes that everybody in our society is entitled to a lawyer and that every opinion, no matter how revolting it may seem, is entitled to expression. In the end, he really doesn't care what other people think, or whether that gets him into trouble or not."[25] Clark's controversial representation of reputed Nazi war criminal Karl Linnas is one powerful example that seems to support Navasky's character analysis.

In 1987, Clark was invited to speak in Los Angeles by the Jewish Federation. The event was canceled, however, because of Clark's defense of Linnas, as well as public comments he had made proclaiming that because so much time had elapsed, Linnas should essentially get a pass. He was an old man, and the government should leave him alone.

> You don't go after septuagenarians 40 years after some god-awful
> crime they're alleged to have committed. . . . If you do, then what
> it really means is, if we find you, we'll kill you, so act accordingly. It
> means that we are going to be condemned to eternal conflict, which
> is my great concern. We've got to find a way to end wars.[26]

Clark's association with Linnas alone was patently offensive to many, but his
overt entreaty for clemency based merely on the passage of time seemed to
add injury to insult. His remarks on Linnas's behalf are difficult to comprehend given the severity of the crimes with which he was appropriately charged.
Why would Clark say such things? Did he feel the same way about the prosecutorial pursuit of an elderly Byron De La Beckwith—the racist murderer
of 1960s civil rights leader Medgar Evers—thirty years after the murder? If
so, it does not appear that he ever publicly voiced this opinion.

It is possible that Clark's statements may have stemmed more from his
antiwar views and strong beliefs in nonviolence, rather than from any la-
tent animosity or insensitivity toward Jews. He equated going after Linnas
with a never-ending battle. From his perspective, at some point we have to
simply move on. This position, though, seems contrary to Clark's personal
disposition. He has never been one to give in when faced with what appears
to be a futile battle. Ironically, that may be both his greatest strength and
his most significant flaw.

Doggedness or zeal—as it is commonly labeled in the realm of legal
advocacy—is held up as a virtue. The most revered courtroom advocates
throughout history are inevitably praised for their zealous advocacy on
behalf of clients. In 1820, Lord Henry Brougham uttered the most famous quote regarding a lawyer's commitment to a client in reference to
his defense of Queen Caroline of England on the charge of adultery. Lord
Brougham graphically explained the lengths to which a true advocate must
be willing to go:

> [A]n advocate, in the discharge of his duty, knows but one person in all
> the world, and that person is his client. To save that client by all means
> and expedients, and at all hazards and costs to other persons, and,

amongst them, to himself, is his first and only duty; and in performing this duty he must not regard the alarm, the torments, the destruction which he may bring upon others. Separating the duty of a patriot from that of an advocate, he must go on reckless of the consequences, though it should be his unhappy fate to involve his country in confusion.[27]

There are few in American history that fit this conception of a lawyer's role better than Ramsey Clark. Many of the causes and clients that he has chosen to champion over the years required him to affirmatively snub his own country, the very nation that he so ably served from 1961 to 1969, ultimately as attorney general. This quality is in many respects admirable. Clark was willing to ceaselessly criticize and defy his own government in pursuit of justice and peace, thereby exposing himself to harsh public criticism and even hatred. On its face, that surely seems courageous, maybe even messianic. However, just because one purports to be acting in the name of justice and peace does not make it so. Those are mere labels that can be stamped on any cause. Former Attorney General Jeff Sessions had claimed to be furthering justice by cracking down on low-level drug offenses; others considered Sessions's actions to be the very antithesis of justice, ensuring the continued mass incarceration of disproportionate numbers of black and brown citizens.[28]

No doubt, everyone is entitled to representation, and fulfilling that role in the American legal system furthers the concept of justice, at least from a procedural standpoint. Procedural justice, though, is different from justice in terms of the cause. If Ramsey Clark injected himself into unthinkable cases in order to ensure that procedural justice was served, few could reasonably argue with that. However, the justice he often seeks also appears to relate to the underlying substance of these matters, not just the potential unfairness of the process. Indeed, rather than simply providing a meaningful defense in order to guarantee fair treatment for his demonized clients, in many representations Clark has positioned himself as a veritable spokesperson, inexplicably rationalizing or even promoting his clients' questionable causes and viewpoints.

David Strachman, an attorney who served as opposing counsel in a number of actions in which Clark represented the Palestine Liberation

Organization (PLO) and Syria, expressed respect for the former attorney general as a lawyer and a person, but consternation over Clark's penchant for embracing the indefensible beliefs espoused by his clients. According to Strachman, it seems as though Clark's objective in his representations is not always to secure justice. If that were the case, he maintains, one would expect Clark to concentrate on making technical procedural arguments. However, Clark instead adopts "loser positions" that frequently embody his clients' messages or else advocates for alternative interpretations of those messages. Is there a method or at least a pattern to this seeming madness? One interesting theory offered by Strachman is that Clark fancies himself as a modern-day Don Quixote. He is attracted to impossible battles, preferring to fight at the thorny margins of society rather than within the comfortable confines of the status quo.[29] This suggests that notwithstanding his aura of integrity, Clark's motivations may be more contrarian than principled, making his perplexing client choices and public policy positions even harder to fathom.

If Clark worked to achieve some type of equitable compromise, even when advocating unwinnable theories, maybe his preference for defending the rights and views of the public's enemies would be more understandable. But that has not been his standard approach. Instead, he digs in his heels, convinced of the justness or correctness of his position, and refuses to inch toward the middle. When it comes to matters of this nature, Ramsey Clark is resolute in his belief that he is right. With such a mindset, he cannot capitulate in the face of that which he *knows* to be wrong; he stands on what he deems to be principle when any reasonable person would seek compromise.[30] This dogmatic rigidity, perhaps more than anything else, is what has hurt him throughout his public and private professional careers. It is what has alienated many and relegated Clark to only passing mention in accounts of seminally important historical events in which he played significant roles.

What is the real answer to the puzzle of Ramsey Clark? The varying assessments reveal that there likely is no satisfactory way to encapsulate who he is. There are multiple layers of complexity that include innumerable contradictions: a peace-loving man who defends war criminals;

a death penalty opponent willing to represent the executioner; a loving husband and father who was an inveterate workaholic, absent from home far more than he was present. In short, Ramsey Clark is a mystifying enigma, with enormously admirable, even heroic qualities, combined with an abundance of confounding imperfections. This is why he is so fascinating and why this book is so necessary. He is an incalculably essential figure in American history, who has been largely overlooked, misunderstood, or else simply dismissed as irrelevant. This is unfortunate, as his life offers important lessons about courage, equanimity, patriotism, and, most of all, justice.

I have been fortunate to get to know Ramsey Clark well over the past eleven years, but our relationship has only added to my confusion. I remember our first official meeting vividly. I had read all sorts of articles about him and had formulated an image that left me simultaneously starstruck (because of the magnitude of his accomplishments) and apprehensive (due to the viral characterizations of him as evil). That meeting and those that followed have alleviated my ambivalence toward Clark, at least on an interpersonal level. He is charming, kind, down-to-earth, and incredibly sincere. I cannot help but like him. My encounters with him, however, have done little to advance my quest to discover the Holy Grail that is his core. Indeed, I have determined that such a quest is as futile as many of the legal battles in which he has inserted himself. The truth of the matter is that an examination of Ramsey Clark's life will yield different conclusions depending upon the perspective of the examiner, as well as the substance of what he or she examines. To one, he may be a hero; to another, the devil's closest ally.

As a result, my objective in this book is not to personally assess Ramsey Clark and communicate my own subjective conclusions about him. Rather, it is to act as an informed reporter, recounting significant events, legal representations, stories, and relationships from his illustrious life, while also adding what I hope will be meaningful observations. From this, one can draw one's own conclusions, though my goal is to give the world a much-deserved glimpse into the substance of a man who is unknown to far too many. The volume of potential material is mind-bogglingly vast and cannot possibly be depicted in studied, comprehensive detail. I have thus selected what I deem to be most historically consequential and revelatory.

Author James Baldwin once wrote that "a journey is called that because you cannot know what you will discover on the journey, what you will do with what you find, or what you find will do to you."[31] This book endeavors to tell the story of Ramsey Clark's life journey, but the real journey is in the examination of that life. I cannot tell you what you will find, or what you will do with it, or how it will affect you. All I can tell you is that it is a journey well worth taking.

CHAPTER ONE

BABY BUBBA

"The birth of a healthy baby is a source of joy that
makes the deepest sorrow seem selfish."
Ramsey Clark[1]

SOME BIOGRAPHIES begin with an abundance of chronological detail, devoting inordinate space to intricate descriptions of family trees and distracting accounts of personal histories before moving into the more interesting aspects of their subject. While I respect such thoroughness, I have no intention of replicating this approach. Portions of Ramsey Clark's early life are important in tracing his journey, as are certain historical tidbits about his ancestors. I will limit myself only to those, comfortable in the knowledge that my chronicling is not complete and that others could make different choices.

It wouldn't be hard to predict Ramsey's initial professional path and the lofty public service status he would ultimately attain based upon a brief examination of his familial pedigree. But nothing in his past could foreshadow the controversial private practice to which he has devoted the majority of his adult life. His mother's father, William Ramsey, served as a judge on the Texas Court of Criminal Appeals and as a justice on the Texas Supreme Court.[2] His paternal grandfather, William Clark, was no slouch either; as a highly regarded attorney, he distinguished himself by serving as the president of the Texas Bar Association.[3] William Clark, however, harbored and vocally espoused some hard-core racially insensitive views,[4] views antithetical to those his famous grandson would later embrace.

Ramsey's father, Tom Clark, surpassed the renown of both his father and father-in-law by rising to the pinnacle of the legal profession as an associate justice on the United States Supreme Court. Although his appointment to the Court was surely the capstone of his legal career, Tom had already made a name for himself prior to that, holding various high-level positions within the Roosevelt and Truman administrations, including serving as attorney general. Before his rise to governmental acclaim, though, he was just a local lawyer struggling to provide for his family.

Ramsey, the second son to Tom and Mary Ramsey Clark, was born in Dallas, Texas, on December 18, 1927. His brother, also named Tom, but known as Tommy, was 2 years old at the time. It's no secret that toddlers are not especially articulate. As a result, Tommy's valiant efforts to say "baby brother" apparently came out sounding like "baby Bubba." Thus, he unintentionally saddled Ramsey with the nickname Bubba, later shortened to Bub and used by family and others close to Ramsey throughout his youth and beyond.[5]

Bub looked up to his older brother, and the two boys had a very close though short-lived relationship.[6] At the age of 6, Tommy contracted spinal meningitis and died shortly after the onset of the illness. This was a devastating blow to the Clark family, with Ramsey's mom taking it especially hard. The birth of Ramsey's sister Mimi, however, helped ease the intense loss that Mary Clark felt and likely is what saved her life.[7]

Given Ramsey's young age, it is impossible to know what sort of impact this tragedy had on him. He probably barely even understood the concept of death. However, it presaged the parade of punishing tragedies that he would face throughout his life, personally and professionally. Many of the people Ramsey respected and loved the most were tragically and unexpectedly taken away at various points throughout his long life. The assassinations of President John F. Kennedy and his younger brother Attorney General Robert Kennedy seem most poignant in this regard. As an enthusiastic member of the Department of Justice under President Kennedy, Ramsey was whimsically hopeful about the future of America. The president's brutal, untimely death changed this rosy outlook, rocking the idealistic Justice Department newbie to his core. John was the older brother of Bobby, Ramsey's boss, and that undoubtedly made him experience the grief in a most profound and familiar way. He had tremendous admiration and affection for Bobby. Their parallel personal losses surely must have contributed in some way to this strong affinity.

The murder of Martin Luther King, Jr.—followed closely by that of Bobby Kennedy—had to have been gut-wrenching for Ramsey. But in each instance, he had to maintain his composure as attorney general, the country's chief law enforcement official. Containing his pain and emotion in order to persevere must have been difficult, but he had been there before, and he would sadly return to the same tragic sphere again and again. First, he dealt with the unexpected loss of his father, who died of a heart attack while staying alone in Ramsey's New York apartment; then, some years later, Georgia, Ramsey's beloved wife of sixty-one years, succumbed to lung cancer, as did his son Thomas shortly thereafter.[8]

I will say more about these deaths in later chapters, but the point for now is that his initial brush with personal loss may have somehow conditioned him for what was to follow. It has been said that familiarity can breed contempt, but it can also foster understanding and compassion. Although I think that every successive death took a powerful toll on Ramsey Clark, he learned something from each one, and he miraculously did not let any of them break him. He pressed on, comforting others when he was in great pain. I witnessed this personally in discussing with him the illnesses and deaths of his wife and son. He deflected any concern I exhibited toward him and instead sought to focus on me and my family.[9] Maybe this was a coping mechanism to avoid displays of grief or perhaps it reveals something more penetrating about the substance of Ramsey's character—an innate desire to care for and tend to the feelings of others.

Following young Tom's death, the Clark family remained in Dallas where Tom, Sr. practiced law in the District Attorney's Office and in private practice before being tapped to join President Franklin Delano Roosevelt's Justice Department when Ramsey was 9. Although Tom believed that he was to assume the position of assistant attorney general for the Claims Division, upon arriving in Washington with his family, he learned that this was not to be the case.[10] As a result of some political friction between President Roosevelt and Thomas Connally, Tom Clark's nominating senator, the elder Clark was named a special assistant assigned to the

War Risk Litigation Section, a lowly post in an undesirable section of the DOJ.[11] But Tom worked hard, and with the help of some connections, he was later able to obtain a position working in the Antitrust Division, first in New Orleans and later in California.

These moves, and the demanding nature of the jobs, proved highly disruptive to the family. While Tom was in New Orleans, his family moved to Dallas. When he assumed his California position, Ramsey stayed behind in Dallas with his grandmother in order to finish the sixth grade, but he joined the rest of the family in Los Angeles after that.[12]

It was in Los Angeles that Ramsey met his dear friend Robert Huttenback, who would go on to become the chancellor of the University of California–Santa Barbara and would later be convicted, along with his wife, of embezzlement.[13] Ramsey represented his friend in a subsequent matter related to this conviction. As young schoolmates, Ramsey fondly recalls that his first reaction upon meeting his future friend was one of shock and modest dismay, engendered by Huttenback's wardrobe. Huttenback was apparently wearing lederhosen. Ramsey's initial impression was that Huttenback was pretentious and odd, but even at this early stage in his life, Ramsey was slow to judge and condemn, and he therefore gave his future pal the benefit of the doubt, resulting in an enduring friendship.[14]

Ramsey happily remembers family leisure time in Los Angeles when his dad was not otherwise preoccupied with work. The Clarks' stint in California, however, took a dramatic and unfortunate turn after the Japanese bombing of Pearl Harbor and the onset of World War II. Tom got the dubious distinction of being appointed to oversee the notorious internment of Japanese Americans as the civilian coordinator of the Alien Enemy Control Program for the West Region, described by one DOJ official as the "toughest and nastiest job in the Department."[15] Though Tom fulfilled his responsibilities in this role, he would later express grave regret for the part he played in this dark chapter in American history. In 1966 he publicly apologized for the episode by conceding that "I have made a lot of mistakes in my life, but one that I acknowledge publicly is my part in the evacuation of the Japanese from California in 1942."[16]

Tom Clark, though a conservative, always supported the civil rights of all people, notwithstanding his father's vocal and adamant denunciation of race mixing.[17] In fact, it may have been William Clark's harsh racial vitriol that pushed his son in the opposite direction. In any event, his public act of contrition should not have been a surprise. Rather, the surprise, in hindsight, is that he dutifully accepted such an ignoble assignment in the first place. This may reveal an important difference between Tom and Ramsey. Tom was surely a principled man, but he seemed more willing to go along with the mainstream than would prove to be true of his son. Johnson's special counsel Larry Temple observed that he never saw the president order Ramsey to do anything. Even when Johnson strongly expressed certain views, if Ramsey disagreed, he did what he thought was right.[18]

Given this independent disposition, one would suspect that young Ramsey might have been angry with his father at the time for not standing up to President Roosevelt. However, he was only 13 when the Japanese bombed Pearl Harbor, and thus his staunch antiwar backbone had apparently not yet formed. As a result, his response was rather typical for a boy his age during that era. Ramsey was so moved by the attack on his country that he wanted to do something about it, something significant. He sought to join the war effort by attempting to enlist in the Marines.[19] The future putative "hater of all things American" volunteered to defend our nation on the frontlines. He willingly applied for membership in what he would later refer to as the corrupt U.S. military-industrial complex. Even if he fully understood his father's role in the Japanese internment, it does not seem that this would have necessarily upset the youthful, gung-ho Ramsey.

Although his young age blocked his first attempt at military service, Ramsey's desire to participate in the U.S. war effort did not wane, and at age 17 he joined the Marines. He dropped out of high school in order to do so, over the stern objections of his father, who was obviously concerned for his son's safety. After recovering from hernia surgery and completing boot camp, Ramsey embarked upon what would be a transformative war adventure as a corporal in the U.S. Marine Corps. World War II was nearing its end, and Ramsey never took part in battle, but he did witness up close and personally the devastating effects of the prolonged armed conflict.

Stationed first in London and then in Paris, Ramsey served as a courier delivering confidential diplomatic and military information from Washington to Paris and then to various locations in Europe and North Africa.[20]

His role required extensive travel throughout those regions, and after the war ended, he continued his courier work as a State Department employee, making further trips to eastern and western Europe and various countries in Latin America where he was stationed. Ramsey was appalled at the death and destruction he saw during his travels, and it left an indelible impression upon him.[21] He also experienced what life was like in foreign lands as compared to the United States. He felt drawn to many of the countries that he visited, especially those in Latin America, to which he would ally himself in later years. Ramsey developed a particular affection for Cuba, which foretold his subsequent close association with that nation's much-maligned leader Fidel Castro. Interestingly, Brazil likewise earned a special place in Ramsey's heart. He was amazed at the beauty and diversity of its people and the utopian manner in which all races seemed to blend together.[22]

While Ramsey was still stationed in Europe toward the tail end of the war, Tom Clark was appointed U.S. attorney general by President Harry Truman. Truman had been Roosevelt's vice president, but Roosevelt died in April of 1945, and Truman assumed the presidency. In his capacity as attorney general, Tom and his wife Mary traveled to Europe to observe the Nuremberg trials, though Tom had no official role in the proceedings. Ramsey joined his parents in Nuremberg and watched portions of the trials with his father. The trials were of alleged Nazi war criminals and were conducted before international military tribunals established by the victorious Allied forces. Ramsey's later representation of reputed Nazi war criminals, and his well-documented opposition to anything resembling "victor's justice," suggest that the trials may have influenced this gravitation to the side of the condemned.

Some have suggested that he is anti-Semitic—a topic that will be examined more thoroughly in a later chapter—and Ramsey's Nuremberg experience, along with the odd story of his acquisition and longstanding retention of a large bust of Adolf Hitler, could fuel further speculation in this regard. In the late summer of 1946, not long before Ramsey was discharged, he went on several courier missions to Moscow. In making these trips, he had a stopover in Berlin for up to two days. During one of these stopovers, he went with a few fellow soldiers to visit Reich Chancellery, which housed

the office of Germany's chancellor, Adolf Hitler. It had been badly damaged during the war. While walking through the extensive rubble down a
corridor, Ramsey stumbled upon Hitler's ceremonial office and then noticed a detached wooden door on the ground that was similar to the one
leading to the führer's office. He lifted the door and beneath it he found
a large, 20-pound bronze bust of Hitler. He wrapped it in his jacket and
smuggled it back to the United States and has either stored or carted it
around with him ever since.[23]

Why has Ramsey Clark kept a replica of perhaps the evilest, most despised individual of all time? At age 84, still in possession of the metallic
head, he contended that he did not "want [it] to fall in to the hands of
anybody who could use it politically—either Neonazis [sic] or those who
would use it to demonize Germany."[24] He was contemplating donating it
to a museum at that time, but apparently did not do so. During a visit with
him in June 2016, he asked me if I wanted to see the bust. Of course I did.
He searched throughout his apartment, but he was unable to locate it. I
suspect that it may be in storage somewhere, or else he finally got around
to donating it. I think his plan had been to give it to a museum in Dresden.
Maybe that is its ultimate resting place.

Objectively, Ramsey's salvaging of the Nazi leader's bust seems quite
strange. Why smuggle it back to the United States and retain it for over
seventy years? It is a peculiar novelty item if that is how he viewed it—not
something that one would typically want to show off to family and friends.
It evokes disgust and disdain, not exclamations of "awesome!" Why preserve this?

Interestingly, he did not openly display the bust in his home. He kept
it out of sight—retained but not flaunted. In contrast, until very recently a
large bronze bust of Mahatma Gandhi occupied a prominent place in the living room of Ramsey's Greenwich Village apartment. This one makes more
sense. It is no surprise that a man who deeply admired Martin Luther King
would have a makeshift shrine devoted to Dr. King's inspiration—Gandhi.
However, it makes his ownership of Hitler's head all the more perplexing.
I just don't get it, but his obsession with demonization and the recurring
use of that concept as a justification for representing a litany of accused war

criminals and terrorists lead me to believe that there is more to the story of the bust. As we see in Chapter 11 "Saddam Hussein," many of Clark's clients have been compared to Hitler, particularly Hussein himself. Is there some connection? More on this later.

Ramsey Clark was honorably discharged from the military in September 1946 and was ready to enter college, but his timing was off; plus, he had not yet finished his high school work. Consequently, he took some correspondence courses in order to obtain his diploma and get a jump on his college work. In the spring semester of 1947, he enrolled at the University of Texas–Austin and in just two years obtained his bachelor of arts degree. More importantly, he met and married the love of his life, Georgia Welch, in April of 1949.

After receiving their degrees in June of that same year, the couple moved to Chicago to begin studies at the University of Chicago—Ramsey in law and history and Georgia in political science. Chicago allowed Ramsey to count his last year as an undergraduate (in which he took various required law courses) as his first year in law school.[25] This enabled him to move through school more quickly. By the end of 1950, Ramsey had earned both a J.D. degree and a master's degree in history, and Georgia had earned her master's in political science.[26] He ridiculously crammed what should have been eight years of schooling into less than four, a feat he was able to accomplish by taking classes nearly year-round.[27]

Ramsey's decision to attend Chicago was contrary to his father's preference, which was Harvard. Tom, however, did not exert undue pressure on his son to attend Harvard, nor even to become a lawyer. He had endured a father who was very domineering and controlling, and he was intent on not making the same mistake with his son.[28] According to Ramsey, "My father was determined that I wouldn't be told what to be, which was probably the only circumstance, considering my generally ornery disposition, whereby I could become a lawyer."[29] Some have suggested that his decision to attend Chicago was an act of rebellion by Ramsey, but it appears that it was principally influenced by the president of the University of Chicago, Robert Hutchins, whom Ramsey greatly admired and with whom he would become very close. Hutchins's strong independent streak and sound moral character were attributes that resonated with Ramsey and undoubtedly helped shape aspects of his own personality.[30]

Besides its influential president, Chicago also had some noteworthy future legal stars during those years, apart from Ramsey Clark. Among them, Abner Mikva, who would later be a U.S. congressman and a judge on the prestigious U.S. Court of Appeals for the D.C. Circuit; Robert Bork, who would likewise become a judge on the D.C. Circuit, but who is more famously known for his failed nomination to the U.S. Supreme Court in 1987; Patsy Mink (then, Takemoto), who would later serve as a U.S. congresswoman and the first Asian American to seek the presidential nomination; and George Anastaplo, who is best known for being denied admission to the Illinois bar for refusing to answer a question about whether he was a member of the Communist Party. Although Ramsey was too busy to establish any truly close friendships while in law school, he did become friends with Mikva and Mink and developed a particularly interesting connection to Anastaplo, which I will elaborate upon in a later chapter. Not surprisingly, Ramsey does not appear to have had any relationship to speak of with Bork. While it could have been his conservative politics, it is more likely simply attributable to the fact that Bork's law school career was interrupted by military service. Hence, Bork actually ended up graduating a few years after his esteemed classmates.[31]

After graduation, Georgia and Ramsey moved back to Texas; they settled in Dallas, where Ramsey would work in the family law practice, first known as Clark, Coon, Holt & Fisher and later as Clark, Reed & Clark, with Ramsey being the second "Clark" in the name. His private practice in Dallas bore little resemblance to the high-profile matters of great public concern that he would later handle in both his government and post-government days. Mostly, he represented business interests, with a heavy emphasis in the area of antitrust. Ramsey said he loved to sue oil companies.[32]

Notwithstanding this commercial focus, he did periodically dip his toe into public interest work, and his inherent attraction to civil rights issues was evident. Besides taking on occasional criminal cases for people that one might refer to as "crazies," Ramsey established Dallas's first legal aid society in 1953.[33] One lawyer at the firm, Bill Keller, had worked for the

National Labor Relations Board and provided Ramsey with insight into how to mediate civil rights disputes. Based on this experience, he would later recommend the creation of the Community Relations Service in the Johnson administration.[34]

While Ramsey enjoyed his law practice, there were two far more important developments in his life during his time in Dallas. In 1952, Georgia gave birth to their first child, Ronda Kathleen. Two years later their second child, Thomas Campbell, arrived.[35] Ronda was born with severe health-related issues—she was deaf, could not speak, and suffered from cognitive deficiencies. At first, Ronda's disabilities were not recognized as permanent, and Ramsey and Georgia sought diligently to ascertain a medical remedy for her conditions. Ronda underwent multiple tests, ordeals that her loving parents endured with her. Reportedly, Ramsey, so intent on understanding what his daughter was going through, insisted that every test she underwent be performed on him as well.[36]

Despite the challenges posed by Ronda's health issues, by all accounts the Clarks lived a relatively happy and serene life in Dallas. Over time, however, Ramsey tired of private practice and wanted to put his legal skills to use in a more meaningful way. He would embark on a public service path as a member of President Kennedy's Justice Department.

CHAPTER TWO

THE PREACHER

"By instinct, I am a maverick. I rather like the
outside way. It's more fun."
Ramsey Clark[1]

ON NOVEMBER 8, 1960, the nation narrowly elected John F. Kennedy as its thirty-fifth president. The victory of this young, charismatic, and inspiring leader seemed to usher in a new day for America. Much like the historic election of President Obama in 2008, Kennedy's ascension to the highest office in the land offered hope to many for a new national order, maybe even a new world order. Great things were on the horizon, and Ramsey Clark desperately wanted to be a part of the action. He was not really enjoying private practice, except for his criminal and family law cases, and was itching to do more with his legal training than simply litigate for personal gain. As he put it, he yearned "to be involved in the major and troubling problems of the country."[2] That was his motivation for seeking a position with the new administration. His influential father was shocked but supportive.[3]

Presidents typically tend to reward those who are most helpful during their campaigns with prestigious appointments. Ramsey Clark did not fall into this category. He had voted for the new commander in chief, but beyond that, he really had not done much, except for some very minor work on the campaign locally.[4] He didn't even attend the Democratic National Convention.[5] Clark had been relatively apolitical across the board up to this point in his life. Besides performing some work on the 1952 and 1956 Adlai Stevenson presidential campaigns and on his good friend Harold Barefoot Sanders's legislative campaign in Texas, Clark had no political involvement except as a voter.[6]

In order to land a spot in Kennedy's Department of Justice, he would need to cash in on some high-powered, family-related political connections. Fortunately, his father was a close friend of Lyndon Johnson, Kennedy's vice president. Larry Temple, one of Tom Clark's law clerks and later President Johnson's special counsel, described the two men as "fast and famous friends" and indicated that Johnson was "one of the half dozen people of whom Tom Clark was most fond."[7] This warm relationship enabled Johnson to get to know Ramsey personally over the years.[8] Young Ramsey frequented the Johnsons' home to use their manual crank ice cream freezer. More significantly, it appears that Johnson may have had something to do with Ramsey obtaining a job with the Department of the Interior during two of his teenage summers working as a surveyor.[9] On top of Johnson's personal familiarity with Ramsey, Tom also openly lobbied his friend to speak with President Kennedy about his son.[10]

Besides the Johnson connection, Congressman Sam Rayburn from Texas, then Speaker of the House, was likewise a dear family friend who thought highly of Ramsey and made a personal visit to President Kennedy on his behalf. Furthermore, Tom's colleague on the Supreme Court, Associate Justice William O. Douglas, was a big fan of Ramsey and fortuitously also happened to be very close with the Kennedys.[11] The combined influence of all of these powerful individuals enabled Ramsey to receive serious consideration for a Justice Department position.

Fancying himself as an antitrust specialist, he was most interested in being assistant attorney general for the Antitrust Division. However, the political forces backing him were not enough to get Ramsey that gem of a post. Kennedy appointed Lee Loevinger instead, leaving two possible positions—the Office of Legal Counsel (OLC) or assistant attorney general for the Lands Division. Although OLC was by far the more glamorous of the options, Ramsey believed that it was too political and would not afford him the opportunity to perform hands-on legal work.[12] Therefore, at the youthful age of 33, he accepted the nomination to head the Lands Division, somewhat to the surprise of his father, who understood that area to be the graveyard of the DOJ.[13]

Notwithstanding the perceived mundanity of the work of the Lands Division, Ramsey characteristically took his role quite seriously and performed exceptionally well, converting the so-called graveyard into an important and efficiently run operation.[14] He was actually somewhat well suited for the position. In addition to being an avid outdoorsman, Ramsey spent two summers (1943 and 1944) working as a surveyor out west for the Department of the Interior in the General Land Office, learning the mechanics of making land measurements to ascertain the correct legal boundaries of pieces of property.[15] Ramsey loved this work, describing it as one of the most transformative experiences of his life, along with his military service.[16] Although he claimed no legal specialization in the field of property law, he did have some exposure to the handling of condemnations and other real estate matters while in private practice.[17]

Much of Ramsey's work related to water rights issues and acquisition of land for federal purposes. When he took over as head, there was a sizable backlog of cases, which he was successful in reducing fairly quickly. One area of particular significance in this regard pertained to Native Americans' property rights claims. Attorney General Bobby Kennedy was passionately empathetic toward America's indigenous people and pressured Ramsey to ensure that the DOJ did right by them. This impressed Ramsey and added to his high regard for Bobby, whom he and others in the DOJ referred to as Bob. As directed, Ramsey labored intently to resolve favorably the voluminous docket of cases. Interestingly, as someone who was normally loath to compromise, preferring instead to persevere to achieve what he deemed to be right, Ramsey actively pursued settlements in the Native American cases, as well as in many of the other matters handled by the division.[18] Although the results were not necessarily lucrative for the claimants, the division's approach was compassionate and pragmatic, yielding many positive outcomes.[19]

Ramsey was a notably effective bureaucrat from an administrative standpoint. Apart from shepherding the reduction in the division's caseload from 33,000 to less than 10,000 in two years,[20] during his first year he streamlined its staff by 10 percent and its budget by 5 percent. His efficiency did not go unnoticed. When his father went before Congress to present the Supreme Court's budget request, it was observed by one congressman that he hoped the justice's budget was as good as his son's. In response, Justice Clark demurred: "Well, you see, he takes after his mother."[21]

Although Ramsey enjoyed his work in the Lands Division, the true passion of his tenure in the Justice Department was civil rights, and fortunately for him, Bobby Kennedy, out of necessity, took a team approach to this exploding area of the sociopolitical landscape, as well as to other important issues facing the DOJ.[22] In 1954, a unanimous Supreme Court, which included Tom Clark, held segregated public education to be unconstitutional in the landmark case of *Brown v. Board of Education*.[23] What seemed to portend a seismic shift in the nature of race relations in the country proved to be little more than a tremor, with school systems intentionally dragging their feet in making any meaningful progress toward integration. While society was supposed to be moving in the direction of a more equal and unified existence, debilitating segregation and inequality in terms of voting rights, public accommodations, employment, and public safety, as well as education, remained the order of the day. The Kennedy administration sought to make actual inroads into this pervasive social condition, albeit with slow deliberation and caution.[24]

One of the obvious areas that needed tackling was education. The law of the land had been declared by the nation's highest court, and the federal government was obligated to ensure that it was followed. Accordingly, Bobby dispatched selected DOJ officials to various locations throughout the South to monitor and enforce local compliance with the *Brown* decision.[25] With his youthful appearance and good-old-boy southern ways, Ramsey was a natural for this assignment. No one would suspect him of being a federal operative. As he has put it, he could "pass,"[26] borrowing a euphemism frequently employed by blacks in referring to the ability of light-skinned individuals to "pass" themselves off as white. Ramsey could pass as a traditional white southerner, and that made his job easier or at least more clandestine.

Throughout late 1962 and 1963, he worked in Alabama, Georgia, South Carolina, and Louisiana to enforce the federal school desegregation mandate. His efforts were very direct, pursuing in-person meetings with principals, teachers, sheriffs, school board members, and even judges. As one might expect, his diligence was not typically welcomed. He recalls that one federal judge in Baton Rouge actually refused to even meet with him.[27] Nevertheless, he was undeterred in his mission. Ramsey thoroughly investigated the school districts and made thoughtful recommendations concerning the additional measures that needed to be taken to effectuate the law of the land, at one point proposing to Bob Kennedy a "radical revision in the Administration's anti-segregation litigation policy."[28]

Ramsey played a major role in monitoring the historic admission and early matriculation of James Meredith as the University of Mississippi's first African American student beginning in September of 1962.[29] Initially, he acted as the communication liaison between various federal law enforcement agents deployed to the campus to maintain peace, the university's administration, and the attorney general, who was at the White House during this tense episode. Later, Ramsey acted as the DOJ official in charge on campus in relief of Deputy Attorney General Nicholas Katzenbach. He continued to monitor the situation into the spring of 1963 and eventually approved of the scaling back of the federal military's presence. This opening foray into the heart of the civil rights arena captivated Ramsey's sense of justice and fairness and would profoundly influence his tenure in the DOJ, as well as the path that his professional journey would take thereafter.

Consistent with his now characteristic self-righteous persona, during his stint in the Kennedy Justice Department, Ramsey was predictably known for his willingness to speak his mind, even if he was alone in his opinion. From early on, it was evident to his colleagues that he was a man of high moral character, not shy about adhering to principles in which he believed, no matter what the consequences. Ed Guthman, a Kennedy DOJ spokesperson, observed that "Ramsey usually was the one who raised the moral questions about issues."[30] John Seigenthaler—Bobby Kennedy's executive assistant and later noted editor of the Nashville newspaper *The Tennessean*—had a similar take on Ramsey's willingness to share his views. He recalled that his boss hosted regular lunches for all of the assistant attorneys general at which he expected those in attendance to provide him with forthright answers to questions posed. He noted that Ramsey especially stood out in these sessions, demonstrating his independent, civil libertarian streak and never shying away from forcefully articulating his opinions.[31]

Later, during Ramsey's service under President Johnson, some thought that the president "seemed to go almost too far in allowing [him] to serve as the moral conscience of the White House, to the point of obstructing policy."[32] Fred Graham, a reporter with the *New York Times*, once expressed the view that Ramsey's "Achilles' heel, if any, [was] not complaisance to pressure from above but a tendency to stand on principle when practical men would compromise."[33] Johnson's special counsel Larry Temple went even further, observing that Ramsey was "tough-minded," preferring to resign rather than do something with which he disagreed.[34] His uncompromising approach led to his being nicknamed "the Preacher" by his Justice Department contemporaries.[35] The Preacher would soon have his rigid orthodoxy shaken by a tragedy of unthinkable proportions.

On November 22, 1963, President Kennedy was taken away by an assassin's bullet, and with that Ramsey Clark lost a great deal of the hope that he'd harbored for America. The president's death likely conjured up childhood memories of the loss of Ramsey's own brother, on top of the palpable sadness emanating from the country's tragedy. It was devastating. He wondered whether he would ever be happy again, and on more than one occasion, while driving from work to his home on Lake Barcroft in Falls Church, Virginia, he contemplated taking a fatal plunge off the Memorial Bridge. Thankfully, he never did. I once asked him what stopped him from driving his car into the Potomac River, and he smiled and pointed to his daughter Ronda (64 years old in 2016).[36] She would have been 11 at the time of President Kennedy's tragic death. The president was gone, but life went on, and Ramsey had a great deal to live for.

Following the assassination, Vice President Johnson ascended to the presidency, much to the dismay of the grief-stricken attorney general. It was well known that Johnson and Bobby did not like each other. Bobby's disdain for the new president was particularly strong, especially now that he had assumed the position formerly occupied by his beloved brother. Johnson, on the other hand, was now somewhat willing to bury the hatchet, at least superficially, and work with Bobby, believing that this would be politically prudent. He therefore left the DOJ intact and endeavored to establish a meaningful working relationship with his attorney general. Bobby was not interested. He was intensely distrustful of Johnson and viewed every move that the president made with skepticism.[37] As his Deputy Attorney

General Nicholas Katzenbach later put it, the dream that Bobby had for his brother's presidency had been "usurped by Johnson, a man Bobby saw as an unprincipled and crude politician who would lie and cheat to attain his personal objectives. . . . Bobby simply did not want to share the Kennedy dream with this man."[38]

Although Johnson tried to make things work with Bobby, he was as suspicious of his predecessor's brother as Bobby was of him. Bobby remained as attorney general, at least in title, through the fall of 1964, but his departure was inevitable. There was some speculation of Bobby as a possible running mate for Johnson, but the president did not want a Kennedy that close to the number one post. Johnson diplomatically put the prospect of the vice presidency to rest. Instead of teaming with Johnson or accepting some other lesser conciliatory appointment, Bobby opted to run for the New York Senate seat. Following Bobby's nomination, President Johnson named Nick Katzenbach "acting" attorney general. Katzenbach was a loyal Kennedy follower, and hence it seems plausible that Johnson may have held some misgivings about him, which may explain why the president kept him in the "acting" role for several months after his 1964 campaign victory over Republican presidential nominee Barry Goldwater. Eventually, Johnson made Katzenbach his formal choice for attorney general, and he was easily confirmed.[39]

Meanwhile, following Kennedy's assassination, President Johnson moved Ramsey Clark from the Lands Division to the White House for a brief stint as a presidential assistant, working on appointments and other special matters for the president.[40] In that capacity, Ramsey got to know Johnson better from a working standpoint and also learned a great deal about how the White House operated, lessons that would be beneficial to him in his next role as deputy attorney general.[41] Katzenbach was amenable to having Ramsey as his number two and recommended him to Johnson. However, Katzenbach was aware that Ramsey's elevation may have been a foregone conclusion. It seems likely that the president wanted someone whom he viewed as loyal to him as a check on the attorney general.[42]

Though the Yale-trained Katzenbach was not particularly impressed with Ramsey's educational pedigree or legal abilities, he liked him, believed that he was good on civil rights, and considered him to be a person of great integrity and high moral principles, maybe to a fault. According to Katzenbach, "[t]here were better lawyers available, but none more idealistic in his view of what law should accomplish."[43]

Besides Johnson's apparent desire to have a family friend in a high position in the Justice Department and Katzenbach's comfort with that choice, it also seems that Tom Clark may have played a role in Ramsey's selection. While many have downplayed the importance of Tom's relationship with President Johnson as influencing Ramsey's DOJ trajectory, there is certainly evidence to the contrary. One significant example was Tom's overt effort to promote his son as a potential operative within Johnson's 1964 presidential campaign. In July of that year, Justice Clark sent his close personal friend a letter extolling Ramsey's credentials:

> He knows all the U.S. Attorneys well—is President of the Federal Bar and I find has lots of good friends in the Reclamation states on account of his work in the Lands Division. He could do a grand job on any confidential work at the convention and during the campaign.[44]

If nothing else, communications of this sort helped keep Ramsey on the president's radar, which helped secure his nomination as the DOJ's second in command.

Once nominated, the confirmation process was completely without controversy. Bobby Kennedy enthusiastically endorsed Ramsey before the Senate Judiciary Committee, which accepted his qualifications for the deputy attorney general post without dissent.[45] Ramsey had amassed an impressive record as head of the Lands Division and had otherwise distinguished himself through his professional service. While his hands-on experience in the civil rights area was not a point of discussion during his confirmation hearing, that exposure would quickly pay significant dividends in his new role, as the nation plunged into the most tumultuous period of the civil rights movement. Ramsey's cool head, steady hand, and compassionate heart were much needed attributes when America's cities began to erupt in 1964.

CHAPTER THREE

"LANGUAGE OF THE UNHEARD"

"I recognize then, as I have before, that pent-up frustrations and
anger frequently overwhelm reason in people who have suffered
great deprivation. My objective was to communicate."
Ramsey Clark[1]

THE 1960S WERE generally a tumultuous time in our nation's history in
terms of civil rights. Although President Kennedy, for political reasons, had
been reluctant to make civil rights a signature component of his administration, the exigency of the times ultimately left him little choice. Discrimination in education and public accommodations was squarely within the
crosshairs of the civil rights leadership during the early 60s. Kennedy took
some proactive measures on the education front with regard to school desegregation, really out of necessity, as southern states were all but ignoring
the Supreme Court's *Brown v. Board of Education* decision. In the area of
public accommodations, however, he seemed content to let the status quo
plod along. But a provocative and effective strategy known as the Freedom
Rides powerfully disrupted that mindset.[2]

The Freedom Rides, which began in May 1961, were initiated by an
organization known as the Congress of Racial Equality (CORE), led by
James Farmer.[3] CORE recruited and trained civil rights activists—African
American and white—in the techniques of nonviolent direct action as a
means of challenging segregation in interstate commerce throughout the
South, which persisted notwithstanding a Supreme Court decision that had
declared the practice unconstitutional.[4]

The Freedom Riders traveled on Greyhound and Trailways buses
throughout the South openly flouting the vestiges of Jim Crow separation in
bus terminals and facilities.[5] Their direct action was effective in antagonizing

the holders-on to racial segregation and exposing their continued discriminatory conduct, but at the price of personal safety. Southern racists did not take kindly to blacks using "whites only" restrooms or dining at the same counters as "law-abiding" white people.They threatened, intimidated, and often physically assaulted the nonviolent Freedom Riders, most brutally in Anniston, Alabama, where a bus filled with Freedom Riders was attacked by the Ku Klux Klan and set on fire, as local law enforcement looked the other way.[6] The juxtaposition of the pacifism of the black and white Freedom Riders with the barbaric cruelty of white mobs created a potent and moving image that was broadcast across the country.

The objective was to make the powers that be take notice and address the racist recalcitrance of the Deep South, and in this regard the Freedom Riders were ultimately successful. President Kennedy indeed took note, but he was not at all happy about what was taking place. As historian David Halberstam recounted in his seminal civil rights book *The Children*, Kennedy viewed the Freedom Riders as "a pain in the ass."[7] His brother Bobby was equally frustrated with the group, especially when the young members of the Student Nonviolent Coordinating Committee (SNCC) took over the mantle of the Freedom Rides from the older CORE membership and insisted upon continuing with the same strategy.[8]

The Freedom Rides created great risk of physical violence, forcing the federal government to intervene to provide protection, which in turn had the potential of alienating conservative Southern Democrats.[9] In an effort to avert this political quandary, Bobby enlisted his executive assistant and close friend John Seigenthaler to endeavor to persuade Diane Nash, the leader of the SNCC students from Nashville, to call off the group's planned Freedom Ride to Birmingham, Alabama, but Nash refused.[10] As concerns increased, Bobby directed Seigenthaler to work with Alabama's governor to make certain that state officials would protect the Freedom Riders. After a grueling session with Governor John Patterson, Seigenthaler eventually received the assurances that he sought.[11] Nevertheless, the journey of the Freedom Riders did not end well.

Escorted by police while traveling from Birmingham to Montgomery, the law officers abandoned the Freedom Riders upon arriving in the state's capital city, and they were intentionally left at the mercy of a violent mob.[12] Among those viciously attacked in the melee were John Lewis, future civil rights icon and congressman, and, even more significantly for purposes of the desegregation effort, John Seigenthaler himself. While trying to help two Freedom Riders escape the violence, Seigenthaler was struck with a lead pipe and lay unconscious in a gutter for an extended period of time.[13] Although Seigenthaler eventually was taken care of and escaped more serious harm, the episode so infuriated Bobby Kennedy that the entire tenor of the federal government's enforcement of the Supreme Court's desegregation mandate changed dramatically. Indeed, in retrospect, John Lewis views the attack on Kennedy's right-hand man as the turning point in terms of the administration's focus on civil rights more broadly.[14]

All those around Bobby noticed a change in his perspective and approach. As Halberstam put it, "His attitude toward the segregationists changed overnight to cold anger."[15] Concerns about political appeasement of white Southern Democrats were no longer a part of Bobby Kennedy's civil rights calculus.

Ramsey Clark witnessed up close his boss's palpable transformation, and it suited the young assistant attorney general just fine, affording him greater opportunities to personally engage in the promotion of civil rights. Ramsey was instrumental in proactively guiding the administration toward securing justice and equality for America's black citizens. Specifically, in the aftermath of his experience with James Meredith's admission to Ole Miss, he drafted a memo to the attorney general that outlined and called for the enactment of far-reaching civil rights legislation.[16] Among other things, Clark proposed the creation of what would later become the Community Relations Service,[17] an agency of the DOJ with primary responsibility for dealing with tense racial situations, such as those endured by the Freedom Riders. Although President Kennedy did not live to see this legislation enacted, he initiated and championed the concept, with his brother's able assistance, and President Johnson followed through by passionately and skillfully shepherding it to fruition. On July 2, 1964, he signed into law the landmark Civil Rights Act of 1964, for which Ramsey Clark had provided the principal early inspiration.[18]

As his tenure in the Justice Department progressed, Clark's commitment to and involvement in the civil rights area became increasingly pronounced. In early 1965 President Johnson decided to move Clark from his position in the White House to the Department of Justice, in the position of deputy attorney general. His new role was fairly well defined, dealing primarily with overseeing the day-to-day operations of the DOJ and serving as a liaison between the department and Congress, especially with regard to judicial nominations. In addition to many other responsibilities, Clark worked diligently on the president's behalf to secure passage of the Voting Rights Act of 1965.[19] As a prelude to this, however, he was fully thrust into the very heart of the civil rights movement when he was assigned to oversee for the federal government the march from Selma to Montgomery on March 21, 1965. This was the third march, the previous two having been unsuccessful—one ended in violence, and the other was intentionally aborted.

Martin Luther King, Jr.'s purpose in organizing the marches and other protests in Selma was to draw greater attention to the voting rights issue and thereby pressure Johnson to expedite his efforts in this critical area.[20] The first march took place on March 7, 1965, and ended tragically, with local law enforcement unleashing a brutal attack on the marchers as they attempted to cross the Edmund Pettus Bridge in Selma. Seventeen marchers had to be hospitalized, and around fifty others were injured, including John Lewis, who famously suffered a fractured skull.[21] The march was technically unlawful, at least as proclaimed by Governor George Wallace.[22] The local police used a so-called commitment to law and order as a convenient excuse for their vile response. This fateful day would later become more familiarly known simply as Bloody Sunday, descriptively capturing the spirit of what had transpired. Media images of pliant black Americans being mercilessly beaten by Alabama state troopers and deputies were telecast around the nation and the world, eliciting widespread reactions of shock and disgust.[23]

Undeterred, Dr. King immediately resolved to march again on Tuesday March 9, and he recruited clergymen from throughout the country to join him. In the interim, however, U.S. District Judge Frank Johnson, on his own initiative, issued a restraining order that prohibited another march until further notice.[24] As a result, Dr. King's plan was really more of a head fake than an actual march, because he had no intention of leading the large gathering of national clergy in open defiance of a federal injunction.[25] The marchers trekked across the Edmund Pettus Bridge, stopped before reaching the troopers stationed on the other side, knelt in prayer, and then turned around and walked back across the bridge, even though the troopers had backed off to allow them passage.[26] Fittingly, this second march was dubbed Turnaround Tuesday.

Later—after hearing testimony from John Lewis, among others, and viewing footage of the Bloody Sunday carnage—Judge Johnson lifted the injunction, ruling that Dr. King and his followers had a constitutional right to carry out their march from Selma to Montgomery.[27] The removal of this judicial impediment, however, was by no means a guarantee that a third march would be peaceful and safe.

Indeed, between the time of the second and third marches, in a fairly transparent attempt to obviate the need for a march, President Johnson accelerated the pace toward legislatively securing voting rights for black citizens. In particular, he publicly announced his personal commitment to guaranteeing voting rights to all citizens and delivered one of his most memorable speeches to Congress in which he formally called for the enactment of legislation. President Johnson famously proclaimed voting rights as not just a "Negro problem" but an "American problem" and shockingly ended his seismic address by predicting victory, coopting the mantra of the civil rights movement: "Because it is not just Negroes, but really it's all of us, who must overcome the crippling legacy of bigotry and injustice. And— *we—shall—overcome*."[28] Although there was great joy and excitement over the president's moving endorsement of the voting rights cause, the march would not be shelved. With Judge Johnson's legal imprimatur, the march was scheduled to proceed on March 21.

There was, of course, great concern about the safety of the marchers. Judge Johnson seemed unwilling to issue his order until he had assurance that the federal government would "back" it.[29] Governor Wallace was perceptibly uncommitted to ensuring that no violence occurred, but rather was more concerned with his not being held responsible in any way for allowing the march to proceed. After privately negotiating with President Johnson,

Wallace publicly decried the march and essentially forced the federal government into providing the necessary security.[30] Ultimately, U.S. Army troops were deployed, and members of the Alabama National Guard were federalized to safeguard the marchers against a repeat of Bloody Sunday.[31] The responsibility for coordinating and overseeing this operation was placed in the able hands of Deputy Attorney General Ramsey Clark.

Upon arriving in Selma, accompanied by Civil Rights Division First Assistant Stephen Pollak and DOJ Director of Public Information Jack Rosenthal, Clark met with Dr. King, Hosea Williams, and other black leaders involved with the planned march. Rosenthal recalls that this initial encounter was quite heated and uncomfortable for Clark. While thankful for the federal government's willingness to provide protection, the leaders were very angry over how long it had taken for this involvement to occur. After all, this was the third march. According to Rosenthal, Clark remained calm and diplomatic throughout the onslaught and, in the end, was able to diffuse what could have escalated into a highly volatile and divisive situation.[32] With this potential crisis averted, the deputy attorney general turned his full attention to protecting the marchers.

Clark was intensely concerned about their safety, and was especially worried about a possible assassination attempt on Dr. King.[33] The latter fear was that a sniper in a building or on a rooftop might try to take King out, ironically a fate that awaited him three years later. Clark and the federal officials that he oversaw worked virtually around the clock to protect the marchers—from traffic-related concerns, because they were literally marching on a highway, as well as from potential violence by what we might today refer to as counterprotesters. He even had to intervene at the outset of the march to avoid what would have been an unnecessarily combative display by the soldiers stationed on the bridge to provide protection. The general in charge wanted all those under his command to have bayonets on their rifles, which Clark viewed as highly antagonistic and threatening to the marchers. He directed the general to get his men off the bridge and to sheath their bayonets. When the general refused, Clark had to enlist the authority of Defense Secretary Robert McNamara to force him to comply.[34]

With this initial crisis forestalled, the march proceeded for the ensuing five days, culminating on March 25 in a massive showing of support, with upwards of 25,000 strong gathering in front of the state Capitol building in Montgomery.[35] Governor Wallace was in the Capitol on that day, and the marchers sought to present him with a petition calling for the protection of blacks who wanted to register to vote. Although he declined to accept it at first, Clark engaged in some negotiations that eventually enabled several members of the group to deliver it to Wallace's executive assistant, as the governor would not personally receive the document—a symbolic victory nonetheless.[36]

The more important achievement, however, was the peaceful and safe completion of the march, thanks in substantial measure to Ramsey Clark. There was a great sense of relief and pride for a mission accomplished. This was a big deal, especially in light of the violent attack that had been unleashed on the marchers during their initial attempt to complete the journey from Selma to Montgomery on Bloody Sunday.

Unfortunately, Clark and his team's moment in the spotlight was fleeting. Before their plane even landed in Washington en route from Montgomery, tragedy struck again. Viola Liuzzo—a white woman who was moved to join the marchers by President Johnson's stirring address on voting rights—was shot and killed. She had been transporting marchers back to Selma, and on a return trip to Montgomery, some local Klansmen followed her and Leroy Moten, who was black, and fired shots into the vehicle killing Liuzzo.[37] Ramsey Clark was crushed. Although he wanted to travel back down to Alabama, he realized that there was not really anything that he could do.[38] The FBI was investigating, and it ended up solving the crime rather quickly with the help of an informant who had been a passenger in the Klan car.[39]

Despite the sad ending to the third Selma to Montgomery march, it was a singularly inspiring event that, combined with the president's articulated commitment to the cause of black voting rights, led to the successful enactment of the Voting Rights Act of 1965. As deputy attorney general, Ramsey Clark had primary responsibility for the legislation and worked long and hard on it, even while dealing with the march-related issues.[40] Signed into law by President Johnson on August 7, 1965, the Voting Rights Act was a groundbreaking advancement in the area of civil rights, perhaps the administration's single most important accomplishment.

Although such developments as the Civil Rights Act, the Voting Rights Act, and the completion of a peaceful civil rights march in the Deep South signified progress, in reality tangible change was painfully slow. Clark himself acknowledged as much, observing that the administration's efforts were always "more cautious . . . than the conditions warranted."[41] This tentative mindset was most prevalent among whites in positions of authority.

Even those sympathetic to the civil rights cause urged Dr. King and other black leaders to be patient in their quest for equality and justice. Indeed, King's fellow clergymen openly criticized him for his impetuousness: "All Christians know that the colored people will receive equal rights eventually, but it is possible that you are in too great a religious hurry."[42] As King pointed out, white moderates "lived by a mythical concept of time," "constantly advis[ing] the Negro to wait for a 'more convenient season.'"[43] They were unhappy with the tension that King's followers created through their nonviolent direct action, preferring to avoid the discomfort of witnessing disturbing clashes between white police officers and black resisters. Let societal inertia work its magic. Good things come to those who wait, right?

Dr. King doubted this truism, resignedly concluding that "wait" had essentially been synonymous with "never."[44] In his classic "Letter from a Birmingham Jail," King poignantly called out clergymen and white moderates for what he perceived as their insulting paternalism and tacit acceptance of the status quo. If his nonviolent civil disobedience could not meaningfully speed the advancement toward equal rights, passively waiting for social attitudes to naturally evolve would most assuredly solidify complacency.[45]

The snail's pace in racial progress suggested to African Americans that their unequal, subjugated status in society lacked national importance; it was as if they were being moderately appeased when necessary, but principally ignored. One of the most frustrating realities for blacks in America throughout our nation's history has been their persistent treatment as a nonentity by the majority of white people. Author Ralph Ellison's masterwork *Invisible Man* powerfully captures this pervasive, debilitating experience, observing that "I am invisible, understand, simply because people refuse to see me."[46] It is bad enough to be overtly discriminated against and vanquished to second-class citizenship, but insult is piled upon injury when blacks are wholly disregarded. Historically, most white citizens have simply trudged along separately from blacks, oblivious or indifferent to the "lesser" race's problems and complaints. Indeed, segregation was America's legally institutionalized method for ensuring that whites could righteously exist in blissful ignorance of the painful indignities that defined black citizens' existence. Out of sight, out of mind.

Dr. King's nonviolent strategy was wearing thin among younger blacks— in particular, because of its perceived ineffectiveness. They were getting beaten up and thrown in jail but little was changing. There was a growing parallel movement to forsake nonviolence and instead to engage in open confrontation, resorting to aggression if necessary. Malcolm X had espoused this view throughout the early 60s, but the movement captured a larger following when Stokely Carmichael, a disciple of Dr. King's and the chairman of SNCC, took up the mantle. He was, by far, the most vocal and charismatic leader of this emerging sect.

Although the organization that Carmichael led was founded on principles of nonviolence, in the mid-1960s he began to take SNCC in an entirely different direction, one that focused on obtaining black power, a mantra that he coined.[47] In a seminal speech on June 16, 1966, following release from his twenty-seventh arrest, Carmichael vehemently maintained that he was not going to jail anymore and asserted: "We want black power! . . . We have begged the president. We've begged the federal government— that's all we've been doing, begging and begging. It's time we stand up and take over."[48]

Black leaders, such as Carmichael, who forcefully spoke out against racial oppression, were pejoratively labeled as troublemakers, agitators, and militants. Even Dr. King, with his decidedly more diplomatic methodology, was often characterized in a similar fashion. Notably, in King's "Letter from a Birmingham Jail," he warned those who denigrated his peaceful approach that such reactions would push blacks in a more volatile and dangerous direction.[49]

The negative propaganda constituted a not-so-subtle effort to undermine the work of civil rights leaders by making them appear sinister and subversive, enemies of civilized society. This tactic, combined with overt physical intimidation and oppression in black communities by local law enforcement, served to discourage more blacks from joining in the movement and to comfort whites by making them feel safe and secure. However, this manufactured stasis was destined to break down. Black people could only endure their efforts being defamed and their troubles ignored for so long. The eruption of bottled up rage was inevitable, and it came in the form of widespread acts of rebellion, commonly referred to as riots, several of which actually preceded the emergence of the Black Power movement and served to inspire Stokely Carmichael's evolution in that regard.

Dr. King once called riots "the language of the unheard."[50] Similarly, Dr. Kenneth Clark has described riots as the exercise of power by the powerless.[51] Throughout the mid-1960s, the unheard began to make themselves known, and the powerless started to flex their collective muscles. America had experienced racial riots at earlier points in its history, some overtly racist in tone, like the Chicago riots of 1919[52] and the Tulsa riots of 1921.[53] However, the riots that took place during the 60s were of a different variety. Rather than affirmative acts of oppression by those in power, these instances of volatile unrest were acts of insurrection, responsively triggered in almost every instance by black mistreatment at the hands of law enforcement. Riots of this nature occurred in 1964 in Harlem, Rochester, and Philadelphia, among other cities.[54] These, however, were but a modest prelude to the explosion that occurred in August 1965, which though clearly foreshadowed, took the nation by surprise in terms of its fury and magnitude.

On August 11, 1965, what began as a routine traffic stop of a young black man suspected of drunk driving in Watts slowly escalated into a combative and disturbing arrest of the man, along with his mother and stepbrother. Local onlookers were angered by what they perceived as a display of excessive police force, all too common to their daily existence. Following that arrest and continuing over the next six days, black citizens of South Los Angeles turned the area into a war zone—burning, looting, and battling with law enforcement officials.[55] In the end, the Watts riots resulted in thirty-four deaths, injuries to over 1,000 people, nearly 4,000 arrests, and property damage in excess of $40 million.[56]

In the face of the widely held view that antagonistic police–community relations had played a significant role in spawning the unrest, Los Angeles

Police Chief William Parker and Mayor Sam Yorty were quick to decry such perceptions, defending police officers and placing the principal blame on the rioters themselves and those "activists" who inspired their anarchistic behavior. Parker believed that the "civil rights zealots"[57] were the heart of the problem, maintaining, "You cannot tell people to disobey the law and not expect them to have a disrespect for the law. You cannot keep telling them that they are being abused and mistreated without expecting them to react."[58] Mayor Yorty echoed this sentiment, mocking the notion that police brutality could have been the cause of the riots and referring to that theory as the "big lie" perpetuated by outside antagonists.[59] More specifically, he asserted:

> Communists, fellow travelers, dupes, and demagogues have . . . deliberately foment[ed] antagonism to law enforcement officers, inciting the residents to resent and resist officers in the proper professional performance of their always difficult and dangerous duty to protect the rights of law-abiding citizens to be secure in their persons and property.[60]

Neither Chief Parker's nor Mayor Yorty's condemnatory reaction reflected any semblance of understanding concerning the underlying circumstances that could have inspired the unrest. Sadly, they were not alone in their myopic law-and-order critique of the situation.

According to most accounts, the overwhelming white response to the Watts riots was "to condemn the lawlessness, the impatience, and the destruction" and to lament the rioters' lack of gratitude for the economic and civil rights advances that were being made within the black community.[61] In other words, blacks were getting what they wanted—and look how they responded. The audacity. Rather than rewarding this bratty conduct with more concessions or a softening of police–community relations, the appropriate response, in the eyes of many citizens, was to increase police control: more law and order, not less.

Similar attitudes were likewise expressed at the highest government levels, with some members of Congress going so far as to attribute the riots to the culture of black civil disobedience promoted by Dr. King and his followers, which was allowed to persist by the federal government and the courts.[62] South Carolina Representative Albert Watson, for example, proclaimed:

The insurrection they are experiencing in California is the responsibility of the President, his Attorney General, the Federal courts and such
professional troublemakers as Martin [Luther] King. . . . Repeatedly
[King] has advocated the violation of local law, and he and his cohorts
have led thousands of Americans in to a life of civil disobedience.[63]

Minnesota Senator Walter Mondale delivered a powerful response to these
types of negative reactions, declaring:

[T]he . . . rioting (in Los Angeles) was a terrible reminder that in
the century since emancipation we have only substituted misery and
hopelessness and hatred for the bondsman's chains. . . . We cannot
respond to this outburst of anguish by continuing the old ways of discrimination and deprivation which brought it about. . . . We must . . .
try to open the doors of hope for these people. . . . And in so doing,
we will [d]efuse the time bombs [that] are ticking away in the slums
of our cities.[64]

How would the president respond? The answer requires a brief step
back in time, just before the riots began. On August 7, the president signed
into law the Voting Rights Act—legislation for which Dr. King and his
followers had literally shed blood. It was of utmost importance to black
citizens. With this power secured, blacks could meaningfully participate in
the American democratic process. Politicians would have to listen to their
concerns and respond, or else risk being run out of office, or at least that
was the belief at the time. In reality, black citizens would still not wield
the power that they sought, nor garner the attention and dignity that they
desired. As their frustration escalated and boiled over, Ramsey Clark was
one man of authority who was willing to listen and take them seriously.

CHAPTER FOUR

TAKING POOR BLACK PEOPLE SERIOUSLY

"We cannot run away from problems. We must face the facts of
slavery and lynchings. The history of blacks both in Africa and
in this nation has been ignored and distorted in the past."

Ramsey Clark[1]

A MERE FOUR DAYS AFTER the monumental enactment of the Voting
Rights Act, the Watts riots erupted, much to the consternation of President
Johnson. He seethed over what he perceived to be the palpable ingratitude
of black people. After all he had done for them, this is how he was repaid?[2]
Johnson's reaction was rather bewildering given his lofty, empathetic rhetoric regarding the difficulties of black Americans and his own prediction that
in the absence of meaningful change, violence could ensue. Specifically, in
his well-received commencement address at Howard University on June
4, 1965, the president eloquently observed:

> Men are shaped by their world. When it is a world of decay, ringed by
> an invisible wall, when escape is arduous and uncertain, and the saving
> pressures of a more hopeful society are unknown, it can cripple the
> youth and it can desolate the men. . . . Blighted hope breeds despair.
> Despair brings indifferences to the learning which offers a way out.
> And despair, coupled with indifferences, is often the source of destruc-
> tive rebellion against the fabric of society.[3]

Notwithstanding this outward manifestation of understanding, President Johnson at first greeted the riots with paralyzing dismay and disbelief,
refusing to speak to any of his aides for several days.[4] When he eventually
gained some semblance of composure, the president contacted Attorney

General Katzenbach, who was in Martha's Vineyard on vacation at the time, to discuss the situation. Katzenbach advised Johnson to simply let the state and local authorities handle it, advice echoed by Defense Secretary Robert McNamara who was with Katzenbach.[5] While sensitive to the federalism concern of not stepping on the toes of local authorities, Johnson felt that he could not stand idly by and do nothing.[6]

When he finally spoke out publicly about the riots, the president's initial statement was highly political, studiously crafted to appease the white masses by condemning the rebellion and drawing an insensitive analogy between the black rioters and the Ku Klux Klan:

> A rioter with a Molotov cocktail in his hands is not fighting for civil rights any more than a Klansman with a sheet on his back and a mask on his face. They are both . . . lawbreakers, destroyers of constitutional rights and liberties, and ultimately destroyers of a free America.[7]

Privately, he fairly quickly back-pedaled, softening his caustic stance by going directly against the advice of Katzenbach and McNamara and approving a number of federal initiatives carefully directed toward black families in the troubled area. Because he did not want to draw attention to these efforts, which might have been interpreted as coddling wrongdoers, Johnson maintained a low profile, eschewing any publicity about the federal government's response, including his clandestine dispatching of a small presidential task force to South Los Angeles, with his Deputy Attorney General Ramsey Clark as the group's chair.

The president gave his low-profile task force a tall assignment, charging it with the responsibility of "develop[ing] with Governor [Pat] Brown, Mayor Yorty and other officials, a combined program to restore and rehabilitate the damaged areas of Los Angeles" and "to wipe out the causes of such violent outbursts."[8] Clark took this assignment very seriously, and in his role as chair, he did what most of white America had resisted doing for so many years: He listened and actually heard what the people of Watts had to say about their situation.

While his southern, white pedigree had been an asset in his previous civil rights missions in the Deep South, this profile was more of a liability in endeavoring to communicate effectively with an angry, urban constituency. Even Clark's principal comrade during the investigation—Roger Wilkins, the nephew of National NAACP Chair Roy Wilkins—was initially skeptical and dismissive of the deputy attorney general.[9] His view was quickly changed, however, by Clark's compassionate and diligent approach to the work of the task force.

In carrying out his duties as chair, Ramsey Clark employed a grassroots strategy, personally meeting with pertinent city officials and conducting numerous town hall–type gatherings during which he afforded virtually every resident of Watts who was interested in speaking an opportunity to voice frustrations and concerns.[10] The key, though, was that Johnson's deputy attorney general did not come across as simply going through the motions, pretending to see and hear the black people who appeared before him. He evinced attentiveness, open-mindedness, and extraordinary empathy.[11] Wilkins was moved to remark that he had never witnessed a "powerful white man take poor black strangers seriously before. . . . [Clark] was more sensitive to the problems of poor blacks than [Wilkins] imagined any white man could be."[12]

Much of the language hurled at Clark by the Watts citizens was harsh and accusatory. Though not directed at him personally, he was the messenger and therefore absorbed the brunt of the rage expressed almost exclusively against members of his race—white police officers in particular. He calmly and respectfully took in everything that the people had to say. Roger Wilkins noted: "[Clark] didn't get flustered by the rage. It went on hour after hour. He was never angry or self-righteous, never lost his manners or his interest."[13] The people had a great deal to share, but no one in power had seemed willing to listen, until this tall, southern stoic man came along. Clark got it in a way that few whites could. He grasped their frustrating sense of isolation and virtual invisibility and understood that this contributed significantly to the societal explosion that began on August 11.

The substance of the task force's report is perhaps the best evidence of Ramsey Clark's commitment to conveying the actual feelings and perceptions of the people of Watts in their own unfiltered words. Although the entire task force—Clark, Andrew Brimmer (assistant secretary of economic affairs for the Commerce Department), and Jack Conway (deputy director of the Office of Economic Opportunity)—ostensibly authored the report, Clark and Wilkins were its principal drafters. Revealingly, the most prominent concerns depicted in the report were those about which the people spoke most passionately—namely, employment, education, and police–community relations. This toxic combination of social ills created a crippling sense of isolation and hopelessness in Watts and elsewhere in America at that time.

With regard to employment, the report acknowledged that addressing this concern was the "most important and immediate task."[14] It also ominously observed that "[t]he high unemployment statistics and low income figures . . . [told] only part of the story,"[15] failing to fully capture the debilitating emotional effects, particularly on the psyche and motivation of black men.[16] Clark and his task force recognized that various factors contributed to the black employment dilemma, including years of legally sanctioned discrimination in education and work-related opportunities. Successfully tackling this problem would entail far more than the mere enactment of antidiscrimination laws. The task force report emphasized that solving unemployment and other related troubles would "require patient, determined, and massive effort."[17] More specifically, it maintained that "[t]he needs [could] be filled only by all-out effort of every component of government—local, State and Federal; of every element of nongovernmental group action; and of the individual citizens, particularly those involved."[18]

The report further observed that the employment and education problems went hand in hand. Without true equalization of educational quality and opportunity, the employment crisis would never be resolved.[19] Perhaps most disturbingly, however, Clark articulated the unshakable perception among blacks in South Los Angeles that the police viewed their community as "hostile territory to be kept in check by a continuous show of force." Apart from the sheer physical abuse often inflicted, blacks felt that officers generally "were unnecessarily impolite and even insulting" in their day-to-day encounters. The ongoing antagonistic relationship spawned an intense sense of mutual distrust and fear.[20]

Clark believed that this reciprocal antipathy could be nullified, in part, through the establishment of "community policing"—a concept that is still being popularly touted today.[21] This approach changes the focus of the police from pure law enforcement to crime prevention and protection, with the goal of creating a sense of unity between citizens and police officers.[22] Clark's exposure to the longstanding, volatile dynamic between law enforcement and the black community would later inspire him as attorney general and thereafter, as he strongly advocated for the professionalization of America's police and for the widespread institution of community policing.

Employment woes, inferior education, and hostile police–community relations were primarily responsible for the ubiquitous, demoralizing alienation experienced by blacks in South Los Angeles, which the Task Force concluded was central to the riots.[23] Although the Clark report abjured casting blame on the black community, it stressed that black citizens needed to play a major role in solving the problems identified. Clark wisely recognized that excluding citizens from the solution, as had been the case to that point,[24] would render the blighted circumstances impenetrable, as blacks were the only ones who fully understood what it felt like to be in their shoes.[25]

Undeniably, the riots themselves were unmistakable evidence that reform efforts by the government and disconnected civil rights leaders were doing little to alleviate the desperation felt within urban black communities. Securing voting rights and dismantling legal segregation meant virtually nothing to blacks in Watts who could already vote and were largely under – or unemployed, confined to inferior de facto segregated schools, brutalized by those ostensibly tasked with keeping them safe, and generally subject to abject poverty and wholesale societal indifference.[26]

Ramsey Clark formally submitted the report to President Johnson on September 17, 1965. It was an authoritative, candid document that exposed painful realities about the condition of black citizens in Watts, emblematic of broader racial inequities throughout the nation. It called for vast and sustained action to treat or at least alleviate these socioeconomic ills.[27] Even more importantly, Clark wrote of the critical need for a reformation of the national conceptualization of black people. In his words, "the task of thinking of the minority poor as a vital and important part of the national scene and treating them with the dignity and decency they deserve as people—American people—must be mastered if we are to succeed in dealing with the problems."[28] Though pragmatic, the report was at the same time optimistic and inspiring, proposing unprecedented teamwork between elite white leaders and African American working-class poor.

It provided sound vision and offered great hope; but, notwithstanding its promise, President Johnson declined to release the report publicly in light of "larger political concerns."[29]

It was the president's protocol to have items on which he needed to act presented to him in written form with "Approve" and "Disapprove" typed on the document. Johnson would check one or the other after reviewing the material. After reviewing the report, White House Counsel Joseph Califano prepared a memo for the president suggesting a desire to release it, but with Johnson distancing himself from the document. As usual, on the second page of the memo there were spaces for Johnson to check "Approve" or "Disapprove." He checked neither, but rather simply wrote "see me."[30] This cryptic message foretold the report's fate. While circulated privately among a number of "permanent government" bureaucrats, copies of the report ultimately were secreted in an undated envelope, bearing the forbidding and duplicitous legend: "Confidential Reports which we have announced have never been prepared. Do not give out to anyone, or acknowledge we have."[31]

Various theories have been posited as to why the president buried the report, ranging from its graphic depictions to political concerns about encroaching on state and local authority. Whatever the reason, its suppression was disappointing and frustrating to Ramsey Clark. Although a copy of the report was provided to the McCone Commission—a California-based body appointed by Governor Pat Brown and led by former CIA Director John McCone—to use in connection with its examination of the riots, that group failed to comprehend and articulate the hopelessness and despair of the people with the same sincerity and candor of the Clark report. More troubling, the McCone report's moderate assessment of law enforcement's contribution to the disturbance, permitted leaders to ill advisedly continue in their calls for more law and order as a viable response to the rioting.

Ramsey Clark's Watts experience opened his eyes and heart to the deplorable plight of black Americans. Legislative strides like the Civil Rights Act and the Voting Rights Act looked good in the headlines, but on the frontlines, conditions remained relatively unchanged. He was convinced that the widespread urban unrest was the product of underlying causes. Punitively treating the symptoms—looting, property destruction, physical injury—would do nothing to squelch the riots. In fact, such measures were likely to further enrage those prone to insurgence. In Clark's view, the only way to meaningfully address rebellion in the streets was to deal head on with the fundamental factors that fueled it—poverty, inferior education, unemployment, and hostile police–community relations. If these issues were not tackled, the unrest was almost certain to continue and escalate. That is precisely what happened, but those rebelling did not know that there would be a new attorney general at the helm with an especially receptive ear and compassionate soul, one who understood their situation in a way that no one before him had.

After two years as attorney general, Nick Katzenbach grew weary of the work of the Justice Department. Around this time, President Johnson approached Katzenbach for his advice on potential names for the position of undersecretary of state. To the president's surprise, his attorney general said that he would be interested. Although Johnson was immediately dismissive of the suggestion, the conversation clearly got his wheels spinning. In a relatively short period of time, he decided that he would nominate Katzenbach for undersecretary, and Ramsey Clark automatically assumed the position of acting attorney general in October 1966, and he remained in that role while the president pondered whether to remove the "acting" designation. Initially, Johnson told Clark that he would not be considered for the actual post, mainly because they were fellow Texans, and even went so far as to seek his advice regarding other possible nominees.[32]

However, as the months passed, support for Ramsey Clark grew strong. John Macy, President Johnson's personnel advisor, recommended Clark very highly, concluding that he was "most deserving of [the president's] consideration."[33] In a memo to Johnson, Macy glowingly lauded the acting attorney general's qualifications:

> He has the legal ability; he understands the political process; he is an able administrator; he has courage and high personal standards; he holds the respect of Congress, the Cabinet, the bar, the courts and the bureaucracy; and he is sensitive to your needs and your problems and is thoroughly loyal to you.[34]

Quite the endorsement, and other influential figures concurred with Macy's appraisal. Even Nick Katzenbach had previously acknowledged that Ramsey would be a "good appointment."[35] In discussing the matter with him, Johnson quickly added that appointing Ramsey would mean that his father Tom Clark would have to resign from the Supreme Court because of a conflict of interest. Katzenbach disagreed, but Johnson insisted that this was the case and added that Tom agreed.[36]

At first, the potential for this conflict of interest may have been part of the reason why Johnson hesitated to appoint Ramsey,[37] but ultimately it seemed to morph into one of the primary motivating factors. Many surmise that the entire episode was a carefully crafted dance to enable the president to make history by appointing the first African American Supreme Court justice, Thurgood Marshall.[38]

However, Johnson certainly had other, more substantive reasons for making Ramsey Clark his choice. The president "loved his powerful and succinct speaking ability, and had great respect for [his] moral character."[39] In addition, Ramsey was imminently experienced and qualified and had the support of the former attorney general as well as both the Kennedy and Johnson wings of the DOJ.[40] He was the quintessential consensus pick, and his nomination proved to be a veritable no-brainer for the Senate.[41] Confirmation was quick and uneventful, without even a hint of controversy—nothing whatsoever to suggest that the new attorney general would become one of the most controversial figures to ever hold that office.

Following his official elevation, Clark authored a humble and moving thank-you note to the president:

> I am deeply honored that you have chosen me to be your Attorney General. The opportunity to serve a cause deemed mighty is the most

that one can ask in life. This you have given me. The quest for the Great Society, for justice for all, is the high adventure of our times. I hope to help us find them. Sincerely, Ramsey.[42]

The note is revealing. It conveys what motivates Clark. His primary objective is the attainment of justice for all, and his appointment as attorney general placed him in the optimal position, so he thought, to assist in fulfilling this aspiration. He was true to this mission, perhaps to a fault, but over time he came to realize that politics often take priority over what may be subjectively fair and just. His commitment to the ideals of his office was both his greatest strength and his greatest weakness.

As anticipated, Watts was not the end of the rioting. If anything, it served as the catalyst for more unrest, especially in light of the placid political response to the message that black citizens were trying to convey. In 1966 and 1967, the most devastating uprisings occurred in Cleveland, Newark, and Detroit.[43] The latter two riots occurred on Ramsey Clark's watch as attorney general and provided him with the opportunity to put his Watts experience to use. The problem of course was that his previous mindset had been one of riot prevention: addressing the underlying causes in order to alleviate the motivation for the unrest. As attorney general, his role was more in the nature of law enforcement: strategizing with local authorities on how best to respond. Even with someone like Clark in this position, there really is no way to peacefully and compassionately contain a riot. However, police can clearly go too far in their efforts to quell civil disturbance, and that dynamic was on full display in the official response to the Detroit riots, with frustrated officials retaliating against rioters through the excessive use of force, which some described as "a riot of police against blacks."[44]

To his credit, Ramsey Clark was not in the least bit shy about pursuing charges against officers who allegedly overstepped their authority by depriving black citizens of their civil rights.[45] As is often the case, even in present times, a lack of evidence made most of these prosecutions ultimately impossible.[46] The one prosecution that did go forward in the aftermath of Detroit stemmed from the notorious Algiers Motel incident in which a group of young people (mostly black men, but also two white women) were purportedly brutalized for hours by Detroit police officers, and three of the black men ended up dead from gunshot wounds.[47]

Three officers and a security guard were indicted and tried for conspiracy to injure various individuals in "the free exercise and enjoyment of their constitutional rights by inflicting punishment [on them] by injury and death . . . without due process of law."[48] Predictably, none was ultimately convicted.[49] A disconcerting result. But Attorney General Clark had demonstrated his willingness to hold law enforcement officials accountable, something that he would do on a number of subsequent occasions when he concluded that police had abused their authority, usually against black citizens.

Although legal avenues proved futile, on the political stage, President Johnson took decisive, public action in response to this series of riots, contrary to his clumsy, clandestine handling of the Watts riots. He announced the creation of the National Advisory Commission on Civil Disorders (the Kerner Commission), which he tasked with answering three questions: "What happened? Why did it happen? What can be done to prevent it from happening again?"[50] In its chilling overall assessment, the Kerner Commission noted that the "nation [was] moving toward two societies, one black, one white—separate and unequal."[51] In addition, it laid primary blame for the conditions that led to the riots on "white racism": "Race prejudice has shaped our history decisively; it now threatens to affect our future. White racism is essentially responsible for the explosive mixture which has been accumulating in our cities since the end of World War II."[52] The commission went on to note that among the ingredients that comprised this "explosive mixture" were "[p]ervasive discrimination and segregation in employment, education and housing, which have resulted in the continuing exclusion of great numbers of Negroes from the benefits of economic progress."[53]

The Kerner Commission's clear appraisal was that the causes of the riots were complex, longstanding, and deeply entrenched. Fortunately, it proceeded to observe that its bleak prediction regarding America's racial future was not inevitable and could be reversed with the realization of "common opportunities for all within a single society."[54] As with the Clark report, the Kerner report made plain just how difficult the mission ahead would be—the end goal could be achieved only through compassionate, massive and sustained [commitment], backed by the resources of the most powerful and the richest nation on this earth. From every American it will require new attitudes, new understanding, and, above all, new will.[55]

President Johnson was not pleased with the substance of the Kerner report and consequently greeted it coldly, void of any pomp and circumstance. His reaction seemed principally attributable to the fact that the commission, in his view, had failed to accord him due praise for his civil rights successes.[56] The president felt that he had been put in an impossible situation by the commission's announcement of sweeping recommendations that were economically unrealistic. Moreover, Johnson seemed particularly uncomfortable with the pronouncement that "white racism" was at the heart of the riots.[57] Although he could not deny that this played a role, he at least partially harbored the belief that rioters and looters were fundamentally "lawbreakers."[58]

There was no denying the existence of an opportunistic, criminal element in all of the disturbances—there were those who viewed rioting merely as a convenient excuse for committing crimes.[59] However, to dismiss the unrest out of hand on this basis, as many white conservative leaders did, was to self-interestedly gloss over the true nature of the problems for black Americans.

Consistent with this mentality, there was also an extensive belief among the same group of leaders that black militants had conspired to ignite the unrest with the aid or inspiration of communist agitators.[60] To make matters worse, President Johnson himself could not fully shake the political temptation of being able to lay blame for the riots at the feet of black radicals or communists.[61] Indeed, as will be discussed in a later chapter, he would obsessively pressure Ramsey Clark to prosecute Black Power activists Stokely Carmichael and H. Rap Brown, whom the president felt were the primary instigators of the riots. Put them out of commission and peace would reign again.

Clark, however, knew better and was scornfully dismissive of conspiracy allegations, later maintaining that

[t]he conspiracy theory provided the happiest answer: it implicated only a few evil people, people we could all hate. . . . Everything in our nature wanted to find a scapegoat. Conspiracy alone could relieve us of a sense of national guilt. The most unpleasant fact ignored, that the ghetto is rampant with crime and that black rage is real.[62]

Clark also had an outwardly sound legal basis for not pursuing Carmichael and Brown—a lack of evidence tying the riots to any of their conduct.

More importantly, though, in retrospect it is clear that Clark's reluctance to blame or prosecute black militants was a harbinger of his gravitation toward the public's enemies, or at least those "demonized" as such, to use one of his favorite words. While he would later align himself with individuals labeled as international terrorists, in the late 1960s, he foreshadowed this future calling by, in effect, protecting radical black leaders, the purported domestic terrorists of that era. FBI Director J. Edgar Hoover even characterized the Black Panther Party as "the greatest threat to the internal security of the country."[63] To him and many white Americans, the members of the Black Panther Party, and other black militants such as Carmichael and Brown, were akin to what many refer to as radical Muslims today. They represented a danger to be neutralized. Ramsey Clark didn't buy it. He had listened to the people of Watts and understood their pain and fury. Their discomfort was intense and their anger legitimate. They needed to be heard, not silenced.

In reflecting on the riots after leaving the DOJ, Clark ominously observed: "[A]s terrible as riots are, they are far from the worst that could happen. If despair and hopelessness reach a level where guerilla warfare can occur, this could cause an irreconcilable division of the country."[64] Although he was adamantly opposed to violence as a general matter, calling it the "ultimate degradation," Clark rationalized the riots as "violence manufactured by injustice."[65] He believed that white Americans were "guilty of immense neglect, and the rage of the ghettoes [was] the 'ultimate product of our inhumanity.'"[66]

Clark's concern over this dark reality undoubtedly inspired him to dedicate his life's work to achieving equality and justice for the least among us.

In 2015, I asked him what he thought of contemporary instances of police violence and protest, such as in Ferguson, Missouri, in 2014. His response reflected his Watts experience, noting that the heart of the problem, now as then, is the absence of the intensity needed to effect meaningful change.[67] Nevertheless, ever the optimist, he is hopeful, as he has been throughout his life, unwilling to concede defeat.

Consistent with his positive, determined spirit, after Watts, Ramsey Clark never stopped listening. He understood the importance of human dignity; ignoring black people and operating with an attitude of "we know what's best for you" deprived them of this critical quality. Clark sought to ensure that African Americans had a voice, as well as an active hand in addressing their collective plight. As much as others may want to fix a problem, they can never truly arrive at a solution without the dynamic participation of those affected. In Clark's view, if black citizens were not listened to and meaningfully allowed to take part in making things better for themselves, the civil unrest would continue. Expectedly, the status quo marched on, and as prophesied, so did black rebellion in the streets.

CHAPTER FIVE

"I AM A MAN"

"The lesson, roughly, is this: that poverty, in all of its
manifestations, is not only ugly and demeaning but also
something that the American people do not want to see."
Ramsey Clark[1]

ALTHOUGH RAMSEY CLARK had dealt with Martin Luther King, Jr. at
various points throughout his tenure in the Justice Department, he did not
have a close personal relationship with the civil rights icon.[2] He respected
and admired King, but mostly from afar—until the march from Selma to
Montgomery in 1965. During this tense and momentous event, Clark came
to know and understand Dr. King on a much more intimate level.

As the leader and most high-profile figure associated with the march,
Dr. King was obviously a prime target for racist violence. Angry whites,
threatened by and upset over confrontational black pressure to bring about
change in America, viewed King and his followers as lawbreakers who
needed to be taught a lesson and kept in their place. These are the people
who terrified Clark. He understood their capacity for brutality, as demonstrated on a number of previous occasions, most notoriously on Bloody
Sunday, and he knew that an assassination attempt on Dr. King was a very
real possibility. Clark considered it his principal responsibility to ensure
that this did not occur. He obsessed over it, especially toward the end of
the march when he thought that King might be particularly vulnerable to
a sniper's bullet.[3]

Clark's angst over Dr. King's safety was somewhat atypical for the normally
unflappable deputy attorney general and was in stark contrast to the equanimity exhibited by King himself. King knew that he was in great danger and that
he could be killed at any moment, but he was not afraid. He refused to let

fear alter his path toward the attainment of equal rights for black Americans. According to Clark, the fear in the air was palpable because of the earlier violence, but also because of reports that this time there were 1,200 white men who had traveled to the area with rifles, prepared to preserve their desired social order.[4] At the end of the first day of the march, while others were uptight and unable to rest, Dr. King slept like a baby in his tent.[5] Clark marveled at this, viewing it as clear evidence that King truly feared no evil even though he was surrounded by hatred and anger.[6] While he may have exuded serenity in the face of hostile whites, Dr. King was not so tranquil with regard to emerging discord among factions of his followers.

This was 1965, and over the ensuing years disdain for him would escalate—within the civil rights movement as well as outside of it. As noted earlier, young disciples of Dr. King had grown weary of his nonviolent approach. Led by such firebrands as Stokely Carmichael and H. Rap Brown, a new breed of civil rights activist wanted to engage in aggressive confrontation and armed retaliation in the face of white oppression. In his famous speech in Cambridge, Maryland, in July 1967, Brown urged black people to exact revenge and combatively rebel:

> An eye for an eye; a tooth for tooth. Tit for tat, brother, that's the only kind of war that man knows. . . . Freedom is not a welfare commodity. It ain't like that old bad food they give you. They can't give you no freedom. You got to take your freedom.[7]

Carmichael charismatically substituted impassioned chants of "black power" for the sedate singing of Negro spirituals such as "We Shall Overcome."

Dr. King's allure was waning, largely because of frustration over the slow pace of progress. One prime example was King's visit to Watts in the aftermath of the riots. Rather than being received warmly, he was greeted by an unreceptive black audience and was even jeered by many.[8]

Those who had always despised King and what he stood for remained steadfast in their contempt. That was no surprise, and likely not particularly disconcerting for Dr. King. Though he was surely tired of this type of resistance, he had come to expect and accept it.

Not so with those who had previously been in his corner. Most notably, President Johnson. The two men had collaborated, albeit under pressure from King, on the Civil Rights Act of 1964 and the Voting Rights Act of 1965.[9] As a result, Johnson somewhat understandably trusted that Dr. King was an ally—or, at a minimum, that he was not someone who would actively oppose the president on major issues. King, however, breached this trust in the most profound way possible from the president's perspective: King publicly denounced the Vietnam War and had the audacity to go so far as to proclaim that the American government was "the greatest purveyor of violence in the world."[10] Johnson was furious and refused to even speak to King following his announced position on the war. Once a frequent visitor to the White House, Dr. King was no longer welcome.[11]

At this point, he had endured many years of virtually constant persecution, beginning with his courageous leadership of the Montgomery bus boycott in 1955. By 1967, he felt beaten down, and his increasing marginalization was acutely discouraging to him. Moreover, despite his persistent, life-risking labors to effect change, only modest advances had occurred. Although he remained a firm believer in nonviolence, King came to accept that perhaps something more drastic needed to be done in order to obtain meaningful reform, not just for black people but for all those who were economically disadvantaged and powerless. He resolved to move his organization—the Southern Christian Leadership Conference (SCLC)—in a more dynamic direction, away from its familiar, nonviolent protest model. He announced what would come to be known as the Poor People's Campaign, an initiative to bring together indigent people of all races and ethnicities to march and camp out on the Mall in Washington, DC, for as long as it took to get the attention of the government. "They would occupy the nation's capital and refuse to leave until their demands were met."[12]

While he recognized that this strategy was somewhat more adversarial than those he had previously pursued, King viewed it as a viable, nonviolent alternative to the riots that were becoming popularized throughout the country.[13] And, like Ramsey Clark, he knew that the root of the rampant civil unrest was principally economic—black people, in particular, were overwhelmingly poor. When coupled with their general second-class citizenship and widespread mistreatment at the hands of the majority, especially law enforcement, rebellion was inevitable. King believed that if something dramatic was not done to address these underlying concerns, the possibility of an all-out race war in America was very real.[14] As such, he firmly committed himself to the Poor People's Campaign. King's wife Coretta observed that her husband approached this project with uncharacteristic exigence—"He worked as if it was to be his final assignment."[15]

Parallel to what would indeed prove to be Dr. King's concluding quest, a remarkable grassroots protest emerged in Memphis, Tennessee—a labor strike by the city's sanitation, sewage, and drainage workers. These individuals—almost all of whom were black—were the very embodiment of the economic injustice and social subjugation that King intended to highlight through his campaign. They were the lowest of the low in Memphis's social order, veritable modern-day slaves, subsisting off of pauper's wages, and lacking any benefits, pension, grievance procedure, or insurance.[16]

To make matters worse, the nature of the work itself was abjectly demoralizing—not to mention dangerous and disgusting. The garbage men were relegated to outdated, unsafe trucks that placed their lives at risk on a daily basis, and their assigned task was to gather and dispose of Memphians' often putrid waste.[17] They were unnoticed and unappreciated. Author Hampton Sides described them as "faceless and uncomplaining, a caste of untouchables" who referred to themselves as "walking buzzards."[18]

Their depressing existence, however, reached a boiling point in February 1968 when these invisible men went on strike, understandably concluding that they no longer could bear their inhumane working conditions. The indignity that they had endured inspired a simple but powerful mantra for their movement, one that succinctly demanded respect and equal treatment—"I *Am* a Man."[19] Ramsey Clark would later remark: "What a message that was. . . . It was one of the most imaginative demonstrations and one of the most powerful symbols that came out of the civil rights movement."[20]

The sanitation workers' strike was led by Reverend James Lawson, a friend and contemporary of Dr. King. Lawson saw a direct connection between the strike and what King hoped to accomplish through the Poor People's Campaign, and he reached out to his comrade for assistance with the cause. Much to the dismay of his closest confidantes, Dr. King agreed to travel to Memphis to participate in a mass meeting.[21] After speaking to a large and enthusiastic crowd there, King was invigorated and clearly saw that the Memphis movement fit squarely within his broader agenda of securing economic justice for all citizens. While he had represented that this engagement would be a one-off undertaking, the striking men captured Dr. King's spirit; he was all in, and he promised to return to take part in a peaceful demonstration later in March.[22]

Unfortunately, the euphoria that King had experienced during his initial involvement with the strike would not be repeated. The March 28 protest event in Memphis was a complete disaster from the beginning, highjacked by militant Black Power activists and general ne'er-do-wells looking for trouble.[23] What had been intended as a peaceful protest march denigrated into an actual riot, conjuring up images of Watts, Newark, and Detroit. While Dr. King's previous demonstrations had often been met with outside violence, this time the demonstrators themselves seemed to be the instigators of the mayhem.[24]

King was forced to abandon the march to avoid being linked to the violence. He hated to do this but understood how damaging his presence could be to his image and ongoing efforts.[25] His ambivalence over leaving, however, paled in comparison to the anguish he felt concerning what had transpired. King had envisioned the Poor People's Campaign as a viable alternative to the rioting that had been taking place. Memphis suggested otherwise. Perhaps his peaceful ways were now simply a relic of the past. Combat seemed to have greater appeal to the younger generation of activists. Distraught and depressed over this realization, King pondered the futility of his life's work. He suggested to his dear friend Ralph Abernathy: "Maybe we just have to give up and let violence take its course. Maybe people will listen to the voice of violence. They certainly won't listen to us."[26]

Notwithstanding his despondency, Dr. King was able to rally the following day for reporters. He ably defended his actions in fleeing the scene of the violence and distanced himself from the perpetrators, expressing resolve to peacefully persist in his labors on behalf of the sanitation workers and all poor people.[27] Although his close associates were, by and large, skeptical of the Poor People's Campaign and vehemently opposed to King returning to Memphis, he was unmoved, believing that the movement's only hope for continued viability was through the successful completion of a peaceful march in Memphis. Without that, his Poor People's march on Washington would not be possible.[28]

Dr. King's entourage eventually embraced his vision of the necessity for a Memphis march. They all traveled to the city on April 3 in anticipation of the demonstration. However, Dr. King would not live to see it. He was tragically struck down by an assassin's bullet as he stood on the balcony of the Lorraine Motel, preparing to leave for dinner on the evening of April 4.

One of the first federal officials to be notified of Dr. King's assassination was Ramsey Clark, now President Johnson's attorney general. He considered the great leader's death not only a "tragic setback" for the civil rights movement, but a personal loss as well.[29] He had grown fond of King and had tremendous respect and admiration for the slain legend. To some extent, Clark had already begun to model his worldview after the peaceful, nonviolent ways of Dr. King. Clark's humane treatment of black citizens and his strident efforts to curtail police excesses were defining examples. Over time, he would gravitate even further in the direction of King's teachings and beliefs, especially with regard to his opposition to armed conflict and his critique of the American military-industrial complex. The large bronze bust of Mahatma Gandhi that graced Clark's living room for years is an abiding testament of his devotion to the Gandhian ideals that Dr. King preached and lived by.

Ramsey Clark immediately concluded that the assassination was not a matter to be handled by local officials. The investigation needed to be led by the FBI. There were potential federal crimes that could be pursued, and the suspect had already crossed state lines, which made Clark comfortable with seizing control of the case. He communicated his decision to Assistant FBI Director Deke DeLoach—for him, in turn, to relay the message to Director J. Edgar Hoover. One might reasonably assume that Clark could have personally conveyed this information directly to Hoover. Why use DeLoach as his emissary? Well, to put it mildly, Clark and Hoover did not have the best working relationship. This was principally due to Hoover's enormous ego and addiction to power. As attorney general, Clark was technically the FBI director's boss, which did not sit well with Hoover, who had known Clark since he was a young boy roaming the halls of the DOJ when his father Tom Clark was President Truman's attorney general.[30] What did this youngster know, and who was he to tell the FBI's first and only director what to do?

It was not simply Ramsey Clark's youthfulness, however, that irked Hoover; he was more outraged over the 40-year-old attorney general's political views and attitude toward crime and law enforcement. He felt that Clark was too liberal and far too sympathetic to the civil rights cause. Hoover, a strict law-and-order man, was mortified by Clark's understanding and genteel treatment of those who took part in the riots. He was particularly disturbed by Clark's rigid opposition to Hoover's favored investigative practice of wiretapping. Clark essentially put a moratorium on wiretapping, except when it could be sufficiently demonstrated that a risk to national security was involved. Accordingly, he routinely denied the FBI's requests for wiretaps, requests that had just as habitually been granted under previous attorneys general, including Ramsey's father. Further, Hoover hated Dr. King and was obsessed with exposing the reverend's moral failings as a way of undermining his effectiveness.[31] Clark's unswerving refusal to approve King-related taps pushed Hoover over the edge, prompting him to derisively nickname Clark "the Jellyfish."[32]

All the more galling to Hoover, though, was the fact that he had no dirt on Clark. With some record of marital infidelity or sexual debauchery, as he had on Dr. King and other influential leaders, Hoover could exert negotiating leverage to get what he wanted. However, with regard to Clark "[t]here was no file of indiscretions."[33] The irony of this is piercing. Hoover fancied himself the chief policer of morality and decency. He detested those who failed to exhibit these qualities. But when he came face-to-face with a leader who seemed to be the epitome of moral decency and matrimonial stability, that somehow enraged him even more. What Hoover clearly wanted, at least in his mind, was to be the lone occupier of the moral high ground. Even without Ramsey Clark in the picture, Hoover's ability to stake a legitimate claim to such status was dubious, at best; with Clark on the scene, it was infuriatingly impossible.

Hoover's acrimony toward Clark was not exactly mutual. The mild-mannered attorney general accorded respect to the much-maligned Hoover and abstained from overtly criticizing him or his department, actually attesting that he believed the FBI always operated with integrity.[34] The latter seems like quite a stretch on Clark's part, as does his generous characterization of their relationship as "cordial."[35] While this may have been superficially accurate, beneath the surface there was a seething disdain from Hoover's corner.

Clark's use of DeLoach as his agent thus makes sense—the directive might seem slightly more palatable to Hoover coming from his trusted assistant. When DeLoach contacted the director about Dr. King's death, Hoover's immediate, visceral reaction was to avoid any involvement in the investigation. He insisted that this was a matter for the local authorities. Eventually, DeLoach was able to make it clear to Hoover that the attorney general had not given the FBI any choice in the matter.[36] The director reluctantly acquiesced but endeavored to preserve at least the semblance of authority by proclaiming that the FBI had to maintain complete control of the case.

Hoover's strong aversion to Dr. King made him an unlikely source for solving the murder. However, it may have been precisely this disdain that made him ideal for the task—he did not want to have an accusatory finger pointed at him with regard to the assassination. Thus, he had a vested interest in conducting an exceedingly thorough investigation.[37] And thorough it would be—an international manhunt more extensive and costly than any in history to that point.[38]

Clark believed that an expeditious resolution may have been the only hope for avoiding violence in response to Dr. King's killing. Although that may have helped curtail some of the volatile response, the assassination struck too raw a nerve with black citizens for them to placidly mourn their great leader's passing. President Johnson's calls for calmness and nonviolence consistent with Dr. King's teachings were futile, as were similar entreaties from black leaders.[39] Stokely Carmichael was far more accurate in his assessment of what was to come: "When white America killed Dr. King, she declared war on us. The rebellions that have been occurring around this country—that's just light stuff compared to what is about to happen."[40]

Sure enough, explosions of rage permeated the country, even Washington, DC, a city that many felt was impervious to civil unrest. Rioting, looting, and arson quickly erupted in the nation's capital and in over a hundred other cities over the course of the week following the assassination.[41] In observing the rebellion in his city, the president resignedly commented:

> What did you expect? . . . When you put your foot on a man's neck and hold him down for three hundred years, and then you let him up, what's he going to do? He's going to knock your block off.[42]

The wholesale uprising was unprecedented, demonstrating that these types of disturbances could literally happen anywhere.[43]

Ramsey Clark's response was predictably measured, undoubtedly influenced by his prior experiences with these types of situations, specifically Watts. He knew that Dr. King's death was not the lone cause of the mass revolt; it simply represented a profound manifestation of the powerlessness that many black Americans felt. They were in a very hopeless state, and the man who symbolized perhaps their greatest prospect for a better tomorrow had now been violently taken away. Though senseless and destructive, when considered in these terms (as the president had observed) the rioting seemed understandable, almost appropriate. As a result, Clark would not condone an overly aggressive law enforcement response. Order needed to be restored, but citizens had to be treated with dignity and respect. He warned local leaders throughout the country that "either overreaction or under-action can lead to rioting. You have to exercise a very careful control."[44]

Clark traveled to Memphis on the day after Dr. King's assassination, accompanied by Deke DeLoach and Roger Wilkins, among others. Upon his arrival, he noted an intense militaristic presence in the city that troubled him. He was insistent that excessive force not be utilized in dealing with the unrest and felt that the National Guard's use of armored tanks was unduly confrontational.[45]

Ramsey Clark's empathetic and cautious reaction to the nationwide un-rest was in sharp contrast to that of conservative politicians, who were quick to condemn the lawlessness and demand increased law and order. Indeed, this became the centerpiece for Richard Nixon's successful 1968 presiden-tial campaign, and it was a consistent rallying cry for American Independent Party candidate George Wallace.[46] They both manipulatively played on the fears of white Americans, forbiddingly predicting that the rioting could be coming to a neighborhood near them unless a law-and-order candidate was elected, unashamedly fomenting further racial division.

Interestingly, in 1968, Nixon's focus was not simply on the need for more "law and order" in general. Rather, he specifically targeted Ramsey Clark personally and declared that President Johnson's weak, soft-on-crime attorney general was the problem. Nixon promised the American people that the first thing he would do if elected was get a replacement who would make them safe again—"If we are to restore order and respect for law in this country, there's one place we're going to . . . begin. We're going to have a new Attorney General of the United States."[47] Nixon's scapegoat-ing of Clark, which was echoed by other conservative politicians, gained significant traction with the public at large. Reams of critical, hateful mail poured into the White House and the DOJ in response to Clark's compas-sionate approach to the riots.

A significant portion of these letters were in reaction to his denunciation of Chicago Mayor Richard Daley's assessment of what went wrong with regard to the handling of the riots in his city following Dr. King's assassina-tion. According to Daley, the police "should have had instructions to shoot arsonists and looters—arsonists to kill and looters to maim and detain."[48] Clark blasted the Chicago mayor's position and threatened him with personal prosecution if any looters were shot in the future,[49] not an unlikely scenario given the forthcoming Democratic National Convention in that city and the anti–Vietnam War protests that were certain to occur.

The public let the attorney general have it. One citizen, for example, pro-claimed: "When a man of the stature of Mayor Daley . . . indicates that he is going to try to preserve law and order, the Attorney General should have been the first one to back him up. But obviously, this Ramsey Clark does not believe in law and order."[50] Another directly accused Clark of being the cause of the arson and looting—"You have taught negroes they don't have to work and save for what they want; just burn and rob."[51] Even Senator John Tower, from Clark's home state of Texas, called out the attorney general and demanded that he be replaced. In a speech following the riots, Tower expressed the view that Clark was "more concerned with the civil rights of law *violators* than he [was with] the civil rights of law *abiders*."[52]

The sentiment was undeniably widespread that the attorney general had to go. Criticism, however, was not going to alter Clark's course, nor would it prevent him from doing his job. Accordingly, while being lambasted both publicly and privately, he maintained a careful watch over the FBI's international manhunt for Dr. King's assassin.[53] After a tortuous sixty-five-day chase that seemed destined to fail, King's killer James Earl Ray was apprehended in London and extradited to the United States, where he eventually entered a guilty plea and was sentenced to ninety-nine years in prison.[54] While by most accounts, including Ramsey Clark's, Ray most likely acted alone, many still harbor conspiracy theories, just as is the case with President Kennedy's assassination.[55]

Although the capture of James Earl Ray was definitely a positive development for Ramsey Clark from both a personal and professional standpoint, it did little to quell the mounting criticism of his perceived delicate treatment of "lawbreakers." Things had already gotten worse for him in terms of public opinion with the realization of Dr. King's vision for a Poor People's march on Washington. In the aftermath of King's death, his followers pledged to complete the sanitation workers' march in Memphis, as well as to lead a diverse assortment of America's poor to the nation's capital to camp out on the city's historic Mall in the hope of exacting meaningful reform.[56] King's closest friend and confidante Ralph Abernathy would serve as his successor, leading both efforts. There was great fear that the sanitation march would be marred by the same sort of violence that had ruined the first aborted effort led by Dr. King. In truth, the concern was even more pronounced this time around in light of the ubiquitous intervening violence that had erupted after King's assassination. This trepidation, though, proved unfounded.

Seemingly, in respectful homage to Dr. King, a peaceful, silent protest march was successfully completed on April 8, movingly led by his widow Coretta Scott King and Reverend Abernathy, along with King devotees Andrew Young and Jesse Jackson, as well as renowned entertainer Harry Belafonte.[57] Not only was the nonviolence of the march a victory of sorts, it was likewise an effective protest vehicle that helped push Memphis's mayor to eventually acquiesce to many of the workers' demands. This was a major accomplishment and a promising first step toward achieving more significant gains for all indigent Americans through the Poor People's Campaign.

About a month after the completion of the Memphis march, large caravans of an ethnically diverse assortment of America's poor, including white citizens, fittingly departed from outside the Lorraine Motel in Memphis—the very site of their visionary's demise—en route to Washington, DC. The SCLC had secured an extended permit for a portion of the Mall on which the protesters planned to erect a shantytown where they would reside until their demands were adequately met.[58] As a tribute to Dr. King, the makeshift municipality would be called Resurrection City, connoting the "idea of rebirth from the depths of despair," according to Andy Young.[59]

There was great concern in Washington about the potential effect that this demonstration could have on the city. J. Edgar Hoover was convinced that a march on Washington would be disastrous and was certain to end in the same sort of violence and lawlessness that had marred the first sanitation workers' march in Memphis. To better prepare for this assured debacle, he sought Ramsey Clark's permission to wiretap the SCLC's offices in Atlanta and DC, but the attorney general thwarted these efforts.[60]

Other political leaders shared Hoover's concerns, most notably, the president himself. To Johnson and those of like mind, the nation's capital did not seem like a fitting location for such a demonstration; it would sully the pristine city. But that was the point—to show the powers that be the gut-wrenching face of poverty. The convenient political excuse that crime and violence would overtake DC was simply a more palatable justification for denouncing the campaign. The reality was that the president and other white leaders simply did not want a bunch of poor, mostly black people debasing the sacred Mall with their presence.

Notwithstanding the resistance, the Poor People's Campaign went forward as planned, much to the dismay and disgust of President Johnson. As recounted by Clark, "Resurrection City appalled [the President]." For Johnson, Washington "represent[ed] everything good that he believ[ed] in. . . —physical beauty, grace in government, heroic monuments, human dignity. To see these pitiful poor people with their psychotics and their ugliness and misery sprawled on the monument grounds really hurt him—deeply hurt him."[61]

The attorney general respected Johnson's willingness to allow the demonstration to proceed, but his assessment of the scene was quite different. Clark saw Resurrection City as the truth, which, unfortunately, was "awfully ugly."[62] He perceptively observed:

[Y]ou just can't hope to confine [poor people] in the ghettos and never think about them. And what the American people really said was, "We don't want to see it. We don't want to know about it. If it has got to exist, keep it out of our sight. Keep it off the monument grounds.[63]

Clark knew from experience that trying to repress or isolate the ugliness—the truth—would only fuel further rage and rebellion. Consequently, he felt that it was "imperative for leadership to try to reach across and communicate."[64]

Although the concept of Resurrection City was creative and thought-provoking, in the end it proved to be a disaster. Inept, feuding leadership (combined with a nefarious criminal element) doomed the operation before it could have any consequential impact.[65] If this were not enough, two weeks of unrelenting, torrential rains sealed the deal, physically ruining whatever semblance of a city had existed.[66]

Besides being a catastrophe for the movement, it was also a terrible blow to the Johnson administration, largely because of the perception of Ramsey Clark's handling of the situation. The participants viewed Clark's law enforcement oversight of the demonstration as too draconian, while the general public, white Americans in particular, viewed it as far too lax.[67] The truth was likely somewhere in the middle, but there was only so much

that the attorney general could do under such difficult circumstances. He
was in a no-win predicament. An all-out, law-and-order crackdown would
have pleased conservatives and the fearful public, but it would have greatly
offended Clark's moral sensibilities. Completely giving in to the demonstrators and letting them have free rein, on the other hand, would have created
uncontrollable chaos throughout DC. In any event, Clark's Solomon-like
approach caused significant damage to his public image.

Already being portrayed as weak and overly sympathetic to liberal, civil
rights concerns, compromising visuals of Clark related to Resurrection
City only served to validate and heighten these characterizations. At one
point during the demonstration, with television cameras rolling, he invited
a group of protesters into the Department of Justice to hear their griev-
ances, allowing their caustic rebukes of him to be broadcast across the
country.[68] Reminiscent of his composed willingness to listen in the face of
similar rage in the aftermath of the Watts riots, Clark serenely took in the
concerns voiced by the citizens of Resurrection City.[69] At one point, an
angry woman actually shook her fist in the attorney general's face.[70] Perhaps channeling Dr. King, Clark remained calm.

It took great courage and fortitude for him to peacefully receive the
message of the angry demonstrators. To the viewing audience, however,
Clark did not appear courageous and compassionately reserved. Rather,
he seemed afraid and incompetent, too fearful to even know how to respond.[71] This prominent display of apparent vulnerability was a campaign
gift to Nixon and Wallace, providing them with more law-and-order fod-
der and tangible evidence of the pressing need for a new attorney general.

Nixon's opportunistic ploy, of course, worked, and once in office, he
quickly fulfilled his promise to rid the DOJ of Ramsey Clark by making
John Mitchell his attorney general. Nixon could not have made a choice
more diametrically opposed to Clark. The new attorney general quickly
undid much of the progress that Clark had made on the civil rights front.
The days of listening were over, instead replaced with law-and-order rhetoric and policies to match.[72]

The pressure on Ramsey Clark during this period was undoubtedly exacerbated by the tragic loss of his former boss and cherished friend Bobby

Kennedy, who was assassinated in June 1968 following his victory in the California Democratic primary for president. Dr. King's death was traumatic for Clark, but at least the country still had Bobby. Sirhan Sirhan's bullet, however, extinguished what seemed to be America's future guiding light, its greatest hope for a better country and world.[73] Kennedy seemed to understand poverty and race at a level on par with Clark, and the least among us felt that they might actually have a voice going forward if he were elected. Attorney General Clark surely harbored that belief, and with his kindred spirits—Martin Luther King, Jr. and Bobby Kennedy—gone from this world, he must have felt very much alone in his quest to ensure justice and human dignity for all people.

Without Kennedy, Clark lacked almost any high-profile support for his humane treatment of the indigent residents of Resurrection City, and for his reaction to their protests. Although the demonstration was a complete fiasco in virtually everyone's eyes, the sheer rawness of it deeply affected him, as did white America's response, which was overwhelmingly manifested through displays of disgust, anger, or indifference. This confirmed Clark's theory that fear played a major role in preventing progress in addressing the underlying ills within society, particularly poverty in the black community. According to him,

> When you are afraid, you lose all compassion for other people. . . .
> Frightened, you fail to fulfill the obligations of a compassionate and
> just people—to educate and employ and house and give health to the
> poor. [F]ear deprives you of any concern for justice itself.[74]

Clark's deep understanding of and appreciation for the effects of fear seem to have been spawned by his exposure to Dr. King. King once told him that "fear will corrupt your soul," and further admonished that "you can never be afraid."[75] That notion can be taken in various directions.

Fear can corrupt by causing individuals to refrain from acting in a fashion consistent with their conscience, such as by tacitly accepting segregation in order to avoid any sort of confrontation. It can also inspire overtly corrupt behavior, as was the case with those who responded violently to peaceful civil rights protests. Fear of what the success of the movement might have meant for their positions in society caused these individuals to act repressively in an effort to preserve the status quo. Further, then and now, fear can cause police officers to overreact to tense situations or to carry out their responsibilities blinded by stereotypes.[76] Clark fully grasped the boundless distorting power that fear wields, cognizant of its ever-present potential to cloud his judgment and that of others.

Throughout his life, if Clark had been a fearful man, he would have evaded the many arduous challenges that he embraced—defending the indefensible and standing up for the demonized. Although he has not necessarily put his life on the line in the same manner as Dr. King, he has been just as willing to expose himself to the predictable anger and hatred of others, secure in the knowledge that he was advocating for what he believed to be right and just. I can't help but think that Clark's relationship with Dr. King and his intimate observation of King's peaceful resolve in the face of tumult inspired his outlook on life, his country, and the world. He watched Dr. King walk in the valley of the shadow of death, nonviolently fighting for the rights of his people, without exhibiting any tangible fear or reluctance. This ultimately cost him his life. If Dr. King could persevere undaunted under the incomparable circumstances that he faced, Ramsey Clark resolved that he surely could endeavor to protect the oppressed, the underdogs, and the outcasts, unencumbered by fear.

Fear did not distort Ramsey Clark's view of Resurrection City, or of the rioting and righteous anger on display. Seeing clearly, he was empathetic, not hostile or indifferent. He had witnessed the despair, hopelessness, and isolation experienced by the citizens of Watts, and he knew that their circumstances were emblematic of a far more expansive problem. He understood black citizens' rage and to some extent had to acknowledge its legitimacy.

This is especially so when juxtaposed with the U.S. propensity to address problems militarily, purportedly to spread its brand of democracy. The Vietnam War itself reeked of hypocrisy when those who condoned that conflict decried the upheaval by blacks at home who were frustrated with being subjugated and ignored. If violence was the answer in Vietnam, why should it not be the answer in Washington, DC, or Chicago or Detroit? In speaking out against the war during his famous Riverside speech in 1967, Dr. King poignantly observed that he could not denounce violence carried out by oppressed black people "without having first spoken clearly to the greatest purveyor of violence in the world today: my own government."[77]

King's portrayal of America resonated with Ramsey Clark at the time. He considered it to be one of the most important and courageous statements that he had ever heard,[78] and he subsequently adopted it as a descriptive mantra, frequently quoting it in speeches critical of America's ongoing penchant for militarism.[79] Although Clark did not witness the famous speech live, he has an autographed copy that was sent to him by Dr. King. Little did he know that this small gesture would amount to a passing of the antiwar torch.

The Vietnam War weighed as heavy on Clark as it did on Dr. King, but as attorney general, he faced a potentially debilitating conflict between his law enforcement duties and his nonviolent heart. He also recognized and struggled with the mendacity of America drafting black men to fight for a country that denied them equal rights. On the other hand, he respected the rule of law and was committed to preserving its integrity, and the law of the land—the Selective Service Act—provided for the drafting of men into the armed forces. Refusal to be inducted was thus a federal crime, as was aiding and abetting such an act of defiance. War was wrong, but the law had to be enforced. What was the attorney general to do?

CHAPTER SIX

"HELL NO, WE WON'T GO!"

"I joined the Marines during World War II, but a bunch of my
buddies were conscientious objectors. Even then, I realized that they
were better men than I, that what they did took more courage."

Ramsey Clark[1]

WHAT WE REFER TO as the Vietnam War began in 1955 with efforts by
the South Vietnamese government, led by Ngo Dinh Diem, to rid the region of all communists and others opposed to the government. Diem was
brutal in his treatment of these individuals, subjecting them to imprisonment, torture, and execution. Though not necessarily in sync with Diem's
tactics, the United States was supportive of his anticommunist motivation
and therefore allied itself with South Vietnam with the goal of forestalling
the efforts of Ho Chi Minh, the president of the communist-supported
Democratic Republic of North Vietnam (DRV), to unify Vietnam. The
American government was concerned about the potential domino effect of
South Vietnam becoming communist—other Asian nations would follow
suit, falling like dominos.[2]

Over time the conflict escalated between North and South, as did America's participation. Initially, the United States refrained from sending "combat"
troops, but eventually became fully engaged in what morphed into an incredibly savage confrontation. The tactics utilized by both sides were barbaric and
the casualties horrific. The extensive use of chemical warfare—Napalm and
Agent Orange—was unprecedented, torturously killing millions and exposing countless others to debilitating long-term side effects.[3]

Although early media reports regarding America's involvement were
largely positive, as the war waged on, it became increasingly apparent that
this rosy picture was far from the truth. The reality of the violence in

Vietnam, especially that which the U.S. government actively condoned and took part in, would be unthinkable were it not true. Vast numbers of innocent civilians were being killed, and it seemed to many that our motivation for doing so was arrogant imperialism, driven by self-interest and sustained by tragic hubris.[4] Scores of U.S. citizens not only became disillusioned with the war effort, but they began to actively oppose it, speaking out and waging large-scale protests.

Though not always lodged at him individually, President Johnson took every piece of Vietnam-related criticism as a personal affront.[5] He was obsessed with the war for a number of reasons, but mostly because he feared that an embarrassing defeat would be his lasting legacy, negating historic civil rights advances and overshadowing the ambitious Great Society agenda.[6] Any questioning of the war—a conflict to which he was myopically committed—infuriated the president.[7] As mentioned in the previous chapter, when Martin Luther King, Jr. sided with those opposed to the war and caustically labeled his government the "greatest purveyor of violence in the world," the once-collaborative relationship between the two was forever broken.[8]

Others shared King's perspective on the American government. They had grown uncomfortable with the war effort and questioned the U.S. motivation and resolve to remain engaged in what seemed to be a futile, unjust conflict. We had inserted our nose where it did not belong, killing people who had done nothing to harm us, and we were too stubborn and certain of our moral and military superiority to admit our folly and withdraw.

Sincere belief in this critique spawned a powerful anti–Vietnam War movement throughout the country. Besides staging sit-ins and public demonstrations, many young men began burning their federally issued draft cards or else openly refused induction into the military when drafted. At the time, the United States drafted men under the Military Selective Service Act (SSA), which required formal registration within a specified number of days following one's 18th birthday. Evading or refusing to register or report for service was a federal crime, punishable by up to five years in prison.[9] Hence, so-called draft dodgers—taking a cue from the civil rights movement—engaged in active civil disobedience, willing to risk imprisonment to demonstrate their opposition to the Vietnam War.

While Dr. King opposed the war generally and in a fashion similar to other protesters, it is important to note one critical distinction: His aversion had a decidedly racial theme. Specifically, his disapproval primarily arose from his recognition of the acute paradox displayed by the United States in calling upon black men to fight side by side with white men in Vietnam on behalf of a nation that did not treat them in a manner equal to white men at home. In other words, African American men were being called to fight for democracy abroad when they were not yet entitled to full, democratic citizenship in their own country. Moreover, the hypocrisy of America condemning racial rebellion in its streets while fully engaged in the most violent of battles internationally was impossible to reconcile.

By the time that Ramsey Clark was attorney general, opposition to the war had reached a fever pitch. As attorney general, he was responsible for enforcing the law of the land, including the SSA—indeed, some might have claimed *especially* the SSA, given President Johnson's absolute obsession with the war. Dependably progressive on so many issues of that era, including civil rights, the president had no tolerance whatsoever for those who evaded the draft or encouraged others to do so. His sensitivity about this was nothing short of manic.[10] It therefore should come as no surprise that he placed tremendous pressure on his stridently independent attorney general to pursue prosecution of both draft dodgers and their aiders and abettors.

If one were to predict how Clark would respond to this pressure, the odds-on guess would be that he would not go forward with prosecutions. Logically, his understanding and compassion regarding civil rights protesters' exercising their First Amendment rights in an effort to effect change would translate to Vietnam War protesters as well. They too saw government-sanctioned injustice being carried out in Vietnam and engaged in demonstrations designed to encourage the United State to rethink its position on the conflict.

The attorney general would refrain from pursuing criminal charges against these protesters, especially given his personal aversion to violence generally and to the bombing in Vietnam in particular. Perhaps the only attorney general in history to be excluded from regular National Security Council meetings, Clark expressed his views to the president that the United

States should stop all bombing of North Vietnam. On the occasions when Clark was invited to meetings with presidential advisors, he offered this same view. Clark has theorized that the president included him so that he would have at least one person in the room who would express an opposing view on the bombing.[11]

In any event, notwithstanding his empathy for civil rights protesters and his known position on the Vietnam conflict, the attorney general, to the consternation of many, authorized antiwar-related prosecutions, the most notorious of which was the pursuit of the Boston Five on charges of conspiracy to aid and abet draft evasion.[12] This alone was puzzling, but his simultaneous refusal to prosecute Black Power activist Stokely Carmichael and other black leaders who were engaged in the same alleged unlawful behavior as the Boston Five was completely dumbfounding. The only observable difference was that the Boston Five were white and entitled, while Carmichael and the others who escaped indictment were black and socially oppressed.[13] Did these distinctions make a difference to Clark? And if so, was that appropriate, particularly for someone so rigidly committed to the sanctity of the rule of law?

By the mid-1960s, Stokely Carmichael, along with his compatriot H. Rap Brown, had become a source of intense frustration for President Johnson. Carmichael, who assumed the chairmanship of the Student Nonviolent Coordinating Committee (SNCC) in 1966, guided that organization in a confrontational direction that belied its name. He once menacingly observed: "We have been lynched, our houses have been bombed and our churches burned. Now we are being shot down like dogs in the streets by white racist policemen. We can no longer accept this oppression without retribution."[14] Rather than civilly disobey unjust laws in the hope of inspiring change, Carmichael promoted the acquisition and exercise of "black power" in order to take that which was rightfully owed to black citizens.[15]

Besides his harsh rhetoric aimed at white America generally, Carmichael directed considerable ire at the government's involvement in the Vietnam War, especially with regard to the drafting of black men for military service in a conflict that he viewed as racist. In the spring of 1967 during a large antiwar rally in New York, Carmichael stole the spotlight from Dr. King and Dr. Benjamin Spock by caustically indicting the American government's involvement in Vietnam as the height of dissimulation:

> We maintain that America's cry of "preserve freedom in the world" is a hypocritical mask behind which it squashes liberation movements which are not bound, and refuse to be bound, by the United States' cold war policies. We see no reason for black men, who are daily murdered physically and mentally in this country, to go and kill yellow people abroad, who have done nothing to us and are, in fact, victims of the same oppression. We will not support LBJ's racist war in Vietnam.[16]

On another occasion, Carmichael again highlighted the duplicitous audacity of the government's enlisting of black men to fight in the war, using a catchy tag line that he adopted and popularized: "Hell no. We won't go. They expect us to run in Harlem and fight in Hanoi? They must be crazy."[17] He elaborated, "Even if I believed the lies of Johnson, that we're fighting to give democracy to the people in Vietnam, as a black man living in this country I wouldn't fight to give this to anybody."[18] One other markedly fiery antiwar speech that he delivered in Tougaloo, Mississippi, inspired almost five minutes of shouting by the assembled crowd: "We ain't going, hell no!"[19]

Johnson already had concerns about Carmichael, firmly believing that he and H. Rap Brown were fomenting the widespread urban rioting that was taking place during this period. He found Carmichael's confrontational approach personally distasteful, and he clearly preferred dealing with the more traditional civil rights activists of the old guard, such as NAACP President Roy Wilkins and Urban League Chair Whitney Young, who were very supportive of and cooperative with the president's administration.[20] Sympathetic to the plight of black citizens, Johnson willingly worked with these leaders to improve the status of blacks in America, albeit at a somewhat patient, measured pace.[21] Carmichael and other principals of the new guard, however, were convinced that the only way to achieve equal stature in American society was through the establishment and assertion of black power, which included resorting to violence, if necessary. Johnson viewed this as a significant impediment to progress in civil rights. In particular, white voters felt threatened and angry, which translated into hesitance on the part of their elected officials in Washington.[22]

Equally disturbing to President Johnson was Carmichael's blatant, vocal disdain for the Vietnam War, which was obviously capturing the imagination of many young people, both black and white. Given the importance of victory in Vietnam to his legacy, it became Johnson's prime objective to remove Carmichael from the antiwar picture. A successful federal prosecution seemed like an effective strategy for accomplishing this.[23] While a potential charge against Carmichael under the SSA for knowingly aiding and abetting draft evasion appears to have been the most logical and viable basis for indictment, this was not the crime for which he was investigated. Instead President Johnson pushed for charging him with conspiracy to incite a riot.

During a notably intense Cabinet meeting on August 2, 1967, the principal topic for discussion was the issue of whether Carmichael and Brown could be indicted on this charge.[24] In his report to the Cabinet regarding the recent riots in Detroit and elsewhere, Ramsey Clark concluded that there was "no hard evidence of a Negro conspiracy."[25] Though he conceded that "we know there are lots of leaders and roving trouble-makers[,]" Clark attributed much of the severity of the unrest to overreactions by "irresponsible officials."[26]

Secretary of State Dean Rusk incredulously retorted, "Don't we have any remedy for these people?"[27] Clark responded by noting that the Justice Department was closely following both Carmichael and Brown but reiterated that there was no basis for prosecuting either of them.[28] Though a conviction might have been possible at the trial level, according to Clark, it would undoubtedly have been overturned on appeal, which would have only served to further elevate the stature of Carmichael and Brown.[29] Nevertheless, various Cabinet members persisted in their calls for prosecution. John Gardner, secretary of Health, Education, and Welfare, rhetorically scoffed: "Surely there must be a limit to what a man can say?"[30]

The bottom line seemed to be that as unsettling as Carmichael's and Brown's words and methods may have been to many, they simply did not rise to the level of a conspiracy to incite a riot.[31] Although the president eventually acquiesced to his independent attorney general's position concerning the prosecution, he and others within the administration never fully embraced that decision.

But what about a prosecution for aiding and abetting draft evasion? There was unquestionably ample evidence to support such a charge. Yet, this was not an avenue that Ramsey Clark chose to pursue. Instead, he somewhat inexplicably went after five, well-established white men on the charge of conspiracy to aid and abet draft evasion. To be sure, these were not the only individuals who were prosecuted for violating the SSA, but this particular prosecution was singularly noteworthy because Clark took the lead in authorizing and overseeing it. Nicknamed the Boston Five because their prosecution took place in Boston,[32] the group consisted of Dr. Benjamin Spock, Reverend William Sloane Coffin, Jr., Marcus Raskin, Michael Ferber, and Mitchell Goodman.[33] All of the men were highly regarded professionally and active members of the antiwar movement, but Dr. Spock and Reverend Coffin stood out because of their national reputations. Dr. Spock was one of the country's best-known pediatricians, having authored the hugely popular bestseller *The Common Sense Book of Baby and Child Care*.[34] Reverend Coffin had been the chaplain at Yale University since 1958 and was an outspoken, influential activist for human rights.[35]

Although the Boston Five organized and took part in activities that were no more overt or provocative than the antiwar efforts of Stokely Carmichael, Clark and his team focused on several of the group's most conspicuous acts. One of these incidents was a major press conference on October 2, 1967, that publicized all of the anti-draft activities occurring around that time.[36] Another was an infamous demonstration on October 20, 1967, during which a briefcase filled with draft cards and other draft-related materials was hand-delivered to the Department of Justice.[37] It was at this event that Reverend Coffin, on the steps of the DOJ Building, famously called on the draft-eligible men present to refuse induction and announced his commitment and that of his cohorts to "aid and abet" the young men in any way possible.[38] He went on to essentially invite federal prosecution, asserting: "This means that if they are now arrested for failing to comply with a law that violates their consciences, we too must be arrested, for in the sight of that law we are now as guilty as they."[39]

Coffin's speech clearly laid the foundation for an "aiding and abetting draft evasion" prosecution under the SSA, even if the choice of these particular individuals for indictment seemed dubiously selective. Despite this, rather than proceeding with such a straightforward case, Clark chose to pursue a far less substantial conspiracy theory, one that ultimately proved unsuccessful: Raskin was acquitted; Spock and Ferber had their convictions overturned on appeal; and the government opted not to retry Coffin and Goodman after their successful appeals.[40] The problem with the conspiracy theory was that there was little, if any, tangible evidence that the five men "conspired." Some contend that they had minimal personal interaction with one another prior to the indictment and apparently had never come together as a group until that time.[41]

Why then did Ramsey Clark's team pursue the Boston Five, out of all the other possible targets, and why on a charge that was almost certain to fail? One theory is that the prosecution was an attempt by the DOJ to save face after Lt. General Lewis Hershey, the director of the Selective Service, issued a draconian pronouncement that all draft-eligible resisters should be declared delinquent, denied deferment, and reclassified for immediate induction.[42] Clark dialed back this over-the-top edict through a joint statement issued with Hershey announcing the creation of a special unit within the Justice Department that would concentrate on investigating and prosecuting Selective Service violations, but on a much narrower scale than the general's original strategy. Special attention would be paid to the "counsel, aid, or abet" provisions of the SSA, which appears to have been a significant part of the impetus behind the Boston Five prosecution.[43] Indeed, the unit's head, John Van de Kamp, confirmed as much and indicated that the group was selected because of their notoriety and the large volume of available public evidence against them.[44] Furthermore, it is also possible that the indictments may have been intended "to send a message that although criticism of the war and the draft would be tolerated, 'inducing or procuring evasion' would not."[45]

Although there may be some validity to these explanations, Ramsey Clark has offered different, conflicting rationales over the years and has never been entirely forthcoming about the episode. One justification hinges on his commitment to the role of the DOJ—to prosecute violations of the law. According to Clark, "if the law says that you cannot do this and you do it, then you've got an obligation to enforce the law."[46] The Boston Five's open and notorious violation of the letter of the SSA necessitated prosecution—failing to have done so would have effectively robbed the justice system of integrity.

Somewhat paradoxically, Clark has similarly maintained that this integrity rationale supported his refusal to prosecute Stokely Carmichael because he viewed the factual basis for a violation of the law to have been deficient. Elaborating on the centrality of systemic integrity to his prosecutorial decision-making process, Clark emphasized:

> [T]he system has to have integrity. If you don't prosecute violations of the law, you don't have a government of laws. On the one hand, in my judgment, if we had prosecuted Carmichael without facts, we would be guilty of, you know, most serious abuse. But if we didn't prosecute Spock and Coffin where we did have the facts of violation in our judgment—this is a matter of judgment—we would be guilty of just the opposite abuse. It's not a question of morality—who's right. . . . It's a question of whether the system has integrity.[47]

Clark has also suggested that the Boston Five's conduct was singularly egregious because their purpose was to destroy the Selective Service System, a goal more nefarious in his mind than simply expressing opposition to participation in the Vietnam War.[48] It is hard to understand, however, why such an overt objective would have made a difference. If the efforts of others, though not expressly intended to defeat the system, nevertheless had the potential effect of doing so, what is the point in drawing a distinction?

More recently, Clark offered yet another riff on his prosecutorial motivation, contending that his pursuit of the Boston Five was intended to provide a forum for debating the efficacy of the draft.[49] He professedly wanted "to show [President] Johnson that opposition to the war wasn't limited to draft-dodging longhairs but included the most admired pediatrician in

America, a prominent and revered patrician minister, and a respected former Kennedy Administration official."[50] There may be some truth to this explanation, particularly given Clark's formal request that the trial judge in the case impose no penalty in the event of conviction.[51] But if true, this reasoning only serves to further complicate the story. Let's get this straight. The conduct in question was so bad that it had to be prosecuted; however, it was not bad enough to warrant any punishment. This seems like nonsense coming from the same man who proclaimed the overarching importance of integrity within the system. A sham prosecution in order to evoke a high-profile debate concerning the draft does not sound like the approach of an integrity-driven attorney general.

Perhaps sensitive to this potential critique, Clark sought to justify his "no punishment" position by contending that the Boston Five violated the law out of a sense of "moral rightness";[52] their morality placed them on a different penal plane. This suggests that Clark agreed with the moral propriety of their conduct even though he recognized its unlawfulness.[53] That this subjective belief led him to oppose punishment is troubling. Such subjectivity should not color the decisions of an ostensibly independent prosecutor. Where would Clark draw the line? What if he had been vehemently in favor of the Vietnam War and its legitimacy? Should that have led him to seek a more severe sentence because he viewed the Boston Five as morally wrong? Surely not, which exposes yet another confounding wrinkle in Clark's revisionist account of the Boston Five saga.

Ultimately, Ramsey Clark's tortured explanations regarding this prosecution sound more like a man trying to convince himself that what he did was consistent with his principles, rather than inform others of what was really at play. He seemingly acknowledges that he could not reasonably carry his integrity rationale to its logical extreme, which would have meant that he should have prosecuted everyone who violated the SSA in order to ensure that the law had the all-important element of integrity. That would have been impossible. No prosecutor can pursue every criminal act with the same vigor. Priorities must be taken into account, and prosecutors have virtually unfettered discretion in making charging decisions. Clark maintains that it made more sense to pursue individuals who were capable of defending themselves in court, in essence, making the prosecution a fair fight.[54] He was not interested in going after sincere and powerless draft dodgers.[55]

Whatever the actual reason for Clark's suspicious choice of defendants, the seemingly irreconcilable question that remains is how he could, with a straight face, prosecute the Boston Five but not Stokely Carmichael. Carmichael's rhetoric was far more direct, tending toward the incitement of violence. Not only did he urge black men to evade the draft, he suggested that the rest of the black community should physically protect those men to prevent their imprisonment—"there're enough people in that community around him, so that if they dare come in, they are going to face maximum damage in their community."[56] Moreover, he directly aided and abetted draft evasion, to the point of escorting fellow SNCC leader Cleveland Sellers to his Army induction ceremony and whispering words of encouragement as Sellers famously refused induction.[57] How could Clark ignore this, especially with the president breathing down his neck, pining for Carmichael to be locked up?

Strangely, Clark contends that he never really considered prosecuting Carmichael for violating the SSA.[58] Although there is ample evidence to suggest that others pressed for such a prosecution,[59] and that the Justice Department may have affirmatively declined to act based on a lack of evidence,[60] it seems obvious that Clark did not even view Carmichael as being in the same category as other anti–Vietnam War activists.

He assessed Carmichael's conduct through a civil rights, rather than an antiwar, prism. He tellingly conceded this point to me, admitting that he did not view blacks, such as Carmichael and Brown, who were resisting the draft, in the same way that he viewed whites who did so.[61] This admission helps explain his singular focus on the potential charge of "conspiracy to incite a riot." In his mind, Carmichael was all about securing equal rights for black people; rioting was a reaction, in large measure, to their unequal status in society. The drafting of black men for the Vietnam War was but another manifestation of the inequitable treatment of black citizens by the American government—they were being denied rights by a system at home, yet were expected to defend the ideals of that very system abroad.

This concern was exacerbated, in Clark's view, because African American men were actually being sent to Vietnam (some voluntarily) in disproportionate numbers.[62]

To Clark, disparate treatment based on race was at the heart of Carmichael's antiwar rhetoric. It was not about tearing down the draft; it was about advocating for the rights of his people.[63] And the attorney general understood this in a way that his Johnson administration contemporaries could not comprehend. Again, his Watts experience likely preconditioned him to empathize with the plight of black America. He knew what the real causes of the riots were—poor education, unemployment, and general mistreatment, particularly by law enforcement. Carmichael and H. Rap Brown may have heightened the disenchantment and unrest in the black community through their oratory, but that was not the cause. Hence, Clark steadfastly refused to indict them on the only charges that he deemed even remotely pertinent.

When assessed in this light, maybe Clark's earnest commitment to the integrity of the justice system can be reconciled. He recognized that African Americans were a subjugated class in society, treated unequally in virtually every realm of American life. They clearly perceived the "law" as a primary tool of white oppression, used to perpetuate and institutionalize their unequal societal status. As such, it is highly plausible that he found it indefensible to place black citizens on equal footing with whites when the question was one of criminal culpability. Instead of establishing the integrity of the system, adherence to equality in this one facet of their existence would have only served to reinforce the perception of the law as unjust and oppressive. In other words, Clark's inequitable treatment of Stokely Carmichael and the Boston Five may have been a covert way of balancing the scales of justice to some degree.[64]

This assessment of Clark's prosecutorial approach, however, is contradicted by another head-scratching indictment that Clark approved—that of heavyweight boxing champion Muhammad Ali.[65] Ali was black and a member of the Nation of Islam. He opposed induction as a conscientious objector based on his religion and, echoing King and Carmichael, further questioned why he—a black man—would be called upon to fight for his country on foreign soil against people of color when that same country treated him and his people so poorly at home. "Why should they ask me to put on a uniform and go 10,000 miles from home and drop bombs and bullets on brown people in Vietnam while so-called Negro people in Louisville are treated like dogs and denied simple human rights?"[66]

Given the apparent rationale for Clark's reluctance to prosecute Stokely Carmichael, one might have reasonably suspected that Ali's logic would resonate with him. Like Carmichael, Ali had a point. How could the U.S. government reasonably seek to force black people to defend its putative democratic ideals abroad in light of the racial injustice that was evident in America's streets? Nevertheless, Clark was somehow okay with the champ's prosecution. Perhaps it had to do with the fact that Ali had the means and renown to put up a vigorous defense. After an initial conviction and the imposition of a prison sentence of five years, Ali was ultimately victorious on appeal to the U.S. Supreme Court.[67] The price of victory, however, was the loss of his prime years as a boxer, having been banned from the sport for three years for adhering to his principles. He would still go on to be the reputed and self-proclaimed "greatest of all time," but his boxing legacy could have been even more substantial if he had those three years back.

Ironically, in the years following his prosecution, Ali became close with Ramsey Clark; he grew to admire and respect his erstwhile adversary. The reverence was mutual. In an interview, Clark told me that Ali was "the most beautiful human being he had ever seen."[68] That was plainly an acknowledgment of the champ's captivating physical appearance, but it also reflected Clark's assessment of Ali's warmth and spirituality, his love of poor people, and his desire to help those in need. Ali's longtime cornerman and chief motivator Drew Bundini Brown, in the buildup to the acclaimed bout between Ali and then-champ George Foreman, perceptively appraised the otherworldly aura of his boss:

> I think Muhammad is a prophet. How you gonna beat God's son? Anybody love poor people and little people, got to be a prophet. He was champion of the world; had a long table filled full of food; had a house for his mother; one for him. And he told 'em to take it and shove it. If he couldn't love his God.[69]

Interestingly, Bundini Brown's characterization of Ali mirrors how many would describe Clark. He was and is prophet-like, eschewing personal wealth and comfort in order to provide for others. Like Ali, Clark has always been willing to stand unflinchingly on principle, no matter what the price. It thus is not really so surprising that the two men gravitated to each other. Ali occasionally dropped by Clark's Greenwich Village law office to visit; Clark represented him in several civil matters. In the early 70s, Ali even asked his former prosecutor to serve as his manager for an upcoming fight in Chicago. Notwithstanding his affection and respect for Ali, Clark declined because of his intense aversion to the sport. He viewed boxing as barbaric and wanted no part of it.[70]

I was with Ramsey Clark several days after Ali's death during the summer of 2016. It was clear to me that he was very sad that his friend was gone. At one point, he absentmindedly picked up a copy of the *New York Times* that was on the table next to him. Virtually the entire front page was devoted to Ali. Clark stared at it, seemingly forgetting for a moment that I was seated across from him, and visibly winced, slightly shaking his head at the same time. It was as if he couldn't believe it. Another person he admired and loved had left this world before him. When would it stop?

Once he regained his focus, Clark talked about a time that Ali visited him at his apartment with one of his young children. Clark recalled Ali practically juggling the child in the air, much to Georgia Clark's consternation.[71] Throughout my two-day visit, Clark kept returning to the subject of Ali, obviously preoccupied with the champ's death. At one point, he searched for the right word to capture the essence of Ali, and he tellingly settled upon "sweet"; to him, that was the best word to describe the greatest pugilist of all time.[72]

Notably, Clark's relationship with Ali was not the only one that he struck up with a former prosecutorial target. He likewise developed friendships with Reverend Coffin and Dr. Spock. Coffin actually performed Clark's son's wedding ceremony. Clark also became close with Stokely Carmichael and H. Rap Brown. Although he protected these two men to a certain extent as attorney general—unlike with Ali, Coffin, and Spock—Carmichael and Brown were constantly in the DOJ's and FBI's crosshairs, their every move carefully monitored. For Clark to later befriend each of them was unexpected, to say the least, but consistent with the path of his life's journey, which led him to be ever-more protective of those most marginalized and vilified by society.

As contemporary evidence of this, in recent years Clark joined in the legal defense of H. Rap Brown, now known as Jamil Abdullah Al-Amin, in an effort to free him from a maximum security prison where he was incarcerated following his conviction for the murder of a Fulton County, Georgia, sheriff's deputy under dubious circumstances.[73] Interestingly, Al-Amin's wife Karima speculates that Clark's relationship with and assistance of her husband may stem from some "sense of responsibility to right a wrong," namely, the manner in which Al-Amin had been targeted and treated during the late 1960s. Even though Clark was not personally responsible for these actions, he was a part of an administration that desperately wanted to bring Al-Amin down.[74]

None of this sheds any further light upon the Boston Five case. If anything, it simply muddies the water more. But the friendships with Coffin and Spock may suggest that Clark harbors regret about the prosecution, even though he has never directly admitted this. The closest he came to doing so was in a speech at Yale delivered shortly after he stepped down as attorney general. Following an introduction by Reverend Coffin, in commenting upon his introducer, Clark revealingly stated that "if to err is human and to forgive divine," then he was human and Coffin was divine.[75] Consistent with this, Roger Wilkins, Clark's close friend and ally during the Johnson years, later expressed the belief the Clark was embarrassed by the Boston Five prosecution.[76]

Others have gone so far as to postulate that this embarrassment or guilt may have profoundly affected the trajectory of Clark's post-DOJ life. In an interview, his predecessor Nick Katzenbach speculated to me that it may be that Clark has spent much of his professional career atoning for some of the Vietnam-related prosecutions like the Boston Five case, matters about which he simply did not feel comfortable in retrospect.[77] Clark's former law partner Melvin Wulf has echoed this sentiment:

Standing by, being Attorney General during the Vietnam War without resigning, is not a particularly heroic position to have taken. . . .
I sometimes speculate—and this is absolute speculation—that what
he's doing is a kind of atonement for having been Attorney General
for Lyndon Johnson at the time of the Vietnam War, and for having
in fact initiated the indictment against Dr. Spock and the others.[78]

Admittedly, all of the post-hoc assessments concerning Ramsey Clark's
Vietnam-related prosecutorial decisions and the effect that they may have
had on him are largely conjecture. There is some factual support, but nothing definitive. Only Clark knows for sure, and he has either been craftily
evasive or else is incapable of personally grasping exactly what drove this
curious chapter in his life journey. One thing seems certain, however. The
rigid, independent streak that he demonstrated in pursuing the Boston Five
and in refusing to indict Stokely Carmichael became even more pronounced
during the balance of his DOJ tenure, as he waged increasingly controversial
battles from the inside, perhaps foreshadowing his path in the years ahead.

CHAPTER SEVEN

BATTLING ON THE INSIDE

"I've tried to keep the sense of legal discipline intact here,
but the pressures against you are tremendous, and, God
knows, you pay a heavy price for resisting them."

Ramsey Clark[1]

RAMSEY CLARK HAD enormous respect and admiration for President Johnson. He felt that Johnson's efforts on civil rights and in endeavoring to end poverty were sincere and courageous. Creating racial equality and elevating the poor were idealistic goals that few, if any, presidents would have been so bold as to undertake. Clark believed that the president truly cared; he was not just going through political motions. To be sure, there was some egotistical narcissism at play as well. Johnson recognized that if he accomplished his grand plans for a Great Society, he would go down as one of the most celebrated leaders in history, and he desperately wanted that distinction. This, in large measure, is why the Vietnam War vexed him so; it was going to irreparably tarnish the glorious legacy that he hoped to leave.

For the most part, Clark's high regard for Johnson was unaffected by any misgivings he may have had regarding the president's underlying motives. He remained loyal to his boss until the end. This loyalty, however, did not stop Clark from doing what he believed to be right. The Preacher moniker from his early days in the Justice Department remained apropos throughout his tenure as attorney general. His rigid opposition to wiretapping, unwavering condemnation of the death penalty, and stubborn refusal to prosecute Stokely Carmichael, even in the face of intense pressure from the president and others within the administration, are but a few examples of his "mustang independence." Johnson had political concerns and objectives; his chief prosecutor did not. Though Clark loved the president, he did not view his role as that of a sycophantic yes-man. When appropriate and called for by the law, Clark was not hesitant to diverge from the president's desired path.

While this was true at various points during his time as attorney general, following the Boston Five episode, Clark's independence drifted toward what the president likely considered to be insubordination and perhaps even outright antagonism. Occasionally standing on principle and integrity in authorizing prosecutions was one thing, but consistently acting, on myriad fronts, in a manner openly defiant of Johnson's wishes was quite another. Clark undertook increasingly controversial actions that the president viewed as detrimental to his legacy. Indeed, things were so bad toward the end that some say Johnson never forgave his attorney general. Whether or not that is true, he was clearly furious with Clark to the point of considering whether to move him to a different position during 1968.[2] That never happened, but Johnson visibly began to treat Clark as an outsider, ultimately declining to even invite him to the administration's farewell luncheon on the day of Nixon's inauguration.[3]

What exactly did Ramsey Clark do to irk the commander in chief in such a lasting fashion? The list is a long one. At the top, though, would have to be Clark's role in permanently damaging Johnson's close relationship with his senatorial mentor, cherished colleague, and dear friend, Georgia Senator Richard Russell. Russell was an unabashed segregationist and staunch opponent of civil rights legislation, but his longstanding ties to the president enabled their union to persevere notwithstanding policy disagreements. Johnson felt that he owed his entire career to Russell and did whatever he could as president to accommodate his friend. One no-brainer of an accommodation was to make sure that the senator's recommendations for federal judgeships sailed through the confirmation process. However, the sailing for Russell's candidate for a seat on the U.S. District Court for the Southern District of Georgia turned out to be far less than smooth, thanks in substantial part to the president's attorney general.

Because the confirmation of federal judges requires the advice and consent of the Senate, a tradition has been established that senators from the president's party recommend nominees for judicial vacancies in their states.

Then, after some internal vetting, the president typically makes official nominations.[4] The attorney general has somewhat of a shepherding and oversight function in connection with the vetting process. Once screening reports are prepared on nominees by the DOJ, FBI, and American Bar Association, the attorney general takes these and puts together files on the candidates that are then sent to the White House.[5] Following that, the president formally puts nominations forward, usually choosing from senators' so-called short list of recommendations, and such nominations are historically confirmed by the Senate, almost without exception.[6] In more recent times, however, the process has become so political that this mechanical certainty is far from a given. When the president's political party does not comprise the majority in the Senate, nominees frequently languish in committee with their nominations never coming up for a vote before the legislative session adjourns.[7]

In 1968, when a vacancy opened up in Georgia's southern district, Richard Russell had the perfect candidate, one with whom he was particularly close—Alexander Lawrence. By all objective accounts, Lawrence was extremely qualified for the judiciary. He was a noted lawyer and legal scholar, had been president of the State Bar Association, and—maybe even more important for appointment purposes—was an active member of the Georgia Democratic Party.[8] Russell was so confident in Lawrence that his was the lone name forwarded for the president's consideration.[9] Unfortunately for the senator, a little digging uncovered some fatal flaws concerning his nominee, at least in the eyes of more progressive segments of the party.

Perhaps not surprisingly, Russell's pick turned out to have a pedigree as a faithful and vocal segregationist. During the prenomination scrutinizing, evidence of his earlier virulent racial views came to light, including one 1958 address in which he scathingly attacked the liberal Supreme Court led by Chief Justice Earl Warren. Lawrence reportedly called the justices "unrestrained 'zealots' who now 'rule[d] by uncontrollable will,'" and characterized the Court's ostensible "independence" as "judicial arrogance."[10] All of this, of course, was viewed as a thinly veiled denouncement of advances that the Court approved on the racial front, namely desegregation. And Richard Russell loved it. Rather than viewing it as a potential disqualifying misstep, he surely considered Lawrence's views to be a preeminent badge of suitability for the bench. At the time it was delivered, the senator had Lawrence's speech reprinted in *The Congressional Record*, praising it as "one of the ablest deliverances on the situation which prevails in the United States today."[11]

A groundswell began to gather around Russell's nominee, with civil rights groups, including the NAACP, mounting a strong opposition push. Nevertheless, it was by no means inevitable that President Johnson would listen to this negative critique, let alone accept it. However, an essential cog in the nomination wheel, known for his attentiveness to matters concerning race, was characteristically listening.

In light of the evidence supporting the conclusion that Lawrence was a segregationist who might undermine the historic civil rights strides made by the Johnson administration, Ramsey Clark harbored grave misgivings about his potential nomination. Clark had witnessed the unsavory results of the appointment of racist southern judges throughout President Kennedy's tenure, individuals whose ascension to the bench was paved by the administration's desire for political favor in the Senate. These judges were anathema to Clark personally and, more importantly, to the integrity of the judicial system and the rule of law. He would not stand for an encore of this dangerous political dance.[12]

While many were content to cross their fingers and hope that Lawrence's views on race had evolved over time, Clark was not willing to take that risk. He actively lobbied the president to refrain from making the nomination. He understood the importance of the relationship with Senator Russell, but moving forward with Lawrence, in Clark's view, had the potential to seriously damage Johnson's historical imprint.[13]

Although Clark's opinion got the president's attention, Johnson still could not stomach going against the wishes of his beloved comrade. He reminded his attorney general that Senator Russell was "the dearest friend he had in the Senate" and observed that he was concerned about offending this very powerful ally.[14] Yet, Johnson's obsession with his legacy counterbalanced his worries about Russell and left him in a hopelessly torn state regarding the nomination. He settled on somewhat of a compromise, telling Clark, in essence, to come up with a way to make Lawrence's candidacy palatable, if at all possible, because he wanted to make the appointment.[15]

The decision seemed to be left in Clark's hands, as Johnson was unlikely to second-guess his judgment. And Clark's plan was to delay the decision until the issuance of the ABA's final report. Russell, however, was not willing to wait. As the vetting process dragged on, he lost patience and began lobbying harder with the president directly. At Johnson's request, Russell provided an additional letter of support for Lawrence, which was passed along to Clark. The letter was not nearly enough, though, as Clark had uncovered more negative information about Lawrence's views on race, and he simply did not believe that the proposed nominee would faithfully apply the law of the land if appointed. Clark therefore determined that he absolutely would not send the nomination forward to the White House, and he informed Senator Russell. Not surprisingly, the senator did not take this news well; he told Clark that if the appointment was not made, he "would never feel the same about" President Johnson.[16]

Russell persisted in his efforts with the president, and it seemed that the nomination was going to move forward. But Ramsey Clark remained an impediment. He continued to delay the nomination, still awaiting the ABA's report. Johnson pressured Clark, proclaiming that he wanted to appoint Lawrence—"If there's a way to posture him where we can nominate him, I want to do that. Now go get after it, and see if there's a way to do that."[17] This was a not so subtle directive. Johnson was now firmly in his friend's camp, but it was too late. His attorney general's delay tactics, which actually continued thereafter, had already irretrievably antagonized Russell. He wrote a blistering letter to the president, essentially accusing him of extortion—claiming that Johnson was delaying the nomination of Lawrence until after the Senate vote on the nominations of Abe Fortas and Homer Thornberry, as chief justice and associate justice, respectively, to the U.S. Supreme Court, in order to ensure Russell's support.[18]

Johnson was devastated by the letter, and he blamed the destruction of his cherished relationship with Senator Russell squarely on his attorney general. He told Clark, in no uncertain terms, that his "foot-dragging on [the nomination had] destroyed one of the great friendships I've had with one of the great men that has ever served this country."[19]

The president was deeply hurt by Russell's missive; however, it only strengthened his resolve to get Alexander Lawrence's nomination moved forward. Now, he directly ordered Ramsey Clark to do so, knowing that this might potentially push his attorney general to resign. Clark did not, though, and instead, complied with the president's instructions, but largely because there was no longer any reason to oppose Lawrence.[20] Everything that Clark had hoped to accomplish had been achieved, and the long-awaited report from the ABA actually found the prospective judge to be "well qualified."[21] The nomination sailed forward with no further controversy, and ironically Lawrence turned out to be an exceptionally liberal judge, who was later vilified in southern Georgia for his decisions promoting the desegregation of public schools.[22]

Ramsey Clark's principled battle over the nomination, irrespective of the costs to others, not only resulted in a lasting fissure between President Johnson and Senator Russell,[23] it also marked the beginning of a similar degeneration of Clark's relationship with the president. One might have expected him to rein it in a bit after this episode. But that would not have been consistent with Clark's character. And so he continued to wage battles from within.

One of the most significant clashes that Clark embraced was with Mayor Richard Daley and his Chicago police force in connection with the 1968 Democratic National Convention (DNC). This was August 1968, the height of the anti–Vietnam War movement, and massive protests were assured. Mayor Daley anticipated rioting and chaos, akin to what his city had experienced in the aftermath of the assassination of Martin Luther King, Jr. just a few months earlier. At that time, Daley famously proclaimed that police should have been given orders to shoot looters to maim and arsonists to kill.[24] The callous and utterly irresponsible nature of this comment outraged Ramsey Clark. He knew that the mayor was completely in the wrong and made his displeasure known publicly, even though members of the administration advised him to hold his tongue.[25] In a speech delivered at the University of North Carolina, Clark dramatically declared:

A reverence for life is the sure way of reducing violent death. There are few acts more likely to cause guerrilla warfare in our cities and division and hatred among our people than to encourage police to shoot looters or other persons caught committing property crimes. How many dead twelve-year-old boys will it take for us to learn this simple lesson?[26]

Fear of large-scale unrest in Chicago led officials to seek assistance from the federal government to ensure public safety and peacefulness. But Ramsey Clark blocked these efforts, viewing any such action as contrary to the First Amendment rights of the protesters. He was adamant in his positon that the federal government should not interfere. The president was incensed by his attorney general's recalcitrance. As a result, Johnson's Chief of Staff W. Marvin Watson personally stressed the severity of the potential situation in Chicago to Clark in an effort to get him to act.[27] However, Clark was unmovable on this issue and offered his resignation rather than going against his principles. Watson refused to accept this offer and noted that only the president could make such a decision. Clark did not offer his resignation to Johnson but instead persisted in his stubborn resistance to involve the federal government in curtailing the demonstrators' right to peaceably assemble.[28]

In a subsequent conversation, Mayor Daley urged Watson to get the president to send troops to Chicago in a show of force to prevent rioting. Watson noted that the President was in favor of this, but he stopped short of representing that troops would be sent. Daley rightly interpreted this as being the handiwork of Ramsey Clark, for whom he obviously had no love.[29] Taking a cue from Richard Nixon's campaign rhetoric, Daley childishly denigrated Clark, maintaining that "What we need is a good Attorney General. We need a new Attorney General. Half the trouble brought upon the President has been brought on him by the Attorney General. After all, he has no guts and never had any guts."[30] Ultimately, there would be a federal presence in the form of U.S. Army troops, but Daley had to go around Ramsey Clark with the aid of the Illinois governor in order to obtain this.[31]

In the lead up to the DNC, antiwar protesters sought permits to enable them to legally march and demonstrate at several locations and to camp in Lincoln Park. All of these requests were denied, but the city did grant permission for one rally to be held on August 28 at the south end of Grant Park. Apart from its stinginess in awarding permits, the city intended to further squelch the protesters' activities by actively enforcing an 11 p.m. curfew. In anticipation of rioting and violence, Mayor Daley placed all 12,000 members of the Chicago Police Department on twelve-hour shifts.[32] Daley planned to showcase his law-and-order credentials through a no-nonsense display of military-style force by his law enforcement officers.

Rather than ensuring safety and calm, the mayor's tactics angered and provoked the protesters. Over the course of five days and nights, the police and demonstrators battled one another, with the officers getting the better of the clash, aggressively utilizing tear gas and batons to subdue protesters and force them out of the parks where they had been camping. Highly respected CBS news anchor Walter Cronkite was uncharacteristically opinionated on the air in describing the Chicago police as "thugs."[33]

Pushed into commercial areas, the demonstrators responded by throwing rocks and shattering windows of local businesses. The confrontation reached its apex on August 28 when the police violently disrupted a large afternoon rally in Grant Park.[34] Although there was no shooting of looters or killing of arsonists, the scene that unfolded was nothing short of horrific.

After an initial melee, calm was restored, and the demonstrators endeavored to obtain a permit to march to the site of the DNC to continue their protests. As with previous requests, this too was denied. Running out of options, the agitated crowd gathered near one of the hotels where convention delegates were staying to discuss strategy. To clear an intersection and maintain "order," the police escalated their tactics to wholesale brutality and viciousness, much of which was captured by television cameras.[35] Author Norman Mailer's portrayal paints a vivid picture of what transpired:

> The police attacked with tear gas, with Mace, and with clubs, they attacked like a chain saw cutting into wood, the teeth of the saw the edge of their clubs, they attacked like a scythe through grass, lines of 20 and 30 policemen striking out in an arc, their clubs beating, demonstrators fleeing.[36]

While there was undoubtedly general wrongdoing and unlawful behavior among the protesters, their conduct objectively paled in comparison
to the police over-reaction. Nevertheless, Mayor Daley's administration
attributed the violence to "outside agitators" whose purpose was to in-
stigate a confrontation with the police.[37] They wanted the demonstrators
prosecuted, as did President Johnson, who had great disdain for those who
actively opposed the Vietnam War.[38]

The president's attorney general and many others, however, were of
a decidedly different mindset. From their perspective, any riotous actions
by the demonstrators were precipitated by the police. Predictably, Clark
wanted the offending officers to be prosecuted and had no interest in pursuing any of the demonstrators.[39] The DOJ's investigation suggested that
there was no basis for charging the latter group with any federal crime.[40]
According to Clark, indictments were prepared against eight police officers
for excessive use of force, but Judge William J. Campbell, the chief judge
for the Northern District of Illinois, ordered the U.S. attorney not to sign
the proposed indictments, which resulted in the cases being delayed until
after the presidential election when they were finally signed and presented
to a grand jury for full consideration.[41]

After the inauguration of President Nixon, his Attorney General John
Mitchell set about securing the indictments of certain protesters.[42] On
March 20, 1969, a grand jury indicted eight protesters, including Black
Panther leader Bobby Seale, and the eight Chicago police officers.[43] The
indicted protesters, except for Seale, were mostly well-known antiwar radicals—Abbie Hoffman, David Dellinger, Rennie Davis, Tom Hayden, Jerry
Rubin, John Froines, and Lee Weiner, the latter two being the least celebrated.[44] The defendants were charged with conspiring to use interstate
commerce to incite a riot and crossing state lines for the same purpose.
Interestingly, the prosecutions were under portions of the Civil Rights Act
of 1968, which Ramsey Clark had been instrumental in getting passed,
although he opposed the sections in question out of concern that they
would deter lawful, peaceful demonstrations.[45] Added as a rider to the act,
the provisions were expressly inspired by and directed toward the conduct
of black activists who President Johnson and others believed to have been
at the heart of the civil unrest throughout the late 1960s, namely Stokely

Carmichael and H. Rap Brown. The antiriot portion of the legislation was commonly referred to as the Rap Brown law.[46]

Bobby Seale did not seem like a logical defendant in this case. His involvement in the demonstrations was limited to delivering two speeches, and when he was finished, he returned to his home in Oakland, California.[47] It seems likely that Seale was targeted because of his Black Panther affiliation and well-known, militant advocacy on behalf of African Americans.[48] After all, Chicago was one of the central locations for the Black Panther Party, and local law enforcement was notoriously hostile to this group.

The defendants were at first known as the "Chicago Eight," but this would later be reduced to "Seven" when Seale was removed from the case. From beginning to end, the trial was uniquely dramatic and preposterous.[49] The federal district court judge who presided over the matter—Judge Julius Hoffman (no relation to Abbie)—unapologetically seemed to be out to get the defendants and their controversial lead attorney William Kunstler—Ramsey Clark's future ally and co-counsel.[50]

The defendants and their lawyers were equally antagonistic toward the court, viewing the entire proceeding as a hit job on the antiwar movement, an unlawful effort to silence social dissent. Seale was furious about his prosecution, especially the judge's refusal to permit him to represent himself when his attorney of choice—formerly lead counsel in the case—could no longer handle the matter because of serious health issues.[51] The Black Panther leader openly berated the judge, calling him a fascist and a racist. Judge Hoffman infamously retaliated by having Seale bound to his chair and gagged during the proceeding.[52] The judge eventually severed Seale's case from the others, found him in contempt, and sentenced him to four years in prison.[53]

With the removal of Seale, the anarchy within the courtroom only increased. Abbie Hoffman and Jerry Rubin brazenly ridiculed the judge, comparing him to Adolf Hitler. The Chicago Seven's scorn for the court's authority had no bounds. As Kunstler biographer David Langum recounts, throughout the trial they "sat at their table, often reading, writing speeches, munching jelly beans, making faces, or laughing. Sometimes they slept. Litter piled up on their table and the carpet underneath it."[54] What may have appeared as spontaneous chaos was later claimed by Kunstler to have been an orchestrated defense strategy designed to keep the government on its heels.[55]

Perhaps most notably, at least from my point of view, Ramsey Clark was listed as a central witness for the defendants. He considered the police to have been the principal wrongdoers and the cause of the unrest. They had overreacted, employing unnecessary and excessive force. If anyone should have been on trial, it was the officers and those officials who sanctioned such egregious law enforcement tactics. This would have served as powerful testimony, especially coming from the nation's former chief law enforcement official. Judge Hoffman, however, never allowed Clark to testify.[56]

In the end, while the jury deliberated, Hoffman found the defendants and their lawyers guilty of 159 counts of contempt and handed down draconian sentences, particularly as to Kunstler. The jury found some of the defendants guilty of crossing state lines with the intent to incite a riot, but it rendered a not-guilty verdict as to the conspiracy charges. Ultimately, all of the contempt findings, including Seale's, were reversed, as was the jury's guilty verdict, based primarily on the obvious bias and unfairness of the proceedings. The government opted not to retry the defendants.[57] As for the parallel prosecutions of the eight police officers—those deemed to be the true culprits by Ramsey Clark and many others—seven were acquitted outright and the eighth had his case dismissed. Clark was deeply troubled by this result, though surely not surprised.[58]

Intriguingly, he sees a parallel between his involvement in the DNC episode and his apparent disparate treatment of the Boston Five and Stokely Carmichael. Clark contends that he could have been just as readily criticized for having approved indictments of the Chicago police while refusing to pursue the antiwar protesters who were the target of the police violence.[59] Objectively, the similarity does not seem to be that strong. The Chicago police were engaged in very different activities from the protesters they terrorized; choosing to prosecute their excessive behavior could not have been difficult. On the contrary, the conduct of the Boston Five and Carmichael was largely the same, and Clark had to make a somewhat complicated judgment call as to whom he should prosecute.

On a subjective level, however, it may be that the parallel that Clark sees is his identification with the individual or individuals whom he viewed as the oppressed. Carmichael, as a black man in the 1960s, clearly was on the outside; so too were the antiwar protesters—they were left-wing extremists, considered by many to be unpatriotic or maybe even communist. I think this is the manner in which Ramsey Clark was able to equate the two seemingly divergent situations, perhaps on a subconscious level. It is certainly consistent with the groups that he has chosen to identify with throughout his post-DOJ days.

Ramsey Clark's visible and vocal role in the drama that unfolded in Chicago that summer, and his principled position regarding who was at fault, made him an even more attractive and vulnerable target for Democratic nominee Hubert Humphrey's conservative opponents—Richard Nixon and George Wallace. They used this episode as further evidence that Clark was "soft on crime," which in turn was a reflection on the Johnson administration and anyone associated with it, including then–Vice President Humphrey. According to the campaign rhetoric, Clark was a coddler of criminals, a protector of lawless rioters, and an enemy of law enforcement—those brave men who sought only to maintain law and order. His outspoken denouncement of Mayor Daley and the Chicago police was poster-board material for this divisive portrayal. The truth about Ramsey Clark's posture regarding law enforcement and crime was far more complicated.

Before the DNC debacle, Clark had amassed a fairly long history of dealing with the police, beginning most notably with his chairing of the Presidential Task Force in the aftermath of the Watts riots in 1965. His Watts experience made him critically aware of the antagonistic relationship that the police typically had with the black community. This was relatively well understood to be the case in the South, but for it to also exist in urban settings, such as Los Angeles, was a revelation. Clark concluded in his Watts report that the acrimonious interplay between white, violence-prone police officers and black citizens was a central cause of the riots. Every riot up to the ones that erupted following the assassination of Dr. King occurred following an incident between the police and blacks. Given this reality, in an effort to prevent future rioting, Clark worked closely with law enforcement, attempting to build a more cooperative atmosphere in terms of how the police carried out their duties in the black community.

In his view at that time, "the foremost problem confronting the nation is the relationship of a policeman to the community, and it will be for decades to come," a statement made in reaction to Mayor Daley's original call for heavy-handed police measures to quell rioting.[60] One aspect of Clark's strategy for dealing with this problem was to ensure the prosecution of those who overstepped their authority and violated the constitutional rights of others, especially blacks. Indeed, this was his number one enforcement priority in the area of civil rights.

Given the highly combative nature of police–community relations, Clark has often rhetorically queried: "Who will protect the public when the police violate the law?"[61] He believed that it was his responsibility to do so, as the nation's chief law enforcement official. "[I]t was imperative that some leadership speak out and say that the police above all must obey the law; they above all must be professional and disciplined, because when they don't follow the law, there's no hope."[62] Clark deemed it essential to get the attention of local police forces to make them think twice about engaging in violent, unlawful behavior against African American citizens.

Though there was support for his position, many felt it was not his place as U.S. attorney general to be meddling in local police affairs. Clark was adamant that sitting idly by waiting for others to address the escalating problem was not an option that he seriously considered.

> When I see massacres like Orangeburg, South Carolina; when I see the stupid violence of police at the Chicago national convention and . . . at Berkeley just recently, I realized that they have to be told from some high source in power that they will be held responsible for their acts.[63]

Though largely overlooked from a historical perspective, the Orangeburg Massacre to which Clark referred infuriated him like no other act of police violence.

In March 1968, state and local police officers in Orangeburg, South Carolina, opened fire on apparently unarmed black students from South

Carolina State College who were protesting the local bowling alley's refusal to grant them access to the facility.[64] Three students were killed and
twenty-seven others seriously wounded, most in the back or in the soles
of their feet, suggesting that they were either lying down or fleeing at the
time of the attack.[65]

True to his stated civil rights enforcement priority, Clark did not hesi-
tate to go after the nine offending officers. Despite the local government's
cover-up, as well as the strong likelihood that a conviction would not be
possible, Clark pursued the officers on the charge of "impos[ing] summary
punishment" without due process of law.[66] Although the officers were ultimately acquitted, as Clark suspected would be the case, he had no regrets
about the prosecution; rather, he was content with the message his action
sent, firmly believing that "[f]rom a law enforcement standpoint, [the case]
would have a sobering, stabilizing effect."[67]

The prospect of inspiring caution in the face of similar public safety
challenges in the future was ample prosecutorial motivation for Clark. He
laid definitive blame for the tragedy at the feet of the government and the
American public for

> our failure to right grievous wrongs, permitting conditions to arise
> and continue where tens of thousands of black Americans were de-
> prived of constitutional and statutory rights—and really their oppor-
> tunity for personal fulfillment in our society.[68]

Although Clark was a staunch opponent of police brutality and mistreatment of black citizens, he knew that merely responding in a punitive
manner to individual officers who overstepped their authority was not sufficient. The problem was endemic, part of the very fabric of police culture.
He needed to disrupt that through the professionalization of the police
and the establishment of community policing.

In Clark's view, because policing is one of the hardest occupations in
our society—requiring high intelligence, great skill, and sound judgment—
rigid professional standards needed to be in place to ensure these qualities.
The ability to shoot a gun and physically overpower a suspect should be

very low on the list of attributes for police officers. Individuals who were long on these skills, but short on judgment and intellect, tended to be the hotheads who caused the most problems.

Sadly, this is still true today. Stories of young, poorly trained officers who overreact to tense situations out of fear and inflict harm or death on citizens remain far too common. Ramsey Clark correctly recognized that until local governments take seriously the necessity for a professional, skilled police force, the situations that give rise to unfortunate police–community encounters will persist.

Wisely, he understood that while the police had traditionally deserved the brunt of the blame, police–community relations was a two-way street. There were undeniably citizens who violated the law or intentionally antagonized officers, but the police still had the power, and they were the ones who needed to be above the fray. Rather than manhandling suspects and beating them into submission, officers must be able to deescalate such circumstances without resorting to unnecessary violence. The officers also need the trust and support of law-abiding citizens within the community. Mutual trust and support create an optimal law enforcement environment and are central to the concept of community policing. In commenting on the dire nature of the relationship between the police and the black community, Clark observed: "As never before, the policeman needs full community support. And as never before, the community needs him."[69]

Clark's proposed police reforms were always couched in supportive terms. He recognized that inadequate allocation of resources was a major impediment to officers doing their job well. Law enforcement to Clark was perhaps the most demanding and important occupation in America. He stated,

> There is no activity of modern times that requires a greater set of professional skills than policework [sic]. Police must know the law.
> . . . The policeman has to be a scientist in a broad range of physical and social sciences. . . . An officer often needs to be a medic and an athlete.[70]

He deemed it appalling, given the difficulty and unbridled significance of the law enforcement profession, that police officers were not trained better and paid more.

> Now, you can do whatever you want to, but until you improve police salaries you're not going to improve police performance because the salaries are pathetically low and you just can't attract and retain and develop and build competence without better salaries.[71]

Understandably, law enforcement leaders widely praised Clark for his efforts on their behalf, contrary to the disparaging, antipolice image of him cultivated by Nixon and Wallace, and attributed more broadly to President Johnson and his administration. For example, the director of the International Association of Chiefs of Police claimed that Clark did more for local law enforcement as attorney general than any of his predecessors. Similarly, Baltimore's police commissioner maintained that Clark provided "more enlightened leadership and demonstrated more sensitivity to the problems of law enforcement than any other Attorney General."[72]

Regrettably, the negative characterization of Clark's approach to policing is what stuck and permitted the Nixon administration to portray itself as the true protector of the public good, firmly committed to the reestablishment of law and order in America. Subsequent administrations, including our present one, followed Nixon's script, resulting in persistent police–community relations problems, often eerily reminiscent of situations that Ramsey Clark passionately battled against as attorney general.

President Johnson had actually been quite aggressive in addressing the issue of crime in America, establishing the President's Commission on Law Enforcement and Administration of Justice—better known as the Crime Commission—which issued a path-setting, comprehensive report calling for meaningful reforms in policing, the court system, and prisons.[73] Thus, Johnson was surely disconcerted by the dominant soft-on-crime impression of his administration that Ramsey Clark had been instrumental in creating. And Johnson's dismay regarding his attorney general would only grow stronger during the waning months of his presidency.

Toward the end of 1968, after the election of Nixon, the president gave explicit instructions to all of his Cabinet members to refrain from starting any new projects that they could not finish. This seemed intended, in part, to ensure a smooth transition with President Nixon. Johnson believed that if any proposed project was worthy of moving forward, it would surely be taken up by the new administration.[74] Ramsey Clark, though, seemed to disagree with this assessment. Knowing that he and his successor John Mitchell did not share many of the same values or views, Clark deemed it necessary to initiate some important litigation before he left office. Otherwise, Clark did not believe it would be pursued.

Larry Temple recalled a major lawsuit filed against a group of large automotive manufacturers, which particularly got under the president's skin. The case was against General Motors, Ford, Chrysler, and American Motors and alleged that the four auto giants had conspired to delay the development and use of devices to control pollution.[75] Johnson directed Temple to find out why Ramsey Clark had filed it. Temple remembers the president rhetorically exclaiming, "Didn't he hear my admonition?" When Temple asked Clark why he did it, the attorney general matter-of-factly said that it was important and that he did not think the new administration would file it. Furthermore, he had purposefully refrained from informing the president of his intentions because he wanted Johnson to be able to deny having any prior knowledge of the actions.[76]

Clark acknowledges that he filed a number of lawsuits based on the same premise, taking matters into his own hands, notwithstanding the president's express orders. He instituted an action to block a merger between Music Corporation of America and Westinghouse, as well as a monstrous antitrust lawsuit against IBM.[77] The latter case not only angered Johnson,[78] it also significantly strained the attorney general's relationship with his predecessor, Nick Katzenbach. Katzenbach was slated to assume the post of general counsel for IBM, taking over from Burke Marshall, who had served as the assistant attorney general for the Civil Rights Division during the Kennedy administration.[79] Katzenbach would have to endure the difficult case for the next twelve years before it was finally dismissed.[80] There is nothing to suggest that the suit was in any way inspired by personal animosity toward

Katzenbach or Johnson, but it is undeniable that Clark was well aware of the ire he was engendering; he pressed forward anyway on principle, notwithstanding the anticipated backlash.

While on some level Ramsey Clark's remarkable independence is worthy of respect and praise, it is difficult to not interpret his renegade actions, on a different level, as simply arrogant. Who was he to know— better than the president of the United States—which issues were in the public's best interest? Who was he to force the future administration to address issues that he had unilaterally deemed to be critical? The impudence—the sheer sanctimony of it all. At the time, his behavior was undoubtedly shocking, but should it have been? After all, this was the man aptly nicknamed the Preacher, characteristically being stubborn and true to his ideals. More importantly, Clark's outlaw-esque exit from the DOJ vividly preordained what was to come once he emerged on the outside.

CHAPTER EIGHT

TAKING THE BATTLE TO THE OUTSIDE

"We must disenthrall ourselves and engage fearlessly and
passionately in the pursuit of truth. Finding it, we should
test it skeptically, tolerantly, openly, ceaselessly."

Ramsey Clark[1]

RAMSEY CLARK WAS STAUNCHLY nonpartisan as attorney general. He
pursued what he thought was right, no matter what the political consequences—a mindset that undoubtedly was of little help to President Johnson or to Hubert Humphrey in his 1968 presidential run. Notwithstanding
the controversy that swirled around him, particularly toward the end of
his tenure, one colleague assessed Clark as "the strongest and most able
Attorney General in history." He went on to suggest, though, that Clark's
apolitical nature would make recognition of this status impossible. As recounted by author Richard Harris,

> he failed to come across [as strong and able] because, wholly unlike
> anyone in the post before him, he was so deeply convinced the De-
> partment of Justice should be above politics that he refused to engage
> in them, even to the extent of defending himself by publicizing his
> record.[2]

Once on the outside, the former attorney general was even more unconcerned about political messaging. He had significantly flexed his independent muscles as he inched toward the finale of his DOJ career. Now,
he was completely free to wage battles as a private lawyer in areas that he
deemed most important for the betterment of his country, regardless of
the costs to him personally.

Rather than jumping immediately into the fray, Clark deemed it appropriate and necessary to wait a year before taking on any legal work. He thought that it could appear that he was using his former government position as leverage in the private sector. Ever the principled one, he wanted to avoid even the appearance of impropriety. Given the arduous work pace that Clark had maintained during his eight-year stint in the DOJ, one might suspect that he would just hang out and lay low for a year. But that was not really his style. This was a man who had not taken a single vacation day during his entire time as a government lawyer. Instead of kicking back and relaxing, Clark wrote a book, with the significant and able assistance of his wife Georgia, in addition to keeping up an active speaking and interview schedule.[3] The book was *Crime in America*, published by Simon & Schuster in 1970, and it would go on to become a bestseller.[4] Highly provocative and progressive, it caused a stir throughout the nation.

The book addressed the omnipresent problem of crime, its causes and effects, and the institutionalized unfairness that Clark believed helped perpetuate a system that was disproportionately skewed against people of color and the poor. Though scandalous to many, its themes and substance should have sounded familiar to anyone who was paying attention to the former attorney general during his years in Washington—crime emanated from poverty and other unequal social conditions; prisons were broken, producing far more criminals than they rehabilitated; lack of well-trained, well-compensated, professional law enforcement officers resulted in poor police–community relations and more crime; more gun control was needed; wiretapping as a tool of law enforcement was nefarious and ineffective; and the death penalty was a barbaric abomination that should be eliminated. Clark also ventured into even more controversial territory, arguing for the legalization of marijuana and the use of indeterminate sentencing for felons, which would afford them the chance to be unconditionally freed or gradually released under restrictive conditions, with the expectation that this would enhance rehabilitation.[5]

Toward the end of his work on the book, Clark took an unexpected professional step, for him, because it represented the conventional path that many former attorneys general take—cashing in on their fame by joining a large, corporate firm. For example, Eric Holder, President Obama's first attorney general, is now a partner at the silk-stocking firm of Covington & Burling. Like his fellow chief prosecutors, Ramsey Clark too appeared drawn by money and prestige to one of the leading firms in the country, New York's Paul, Weiss, Goldberg, Rifkind, Wharton & Garrison (Paul Weiss). Paul Weiss's liberal reputation surely attracted Clark, and the firm, which had fairly recently added former U.S. Supreme Court Justice Arthur Goldberg to its ranks, was no doubt thrilled to have another high-profile attorney on board.

Even though he had joined a lucrative law practice, it was apparent from the beginning that Clark was not in it for the money. He quickly immersed himself in the anti–Vietnam War movement and undertook a significant quantity of non–income-generating public interest litigation. Nevertheless, he did successfully handle a few major commercial matters for Paul Weiss, including his representation of the Alaska Federation of Natives in a land dispute, which resulted in a $962.5 million settlement.[6]

Clark's passion, though, was clearly in the public arena, pursuing social justice on a broad scale. His extensive Vietnam-related activities are singularly noteworthy in this regard, given his ties to Lyndon Johnson and his previous prosecution of the Boston Five, among other proponents of draft evasion. Clark had voiced his opposition to the continued bombing in the region while attorney general, but he still remained part of an administration myopically committed to victory in Vietnam, and he authorized criminal charges against those who sought to undermine that aspiration. Perhaps guilt over his complicity in this historic episode is what led him to become such a strident opponent of the war. Some of his former colleagues subscribe to this theory.[7]

When pressed on the television show *Face the Nation* about the perceived hypocrisy of his anti–Vietnam War advocacy in light of his previous cooperating association with Johnson's Vietnam machinery, Clark refused to act as judge of his past involvement. Rather, he somewhat defensively stated why he felt it was his obligation to oppose the war:

> I think each of us has an obligation to judge the present, and work for the future, and I don't feel inhibited by the past. I think we've got to

constantly seek the truth today. I think this country and this world are in trouble, and I think one of the greatest manifestations of it is the war in Indochina. If I felt some mental block because of some position I took in the [past], I wouldn't be worth anything, would I? You have to go on.[8]

Clark's belief in fighting for and preserving the integrity and human dignity of all people is principally what has inspired him to come to the defense of so many individuals viewed as enemies of the United States. By declaring them an enemy, our government suggests that they are somehow inhuman, not worthy of the respect that we typically accord to others; and much of the populace readily accepts this way of thinking. Clark viewed the Vietnam War as one of the most extreme examples of this tragic phenomenon. At the time, he contended:

The dehumanization which the Vietnam experience has inflicted on the American people has been just devastating. We have to wonder what we have done to ourselves. The body-count by which the Vietnam war is officially and journalistically reported is as good an illustration as any of how we have depreciated the value of life. We seem to want to derive some glory from the number of people we have killed.[9]

Clark not only had no qualms about actively opposing the war effort, he actually deemed it his social and patriotic responsibility to do so.

Ramsey Clark's anti–Vietnam War activities were wide-ranging and varied, but his most provocative undertaking by far was traveling to North Vietnam during the summer of 1972. His articulated purpose for the trip was to show the reputed enemy that Americans were not so bad and also to obtain a firsthand account of what was really taking place there; Clark wanted to know the truth and share that with the American people.[10] In later reflecting upon his visit, the former attorney general noted that his sense of morality and patriotism also provided powerful incentives:

> I felt that the United States government was tragically wrong in its military actions in Vietnam and that someone who really loved the country had a high obligation to say so and to stand up and to resist. . . . So I felt the highest moral obligation to do what I did. . . . It was an irresistible moral obligation as I saw it, and not to have done it would have been extremely damaging to me as a human being.[11]

Clark was part of a diverse investigative team operating under the auspices of an entity known as the International Commission of Inquiry into U.S. Crimes in Indochina. The six-member group spent two weeks in North Vietnam, principally investigating the accuracy of reports that American forces had engaged in the strategic bombing of non-military targets in the region, including dams and dikes. Clark was most concerned about the impact of the bombing on civilian populations. U.S. reports denied targeting civilians and generally portrayed its involvement in the conflict in a positive light. Clark was highly skeptical, feeling that the American people were being "saturated with disinformation, misinformation, [and] falsehoods" by the government.[12] He therefore felt morally compelled to ascertain the truth and was undeterred by official efforts to dissuade him from going, including the threat of criminal prosecution upon his return.

What Clark saw confirmed what he had feared: The accounts conveyed by his government to the American people of what was transpiring in Indochina were not true. It was propaganda designed to generate support for the war effort and to counterbalance the widespread activist dissent. The devastation that Clark saw was crippling.

> To see the survivors of bombed villages was almost unbearable. I have seen stunned people in war and peace but the incomprehension of the simple villager, generations in that place never visited by a foreigner, is another dimension in human suffering.[13]

The bombed areas that he visited while in North Vietnam contained "no significant military targets." He maintained:

There are just cities and villages, the few dirt roads, the several small railroad lines, the dikes built over the centuries that support civilization, rockets, guns and the people. If we bomb, we will necessarily hit homes, schools, churches, hospitals and kill old men, women and children. We do. So it goes.[14]

Clark's earlier opposition to continued U.S. bombing while attorney general largely grew out of concern over the inevitable collateral damage that such warfare inflicted. He loathed all violence, but indiscriminate bombing was at the top of his list. Upon his return home, Clark advocated even more strongly for a cessation of the bombing:

[U]ltimately the bombing will destroy the soul of America in the hearts of humanity. As a use of violence, the bombings are the most inhumane, indiscriminate and deadly of all. They burn and destroy little children in the villages, the women and the elderly as readily as combatants.[15]

He saw the truth firsthand, and that reality inspired him to assume an active, vocal role within the broader antiwar movement; this passion cultivated by the Vietnam conflict would endure throughout the remainder of his life.

Some critics argued that Clark was little more than a communist dupe, one who was shown a one-sided, carefully orchestrated view of the bombing in an effort to convince him of his country's evil methods and to motivate him to act as a spokesperson of sorts for the North Vietnamese cause. According to the Clark denigrators, he naively accepted whatever his hosts were selling and did not push to obtain a more balanced picture. Reportedly, he was only shown the evidence of bombing that the North Vietnamese wanted him to see.[16]

Clark, not surprisingly, took issue with such appraisals of his trip, considering them to be attempted dilutions of the truth that he had seen with his own eyes. He contended that he had been "free to walk the streets of the cities where [he wished], to walk along the paths in the villages and the paths on the tops of dikes. There have been no efforts that I could detect to influence me or prejudice my judgment."[17] He was also afforded the opportunity to visit and spend substantial uninhibited time with American prisoners of war, and from everything that he could glean, they were being treated well, contending that their health was better than his own, and "I am a healthy man."[18] Clark insisted that no steps had been taken to curtail his interaction with the POWs, and he believed the POWs' overall assessment of the prison camp's conditions, as well as of those at other locations.[19] Admittedly, however, he only met with a small sampling of prisoners.

Clark's truth-seeking mission to Hanoi would be but the first of many that would take him all over the globe. He made numerous similar trips in subsequent years to various targets of U.S. aggression and misinformation campaigns, including Panama, Grenada, Libya, North Korea, and Iraq, to name only a few.[20] With each journey, his skepticism regarding the U.S. government and his abhorrence for what he perceived as its violent imperialism grew stronger, making him ever-more critical of his nation's leaders and moving him further outside the mainstream of American society. Over time, his detractors increasingly used Clark's tactics and words to paint him as anti-American and unpatriotic.

In discussing that visit during one of our interviews, Clark somewhat jokingly told me that his reception in Hanoi was far better than the one he received when he returned to the United States.[21] This was ironic, but by no means unexpected. Upon landing at the San Francisco Airport, Clark was greeted by a horde of mostly hostile journalists and protesters who sought to cast him in a negative light—as a traitorous, enemy sympathizer.[22] And after that, the hits just kept coming, harder and harder.

John Mitchell, Nixon's former attorney general, could not resist the opportunity to publicly denounce Clark's visit, calling his predecessor's conduct "outrageous." Mitchell also again attempted to make Clark a campaign issue in the 1972 presidential election. Nixon's Democratic challenger George McGovern had suggested that he might appoint Clark as his FBI director if elected (a position in which Clark had no interest, by the way). In light of Clark's North Vietnam visit, Mitchell proclaimed that replacing

J. Edgar Hoover with him would be a "travesty" and demanded that Mc-Govern publicly repudiate Clark's conduct.[23]

Besides becoming a potential lightning rod in the presidential campaign, there were high-level efforts to have Clark criminally prosecuted. U.S. Secretary of State William Rogers described Clark's actions in North Vietnam as "contemptible," and Georgia Congressman Fletcher Thompson urged Mitchell's successor Richard Kleindienst to investigate whether Clark violated U.S. sedition or treason laws.[24] Although no prosecution ever took place or was even seriously considered,[25] public outrage nevertheless persisted.

For some apparent masochistic reason, Clark chose to save much of the hateful correspondence that rained down upon him from his fellow citizens. One expressed "utter disgust" over Clark's televised portrayal of America's bombing of nonmilitary targets in North Vietnam, calling him "gullible enough to believe anything the Communists" told him and charging him with "aiding and abetting the enemy."[26] Another writer voiced indignation over Clark's efforts to raise money to rebuild a hospital in North Vietnam that he contended was destroyed by U.S. bombing. She stated: "I resent bitterly your efforts to raise money to rebuild a North Vietnamese hospital. These people are my enemies. . . . I find it unexcusable [sic], no traitorous, to raise money for our enemies!"[27] Some chose to communicate their distaste more succinctly. One unsigned letter simply read "You Stink."[28] Others suggested that Clark should receive capital punishment for treason: "You ignorant, naieve [sic] SOB. You should be shot for treason."[29] I could go on and on, but I think you get the picture. Clark was vilified; he was now forever saddled with the reputation of being anti-American and a friend of the public's enemy. In the years ahead, he would solidify that perception time and time again.

Not everyone derided Clark for his Hanoi trip. He had a fairly large contingent of supporters, even among American soldiers and their families. The prisoners of war with whom he met were especially positive. Clark seemed to concentrate more on them individually during his visit, rather than on the war itself, which seemed to have been the American government's exclusive focus. The POWs and their loved ones appreciated Clark's sincere attention. One letter in particular was striking in its endorsement of Clark and his Vietnam-related work:

> I was a prisoner in North Vietnam for five years and four months and had the privilege of meeting you in Hanoi. My wife has told me that you contacted her, sent her tape recordings of our conversation and photographs taken at our meeting. I deeply appreciate your taking the time to extend these courtesies to my loved ones. I would also like to express my heartfelt thanks to you for your efforts to bring the truth to the American people about our bombing acts against North Vietnam. It is most depressing to read about the slander and harsh treatment you had to endure as a result of your humanitarian efforts . . . [30]

The wife of another POW was similarly aligned with the former attorney general: "I hear a lot of people blasting Clark but you can't find any bad noise from me. I think he was only trying to do what was right in his heart."[31] Some fellow anti–Vietnam War activists predictably expressed their solidarity with Clark. Jane Fonda, whose earlier visit to North Vietnam was even more maligned than Clark's, wrote to praise him for his effective antiwar advocacy:

> We won't get a chance to talk so I want to let you know by note how much effect your brave actions have had on so many people—people who have never listened before. Your manner of speaking to the public about what you experienced has taught us all a great deal.[32]

Apart from his own public opposition to the war, Clark undertook to defend other antiwar activists in the courtroom, paradoxically, the same types of individuals he had prosecuted as attorney general. Most notably, he served as counsel to the Harrisburg Seven, a group of vocal Vietnam War opponents comprised largely of Catholic clergy. Ostensibly led by Father Philip Berrigan and his future wife Sister Elizabeth McAlister, the defendants were alleged to have conspired "to raid draft boards in nine states, blow up heating pipes in Washington utility tunnels and kidnap presidential foreign affairs adviser Henry Kissinger."[33] Clark's agreeing to join in representing the defendants was particularly poignant because many viewed the case to be on par with his own notorious prosecution of the Boston Five. The *New York Times* described it as "the most politically controversial trial since [Ramsey] Clark, as Attorney General, authorized the prosecution of Dr. Benjamin Spock on anti-draft conspiracy charges."[34]

Clark's attraction to Berrigan seems to have been about more than simply a shared opposition to the Vietnam War. Apart from his antiwar activities, Berrigan had been a devoted civil rights advocate, operating on the front lines of the desegregation movement during its apex. He devoted much of his life to helping the urban black community seek equality in what he considered to be an inherently racist country. Even his antiwar advocacy had an overtly racial tone to it, similar to that of Stokely Carmichael. This undoubtedly resonated with Clark. As he recalls, during the Vietnam era, young black men were not able to get college deferments like their white counterparts. The odds were stacked against them in terms of legally avoiding the draft, and oddly many of them volunteered for service, viewing it as a way to raise their stature in society. Coming home in a uniform with stripes would make them special, particularly in their own communities.[35] Unfortunately, this was misguided, wishful thinking, of which Berrigan was acutely aware. As a result, he worked arduously to keep blacks out of the war altogether.[36]

Although the trial was not a chaotic mess like the Chicago Seven fiasco, it was not without controversy. Acting on a hunch, Clark decided not to call any witnesses for the defense following the close of the government's case, a strategy that divided the seven defendants almost evenly.[37] To the shock of nearly everyone in the courtroom, Clark simply rose from counsel's table and said: "Your Honor, the defendants shall always seek peace. They continue to proclaim their innocence. The defense rests."[38] His unorthodox ploy seemed to have the desired effect, as the jury was unable to reach a verdict on the most serious charges.[39]

Besides the Harrisburg Seven, Ramsey Clark represented Craig Morgan, the student government president at Kent State University, who, along with other students, was being prosecuted for allegedly inciting a riot. After three nights of somewhat combative student protests at Kent State against the

U.S. expansion of the war in Cambodia, the National Guard had been called in and martial law was declared on campus. The university announced that another planned student demonstration had been canceled. The protesters rebuffed this suppressive reaction and proceeded with their intended activities.[40] As a result, the guardsmen directed the assembled demonstrators to disperse, but they refused. This led to a rise in tensions and apparently some rock and stick throwing by students, as well as the tossing back of canisters of tear gas that the guardsmen had fired.

According to the National Guard, this was not the full extent of the students' onslaught. The commander of the troops initially claimed that there was also a sniper shooting at them and that this is what led to their opening fire on the students, killing four and wounding ten others.[41] Eyewitnesses, on the other hand, maintained that the guardsmen suddenly and inexplicably began shooting, and there did not appear to be any other evidence to support the sniper theory.[42] Eventually, the National Guard backed off this justification and instead hung its defense on the argument that its regulations allowed soldiers to shoot when they felt their lives were in danger.[43]

Notwithstanding the fury over what transpired on that ill-fated day, the guardsmen's tenuous defense apparently worked. None of them was subsequently charged with any state crime, and a later federal prosecution for deprivation of the students' civil rights ended in an acquittal of the eight who were charged.[44]

Stunningly, the government seemed most intent on addressing the conduct of the campus protesters, criminally charging twenty-four students and one faculty member for their alleged involvement in either inciting or taking active part in the riotous behavior that preceded deployment of the National Guard troops. Among those indicted was Craig Morgan, whom Ramsey Clark vigorously defended, contending, for a number of legal reasons, that the case against him should be dismissed. In the end, with the assistance of a legal team organized by William Kunstler, one defendant went to trial and was acquitted. Following that, the remaining indictments were all dropped.[45]

In addition to providing legal representation to those who lawfully opposed America's involvement in Vietnam, Clark personally engaged in a number of other antiwar activities designed to address various aspects of the conflict. Two of these—both relating to the draft—were especially noteworthy as they seemed to be patently contrary to positions that he had taken as attorney general. First, after having prosecuted the Boston Five based principally on the premise that their goal was to destroy the Selective Service System, Clark himself, as an outsider, endeavored to accomplish a similar goal (although he did not overtly encourage draft-eligible men to violate the law as Dr. Spock and his "accomplices" had done).

Instead, Clark took his arguments directly to the U.S. Senate Judiciary Committee.[46] Specifically, he argued against the practice of subjecting antiwar activists to the penalty of automatic induction, even ahead of those who had volunteered for service in the military. Clark contended:

> To accelerate the induction of a young man into the armed services for speaking against the war, is clearly constitutionally impermissible whether the action be provided for by Congress, adjudicated in the courts or as in the case under the present law determined through administrative provision by local draft boards.[47]

He favored abolishing this practice altogether and seriously revamping the entire Selective Service process.

Clark was also opposed to formally prosecuting those who violated the Selective Service Act (SSA), except under the clearest of circumstances; this was an obvious retreat from actions he had taken while attorney general. In Clark's opinion,

> [W]e should not force the issue of prosecution until the time comes when the conduct of the individual is clear, the time comes for his actual induction and his then refusal to serve is clear, and then the law has no choice if the system is to have integrity.[48]

He still clung to his "integrity" mantra, but the scope of what he viewed as properly subject to indictment had narrowed significantly. In the event of an actual conviction, post-DOJ Clark was firmly against imposing prison sentences, preferring instead some type of constructive punishment. Sounding like every bit the antiwar advocate, Clark proclaimed that: "War is bad enough without making criminals of those who refuse to serve. Congress has a duty to carefully tailor the sanctions provided to meet the essential needs of the law only."[49]

Within less than a year, Clark had gone from being an insider supporting the integrity of the SSA as written, to an outsider calling for an overhaul of the system. It is impossible not to speculate that he must have harbored serious misgivings about America's draft laws while still in office—hence, the tortured post-hoc explanations for his Boston Five prosecution. However, on the outside, no longer constrained by any semblance of governmental responsibility, Clark was able to unabashedly flaunt his antiwar self. And consistent with this, he later took his contrarian views regarding the draft to another level by strongly advocating that amnesty from prosecution be granted to those designated as Vietnam draft dodgers. At that moment in history, this was even more controversial, especially for a former attorney general, than Clark's previous calls for reforming the SSA.

In a heated debate with noted conservative commentator William F. Buckley, Jr. on his television program *Firing Line*, Clark argued for "absolute and unconditional amnesty" for anyone who resisted fighting in the Vietnam War, whether for reasons of moral conscience or simply out of fear.[50] He maintained that the war was unjust and that those who chose not to join in America's military effort were right in their refusal. Buckley took issue with Clark's position, pointing out the former attorney general's complicity in this "unjust" war. He peppered Clark with sarcastic questions. Did you ever tell the president that he and his war were unjust? Why didn't you quit? Why did you prosecute people under the law that you now say is unjust?[51]

Though a little rattled, Clark did not stoop to meet his host's obvious taunting and simply emphasized his then-current feelings about the war and the draft laws. When Buckley persisted in hounding him on the inconsistency between his DOJ-related actions concerning the war and his righteous advocacy for amnesty, Clark sternly stated, "I want to do justice now. What's wrong with that?" More specifically, he contended: "We ought to open up the gates of America and say come on home. The war is over. We are going to forget those offenses because we believe in justice, and we have the power to control our destiny through law."[52]

As the years following the Vietnam War passed, Clark found new outlets for promoting his antiwar views. In addition to publicly condemning virtually every subsequent act of U.S. aggression—Lebanon, Grenada, Libya, Panama, and more—he emerged as a leader in the international peace movement, making a number of North Vietnam-type visits to "enemy" territory. In each instance, the visits and the conclusions that he drew from them were essentially the same. The United States, in Clark's eyes, had invariably carried out an unwarranted attack that violated international law by either intentionally or recklessly inflicting widespread destruction on civilian populations.[53]

To further hammer home the point, he would routinely punctuate these visits by organizing unofficial, ad-hoc war crimes tribunals to try and convict the United States and various responsible officials, in absentia, for their wrongful actions.[54] He was also at the forefront of the antinuclear movement, founding one of the leading disarmament organizations, Disarm.[55]

Ramsey Clark's increasingly critical view of his country opened him up for exploitation by groups that did not harbor the same earnest intentions. For example, he provided leadership and support to the National Coalition to Stop U.S. Intervention in the Middle East, founded the International Action Center in 1992, and has been active in the antiwar umbrella coalition known as ANSWER—Act Now to Stop War and End Racism. All of these groups undeniably seek to accomplish noble ends, and that is surely what attracted Clark, but they are also reputedly linked to the Marxist–Leninist Workers World Party (WWP),[56] an organization that appears to have significant ties to historically extremist groups and radical governments such as North Korea. It is possible that characterizations of WWP have been exaggerated in an attempt to discredit the organization, a ploy utilized on other entities for which Clark has had an affinity, like the Black Panther Party, a group that the WWP has also supported. Moreover, regardless of negative claims about the WWP, it is important to note that Clark has denied knowing much about the group and has claimed to have "no formal association" with it.[57]

Clark's involvement with associations like the International Action Center stems from his sincere opposition to war, regardless of any ulterior purpose that might lurk within these groups. His forthright commitment to this cause likely emanates, at least in part, from his admiration for nonviolence guru Martin Luther King, Jr. When asked in a 1969 interview which black leader impressed him most during his time as attorney general, Clark mentioned Thurgood Marshall and Roy Wilkins but ultimately settled on Dr. King. His veneration of King stemmed from his firm belief in the validity and necessity of the nonviolent philosophy that King espoused—violence divides and destroys.[58] What's more, Clark's direct exposure to the reality and ramifications of violence served to reinforce his discipleship of Dr. King's message.

> [Y]ou can't see the autopsy photos of John Kennedy and Martin Luther King and Bob Kennedy and you can't read the history of the Philippine–American war, and watch what we were doing in Vietnam, without rejecting violence.[59]

For Clark, the only path to freedom and justice for all is a nonviolent one.

Clark's commitment to nonviolence does not relate solely to opposing armed aggression. In his opinion, the deadliest weapon of all may be economic sanctions. Indeed, he has compared them to the sinister neutron bomb, which kills people but spares physical structures. Sanctions act in a similar fashion: They only harm individuals; physical infrastructure and other manifestations of wealth are preserved.[60] On numerous occasions Clark has passionately spoken out regarding the devastating effects of sanctions on the Iraqi people, particularly children, calling the sanctions genocide.[61] Sara Flounders, director of the International Action Center, perhaps expressed Clark's sentiments best when she wrote, "Sanctions are war. They are the most brutal form of war because they punish an entire population, targeting children, the future, most of all sanctions are a weapon of mass destruction."[62] Apart from verbal condemnation, Clark literally put his money where his mouth was on countless occasions, making annual humanitarian trips to the region to bring food and medical supplies.[63]

Clark believes that America is driven by a desire for global domination, and in order to achieve and maintain that, it must have a strong military, prepared and willing to exert strength. The amount of money spent in this area is astounding, especially when thought of in terms of the other uses to which these funds could be put—eradicating diseases or ameliorating starvation throughout the world, for example. The striking contrast between Clark's passion for and devotion to helping the less fortunate and his own country's plutocratic excesses has rendered him increasingly disdainful of American leadership.

His antiestablishment persona—combined with his extensive experience, plainspoken style, and general likability—made him a popular possibility for the Democratic side of the 1972 presidential race.[64] At the time, Clark seemed more content with pursuing causes as an outsider, and therefore he never seriously considered a presidential run. However, in 1974, he seemed to have had a change of heart, perhaps concluding that he could more effectively seek to solve the ills of society as an elected official. In a move that surely pleased Paul Weiss as much as it did Clark—given his penchant for pro bono clients—he resigned from the firm and shortly thereafter, with the apparent encouragement of future New York Governor Mario Cuomo, decided to toss his hat into the ring for New York's U.S. Senate seat, ultimately taking on popular Republican incumbent Jacob Javits.[65]

Predictably, from the outset, there was nothing conventional about Ramsey Clark's campaign. For one thing, his staff was comprised, for the most part, of individuals who were strong on passion but short on experience. His close friend and campaign aide Lois Akner recounted that the joke during the early stages of their efforts was that "to work on the campaign, you had to have no experience."[66]

Consistent with this theme, Clark tapped noted author and journalist Victor Navasky to be his campaign manager, described by fellow staffer Mark Green as "a person of enormous intellect, integrity, and mirth who's the opposite of a political pro."[67] There was, however, some method to Clark's madness. He wanted someone whom he could trust, and Clark thought that, as a journalist, Navasky would be adept at drumming up a lot of free publicity.[68] Navasky's deputy was Ken Lerer—at the time also a political novice but who would go on to be a prominent journalist and businessman, co-founding the *Huffington Post* and serving as chairman of

Buzzfeed, among other things.[69] Clark was also assisted by his former Paul Weiss associate and future NYU law professor Stephen Gillers, as well as Mark Kaplan and wealthy philanthropist Eugene Lang, who handled legal and financial matters for the campaign for a period of time.[70]

Speaking of finances, this became a significant point of contention. Clark was unwilling to take large contributions. Though he was permitted by law to accept individual contributions of up to $1,000, Clark initially maintained that he would not accept any amount greater than $10. In response, Akner recalls one aide, Monty Kaufman, telling Clark, "the difference between integrity and insanity is $90."[71] Ultimately, Clark agreed to raise his cap to $100, but this too was exceptionally radical; he was clearly ahead of his time in terms of campaign finance reform.[72]

Though this maverick approach to campaigning may have had some popular appeal, the pragmatics of it were hard to swallow and caused some tension among his supporters.[73] In particular, Eugene Lang, one of Clark's wealthiest and most devoted backers, walked away from the campaign out of frustration over Clark's refusal to accept larger donations.[74] The stubborn, principled candidate was unfazed and ultimately ended up raising a very respectable $800,000, despite his stingy contribution ceiling.[75]

Clark also attracted a bevy of support from an eclectic assortment of liberal celebrities. For example, Paul Newman and Chevy Chase hosted a fundraising event for him, and Harry Belafonte was an active and vocal supporter, likewise organizing an event on Clark's behalf at the renowned Apollo Theater in Harlem.[76] His anti–Vietnam War compatriot Jane Fonda was predictably in his corner as well. Other notables included blues legend B. B. King, comedian Steve Allen, R&B star Roberta Flack, actor Tony Randall, singer–songwriter Harry Chapin, Olympic gold medalist and actor Rafer Johnson, and historian Arthur Schlesinger, Jr.

Clark's unorthodox candidacy only got weirder at the Democratic State Convention in Niagara Falls, where he chose a highly unlikely duo to put his name forward for the party's nomination. The first was well-known New York City Police Department (NYPD) Detective Frank Serpico.[77] Serpico is famous for having courageously blown the whistle on the NYPD for its rampant internal corruption. In 1971, Clark agreed to represent Paco (as

Clark likes to call him) in connection with the detective's formal testimony before an investigatory commission appointed by the mayor of New York, John Lindsay—the Knapp Commission.[78]

Clark was undoubtedly impressed by the honesty, integrity, and bravery exhibited by Serpico in speaking out when he knew that this would make him a marked man within the NYPD. Not only did Clark represent him in an advisory role throughout the ordeal, but he allowed Serpico to sleep in his apartment on the night before his scheduled testimony, which proved to be an uncomfortable experience for the former attorney general. Serpico was paranoid that his fellow officers were out to get him—and for good reason. On one occasion, fellow officers had refused to summon medical assistance for him when he was shot in the face while making a drug bust. Though he survived, he suffered damage to his jaw and lost hearing in one ear. Concerned that dirty cops might try to finish him off, Serpico hid around seven pistols throughout Clark's apartment, in the heating system and in the oven, because there was no furniture at the time.[79] The devoutly non-violent Clark found this unnerving.[80] Clark survived the apartment episode and went on to establish a strong and lasting friendship with Paco, one that has endured to the present.

The Senate hopeful's other nontraditional nominator was Herbert X Blyden, a civil rights advocate and one of the principal spokesmen on behalf of the inmates during the infamous Attica prison uprising. Clark had become acquainted with Blyden as a result of his own involvement in the aftermath of the deadly police–prisoner standoff at Attica, and as with Serpico, the two men had grown close.

In 1971, the inmates at Attica—overwhelmingly African American, Latino, and poor—decided to take reform matters into their own hands, when the racially hostile environment and inhumane conditions reached a boiling point.[81] Peaceful efforts to obtain concessions had proven unsuccessful and were seemingly being met with even greater oppression.[82] On September 9, a virulent show of force by correction officers spawned rioting by "A" Block prisoners, which spread throughout the prison population, eventually resulting in their seizing control of Attica and taking numerous civilian workers and guards as hostages.[83]

Almost 1,300 inmates, who were occupying the prison's "D" Yard, created a makeshift community of sorts, led by various democratically elected spokesmen, including Blyden who was chosen as the leader representing Attica's "B" Block.[84] In addition, at their request, a select group of individuals, referred to as observers, was organized to act as a negotiating liaison between the inmates and prison officials. Included among the observers were such notable figures as attorney William Kunstler and *New York Times* columnist Tom Wicker.[85]

Although the list of demands eventually became long and varied, at its heart was the same fundamental concept that had inspired the black sanitation workers in Memphis to commence their iconic strike in 1968. The sanitation workers wanted to be treated with the same dignity and respect as any other city employee, adopting the profound yet simple slogan "I *Am a Man.*" The racial oppression that the Attica inmates experienced paralleled and exceeded that borne by black and brown men on the outside. White prison guards felt wholly justified in doling out sub-human treatment to these incarcerated men, whom they surely viewed as occupying the lowest rung of the societal ladder.[86] In response to this endemic penal mindset, the Attica inmates, channeling the spirit of their Memphian brothers, proclaimed in the preface to their initial list of demands:

> We are men: We are not beasts and we do not intend to be beaten or driven as such. The entire prison populace, that means each and every one of us here, has set forth to change forever the ruthless brutalization and disregard for the lives of the prisoners here and throughout the United States.[87]

After a four-day standoff, the uprising was brought to an end by a devastating assault unleashed by New York State Police. Twenty-six inmates and nine hostages were killed and eighty-nine others were injured, only one of whom was a state trooper.[88] Not surprisingly, numerous prisoners were criminally indicted as a result of the revolt—sixty-two to be exact—but offending police and guards escaped any criminal censure.[89]

The indicted inmates—who, in a show of unity, collectively referred to themselves as Attica Brothers—would have a sophisticated and organized legal defense backing them.[90] Two of the Brothers—John B. Hill and Charley

Joe Pernasalice—were charged with the murder and second-degree assault of Correction Officer William Quinn.[91] William Kunstler was lead attorney for Hill, and Ramsey Clark occupied the same role for Pernasalice.[92] After a trial involving dubious evidence and questionable courtroom theatrics by Kunstler, Clark's steady, methodical approach garnered his client a conviction on the relatively minor charge of second-degree attempted assault.[93] Hill, on the other hand, was convicted of murder. Although he received a lengthy prison sentence, it was later commuted, and he was eventually paroled.[94]

Although Clark was familiar with the harsh realities of prisons in America, his representation of Pernasalice broadened and solidified his perception of the dysfunction and inhumanity of our penal system. Already a vigorous proponent of massive prison reform, his resolve was fortified by what he witnessed. Clark's selection of Blyden, whom he had grown to respect and admire, to second his senatorial nomination evinced a show of solidarity by the nation's former chief law enforcement officer with inmates across the country and was intended to demonstrate the importance of political inclusion.[95] He thought that the dichotomy of having an honest cop and a morally principled ex-con would send a profound message.

Clark's envisioned point, however, seemed to have been lost on the audience. As he recalls, the delegates walked out in protest as Blyden began to speak, perhaps because he was then under indictment for two murders in connection with the Attica uprising, though Clark feels strongly that it was because of Blyden's race.[96] It was likely a combination of the two. Whatever the reason, this exhibition of disrespect angered Clark, who viewed Blyden as a hero for the valor and compassion that he displayed during the Attica episode—he had helped carry injured individuals to safety, protecting them from inmates intent on inflicting more harm.[97]

After the nominating fiasco, Clark withdrew his name from nomination, opting instead to earn his way onto the ballot in a truly democratic fashion—by gathering citizen signatures from around the state on a petition.[98] The popular candidate had little trouble obtaining the necessary signatures and probably gave himself a campaign boost by doing so, positioning himself well to take on the Democratic nominee, Syracuse Mayor Lee Alexander.[99]

Clark prevailed in the primary, winning the right to take on Javits in the general election. The race appeared tight throughout, and it seemed as though Clark might actually win, piling up significant popular support with his straight-shooting, plainspoken style. Consistent with his character, Clark was intensely committed to the truth in his campaign. He said what he honestly believed, regardless of whether it would be politically help-ful. One magazine was so enamored with his refreshingly unconventional approach that it ran a feature story with the following cover teaser next to a full-page photograph of Clark: "Is America ready for a politician this honest?"[100] Despite Clark's popular appeal, Javits's power and connections, along with his political exploitation of Clark's ill-timed North Vietnam trip, were too much for the former attorney general to surmount.[101] The politi-cal novice, though, gave the incumbent a run for his money, receiving 37 percent of the vote to Javits's 45 percent.[102]

Not yet ready to throw in the towel, Clark gave the Senate another try in 1976, but this time he did not even make it out of the primary, finishing third behind Daniel Patrick Moynihan and Bella Abzug.[103] After that, he forever closed the door on future plans for political office, acknowledging that if he had won, he would have been a fish out of water:

> My experience in the Senate would have been miserable. . . . I would have been a misfit. I never would have been a member of the club because I would have been fighting against the very things they were doing without any real chance of converting more than a handful.[104]

With the political bug out of his system, Clark would continue his jour-ney progressively leftward and ever-more radical, at least by all objective accounts.

CHAPTER NINE

BLACK IS BEAUTIFUL

"Integration will be essential in America to avoid violent
conflict and to show the world, which will have billions
more blacks, browns and yellows in three decades, that the
races can live together with dignity, respect and love."
Ramsey Clark[1]

IN THE PERIOD between Ramsey Clark's departure from the DOJ and
his attempted foray into the political sphere, he got involved in a number
of highly notable cases. One of the most significant and meaningful, yet
overlooked, of these was his representation of Ruchell Magee, serving a
life sentence in the California state prison system.[2]

Magee's story is a painfully tragic one. An African American, he was
first sent to prison at the age of 16 for the rape of a white woman, with
whom he was actually having a consensual relationship in rural Louisiana.
The conviction by a jury comprised solely of white men and his subsequent
sentencing were clearly influenced by race. Notwithstanding Magee's age,
he was sentenced to twelve years in Louisiana's legendarily brutal Angola
State Penitentiary.[3] After almost seven years there, during which he steadfastly maintained his innocence, he was paroled in return for his agreement
to leave Louisiana and never return.[4]

Once free, Magee left the South and settled in with relatives in Los
Angeles. Unfortunately, it did not take him long to again find legal trouble. Within six months, Magee was back in jail, charged with robbery and
kidnapping in an incident involving a mere $10. He maintained that the
charges were "trumped up" and that he was severely beaten by the arrest-
ing officers. Magee was convicted and sentenced to life on the kidnapping
charge because of his felony record.[5]

He was convinced that the police and judge had conspired against
him, and his view of the justice system was forever tarnished. Although his

efforts to prove this were unsuccessful, he nevertheless persisted in arguing that both of his convictions were wrongful, resulting in his being subjected to what he considered unlawful slavery.[6] Magee broadened this theory to encompass all of his fellow inmates as well. They too were the targets of involuntary servitude. This mindset positioned Magee to be a willing accomplice to a dramatic courtroom rebellion in August 1970.

While serving his life sentence in San Quentin, Magee and another inmate, William Christmas, witnessed an altercation between fellow prisoner James McClain and a guard, which ended with the guard being stabbed. McClain was charged with assault, and Magee and Christmas were called as witnesses on the defendant's behalf.[7] The trial for McClain at the Marin County Courthouse presented an opportunity for Jonathan Jackson, the younger brother of George Jackson, to carry out a plan designed to free his brother from Soledad State Prison. George Jackson—a revered inmate who was also a gifted writer and noted intellectual—was a cult hero among black activists of that time. Jonathan's scheme was to seize hostages from the courtroom and then travel to a local radio station to negotiate on the air for his brother's release from Soledad Prison, where George and two other inmates, collectively known as the Soledad Brothers, were awaiting trial for the murder of a prison guard.[8]

Jonathan had smuggled guns in to the courtroom. In the midst of Magee's testimony, Jonathan stood up, pulled out the guns, and conscripted McClain, Christmas, and Magee to join his rebellion. Reportedly, Jackson asked Magee, "Are you with us, brother?"[9] True to his slavery narrative, Magee, who was in manacles at the time, shouted: "Get these chains off of me; I'm a free man."[10] The judge, the prosecutor, and three female jurors were taken hostage, and a sawed-off shotgun was taped to the throat of the judge and held there by Magee.

The men escaped with their hostages in a van, but as they were trying to leave the courthouse parking lot, the police opened fire.[11] Magee was seriously wounded, as was the prosecutor, but Jackson, Christmas, McClain, and the judge were all killed.[12] Magee was charged with murder, aggravated kidnapping, and simple kidnapping. The case became particularly intriguing because it was alleged that George Jackson's equally famous girlfriend,

Angela Davis, was involved in the twisted plot to free George; it was contended that the guns belonged to her. Consequently, she too was indicted on kidnapping, murder, and conspiracy charges.[13]

At trial, Robert Carrow initially represented Magee and later enlisted Ramsey Clark to provide more firepower. Magee, however, did not trust anyone involved in the system, especially if he was white. Therefore, he refused to cooperate with Carrow and did not want Clark or anyone else to represent him; he could do it himself. Under pressure, Magee begrudgingly acquiesced to letting the men try the case on his behalf but insisted on being able to tell his story on the witness stand. He also asserted his autonomy throughout the proceeding by unhelpfully engaging in disruptive and argumentative behavior.[14]

To Magee's delight, Clark fully embraced his theory that what had occurred in the Marin County courtroom amounted to a slave rebellion. His client was caught up in the excitement of the potential to be freed from his unjust bondage. More specifically, Clark argued that the courthouse represented a "freedom ship" to Magee. The group of men "was a vessel going to freedom and [Magee] wanted to be on board. He couldn't deliberate. He couldn't analyze. He was in a state of euphoria."[15] Wacky as this may sound, it appeased Magee and enabled Clark to cleverly argue a diminished capacity defense.[16]

By any measure, particularly with a difficult client and unfavorable facts, the defense team did an exceptional job of representing Magee. The trial culminated in a hung jury, with the jurors voting 12–0 in favor of acquittal on the aggravated kidnapping charge and 11–1 on the murder charge.[17] They did, however, lean in favor of a conviction on the simple kidnapping charge by a vote of 11–1.[18] Besides the crafty diminished capacity defense, Clark and Carrow impressively established that the bullet from the rifle was not the one that killed the judge. Rather, in the barrage of police fire, the judge was fatally struck before the rifle held by Magee went off.[19]

After closing arguments, Clark had to leave rather abruptly to travel to Chile, having been summoned there in response to the unrest caused by a coup against the country's Marxist President Salvador Allende.[20] Magee was scheduled to be retried on the kidnapping charges, but in Clark's absence, the defendant appeared before the court, apparently represented by

a court-appointed public defender, and entered a guilty plea to the aggravated kidnapping charge under highly dubious circumstances.[21] The plea
was curiously accepted during the course of a motion hearing challenging
the composition of the grand jury that had indicted Magee. There has
been some suggestion that Magee was either being sarcastic in accepting
the plea or that he may have simply been admitting his frustrations with
the process, not his guilt.[22] Clark recalls that Magee was being dismissively
flippant with the judge and the system, saying something to the effect of
"I did everything. You name it, I did it."[23]

Following this unfortunate development, Magee later sought to withdraw his plea with the aid of Clark and his co-counsel Carrow. Despite
their diligent efforts, the guilty plea stuck.[24] Throughout this time, though,
Clark developed a close relationship with Magee, as did his wife Georgia,
of whom Magee is reported to have been especially fond. In the ensuing
years, the two visited Magee together on occasion. Clark blissfully remembers one instance when he and Georgia spent all night making gumbo for
Magee's birthday.[25]

Ruchell Magee is now in his late 70s and still in prison. Over the past
forty-plus years, he has tried earnestly, but in vain, to gain his freedom
through the filing of innumerable *pro se* habeas corpus petitions and various
other types of motions. To this day, Clark believes in Magee's innocence.
Magee's tragic life noticeably troubles the former attorney general because
he believes Magee never had a chance, largely because of his race. While
Magee may wrongfully be in prison, Clark nevertheless acknowledges that,
at this point, it would be very difficult for his former client to exist on the
outside. He has been an inmate for virtually his entire life—every day since
he was 16, except for six months.[26] Prison is all that he really knows.

The recurrent unifying concept between the Magee representation and
all of Clark's other battles on both the inside and the outside is his commitment to the attainment of social justice—not just courtroom justice
but something more pervasive throughout society. He wants all people—
whether rich or poor, black or white—to receive the same inalienable benefits of American citizenship—quality education, employment, safe and
affordable housing, access to legal counsel, and respectful police–community

relations, among other things. And to achieve social justice, Clark advocates for radical societal change, a systemic transformation that could best be achieved through legal action.

In his view, the law is society's most powerful instrument of social change.[27] In fact, Clark taught a course on the subject for a number of years at Howard University School of Law, hoping to inspire the next generation of Thurgood Marshalls to seek to transform the world through the law.[28] Once on the political outside, Clark expanded his quest for social justice beyond America's borders, promoting international human rights worldwide, often in the land of our so-called enemies, those labeled terrorists and war criminals by the U.S. government. But before venturing there, he had some "enemies" to defend at home.

As attorney general, Ramsey Clark had consistently sought the attainment of social justice for those then viewed by many as domestic enemies, individuals at the margins of society who promoted revolutionary change. He reliably advocated for the civil rights movement and courageously defended its black leadership, even those deemed too incendiary by the mainstream—people like Stokely Carmichael and H. Rap Brown, as well as members of the much-maligned Black Panther Party.

While on the inside, however, his protection of such reputed militants was not overt. Rather, Clark used a recalcitrant strategy. Specifically, unlike other members of the Johnson administration, Clark was unwilling to openly denounce these activists or to authorize cause-curtailing legal action against them. President Johnson, FBI Director J. Edgar Hoover, and many other leaders portrayed the Black Panthers, Carmichael, Brown, and their followers as domestic terrorists, who represented an extreme threat to the American people. President Nixon and Attorney General John Mitchell took this rhetoric to an even more exaggerated level and unleashed Hoover to eradicate the bogeymen they created. Hoover, of course, happily did so by covertly infiltrating and undermining the Panthers through his sinister COINTELPRO operation.[29]

Nothing of this nature had been possible on Ramsey Clark's watch, though he did admittedly authorize the Ghetto Informant Program to obtain intelligence about possible corrupt, organized activity underlying the riots.[30] He understood the growing rage among young black people and knew that it was justified on some level. Consequently, for the most part, Clark simply refused to openly condemn them by word or deed. But it was not until he left the DOJ that Clark was able to take affirmative steps to actively defend these "domestic terrorists" and to condemn those who unjustifiably attacked and demonized them.

Interestingly, one of the principal objectives of the Black Panthers was to confront and address what they viewed as an "epidemic of police brutality."[31] Clark surely shared their view that police abuse in the black community was rampant and needed to be eliminated. He had made this point as early as 1965 in the aftermath of the Watts riots, and throughout his tenure in the DOJ, he persisted in calling for the establishment of community policing and the professionalization of law enforcement. The Panthers' approach to dealing with these police excesses, however, was not so diplomatic.

Fully armed with rifles, members would essentially "police the police," menacingly observing them during their patrols as a deterrent to possible over-policing in the black community.[32] Though this tactic could temporarily avoid official violence, it could also escalate the tension between law enforcement and black citizens, especially those who happened to be members of the Black Panther Party. Rather than mend their ways, some police departments, under the leadership of the FBI, decided that eliminating the Black Panthers was the most appropriate strategy for ensuring the maintenance of law and order. This scheme violently played out in December 1969 in Chicago when local police—with guns blazing and apparent FBI involvement and backing—raided Black Panther offices and murdered Panther leaders Fred Hampton and Mark Clark.[33]

In a press conference after the incident, Cook County State's Attorney Edward V. Hanrahan condemned the nine Black Panthers who had been present at the time of the raid.[34] In particular, he "charged that they had made a vicious, unprovoked attack on police attempting to carry out a legitimate search of the apartment," and he lauded the officers' exercise of "good judgment, considerable restraint, and professional discipline."[35] In other words, the Panthers were the aggressors, and the police acted as benevolently and professionally as they could under the circumstances.

This depiction was nothing short of laughable. In truth, it would later be shown that the police fired between eighty-three and ninety shots, and the Panthers fired at most one shot.[36] Nevertheless, subsequent official investigations by state and local authorities, as well as a federal grand jury, ended with findings that were only moderately critical of the police.[37] Furthermore, a state prosecution of the officers and Hanrahan for conspiracy to obstruct justice ended with the judge's granting of a motion for acquittal.[38]

Understandably, demands followed for an independent investigation into not only the deaths of Fred Hampton and Mark Clark, but also similar incidents that had occurred elsewhere. In response, during summer 1970, the Commission of Inquiry into the Black Panthers and Law Enforcement was formed, and Ramsey Clark was ultimately drafted to serve as its co-chair, along with NAACP President Roy Wilkins. The commission was charged with investigating and making factual findings with regard to various clashes around the country between the police and Black Panthers—most prominently the Chicago murders—as well as the perceived discriminatory treatment of black militant groups by the police.[39]

After a comprehensive investigation, the commission concluded that there was "probable cause to believe that the predawn raid, carried out by officers with heavy armament but without tear gas, sound equipment, or lighting equipment, involved criminal acts on the part of the planners."[40] Specifically, the fourteen police officers involved were equipped with at least twenty-seven different firearms, including a Thompson submachine gun with 110 rounds of ammunition, five shotguns, nineteen or twenty .38-caliber pistols, one .357-caliber pistol, and a carbine.[41] If the officers were truly only interested in executing a search warrant, as they claimed, the commission believed there were obviously less confrontational options for accomplishing this objective.[42]

Although the commission would not unequivocally state as much,[43] the evidence it uncovered demonstrated that the Chicago raid amounted to what can rightly be characterized as a legally sanctioned "hit" on the Black Panther Party.[44] Between 1968 and 1970, twenty-eight Black Panthers were killed around the country at the hands of police officers.[45] Subsequent investigations invariably found no official wrongdoing, a fact noted in the sharply critical report by the Commission of Inquiry. Specifically, the report characterized some of the state and local investigations into the Chicago raid as simply a whitewash, "designed not to determine the facts but solely to establish the innocence of the police."[46]

Clark's involvement with the commission may have been a seminally important engagement in terms of his evolution as a social activist. He had already witnessed the government's overt vilification of the Black Panthers, a group that he had considered worthy of close scrutiny but certainly not deserving of the demonic labeling and fear campaign directed toward it by the Nixon administration. The investigation revealing the violent and unseemly lengths to which law enforcement would resort to achieve their desired ends undoubtedly intensified Clark's distrust of domestic authority. When combined with his Attica experience and anti–Vietnam War activities, it is not hard to understand why the former attorney general increasingly dedicated himself to personally searching for the truth, rather than accepting official pronouncements. Clark made it his mission to bring this truth to the American people, especially in matters that somehow implicated race.

Ramsey Clark has a seemingly innate affinity for people of color. He is reflexively predisposed to see beauty in other races, particularly black people—in my experience, this is an uncommon proclivity for a white person. I have spent much of my life surrounded by white culture—from my schooling to my fraternity to my jobs to my religion. And even to my family—my wife is white. Never in my 54 years, however, have I met a white person who unquestionably views all black people as equal or better except for Ramsey Clark.

This is not to say that I have not met many well-meaning people of the white race who have treated me and other African Americans with dignity and respect, or even admiration at times. But there has always been a hint of exceptionalism. There are black people whose undeniable talents transcend racial identity, to some extent, and those are the individuals whom I have found to be most widely embraced by white society. Even then, however, there is often an imaginary line that the "exceptional" African American cannot cross, some taboo—like dating or marrying a white person—that can change the interpersonal dynamic. My wife and I both routinely wonder how people who treat each of us well separately will react when they see us together or ascertain that we are married. Unfortunately, more times than not, we are disappointed by the response. An enjoyable lunch or dinner can be sullied by our server inquiring if we want separate checks.

Because of my life journey, I am very sensitive to how people react to my race or to the interracial composition of my family. I watch closely to see how people, particularly white people, respond to me. Do they make assumptions about who I am? For instance, when interviewing for a job, do they go overboard in pigeonholing my blackness, ensuring that I meet as many people of my race as possible, and expounding upon what role I could play in the "black" community? This has occurred on more occasions than I care to recount. One prospective employer even made sure that I had a black realtor to show me homes around town, not knowing that my wife-to-be was white.

Given these experiences, I inevitably brace myself for the hit that almost always comes—a comment or action that highlights my blackness in some patronizing, unflattering, or insensitive manner. In all of my dealings with Ramsey Clark, however, I have never felt the need to anticipate or prepare myself for the impending racial letdown. I would by no means characterize him as colorblind. Indeed, I consider colorblindness a hyperbolic myth. Everyone sees and experiences color, albeit it in different ways; no one is sightless to race. Clark's uniqueness is that he sees blackness or brownness, but there is no conscious or subconscious judging that goes with his observations. If anything, he is overly inclined to see the positivity, the beauty.

When he describes black people, Clark frequently exhibits awareness of their color, but not like most people who do so in order to identify someone—"you know Lonnie; he is that black professor." Ramsey Clark discusses black people's appearance in admiring, almost regal terms. Jamil Abdullah Al-Amin (formerly H. Rap Brown), for instance, was a "great, tall splendid-looking fellow."[47] Similarly, Clark once described Ruchell Magee to me as being "like black steel," short but very powerfully built, capable of doing a vast number of consecutive fingertip pushups.[48] In relating this to me, Clark seemed awestruck by Magee's skin color and power, but it did not come across as pejorative in the least bit. And he inevitably harps on what a "sweet" guy Magee is—"sweet, sweet guy."[49] Yet another example comes from remarks that Clark delivered at a fairly recent reunion of his Senate campaign workers and supporters, when he reminisced about his dear friend Herbert X Blyden, calling him a "great, big powerful guy" and a "beautiful piece of mahogany."[50] And Muhammad Ali, of course, was the most beautiful person that Ramsey Clark has ever seen.

His appreciation for people of color seems to have had something to do with his gravitation toward endeavoring to act as their protector in troubled situations. Throughout his life—while others chose to denigrate, demonize, or marginalize—he chose to join the vilified at the margins, defending their rights whenever challenged, whether in the halls of the Justice Department, the urban streets of America, the courtroom, or far away foreign lands. Typically, those for whom he has advocated have been black or brown, but his real concern is broader and encompasses all people who somehow find themselves on the outside of the mainstream, no matter what their color. In battling for such people, Clark inevitably finds that his adversary is, more times than not, the very government that he once had so earnestly served.

His myopic attachment to the concept of human dignity for all has led him to often side with those labeled as enemies of the public good by American leadership. Some of the most perplexing of these associations have caused critics to question his loyalty and even to ponder whether he might be anti-Semitic. Could there be something to this? How could someone so opposed to war and concerned about the persecuted in society align himself with reputed Nazi war criminals and terrorists?

PHOTO 1. Ramsey Clark being sworn in as attorney general by his father, Supreme Court Justice Tom C. Clark. Ramsey's wife Georgia and his son Thomas Clark II observe in the background, as do President Lyndon Johnson, Solicitor General Thurgood Marshall, and Vice President Hubert Humphrey.

SOURCE: Courtesy of the LBJ Presidential Library. Photo by Yoichi Okamoto. March 10, 1967.

PHOTO 2. Newly installed Attorney General Ramsey Clark meeting with President Johnson.

SOURCE: Courtesy of the LBJ Presidential Library. Photo by Yoichi Okamoto. March 23, 1967.

PHOTO 3. (*Left to right*) Ramsey Clark, President Johnson, former Deputy Secretary of Defense Cyrus Vance, and Secretary of Defense Robert McNamara meeting in the Cabinet Room concerning the Detroit riots.

SOURCE: Courtesy of the LBJ Presidential Library. Photo by Yoichi Okamoto. July 24, 1967.

PHOTO 4. Georgia Clark (*second from the right*) with the other wives of the outgoing members of President Johnson's Cabinet. Lady Bird Johnson, President Johnson's wife, is seated in the middle.

SOURCE: Courtesy of the LBJ Presidential Library. Photo by Yoichi Okamoto. January 10, 1969.

PHOTO 5. Ramsey Clark during his controversial visit to North Vietnam in summer 1972.

SOURCE: Photograph from the Personal Papers of Ramsey Clark, LBJ Presidential Library. Courtesy of the LBJ Presidential Library. Photographer unknown.

PHOTO 6. Ramsey Clark shares a laugh with some children in North Vietnam during his summer 1972 visit.

SOURCE: Slide from the Personal Papers of Ramsey Clark, LBJ Presidential Library. Courtesy of the LBJ Presidential Library. Photographer unknown.

PHOTO 7. Ramsey Clark chatting with Lady Bird Johnson at the dedication of his attorney general portrait. The artist Robert Berks is standing next to Clark.

SOURCE: Photograph from the Personal Papers of Ramsey Clark, LBJ Presidential Library. Courtesy of the LBJ Presidential Library. Photographer unknown.

PHOTO 8. Ramsey Clark shaking hands with Iraqi president Saddam Hussein during one of Clark's visits to Iraq in the 1990s. Hussein's interpreter is in the background.

SOURCE: Courtesy of Ramsey Clark.

PHOTO 9. Ramsey Clark seated next to me during a legal ethics symposium at the University of Georgia School of Law in October 2009. Clark delivered the keynote address.

SOURCE: Courtesy of Heidi Murphy. Photo by Heidi Murphy. October 16, 2009.

PHOTO 10. Ramsey Clark and me at his Greenwich Village apartment celebrating his 90th birthday.

SOURCE: Courtesy of Lois Akner. Photo by Lois Akner. December 16, 2018.

CHAPTER TEN

ANTI-SEMITE?

"Do not be mistaken. I do love the Israeli people, but
I always like the people who suffer the most."
Ramsey Clark[1]

AT SOME POINT, Clark's critics came to believe that what may have started
out as healthy skepticism and constructive opposition morphed into something more extreme. It began to seem like there was virtually nothing that
the U.S. government could do with which Ramsey Clark would not somehow find fault. Norman Podhoretz, former editor of *Commentary* magazine, though acknowledging that Clark had a "certain integrity," suggested
that his form of radicalism "seems to consist only of hatred of the United
States and automatic support for anyone opposed to the United States, for
any reason whatsoever in any context whatsoever."[2]

Clark, on the other hand, maintains that his seemingly jaundiced perspective stems from a love for America and a sincere desire to see it do right
by the world. Nevertheless, his unwavering denigration has caused some to
doubt the purity of his motives. His apparent receptiveness to sidling up with
just about any group that denounces America has only served to exacerbate
questions about his direction. Even those who generally support Clark express dismay over a number of his chosen causes and allegiances.[3]

While there are innumerable puzzling affiliations and representations with
which both friends and foes could take issue, one category that has attracted
sharp criticism is Clark's involvement with clients or matters that could be
characterized as anti-Semitic. There are various examples and, of course, there
was his bewildering decision to swipe Hitler's bust as a World War II me-
mento while a teenager in Germany. During his post-DOJ career, Clark has

represented reputed Nazi war criminals Karl Linnas and Jack Reimer, as well as perennial presidential candidate Lyndon LaRouche. His representation of and relationship with the Palestine Liberation Organization (PLO) lasted for many years, with him defending the group in lawsuits filed by the victims of terrorist attacks, including the infamous case arising from the murder of Leon Klinghoffer. Apart from his courtroom-related ties, Clark has vigorously supported the establishment of a Palestinian state as far back as the mid-1970s[4] and has consistently been as critical of Israel's military buildup and aggression in the Middle East as he has of his own nation.[5]

There is, to be sure, legitimacy to these positions, and Clark's concern for the deprivation of a homeland to the Palestinian people and his disdain for the Israeli government's militarism are by no means inconsistent with his well-established advocacy for international human rights. Some, however, question his position because of the various anti–Semitic-seeming cases that he has handled. The juxtaposition raises eyebrows, as does his alliance with groups and nations that have been linked to anti-Israeli terrorism, such as Hamas,[6] Libya, Iraq, and Syria—associations that will be examined more closely in the next chapter.

As a historically persecuted people, it might logically follow that Clark would be a staunch defender of Jews, in the same manner that he has reliably advocated on behalf of African Americans. His persistent identification with the underdog has been a constant theme throughout his life. And consistent with this, Clark has maintained a stark distinction between his criticism of the Israeli government and his feelings toward the Israeli people. The quote that begins this chapter captures this sentiment. Indeed, he has called the effort to label him as anti-Semitic "kind of pitiful," logically contending that criticizing Israel does not equate to disliking Jews.[7] Yet, his flirtation with individuals and entities viewed as anti-Semitic raises questions. The best place to start in analyzing this is with one of Clark's most unsettling representations—his defense of Nazi concentration camp guard Karl Linnas. Certainly Linnas was entitled to legal representation, but why Ramsey Clark?

Karl Linnas aided Nazi Germany with its invasion and occupation of Estonia, his home. Linnas was a member of the Selbstschutz (or Estonian "Home Guard") and was broadly reported to have been the chief of the Tartu concentration camp in Estonia, though he consistently denied that this was true.[8] In the role of chief, he allegedly oversaw and participated in numerous acts of unspeakable violence, including the brutal murders of thousands of innocent men, women, and children, many of whom were Jewish.[9]

Following World War II, Congress enacted the Displaced Persons Act to permit the many refugees who remained in Europe to emigrate to the United States.[10] Under the act, various requirements had to be satisfied to establish eligibility for naturalization—among them, the execution, under oath, of an Immigration and Naturalization Service form, which provided that the applicant had "never advocated or assisted in the persecution of any person because of race, religion or national origin. . . . "[11] Linnas went through the application process and eventually became a naturalized citizen, having falsely claimed that he had been a student in Tartu during the relevant time period, "had never served in the German Army and . . . had not been a member of any political group or organization."[12] He buttressed this deception by swearing that he had never been a party to the persecution of anyone based on race, religion, or national origin. Later, Linnas compounded his falsehoods by maintaining that on no occasion had he ever "committed a crime involving moral turpitude" or "given false testimony for the purpose of obtaining any benefits under the immigration and naturalization laws."[13]

Linnas's multiple fabrications eventually came to light, and the Office of Special Investigations—established pursuant to the Holtzman Amendment to the Immigration and Nationality Act for the express purpose of ferreting out illegal immigrants who were Nazis—began proceedings to revoke his citizenship in 1979.[14] In his denaturalization case, the trial court held that it was "beyond dispute that [Linnas] 'assisted the enemy in persecuting civil populations of countries'" and therefore concluded that he "unlawfully entered the country because of the willful misrepresentations he made."[15]

The United States subsequently initiated deportation proceedings against Linnas, which foreseeably resulted in a decision to deport him. The only viable country that would take Linnas, however, was the Soviet Union, a nation that had previously tried, convicted, and sentenced him to death for war crimes in a suspicious *ex parte* proceeding.[16] Thus, upon his return there, he would be executed.[17]

Following an unsuccessful attempt to have the U.S. decision reversed by the Board of Immigration Appeals, Linnas sought review before the U.S. Court of Appeals for the Second Circuit, principally arguing that the pertinent legislation underlying his deportation order constituted a bill of attainder in violation of Article I, Section 9 of the Constitution. Specifically, he contended that the Holtzman Amendment was expressly directed at "Nazi war criminals . . . for the purpose of punishing those persons without judicial trial." His argument proved unavailing, though, as the Second Circuit denied his petition for review.[18]

This is the point where Ramsey Clark entered the picture in 1986. He stepped in as counsel for Linnas, along with his partner Larry Schilling, to file a petition for writ of certiorari with the U.S. Supreme Court.[19] The contents of the petition provide some insight into why Clark may have chosen to align himself with such a universally vilified client. In particular, the primary arguments centered around various issues that one could reasonably predict might attract the former attorney general's attention. First and foremost, the end result of Linnas's deportation would be his execution by the Soviets.[20] Clark's longstanding aversion to the death penalty had to have played some part in his decision to represent Linnas. When combined with the questionable circumstances surrounding the Soviet adjudication of Linnas's guilt and the imposition of his death sentence, Clark's strong sense of justice and fairness may have drawn him to the case.

If the deportation could not be blocked, Linnas would be subjected to summary execution. Clark could not fathom having his country be complicit in such an offensive process, devoid of any semblance of due process.[21] In his opinion, no human being, not even a suspected Nazi war criminal, should be tried, convicted, and sentenced in absentia as Linnas had been. Notably, when he later defended his decision to represent another notoriously brutal character—former Iraqi president Saddam Hussein—Clark argued that even Adolf Hitler, had he survived, should have received maximum due process:

> It seems to me that it would have been absolutely critical to give him a fair trial, to let him call witnesses and cross-examine the hell out of them. If you don't do that, historical truth will be distorted.[22]

On top of the general justice and fairness rationale related to the effect of Linnas's deportation, Clark's core concern for systemic integrity was seemingly heightened by aspects of the denaturalization and deportation proceeding itself. Most significantly, Clark objected to the denial of Linnas's right to invoke the Fifth Amendment privilege against self-incrimination, as well as to the court's willingness to admit and consider evidence regarding his Nazi ties, which the Soviets had previously obtained without his involvement.[23] Although the U.S. proceeding was technically civil in nature, the practical effect of a decision to deport Linnas would be death, a criminal penalty. Given this, Clark argued that Linnas should have been entitled to Fifth Amendment protection.[24]

With regard to the unfairly obtained evidence, Clark dealt with that in a relatively straightforward manner, contending that its substance was simply not as overwhelming as portrayed. He maintained that the court of appeals, apparently blinded by the sheer harshness of the allegations, "uncritically adopted" the testimony, not taking into account the fact that it had been acquired under highly suspect circumstances by the Soviets.[25]

Overlaying all of this was Clark's ever-present skepticism of the American government, joined with a healthy dose of cynicism concerning the Soviets' involvement and interest in the case.[26] The targeted nature of the Holtzman Amendment, as well as the cooperative relationship between the United States and the Soviet Union on Nazi deportation matters, caused Clark to question the legitimacy of the entire process.[27] One could safely speculate that Clark was troubled by the hypocrisy of the American government having the audacity to condemn alleged war criminals, given his belief that the United States itself was guilty of numerous war crimes, repeatedly and unjustifiably carrying out acts of aggression against other nations. Who were these American leaders to seize the moral high ground when their hands were so dirty?

While one can surely disagree with Ramsey Clark's process-based misgivings related to the Linnas case in light of the appalling nature of the underlying crimes alleged, it is far more difficult to argue that his motivation for defending Linnas was inconsistent with his long-held commitment to ensuring justice and his genuine distrust of the American government. If there were no more to the story, puzzling over whether Clark's taking on such a case suggested anti-Semitic motives would seem rather dubious. It would be synonymous with condemning him for defending a murder suspect by claiming that he must identify with murderers. That, of course, is ridiculous. Everyone is entitled to a defense in America, and lawyers who are courageous enough to make this constitutional ideal a reality do not thereby embrace the substance of the allegations against their clients. If that were so, the right to counsel would quickly lose its force. The issue with Clark's representation of Linnas, though, is that there is much more to the story.

First, Ramsey Clark made public comments about the case to the effect that even if Linnas *had been* a Nazi war criminal, wasn't it about time to move past this lamentable episode in history? In particular, he expressed doubt as to the propriety of "go[ing] after septuagenarians 40 years after some god-awful crime they're alleged to have committed."[28] Even more perplexing, Clark reportedly stated, "There comes a time after the most horrible acts when the possibility of reconciliation outweighs any possible need for retribution or to maintain the integrity of the law."[29] That may sound noble in the abstract, but when considered in the context of the unspeakable horror of the Holocaust, it carries far less moral appeal. It also raises an interesting question: Would Ramsey Clark advocate for the same all-forgiving mindset if violent, racist acts against black people were the issue?

Take, for example, the despicable bombing of the 16th Street Baptist Church in Birmingham, Alabama—a bigoted, cowardly act carried out by four members of the Ku Klux Klan that resulted in the death of four black girls.[30] This tragedy occurred in 1963, but two of the perpetrators were not prosecuted until the early 2000s, roughly "40 years after some god-awful crime they [were] alleged to have committed." It seems unfathomable that Clark would apply his let's-just-move-on logic to this case. Perhaps I am wrong. Maybe he would be consistent. However, I am not aware of any efforts on his part to come to the Klansmen's defense in the same manner that he did for Linnas.

Apart from his defense of Linnas and his public commentary regarding the matter, Clark has added more fuel for anti-Semitic speculation by inserting himself into other cases that raised similar concerns, including his later representation of another alleged Nazi war criminal, Jack Reimer, throughout the late 1990s into the early 2000s.[31]

One little-known case that preceded his involvement with Linnas and Reimer could be what hooked him on this representational path. On May 14, 1979, a bomb exploded in a crowded market area in the Israeli city of Tiberias during a Jewish religious festival, killing two young Israeli boys and wounding thirty-eight others.[32] A Palestinian, Ziyad Abu Eain, was fingered as the perpetrator by the Israeli government, along with several alleged accomplices. At the time that charges were brought against Abu Eain, he was living in Chicago where his sister resided, and therefore Israel sought to have him extradited for trial.[33]

Initially, Abu Eain was represented by Abdeen Jabara—a noted American Arab attorney who would later serve as president of the American Arab Anti-Discrimination Committee and who notably would become one of Ramsey Clark's dearest friends, as well as a trusted and able co-counsel on numerous matters. Jabara was only modestly acquainted with Clark when he undertook to represent Abu Eain. But he had been impressed by the former attorney general's courage in taking a public pro-Palestine position, something that very few high-profile American leaders had done during that period.[34] Clark recently reaffirmed his staunch advocacy for this position: "People of good will must do all within their power to bring a united, strong, independent, secure and prosperous Palestine into existence now."[35]

After losing the extradition case at the trial level, Jabara decided that it might be helpful to have a bit more gravitas at counsel's table on appeal. The case had become a big deal for the State Department, and all stops were being pulled out to ensure that Abu Eain would be extradited. According to Jabara, the State Department's active involvement in the extradition proceeding was unprecedented.[36] Ramsey Clark seemed like the perfect choice to level the playing field somewhat in the courtroom, and when asked, he joined Abu Eain's defense team without hesitation.[37]

Clark took the lead role before the U.S. Court of Appeals for the Seventh Circuit and sought to undermine the testimony of Abu Eain's alleged accomplices, as well as the veracity of their coerced confessions. More importantly, he argued for application of the political offense exception, the purpose of which is to avoid assisting a requesting nation in prosecuting an offense that is political in nature. In the United States, for the exception to apply, the act in question must have been "committed in the course of and incidental to a violent political disturbance such as a war, revolution or rebellion."[38] Here, although the defense maintained that Abu Eain was substantively innocent, even if one assumed that he had planted the bomb, it was a political offense "because there was and is a conflict in Israel that involves violence, and the PLO, to which [Abu Eain] allegedly belongs, is a party to that violence."[39]

The Seventh Circuit, nevertheless, denied application of the exception, finding generally that the bombing "was not shown to be incidental to the conflict in Israel."[40] More specifically and damningly, it held:

> The exception does not make a random bombing intended to result in the cold-blooded murder of civilians incidental to a purpose of toppling a government, absent a direct link between the perpetrator, a political organization's political goals, and the specific act.[41]

This finding by the Seventh Circuit was truly novel, as it represented a significant tightening of the circumstances deemed sufficient for application of the political offense exception.[42]

Even though Clark and Jabara lost what each viewed as a highly politicized case, they were able to negotiate a favorable agreement on Abu Eain's behalf requiring that he be tried in an Israeli criminal court, rather than before a military body. The two men traveled to Israel and attended the trial, which, to no one's surprise, ended in a conviction.[43]

There are four very interesting aspects of this case as it pertains to Ramsey Clark and his potential motivation for representing Abu Eain. First, Jabara's rationale for recruiting Clark is telling. It was because he was a high-profile American leader known to be pro-Palestinian. Perhaps it is just semantics to some, but "pro-Palestinian" seems very different from "anti-Israeli," and one does not necessarily connote the other.

Second, there are parallels here to Clark's gravitation toward matters involving official abuse or overreaching and defense of militant factions of the civil rights movement. His participation as chair of the Commission of Inquiry in the aftermath of the Chicago police murders of Black Panthers Fred Hampton and Mark Clark immediately comes to mind. Clark's investigation uncovered a level of corruption within the Cook County State's Attorney's Office and the Chicago police, as well as the FBI, that cemented his contrarian view of the American power structure. In his mind, there was literally no level to which government officials would not sink to accomplish their objectives, no matter how misplaced they may have been. Hence, Clark was highly predisposed to side with Abu Eain, undoubtedly suspecting that he, like the Black Panthers, could be subject to unfair targeting and demonization simply because of the Palestinian label.

Third, Ramsey Clark was not paid one penny for his representation of Abu Eain. Abdeen Jabara recalls that Clark never even mentioned the subject of attorney's fees.

And fourth, Jabara shared an anecdote with me about the case that he did not learn about until Clark mentioned it to him recently. Apparently, after Clark's argument before the Seventh Circuit Court of Appeals, one of the judges told the former attorney general that his father Tom Clark would have been ashamed of him.[44] The judge was almost surely wrong in his assessment of the elder Clark's likely reaction were he alive, but the rebuke nonetheless had to sting.

To me, these latter two aspects of the representation underscore Ramsey Clark's motives and suggest that his involvement was more about helping Abu Eain than opposing Israel or the United States. Right or wrong, he believed strongly in what he was doing, so much so that neither compensation nor the prospect of evoking the ire of a federal appeals court judge was a consideration.

Although a deep dive into the Abu Eain case seems to reveal a potentially noble, consistent strain in Clark's choice of clients, other matters that he subsequently handled—combined with the heinous nature of the offenses alleged—have caused some to question his motives.[45] To many, one of the most concerning of his later affiliations was his enduring relationship with the PLO. He appears to have been a supporter from fairly early on and throughout the period during which the PLO was widely cast as a leading terrorist organization in the Middle East. Touting itself as the national representative of the Palestinian people, the entity sought recognition as a state and membership in the United Nations. Clark, while campaigning for New York's Senate seat in 1974, expressed the strong view that PLO leader Yasser Arafat ought to be accorded the right to speak before the UN,[46] but he denounced the organization itself. Specifically, candidate Clark stated of the PLO: "It contains terrorist elements and espouses and condones terrorist activities. It is not the legitimate or even substantive representative of the Palestinians in Israel."[47]

He would dramatically change his tune, though, not long after this negative critique of the PLO, subsequently embracing both Arafat and his organization as clients for over two decades and maintaining, "We have to insist upon the recognition of the only representative of the Palestinian people that they themselves have chosen, and no one else can do it, the PLO."[48] Clark espouses a deep-felt concern for the Palestinian people, whom he considers to be subjugated and discriminated against. Indeed, he has gone so far as to equate their situation, in terms of importance, with an issue near and dear to his heart—American civil rights. He once stated,

> I now really believe that the clearest test of our sensitivity for human rights . . . is how we feel about the rights of Palestinians. If you can't be concerned about them, then your commitment to human rights is not universal, and you have a blind spot.[49]

While the United States, Israel, and other nations condemned the PLO as a terrorist organization, Clark stood loyally by its side, diplomatically and in the courtroom. He and his partner Larry Schilling served as counsel of record for the PLO, Arafat, and later, the Palestinian National Authority in numerous lawsuits stemming from terrorist attacks, allegedly sponsored by them. The most notorious of these cases arose from the murder of Leon Klinghoffer, an elderly, disabled Jewish American. In October of 1985, Klinghoffer and his wife took a cruise on the *Achille Lauro*, a large Italian passenger liner, to celebrate their thirty-sixth wedding anniversary. The ship was hijacked by four Palestinian terrorists, allegedly associated with the PLO. In addition to seizing the ship and holding a number of hostages, the terrorists brutally killed Klinghoffer, shooting him in the forehead and chest and then tossing him and his wheelchair into the Mediterranean Sea.

The murder sparked widespread outrage, particularly among the American Jewish community. Klinghoffer's widow filed a lawsuit against the *Achille Lauro* and various additional defendants, as did other passengers on the cruise ship.[50] Mrs. Klinghoffer did not initially sue the PLO, but the other defendants added the entity to the lawsuit, contending that it was ultimately responsible for any damages suffered by the Klinghoffers.[51] Ramsey Clark served as counsel to the PLO, raising a number of technical, procedural defenses, including a sovereign immunity argument that went to the very heart and soul of the organization's existence. Specifically, Clark maintained that the PLO was a sovereign state and therefore was not subject to suit. This, of course, has always been the point of contention with the PLO. The UN had consistently denied the organization full-fledged membership, relegating it instead to permanent observer status. The court predictably rejected the sovereign immunity contention, as well as many of the other theories raised by Clark.

Although the PLO claimed that the hijackers were independent actors not associated with it, the organization ultimately settled the *Klinghoffer* action. Even if the PLO was, in fact, not involved in Klinghoffer's murder, the optics of the litigation nevertheless further tainted Ramsey Clark's reputation. The case was so egregious and high profile that it inspired U.S. enactment of the Anti-Terrorism Act of 1987, an act expressly directed at the PLO that declared it a terrorist organization, prohibited its operation within the United States, and made it unlawful for American citizens to spread the PLO's message.[52]

Notwithstanding the overt castigation and ostracism of the PLO, Clark continued his close connection with the group for almost thirty years, willingly serving as legal counsel in a variety of matters, such as opposing efforts to close the organization's Mission to the United Nations and defending a number of civil suits by families of individuals killed or injured by alleged PLO-sponsored terrorist acts.[53] The longstanding attorney–client relationship ended in 2007; this was not Clark's choice, but rather the decision of the PLO/Palestinian National Authority, which seemingly desired to move its defense strategy in a different direction.[54]

Apart from Clark's PLO association in terrorism-linked matters, he has compounded speculation about his views by taking on other head-scratching cases, such as his representation of Lyndon LaRouche, habitual fringe presidential candidate,[55] and Sheikh Omar Abdel Rahman, the blind cleric who was eventually convicted of "conspiring to carry out a terrorist campaign of bombings and assassinations intended to destroy the United Nations and New York landmarks, kill hundreds . . . and force America to abandon its support for Israel and Egypt."[56] When compared to other similarly controversial clients and matters over the years, one could surmise that Clark simply has an unyielding commitment to those whom he views as persecuted, especially if the perceived persecutor is the U.S. government.

No matter who the person or what the entity, if Clark believes that there is fervent vilification or persecution afoot, he has been willing to step in to oppose such efforts.[57] He did that as attorney general on behalf of black citizens, and he continued to do so on the outside for antiwar activists and draft dodgers, Black Panthers, Attica inmates, and a long line of clients sentenced to death, as well as maligned dictators, such as Slobodan Milosevic and Saddam Hussein. The common thread in every instance seems to be that the person or group was somehow being singled out or targeted in what Clark believed was an unjust manner, even if there could have been some ostensibly valid basis for that targeting. One particularly compelling case that fits neatly within this representational paradigm was Clark's legal effort on behalf of the Branch Davidians. It likewise demonstrates just how far he was willing to go in order to address wrongful official persecution.

The Branch Davidians might best be described as a cult of Christianity. The group originally split with the Seventh-Day Adventist Church, calling itself the Davidian Seventh-Day Adventist Church. Following another rift, a group of Davidians spun off yet again to form the Branch Davidians. Toward the beginning of 1990, a charismatic Davidian named David Koresh would assume the position as spiritual leader of the church.[58] The congregation, which occupied a compound, Mount Carmel Center, on the outskirts of Waco, Texas, believed that Koresh was the Second Coming of

Jesus Christ. He taught his followers that they were God's chosen people and that he was God's messenger on earth. As a result, the Davidians believed that Koresh's teachings were the word of God, on par with the very contents of the Bible. In addition, Koresh maintained that as the Messiah, "all women belonged to him, including the wives and daughters of his male followers."[59] This reportedly resulted in his unlawfully wedding girls as young as 12 years old.[60]

Before Koresh's ascension to power in the church, he was actually ejected from the Davidians Mount Carmel compound. After a couple of years away, he returned with some followers, armed and prepared to violently stake his claim to the spiritual leadership of the church. Apparently, paramilitary training was also a tenet of the Davidians. It is reported that Koresh preached to his followers, "You can't die for God if you can't kill for God."[61] A shootout between Koresh's people and the then-spiritual leader of the Davidians and his flock ended with Koresh's side being charged with attempted murder. Koresh's followers were all ultimately acquitted, and his prosecution ended with a hung jury, but this episode—along with Koresh's alleged marrying of underage girls—surely put him and the Davidians squarely on law enforcement's radar.[62]

The federal Bureau of Alcohol, Tobacco and Firearms (ATF) was more interested in reports that illegal weapons were being manufactured and distributed from the church compound. After a significant investigation into the matter, the ATF obtained and was prepared to execute an arrest warrant for Koresh, as well as a search warrant by way of a raid on the compound.[63] Because of concerns regarding the local newspaper's negative series on Koresh—"Sinful Messiah"—the ATF moved up the timing of its planned raid to February 28, 1993, one day after the first article was published. Although it is unclear who fired first, the raid resulted in a deadly exchange of gunfire between the ATF and the Branch Davidians. Four ATF agents and five Davidians were killed, and numerous others from both sides were injured.[64]

After the failed raid, the FBI took control of the operation and engaged in extensive negotiations with the Davidians for the ensuing fifty-one days. Besides communicating directly with Koresh, the FBI also employed various other tactics designed to wear down the compound inhabitants, such as piping in loud music and shutting off the electricity.[65]

Despite all these efforts, plus the granting of a number of requested concessions, Koresh still refused to surrender. As a result, on April 19, 1993, with tanks and armored vehicles surrounding the compound, the FBI announced that it would begin shooting tear gas, and if the Davidians opened fire, it would be returned. The hope was that the Davidians would emerge from the compound peacefully, but when no one exited following the initial volley of tear gas, the FBI's tanks rammed the compound building in order to place the gas further inside. This continued for six hours with no sign of relent by the Davidians.

At this point the FBI allegedly noticed a fire within the compound. It spread very quickly, and the local fire department was prevented from entering until after the building was fully engulfed in flames. Though some escaped, the overwhelming majority of the congregants were killed, including a number of children, although it appears that some individuals died from gunshot wounds rather than from the fire.[66]

The FBI contended that the tragedy was entirely the fault of Koresh and the Branch Davidians. Not only did their recalcitrance force the FBI's hand, but the Davidians were personally responsible for setting the fires that resulted in their deaths, according to the government. As further support for this blame-free stance, the FBI recovered a tremendous cache of automatic weapons and ammunition from the remains of the compound.[67] Notwithstanding the official finger-pointing, there was widespread public outrage over what seemed like a draconian and inept display of force by the FBI. That numerous innocent children died only exacerbated the situation for the government.

In the aftermath, the surviving family members of those who were killed filed wrongful death lawsuits against the ATF, the FBI, and various individual officials alleged to be responsible for the deaths, seeking $675 million in damages.[68] Along with co-counsel, Ramsey Clark represented some of the plaintiffs and advocated vigorously on their behalf. Sounding much like he did as attorney general in denouncing Mayor Richard Daley's calls for police to shoot rioting looters, Clark condemned the FBI's indiscriminate and excessive use of force and expressed grave concerns for America's future if such extreme conduct went unchecked. Along these lines, he rhetorically queried in his closing argument at trial, "if [the FBI's] acts were so right, how is it that the results of their acts were so disastrous, ending in the deaths of 84 people from two assaults they initiated against a peaceful people?"[69] Even more pointedly, he concluded:

> If the ATF and the FBI conduct at Mount Carmel did not involve excessive force and negligence, then the U.S. Government can employ this exact self-same conduct with impunity against any group in America, and no one here will be free from the violence of their own government. It has to be stopped.[70]

The trial ended in a verdict for the government issued by an advisory jury, which subsequently led to the trial judge dismissing the entire case. Efforts to have the decision overturned because of the judge's alleged bias against the plaintiffs were unsuccessful.[71] Consistent with his closing argument, Clark was extremely dismayed by the outcome.

> I'm terribly, terribly frustrated by the way this case has gone. . . . This isn't a negligence case, it's a constitutional case. How do you drive a tank into a church dozens of times and then call it negligence? The government has made the victims into the violators.[72]

The parallels between Clark's view of the Waco disaster and his earlier encounters with what he deemed to be unlawful, brutal conduct by law enforcement against marginalized groups are impossible to ignore—in particular, his experience with the investigation into the police murders of Black Panthers Fred Hampton and Mark Clark. There, Ramsey Clark's Commission of Inquiry concluded that the Chicago police, through an unnecessary paramilitary show of force, in essence assassinated the two Panther leaders and then sought to cover it up by falsely casting blame on the victims, portraying them as the instigators of the violence.

Up close and personally, Clark had seen the fallacy behind the official justification for the Chicago murders. He had also witnessed what he considered to be similar travesties of justice in Orangeburg, South Carolina, in 1968 and during the Democratic National Convention in Chicago later that same year. In each instance, the police utilized unbridled force to quell dissent of citizens occupying the purported margins of society, and the police conduct went unpunished. As an insider, Clark knew the truth. After all, he had worked closely with FBI Director J. Edgar Hoover and fully recognized the nefarious depths to which Hoover would sink in order to accomplish unsavory government ends, like destroying the Black Panther Party and other "domestic terrorists" (aka black militants).

Clark understood that the labels and characterizations placed on individuals and groups by his government were used as justifications for marginalization, or even worse, extermination. Once you make someone into a demon, you can do anything to that person with little fear of public reprisal. Demons are convenient fictions of the government's imagination, and Clark has been willing to align himself with the demonized: the Black Panthers, Stokely Carmichael, H. Rap Brown, Ruchell Magee, Attica Brother Charley Joe Pernasalice, convicted FBI agent killer Leonard Peltier, the Branch Davidians, and the list goes on and on. Is it really such a stretch for him to likewise side with demons accused of anti-Semitic acts? To him, there is very little difference between the Black Panthers, Carmichael, or Brown, and the PLO, Ziyad Abu Eain, or Karl Linnas. He sees the commonality of persecution, of being cast as the enemy of the people, and he cannot help but come to their defense in an effort to ensure justice and fairness.

Ramsey Clark's representation of certain individuals and groups—particularly Linnas and Reimer—is still troubling and confusing. If he had a record, like the American Civil Liberties Union, of also standing up for the rights of other hateful individuals and groups, such as the Ku Klux Klan, it might be easier to accept that he is simply all about protecting those on the periphery of the mainstream. If he can view Linnas or Reimer as having been demonized, why can't he view the Klan from that same perspective? Knowing Ramsey Clark, however, I cannot imagine that he would ever embrace a client whom he considered to be anti–African American, no matter how persecuted that person may be. And this is why it is difficult to reconcile his willingness to defend those considered to be anti-Semitic.

I decided to pointedly ask some of his friends and former colleagues what they thought about the claim that Ramsey Clark is anti-Semitic. Every single one was adamant that he is not. His dear friend and associate Bob Schwartz, for example, whom he has known and worked closely with since 1974, firmly believes that Clark is not anti-Semitic—though, he did acknowledge his discomfort with the Linnas and Reimer representations. Schwartz also expressed bewilderment over his friend's uncharacteristic statements about putting the past behind us as it pertained to these Nazi war criminals. Schwartz pointed out that Clark's stance on the mistreatment of Native Americans has always been quite to the contrary, maintaining that we should "never forget." Though the apparent inconsistency is puzzling, it does not alter Schwartz's strong view that Clark is not anti-Semitic.[73] There must be some other explanation for his positional incongruity, but what that could be remains a mystery.

Victor Navasky, another close associate of Clark's, does not believe that anti-Semitism has had anything to do with his friend's representations. Rather, he thinks that Clark is inspired by a pure desire for justice. According to Navasky, when Ramsey takes on such cases, he is standing up for someone whose rights he believes have been trampled.[74] While that can explain Clark's decision to serve as legal counsel for Linnas and Reimer, it sheds no light on his confounding advocacy for moving past their alleged offenses.

Clark's Department of Justice colleagues Nicholas Katzenbach and Stephen Pollak likewise dismissed the notion that he might be anti-Semitic.[75] Katzenbach is said to have called the charge "nonsense,"[76] while Pollak offered that Clark simply does not harbor any group prejudice.[77]

My exposure to Ramsey Clark leads me to agree with the general assessments offered by his friends and colleagues, but there is obviously room for debate, and there is no getting around the perplexing choices he has made over the years. Though Clark has rarely defended himself publicly against criticism regarding which clients he chooses to represent, on one occasion he did express agitation after a Jewish group in Los Angeles canceled his scheduled keynote address at a fundraising dinner hosted by the organization. Specifically, the Jewish Federation Council rescinded its invitation to Clark because of his representation of the PLO in the Klinghoffer case and his defense of Karl Linnas.[78] In response, Clark bristled that the group was politicizing human rights:

> The greatest disservice that can be done to human rights is to politicize them. To say that only those who are for me are for human rights is to destroy the role that the idea of human rights must play in the quest for peace and human dignity.[79]

He further pointed out that besides the cases upon which the Jewish Federation focused, he had "also been involved in scores of cases for Soviet Jews going back many years."[80] He continued, "But my belief in human rights is not selective. . . . In 1974, when I was running for U.S. Senate, I insisted that . . . Yasser Arafat had a right to speak at the United Nations. I still believe that. I think people have a right to be heard."[81]

Clark's earnest commitment to civil rights evolved over time into this broader devotion to the protection of human rights, which may be what has led to his propensity to represent those whom the American public has been told are demons. In 2005, the man who once served as our nation's chief prosecutor would show the world the true lengths to which he was willing to go in his ubiquitous quest to defend and secure human rights by taking on the representation of perhaps his most reviled client of all time—his country's archenemy, Saddam Hussein.

CHAPTER ELEVEN

SADDAM HUSSEIN

"I don't believe in demons; I believe in people. And I believe people do
bad things. But if you believe in demons, then you can do anything to
a demon, can't you? They're not human; they have no human rights."

Ramsey Clark[1]

IN 2005 Ramsey Clark officially undertook the representation of perhaps
his most notorious client. With the exception of Osama bin Laden, it is
difficult to imagine a contemporary figure more universally vilified and despised than Saddam Hussein, the former Iraqi president, known to much
of the world as the Butcher of Baghdad. Many have equated him with the
likes of Joseph Stalin or Adolf Hitler—an evil, psychopathic madman bent
on the iron-fist domination of his region of the world.[2] He was ruthless
and power hungry, thin-skinned and brutal. The atrocities against Saddam's
own people carried out under his leadership were horrifying. Indeed, after
U.S. forces captured him in December 2003, he was charged with numerous war crimes stemming from an unthinkable cavalcade of murderous acts.
By some estimates, Hussein may have been responsible for the demise of as
many as 500,000 (likely more), including those massacred in his genocidal
campaign against the Kurdish people.[3]

Why would a man purportedly committed to justice, nonviolence, and
world peace choose to associate with a barbaric dictator reputed to be a
modern-day Hitler, an executioner of his own people, without even a modi-
cum of due process? Everything about Hussein would seem to be the very
antithesis of Ramsey Clark, even if one takes into account his numerous
other controversial and somewhat confounding representations. How could
Clark be true to his articulated principles, the ideals for which he rigidly
stands, and embrace the Dark Lord of the Middle East?

A popular, reflexive response to this question would be to assert that Ramsey Clark is not who he claims to be. Rather, he is what his actions suggest—decidedly anti-American to the point of being willing to side with anyone who is an enemy of his country. The more extreme, the better. From this perspective, it makes perfect sense for Clark to rush to Saddam's defense; he was actually a dream client, who provided Clark with a high-profile platform from which to criticize his nation's president and those who supported him. Those subscribing to this assessment of Clark might also castigate him further by questioning his mental stability. They could maintain that he is an old man whose judgment is fading, making him ever-more receptive to radical stands.

But Ramsey Clark is just not that simple. His decision to represent Saddam Hussein did not stem from some rash, ill-conceived desire to lash out at America. Nor did it emanate from psychological instability. He knew exactly what he was doing, and a studied examination of the journey that led him to Saddam's side vividly demonstrates this. Clark's decision still may not seem sensible, but the path appears logical.[4]

In 1980, sixty-six Americans were taken hostage in Iran at the U.S. Embassy following the Ayatollah Khomeini's overthrow of the shah. Because of Clark's amiable relationship with Khomeini, President Jimmy Carter enlisted him to travel to Iran as a special envoy on behalf of the U.S. government to negotiate for the release of the hostages. Clark was opposed to being sent as the president's official emissary, as he thought this would make negotiations more difficult. Carter nevertheless flew him there on Air Force Two, attracting the attention of the press. As Clark predicted, this trip did not go well, with the representative nature of the visit resulting in the Ayatollah refusing his entry and forbidding any negotiations.[5]

Subsequently, in open defiance of an executive order that banned travel to Iran, Clark made a return trip as a private citizen with nine other Americans, in order to participate in an ad-hoc conference in Tehran preordained to condemn America's actions in the region. Although he personally declared Iran's seizure of the hostages to have been wrong, Clark and the rest of the conference participants sternly denounced the U.S. role in Iran over the years, from its 1980 disastrous military attempt to rescue the hostages all the way back to the 1953 CIA-sponsored coup that brought about the overthrow of Prime Minister Mohammad Mossadegh and the reinstallation of the shah.[6] Clark offered to personally take the place of the American hostages, but this overture was rejected by the Iranian government.[7]

Many Iranians were skeptical of Clark, viewing him as a possible spy, mislabeling him as the "vilest of American agents."[8] Clark could not win. He was reviled even more harshly by his own government—the one for which he was a so-called agent. Attorney General Benjamin Civiletti threatened Clark with prosecution for violation of the executive-ordered travel ban, and Republican Senator Bob Dole legislatively urged for his indictment under the Logan Act. The president, likewise, felt that the former attorney general deserved to be punished for his conduct because it jeopardized the safety of the hostages.[9]

Ultimately, no charges were brought against Clark, but his public upstaging of the president and open condemnation of the United States detracted even more from whatever credibility he retained in the eyes of the American government. It was safe to assume that future presidents would probably not be seeking Clark's services in the area of foreign diplomacy.

The next U.S. president, Ronald Reagan, surely viewed Ramsey Clark as an even-greater nuisance than did President Carter. In October 1983, President Reagan ordered the invasion of the tiny island of Grenada by American military forces, purportedly to ensure the safety of U.S. citizens there, as well as to rectify the instability of the Grenadian government—the prime minster had recently been executed, along with other cabinet officials. President Reagan maintained that U.S. military intervention had been requested by the governments of surrounding territories.[10] In addition to killing, injuring, and detaining large numbers of Grenadian and Cuban soldiers, the United States captured former Deputy Prime Minister Bernard Coard—believed to be responsible for the murder of Grenada's Prime Minister Maurice Bishop—and apparently held him completely incommunicado, even from his family. Coard's pregnant wife was likewise captured.[11]

This is where Ramsey Clark came into the picture, again on the side of the target of America's aggression. Coard's family retained Clark to provide the former deputy prime minister and his wife with legal assistance.

He traveled to Grenada but was initially not permitted to meet with the Coards.[12] Ever persistent, he was eventually able to do so and advised them throughout their legal ordeal. In the end, Bernard Coard and his alleged co-conspirators were convicted of the murder of the prime minister and sentenced to death, seemingly by a tribunal that bore many trappings of a kangaroo court. Among other things, Ramsey Clark reported that the Grenadian government arbitrarily hired a special judge to hear the case under a three-month contract; jurors were selected outside the presence of the defendants and their counsel; and the general public as well as the defendants' families were excluded from the courtroom.[13] Despite the up-hill nature of the battle, Clark was steadfast in his efforts on behalf of the Coards, and in 1994, with the aid of an assortment of notable figures, obtained the commutation of their death sentences, along with those of Bernard Coard's associates.[14]

Not long after the Grenada invasion, President Reagan would once more find himself at odds with the former attorney general. The enemy of choice this time was Libya, an oil-rich country led by a notorious, terrorism-linked dictator—Colonel Muammar Gaddafi. Reagan characterized Gaddafi as a "mad dog," evil and dangerous, a serious threat to the safety and security of the democratic world. Something needed to be done to contain him. In April 1986, the United States, assisted by its trusted ally Great Britain, unleashed attacks on the Libyan cities of Tripoli and Benghazi. This represented a transparent effort to assassinate Gaddafi but was defended as an act of retaliation for Libya's alleged bombing of a West Berlin discotheque, which had resulted in the death of two U.S. soldiers, among other victims. America's military effort, touted as surgical in its precision, in reality wrought significant death and destruction to Libya's civilian population in addition to devastating various targets where Gaddafi could potentially have been present.[15]

Following the bombing of Libya, Ramsey Clark undertook a personal witnessing tour of the region to obtain a firsthand account of the effects of the U.S. raid. This is precisely what he had done in North Vietnam fourteen years earlier and what he would do three years later in 1989 after the U.S. invasion of Panama. Skeptical of his government's self-righteous and positive portrayal of these military episodes, as well as the acutely pro-U.S.A. media reports, Clark wanted to determine for himself the true nature and extent of America's aggression.

He would likely characterize these as truth-seeking missions, while others have not been so generous in their assessments. Journalist John Judis has suggested that Clark was simply an unwitting dupe on these witnessing trips, "reporting as undoctored fact events that had been carefully constructed by local spin doctors and information ministers."[16] Foreign leaders were arguably providing Clark with a skewed picture, and though he was untrusting of his own government's characterizations, he was haplessly willing to buy the bill of goods sold to him by North Vietnam, Libya, and Panama, among others.

Whatever the case, Ramsey Clark's visit to Libya convinced him that the United States and Great Britain had committed massive, unprovoked atrocities and devastation to innocent civilians and their property in violation of U.S. and international law.[17] He maintained that President Reagan, British Prime Minister Margaret Thatcher, and various other officials of each nation had acted intentionally and with malice and, therefore, were personally involved in the commission of war crimes.

Clark memorialized these allegations in a federal lawsuit filed in Washington, DC, styled as *Saltany v. Reagan*, in which he named both countries as defendants, along with their respective leaders, and sought compensatory and punitive damages for the wrongful deaths and property destruction suffered by innocent victims, who included Libyans, Greeks, Egyptians, Yugoslavs, and Lebanese residing in Libya at the time.[18] Although Clark—along with his loyal co-counsel Larry Schilling—represented various individuals and their estates, he was, in effect, on Libya's side. This was not some ad-hoc war crimes conference. This was an actual lawsuit, filed by the former attorney general of the United States, against his own country and its sitting president on behalf of citizens and residents of the very nation that his president and his country viewed as a serious enemy, a threat to the safety and security of the free world.

Clark's legal action was outrageous, or at a minimum, "audacious." That was the word District Court Judge Thomas Penfield Jackson used to describe the lawsuit in deciding whether Clark should have been sanctioned for a frivolous filing. The plaintiffs' complaint was sharp and unyielding in its condemnation of the attack and those who authorized and facilitated it. The defendants were alleged to have

> conspired, acted in concert with, and aided and abetted one another in causing or permitting the attacks to be made, with a purpose to assassinate the Libyan head of state, and/or to "terrorize" the civilian population of Libya to the point of revolt against his government.[19]

In his decision dismissing the complaint—largely on sovereign immunity grounds—and declining to impose sanctions on Clark under Rule 11 of the Federal Rules of Civil Procedure, Judge Jackson held:

> The case offered no hope whatsoever of success, and plaintiffs' attorneys surely knew it. The injuries for which suit is brought are not insubstantial. It cannot, therefore, be said that the case is frivolous so much as it is audacious. The Court surmises it was brought as a public statement of protest of Presidential action with which counsel (and, to be sure, their clients) were in profound disagreement.[20]

Surprisingly, the judge went on to expressly condone this symbolic use of the federal courts: "The courts of the United States, however, serve in some respects as a forum for making such statements, and should continue to do so."[21]

Maybe it was an acceptable approach for Clark to file protest lawsuits, even when not well grounded in law and fact, in order to expose the evils that he perceived his government to be sugarcoating. Yet, on the appeal of *Saltany v. Reagan*, a three-judge panel of the D.C. Circuit Court of Appeals—comprised entirely of Reagan appointees—soundly rebuked Clark as well as Judge Jackson for condoning his legal shenanigans. In particular, the judges agreed that the suit was "audacious" but found that the seriousness of the injuries alleged should not be a factor in assessing the viability of a claim. "[W]e do not see how filing a complaint that 'plaintiffs' attorneys surely knew' had 'no hope whatsoever of success' can be anything but a violation of Rule 11."[22] The court proceeded to assail the notion that a federal courtroom was an appropriate protest venue for the former attorney general. "We do not conceive it a proper function of a federal court to serve as a forum for 'protests,' to the detriment of parties with serious disputes waiting to be heard."[23]

Although Clark's formal legal action proved futile, his clients were eventually able to obtain monetary reparations from the United States, a tacit concession of the wrongful nature of the harm caused to innocent civilians, though, of course, not an admission of legal culpability.[24] Clark also persisted in his attacks on President Reagan, equating him with the very terrorist thugs from whom he presumably was saving the democratic world and actively calling for his impeachment. According to Clark, through his actions in Grenada and Libya, as well as Lebanon and Nicaragua,

> Reagan [had] violated every principle for which America stands. . . . Serving as judge, jury and executioner, he orders military strikes that kill civilians. He attempts to kill foreign leaders. He resorts to surprise attacks. . . . The President has no legal power to order U.S. forces to murder indiscriminately and terrorize those he styles his enemies. Such acts constitute high crimes and misdemeanors.[25]

In Clark's view, Reagan, rather than foreign dictators or terrorists, represented "the greatest threat facing the American people and indeed the world."[26] To him, the president was the real enemy, not those whom he and his subordinates chose to oppose.

The seeds of Ramsey Clark's perception of authoritarian corruption at the highest levels of American government were no doubt sown during his time with the DOJ. Observing the lengths to which such governmental actors as FBI Director J. Edgar Hoover and even President Johnson would go in order to accomplish some clandestine objective made Clark skeptical. Clark had witnessed Hoover's obsession with Martin Luther King, Jr. and his desire to defame and delegitimize a revered civil rights leader for whom Clark had deep personal respect and admiration. Clark had to battle Hoover

over the director's desire to engage in the surreptitious wiretapping of King, which was purportedly intended to uncover his licentious ways and links to communism. Clark saw through this charade and also questioned more broadly the efficacy of this law enforcement technique, and he therefore refused to legally sanction Hoover's efforts; however, Hoover almost surely did as he pleased anyway.[27]

Clark had observed at close range President Johnson's maniacal fixation on the Vietnam War and his unhealthy concern with the potential effect it would have on his legacy. Anyone who opposed America's involvement in Vietnam or criticized Johnson's leadership on the issue was an enemy of the president. Dr. King, for instance, once a valued member of Johnson's civil rights inner circle, was abruptly excommunicated when he vocally expressed opposition to the war and questioned the moral authority of America to act as international peace police when it was "the greatest purveyor of violence in the world."[28] The hypocrisy of it all, especially from a man—Lyndon Johnson—whom Clark held in high esteem, undoubtedly troubled his principled conscience.

Johnson's successor, Richard Nixon, cemented Clark's jaundiced perception of his country's leadership. Once elected, Nixon, John Mitchell (Nixon's attorney general), and Hoover made "law and order" code for reining in what had become a more assertive form of civil rights and antiwar protests. Civil disobedience had taken a backseat to open confrontation and even rioting. The Nixon administration couched this as lawlessness and set about to systematically demonize those who engaged in such behavior. Hoover famously proclaimed the Black Panther Party as the "greatest threat to the internal security of the country."[29] And war protesters and so-called militant black leaders were similarly characterized as dangerous criminals, the domestic terrorists of that era. Once demonized, it was much easier to marginalize and denigrate these groups and to transform them into enemies of the people. The government was simply trying to protect society from those who would jeopardize the safety and security of American citizens.

Ramsey Clark, however, had dealt with these demonized groups firsthand; he knew them, and he understood that there was far more substance to them and their positions than was being portrayed by those in power. He adopted, from experience, a mindset that things are rarely what they seem to be, particularly when those things may be viewed as disruptive to the status quo. As Clark has stated, "truth is hard to find. You don't really know, you have to search for it—you have to inquire diligently, be very skeptical."[30]

If America's leaders say the sky is falling, Clark must examine the sky for himself. If the United States purports to have surgically bombed a foreign enemy, only striking military posts, Clark is unbelieving. There must be more there, and so off he goes. He believes that America's leadership is neurotically guided by profound self-interest, mostly economic in nature, which causes those in control to do whatever is necessary to maintain and maximize wealth and power. As such, he is committed to ferreting out and exposing the reality behind all that his country does. Once, in reflecting upon the assassination of Dr. King, Clark proclaimed, "We should never abandon our duty to learn the truth about what our government does and has done."[31] That sounds noble, but Clark's ever-questioning of his government's motives, no matter what the context, borders on fanatical and over time has undermined his credibility. The United States cannot always be wrong, can it?

Clark's inveterate distrust of American leadership, whether justified or not, helps to explain his penchant for witnessing trips, as well as his decisions to side with the opposition when he concludes that his skepticism was well founded. However, it may not provide a complete rationale for all of his client choices. Two matters in particular stand out—his representation of Rwandan pastor Elizaphan Ntakirutimana and Yugoslavian president Slobodan Milosevic.

The Reverend Ntakirutimana was the leader of the Seventh-Day Adventist Church in western Rwanda. During the genocidal ethnic cleansing that was being carried out in 1994 by the Hutus against the Tutsis in Rwanda, Ntakirutimana, a Hutu himself, apparently offered sanctuary to fleeing Tutsis at his sprawling Mugonero church complex and a nearby Kibuye hospital complex where his son Gerard was a physician. However, the safe haven that the Tutsis thought they had found proved to be a trap. Ntakirutimana allegedly led Hutu soldiers to the complex where they brutally slaughtered nearly 8,000 defenseless Tutsis, many of them women and children.[32]

For his role, Ntakirutimana was indicted, along with his son, for various war crimes, including genocide by the International Criminal Tribunal for Rwanda, a UN-sanctioned body created to adjudicate war crimes stemming from the 1994 massacre. At the time of his indictment, Ntakirutimana was in Laredo, Texas. He was arrested there following the tribunal's extradition request. Ramsey Clark stepped in to represent Ntakirutimana in this proceeding and successfully argued that the extradition would be unconstitutional. That victory was short-lived, though, as a federal judge later approved a second extradition request.[33]

The weight of the international community was almost uniformly against Ntakirutimana. What he was charged with, and for which there were surviving eyewitnesses, was beyond reprehensible. Although he did not personally kill anyone, he was alleged to have acted in various ways that facilitated the mass murder. Among other things, he duped the Tutsis into a false sense of security. They placed their trust in the goodness of a man of God, even though he was a Hutu, and Ntakirutimana repaid that trust with a savage betrayal, setting them up for a horrific slaughter.

This is the account that the world widely accepts, and if it is the story that one believes, it is truly difficult to understand how Ramsey Clark, peace lover that he is, could come to the aid of the reverend. Clark, however, viewed Ntakirutimana and the entire conflict between the Hutus and the Tutsis in a dramatically different light; he was not only comfortable defending him but seemed self-righteous about doing so.

How does a former attorney general end up as counsel of record before an international tribunal in Africa on behalf of an alleged war criminal? Clark's first association with Rwanda took place in 1965 during his brief stint as an assistant to President Johnson. He worked on the nominations of the first U.S. ambassadors to Rwanda and Tanzania, newly created states at that time. Although this exposure did not lead to any other substantive involvement with Rwanda, it did educate Clark about the country and helped sensitize him to issues in that region. His next formal contact with the country was not until 1996 in connection with Ntakirutimana's case.

After the International Criminal Tribunal issued its extradition request concerning the reverend, family members contacted Clark seeking his assistance. Given the fervor of his defense in the matter, it does not appear that Clark had any hesitation about taking on the representation. Specifically, he maintained before the federal trial court in Texas that the extradition of Ntakirutimana was unconstitutional because there was no U.S. treaty with the tribunal, and he more broadly questioned the authority of the body itself to adjudicate the crimes alleged. According to Clark, "No nation, or person, should be subject to judgment and punishment by a court created by a power entirely foreign to it."[34]

He was not only convinced of the illegitimacy of the proceedings, but he was equally certain about the innocence of his client. From his perspective, the Hutus and Reverend Ntakirutimana in particular, were the subjects of persecution. He viewed the Tutsis as the oppressors, and as evidence of this he pointed out that they ultimately ended up in control after the 1994 genocide. The effort to punish the Hutus, to him, was quintessential victor's justice, a concept that he loathes and has relied upon in other contexts to facially justify his controversial representations.

Clark appeared to believe that his client was framed and that the evidence presented against him before the tribunal was concocted and not credible. To make matters worse, he was not even permitted to know the identity of the sixteen so-called eyewitnesses who testified against Ntakirutimana. In addition, there were objective factors indicating the reverend's innocence: He was married to a Tutsi woman and had an unblemished record in terms of his peacefulness, moral character, and respect for the law up to the point of the 1994 genocide. One of the Fifth Circuit Court of Appeals judges, who agreed with the decision to deny Ntakirutimana habeas corpus relief from the extradition request, nevertheless issued a concurring opinion that spoke out strongly in the reverend's favor on the merits:

> It defies logic, and thereby places in question the credibility of the underlying evidence, that a man who has served his church faithfully for many years, who has never been accused of any law infraction, who has for his long life been a man of peace, and who is married to a Tutsi would somehow suddenly become a man of violence and commit the atrocities for which he stands accused. . . . To the extent that

it may be relevant to the Secretary [of State's] decision [as to whether to surrender Ntakirutimana to the tribunal], I merely add, based on all the information in this record, viewed from the perspective of a judge who has served fifteen years on the trial bench and five years on the court of appeals, that *I am persuaded that it is more likely than not that Ntakirutimana is actually innocent.*[35]

Like this judge, Clark is skeptical of the popular story, apparently even when it is not his own country that is responsible for spinning it. Things are rarely as they first appear, and at a minimum, there is inevitably an alternative side to any narrative. Clark is seemingly pathologically drawn to the contrary account, and when that tale plausibly reveals persecution, he is hooked.

Persecution truly appears to be the one thing that Clark simply cannot stand. If he believes that anyone has been persecuted, no matter how heinous the person may be, he is willing to step up on that person's behalf, even for the likes of reputed war criminals and brutal dictators. He has stated that in order to represent someone, he must "believe in the morality of what the person has done or is accused of having done," unless, however, he determines that "the person is being persecuted."[36] This, along with a fairly compelling alternative version of the facts, undoubtedly helps explain Clark's willingness to embrace Ntakirutimana, even after his conviction on aiding and abetting genocide charges, calling it a "tragic miscarriage of justice."[37] Clark's unyielding commitment to principle demonstrates why he was inclined to do so, notwithstanding the overwhelming international sentiment to the contrary. Ramsey Clark *knew* that the Tutsis were out to get his client, and therefore it simply did not matter what others thought.

Could this persecution theory also explain Clark's mind-boggling association with former Yugoslavian president Slobodan Milosevic, a figure viewed as even more despicable than Ntakirutimana? Milosevic, a Serb, was widely considered to be a nationalist who perpetrated a modern-day holocaust, sanctioning the deportation of almost 1 million ethnic Albanians from Kosovo, as well as the callous murder of innumerable non-Serbian residents of Kosovo, Bosnia, and Croatia.[38] He was indicted in 1999 by the

UN International Criminal Tribunal for the former Yugoslavia during the Kosovo war and charged with multiple crimes against humanity, including genocide.[39] By most accounts, he was a brutal dictator who ruled by force and intimidation, fomenting ethnic discrimination.[40]

Milosevic was extradited under questionable circumstances. There were concerns about the authority of the tribunal, and then-Yugoslavian president Vojislav Kostunica believed that extradition would violate his country's constitution. Against what seemed to be the will of his people, Milosevic was extradited, in part, as a result of the U.S. threat of economic sanctions.[41]

This contributed to Clark's unwillingness to assess the substantive validity of the war crimes with which Milosevic was charged and led Clark to volunteer to represent him. However, Milosevic challenged the legitimacy of the tribunal because it was not established with the consent of the UN General Assembly, and he refused to allow counsel to be appointed in his defense. Milosevic, an attorney, defended himself, with the assistance of appointed advisory counsel. Clark and a few other attorneys filled the latter role, essentially acting as what we refer to in the United States as standby counsel.[42] In commenting on his willing affiliation with Milosevic, Clark stated, "I don't judge him one way or another. But when I saw [Yugoslavia] turn him over against the will of its people, I perceived that as just power politics *persecuting* a guy."[43]

As with Ntakirutimana, Clark seemed to be convinced that Milosevic was innocent of the charges against him. Milosevic died while imprisoned before his trial could be completed. Consequently, he was never actually convicted.[44] And no significant evidence was apparently presented to establish that he affirmatively ordered the heinous acts of which he was accused.[45] In a eulogy delivered at his memorial service, Clark proclaimed, "History will prove that Slobodan Milosevic was right."[46] There was most assuredly an overwhelming narrative to the contrary, but that is not the one that Ramsey Clark chose to believe. Again, he sensed the aroma of victor's justice at play and was predisposed to accept that Milosevic's public, international image was, more likely than not, the product of demonizing propaganda.

Clark went even further in defending Milosevic and condemning the

United States in a letter to UN Secretary General Kofi Annan. In that correspondence, he attacked the American government for its alleged complicity in concocting unjustified charges against Milosevic. Specifically, he contended that the initial indictment against Milosevic "was a purely political act to demonize [him] and Serbia and justify U.S. and NATO bombing of Serbia which was itself criminal and in violation of the U.N. and NATO Charters."[47] Clark maintained that Milosevic was on trial for having done nothing more than defend his country, while the United States, by contrast, had acted far more egregiously in "openly and notoriously commit[ting] war of aggression . . . against a defenseless Iraq killing tens of thousands of people," yet President Bush faced no war crimes charges.[48] Even in ostensibly advocating on behalf of one of the most reviled leaders in the world, Ramsey Clark could not resist the opportunity to publicly berate his own government for its purported wrongs.

Clark's embrace of Milosevic angered many, including some of his supporters. Michael Ratner, then-president of the Center for Constitutional Rights (a nonprofit human rights litigation organization), removed Clark from the group's advisory board because of the Milosevic representation. When informed of his removal, Clark was characteristically unaffected, stating "I didn't ask to be on it in the first place."[49]

Which brings us back to Clark's most infamous affiliation: his relationship with and representation of Iraqi president Saddam Hussein. Most people are probably only aware of Clark's involvement as part of Hussein's defense team in connection with his prosecution before the Iraqi High Tribunal (formerly the Iraqi Special Tribunal) for various alleged war crimes in 2005 and 2006. However, their relationship actually dates back as far as 1990 and the lead-up to the Persian Gulf War.

As a by-product of Clark's representation of the PLO, he came to know and established a rapport with Tariq Aziz, Iraq's foreign minister, whom he first met in 1985.[50] He did not have a personal meeting with Saddam until 1990, when Clark was invited to Baghdad to provide advice in advance of the commencement of the war. Clark accepted the invitation, so he claims, in order to facilitate a dialogue between the United States and Iraq, which had not been constructively communicating with each other. He was also motivated by humanitarian concern for refugees in Iraq and foreign hostages that were being held.[51]

Following this inaugural encounter with Hussein, Clark became a regular visitor to the region, making annual treks to provide humanitarian aid to the Iraqi people. His witnessing of the effects of the U.S./UN trade embargo, commonly referred to as economic sanctions, inspired him to be a committed, vocal opponent and, more broadly, convinced him that this type of warfare was even more devastating and inhumane than actual physical combat: Sanctions were killing scores of innocent civilians, many of them children.[52]

The Persian Gulf War, code name "Operation Desert Storm," began on January 17, 1991, and Ramsey Clark quickly established himself as one of its harshest and most outspoken critics.[53] He allied with the Coalition to Stop U.S. Intervention in the Middle East, a reputedly leftist, extremist group tied to the controversial pro-Hussein Workers World Party.[54] Although Iraq's wrongful invasion of Kuwait was the alleged precipitating event for Operation Desert Storm, Clark never criticized or blamed Hussein personally with regard to the conflict. This stemmed from his belief that the United States and Kuwait intentionally provoked the Iraqi invasion in order to create a convenient justification for America's attack.[55] Whether baited or not, the invasion was still wrong, and Clark grudgingly conceded this, but nevertheless he viewed his nation as the principal wrongdoer.[56] He believed that the United States had a sinister strategy to compound the impact of the economic sanctions by targeting Iraq's infrastructure and life support systems, intentionally inflicting untold harm upon the Iraqi people.[57]

After the initial attack, he undertook to expose the extent of the civilian casualties by visiting Iraq with a film crew in February 1991. By his assessment, the recorded footage confirmed that the victims were mostly civilians, rather than military, contradicting U.S. government reports of the surgical nature of the strikes. Outraged over what he witnessed, as well as the mainstream media's refusal to broadcast his visual evidence, Clark submitted a formal letter to President George H. W. Bush and UN Secretary General Javier Pérez de Cuéllar that, among other things: (1) documented the atrocities he saw; (2) condemned the U.S. actions; (3) demanded aid for the Iraqi people;

(4) requested a full-scale investigation into the legality of the attack; and (5) sought a cessation of the bombing of cities, civilian populations, and life support systems.[58] Not surprisingly, he received no official response.

Undeterred, he took a page from his Iran experience and helped organize and convene a war crimes tribunal to adjudicate charges against President Bush and various other U.S. officials for a variety of alleged war crimes. The investigative body for the tribunal was called the Commission of Inquiry for the International War Crimes Tribunal. The "Commission of Inquiry" label had been used previously for the delegation investigating the Chicago police murders of Black Panthers Fred Hampton and Mark Clark in the early 1970s, for which Ramsey Clark served as co-chair. The Iraq-related commission, however, was not viewed in the same legitimate light as its 1970s namesake. Though notified of the proceedings and afforded an opportunity to appear and respond, the U.S. government never even acknowledged the existence of the commission or the tribunal. Predictably, President Bush and the other officials were found guilty of all charges.[59]

Ramsey Clark's concern for the Iraqi people and his ire over U.S. actions and policies in the region persisted after the conclusion of the war. In each succeeding year, he returned to Iraq to bring medicine and to publicly rebuke his government for its promotion of the genocidal economic sanctions.[60] Clark naturally maintained a link to Saddam Hussein throughout the intervening period leading up to the second military conflict between the United States and Iraq, commonly referred to as the Iraq War. The two men met in person in February 2003, shortly before the war began.[61]

Following Saddam's capture by American forces, Clark promptly sought to contact "the president"—a title that Clark often used when referring to Hussein—and thereafter maintained communication with the president's family. In December 2004, he traveled to Amman, Jordan, at the invitation of a group known as ISNAD, more formally, the "Defense and Support Committee of President Saddam Hussein, his Comrades and all P.O.W.s and Detainees in Iraq."[62]

After this trip, Clark immediately took an active and vocal role in Saddam's defense, condemning the unfairness of the process and issuing urgent demands to his government for a meeting with his client. In a letter to President George W. Bush, Clark requested that he and other lawyers be granted "regular access to President Hussein so that he can make an informed choice of counsel and participate in his defense at every stage and on every issue of importance."[63] In that same correspondence, Clark admonished the American government for its treatment of Saddam while in captivity, claiming that it "violate[d] the Constitution of the United States, international law, the most fundamental human rights and threaten[ed] the possibility of a fair trial."[64] He apparently sent identical letters to then–Attorney General John Ashcroft and Secretary of Defense Donald Rumsfeld. The official response from the United States was that Hussein was no longer in its custody, but rather was being held by the Iraqi Interim Government, and that his request should accordingly be to those officials.[65]

As with many of his other divisive international clients, Clark did not simply participate in the mechanics of the representation, carrying out acts to merely ensure that his client received procedural justice. He did much more. Clark embraced Saddam the man, his family, and his cause. After joining the defense team, he was instrumental in establishing and participating as a co-chair of the Emergency Committee for Iraq, which, in addition to supporting the defense of Hussein and other former high-level Iraqis, advocated for the complete withdrawal of the U.S. military presence from Iraq, the cessation of economic sanctions, and the payment of reparations, among other things.[66] The committee was established as an entity separate from ISNAD because of some concerns about the manner in which that group had been operating and to provide a more effective independent voice on behalf of Hussein.[67]

Further, the affection of Saddam's family for Clark was palpable. In one letter from Hussein's daughter, Raghad Saddam Hussein, she addresses him as "Dearest Mr. Clark," praises his "fabulous character," and thanks him for his involvement with the Emergency Committee and his support for her father's case.[68] In a subsequent letter, she lauds Clark's "brave, wise, and sincere effort" in forming the Emergency Committee and expresses her hope that it would be "the corner stone of our struggle not only to protect the legal rights of my father, but also to enhance the rule of law in our world."[69] The fondness and admiration was mutual. Clark ended correspondence with Saddam's daughter with such closings as "my love to you and the family"[70] or "With love, Ramsey Clark."[71]

Clearly, Clark was not just a token American participant on Saddam's defense team. Besides spearheading the broader effort to bring peace and justice to all of Iraq, he and fellow American lawyer Curtis Doebbler were integral in actually formulating and carrying out the legal strategy in Saddam's case. It was specifically agreed that Clark would "head" Hussein's defense team (that is, he would be lead counsel),[72] but he demurred to this official status believing it would be more prudent for an Iraqi lawyer to lead the team. Clark routinely acted as the spokesperson for the defense, commenting to the media or issuing press releases, often highly critical of the process and of the Bush administration.

In announcing the formation of the Emergency Committee for Iraq, Clark stated that the "Bush administration has deliberately deprived President Hussein and other officials of the right to counsel of choice, family visits, and any access to information."[73] He also accused the administration of flaunting "unprincipled power, beginning with its war of aggression in Iraq" and blasted its creation of the Iraqi Special Tribunal, which he maintained was legally illegitimate and designed "to prepare and propagandize for prosecution."[74] Clark took his concerns to UN Secretary General Kofi Annan in a scathing letter in which he sought UN intervention to stop what he contended was an unlawful trial. He maintained that the tribunal was

> intended by the U.S. to vindicate its aggression, justifying the U.S. occupation and extend U.S. dominion over Iraq while assuring unilateral, selective prosecutions and further demonization of Saddam Hussein and his administration.[75]

Saddam himself openly expressed admiration for and confidence in his counsel and "friend" Ramsey Clark in a lengthy letter to the American people harshly denouncing U.S. officials and their policies, written at the behest of Clark.

> I address you today as my attorney the eminent lawyer and Professor Ramsey Clark has asked that I write this letter of mine to you. Profes-

sor Ramsey has presented an excellent example of a humanitarian in his person and in his colleague Professor Curtis Dobler [sic], both of whom left a positive personal impression on me.[76]

In the letter Hussein also defends his failure to send condolences directly to President Bush in the aftermath of the September 11 terrorist attack, indicating that he did agree to Deputy Prime Minister Tariq Aziz's telegram expressing condolences on behalf of the Iraqi government to "our friend Ramsey Clark and through him to the stricken families."[77]

Given Clark's sanctioning of Saddam's letter, one cannot help but surmise that he agreed with its venomous verbal assault on American officials; some of it even sounded like it could have been crafted by Clark himself. For instance, how about this?

It was American officials and their policies themselves that have created an atmosphere of anti-American hatred in the world by means of their arrogant behavior, their haughty aggressive attitude, their lack of respect for international law and the security of the world. . . . [78]

For his part, Ramsey Clark seemed to harbor respect and admiration for Saddam Hussein. More than one criminal defense lawyer has said: "I don't have to like my client; I just have to defend him." Clark appeared to actually like this particular client.[79] In a letter reacting to Saddam's execution, Clark stated the following to Raghad Hussein:

Your father, the President, lived to serve the people of Iraq with honor and he died for the people of Iraq with honor. I know you have the courage and strength to be faithful to his spirit and that with all the President's family, you and your children, beautiful in your image, will face the future bravely and prevail.[80]

The close connection between Clark and Saddam seems evident, and their common views on the hypocrisy and culpability of America for much of what ails the world adds an air of rationality to their superficially perplexing relationship. But the nature of the crimes with which Saddam was charged greatly complicates the smooth logic that appeared to underlie their attorney–client bond. How could Clark represent him and remain true to the many ideals to which he purports to unwaveringly adhere?

Although Saddam Hussein faced a litany of egregious criminal charges involving the murders of vast numbers of innocent people, he was to be tried first only on those related to the killing of 148 Iraqi Shiites in Dujail, which he contended was legally authorized because of an alleged assassination attempt directed at him. Those would-be assassins were imprisoned for an extended period of time and reportedly subjected to brutal conditions and torture. After around two years of detainment during which a number of the accused died, the surviving prisoners were sentenced to death following an investigation and the entry of guilty pleas to the crime of treason. The executions were subsequently carried out with Saddam's blessing. As a staunch opponent of the death penalty since childhood, how could Ramsey Clark defend someone who was alleged to have orchestrated the indefensible torture and dubious executions of his own people? Wasn't Clark then, in effect, defending the efficacy of the death penalty itself?

Clark's responses to such questions at the time were unsatisfying. When asked by CNN correspondent Wolf Blitzer whether the people killed at Dujail deserved to die, Clark characteristically responded that no one deserves to die and emphasized his opposition to the death penalty.[81] However, he proceeded to rationalize that, notwithstanding his personal aversion to capital punishment, especially when summarily imposed, this was the law in Iraq.[82] "They'd been sentenced after two years of investigation, based on confessions, to death. And it was a mandatory law. We used to have in the United States mandatory law. If you're convicted of treason, death."[83]

Such a rationalization rings hollow when uttered by one so high-minded in his commitment to principle, always prideful in his unwillingness to yield on fundamental issues of justice and morality. How could his position on the death penalty not fall within this category, a barbaric punishment that he has ardently denounced for virtually his entire life? The manner in which the death sentences were meted out by Saddam Hussein reeked of a systematic denial of any rights to the accused, a procedural inequity that Clark would never tolerate at home and indeed one that he would repeatedly hoist in Hussein's defense, asserting the patent unfairness of the process set up to adjudicate his charges.[84]

Is there any way to square this apparent troubling hypocrisy of values and character in a man so wedded to the concept of integrity? With regard to the death penalty, it could be that other principles at stake—foremost among them the integrity of the justice system itself as applied to Hussein—were more important to Clark than his anti–death penalty stance. He was dismayed by what appeared to be blatant victor's justice, with the United States acting as puppeteer for a sham juridical process with a preordained result. The discernible unfairness, in his view, likely outweighed other important moral values.

This, however, begs the question of how Clark could defend a client based on the professed unfairness of the proceedings, when that client is accused of having methodically deprived that fairness to his own people in securing the executions that he undoubtedly desired from the beginning.

The nature of Clark's lengthy involvement with Iraq before signing on with Hussein suggests that more had to be at play here in his choice of client. Specifically, it is hard to imagine that the active involvement of his nation's government in Hussein's prosecution, as well as Clark's vocal opposition to U.S. policy toward Iraq over the years, did not play a major role in his decision to act as defense counsel. He long believed that both of the Bush presidents were themselves guilty of the war crime of genocide, especially with regard to the inhumane maintenance of economic sanctions against Iraq that had killed far more than 148 people, many of them children. So, in a way, Clark's representation likely involved a bit, if not a lot, of "America, who are you to judge?" It was an opportunity for him to call out his country's government for a high-profile example of its own brutal hypocrisy.

Many have declined to engage in deep analytics about Clark's possible motivations for his puzzling representations and acts of private diplomacy. Friend and former Johnson administration colleague Larry Temple expressed wonderment concerning Ramsey's choice of clients:

> It's one thing for Ramsey to represent individuals in this country whom he believes have been wrongly pursued by our government in violation of their constitutional rights; but to voluntarily go half way

around the world to represent Saddam Hussein and others like that . . .
under their system, that's inexplicable from my standpoint.[85]

 Others cling to what superficially seems to be an obvious common
theme: that Clark is anti-American and simply chooses to oppose any cause
that his nation supports and to defend those whom it attacks.[86] Although
Clark is far too complex and sophisticated for such a tidy encapsulation,
such critics may have a point. Given the volume and consistency of his opposition to U.S. policies and actions, along with his habitual identification
with the "enemy," it is difficult to avoid a "there he goes again" dismissive
mindset. Clark is as predictable, or more so, than those he criticizes. His
rigidity, at least superficially, seems to allow for no nuance.

Perhaps there is another pattern at work here, alluded to earlier: the
concept of demonization. Clark has on numerous occasions voiced his
opinion on this subject. In his experience, many governments tend to em-
ploy demonization in order to create a public enemy and unify support for
their agendas. As Clark has said, "Once you call something evil, it's easy
to justify anything you might do to harm that evil. Evil has no rights, evil
has no human dignity, it has to be destroyed."[87] Personally, Clark does not
believe in demons; they are a convenient fabrication to further "political
ends and big-business interests of the U.S. military-industrial complex."[88]
To him, the Saddam that the world hated was the product of U.S.-orches-
trated demonization.

Demonization to Clark is a characterization, a portrayal, theater—it can't
be reality. He learned this firsthand as attorney general in observing the
truth underlying the Black Power movement juxtaposed against the image
that the government, largely through J. Edgar Hoover, chose to portray to
the American public. According to Hoover and other officials, these radicals
were home-grown terrorists who needed to be feared and contained. They
were enemies of the people. Time and again, Clark witnessed this drama
play out, creating an innate skepticism in him about virtually everything
that our government does. There has to be some ulterior motive, likely
related to money or power. His suspicious disposition has led him to take
various witnessing trips to the lands of our enemies to see if the story the

American government has spun is true. This is why he went to Vietnam, Iran, Grenada, Libya, Panama, and of course Iraq.

There is some appeal and rationality to this conception of Ramsey Clark's motivation, and perhaps for a period of time it could be embraced and defended as courageous, admirable, and necessary. This path, however, may have blinded him to other possible alternative realities and made him do to his nation what he contends his nation does to others. He has demonized America, or at least the American government. As he has said, when you make something into a demon, it's easy to hate it. Everything a demon does is evil and wrong. The enemy of a demon is inevitably an angel of sorts. Somewhere along the way, America seems to have become Ramsey Clark's demon and that led to his persistent evangelical denouncement of and opposition to it. This perspective attracted him to individuals and causes that cannot reasonably be explained, especially with regard to someone so unfailingly moral and principled.

Given Clark's association with Iraq and Saddam Hussein, it should come as little surprise that he subsequently aligned himself with one of the American government's contemporary targets of condemnation, Syria, led by its maligned President Bashar al-Assad. However, in Iraq, Clark could plausibly link much of the citizenry's suffering to the effects of outside economic sanctions. Whether misguided or not, this at least provided him with some semblance of moral cover for his involvement. A similar basis for offering his services in aid of the Syrian government seems less compelling. From all accounts, the oppression and death the Syrian people are enduring seems largely attributable to Assad's sinister leadership.[89] As with Reverend Ntakirutimana and Slobodan Milosevic, maybe there is a possible alternative story that Clark has latched onto. Perceived persecution of Syria and Assad, particularly by the United States, probably amounts to a plausible justification for him.

Syria is on the U.S. State Department's list of state sponsors of terrorism. Indeed, all of the matters on which Clark has represented that nation have involved private lawsuits seeking monetary damages under the U.S. Anti-Terrorism Act, a statute that Clark has vigorously maintained is unconstitutional and violates international law. The U.S. government has singled out

Syria and others, such as the Palestinian National Authority and the PLO, because of their alleged condoning of terroristic acts. Clark undoubtedly finds this ironic, at best, given his furtive agreement with Martin Luther King's famous lament that his own country is the greatest purveyor of violence. The perceived duplicity of the proverbial pot calling the kettle black arouses the advocate in Clark. He may envision himself as standing up for Syria, truth, and the rule of law in opposition to illegitimate demonization by the American government, just as he did with Saddam Hussein.[90]

During one meeting with Hussein, Clark recalls venturing into a discussion about President Johnson and his recounting of sad memories of the extreme poverty that he witnessed during his teaching days in Texas. Johnson remembered how seeing young Mexican children come to school with no shoes on their feet would bring tears to his eyes. Following such a touching account, according to Clark, Johnson could, without batting an eye, proceed to the Situation Room and celebrate the rising North Vietnamese body count. The contrast in Johnson's emotion and character were stark, and Hussein responded to the story by poignantly offering up an Islamic saying: "A prophet is someone who can love at a distance."[91] Clark has never forgotten these words and relays them often in varying contexts. Why did these words resonate so much with him?

One thought is because they nicely capture the distinction between Clark and President Johnson, as well as other political figures like the president. Though Clark would unquestionably eschew dubbing himself as a prophet, he surely does not need to witness suffering firsthand in order to feel empathy toward those enduring it. He has said that he always loves those who suffer, near or far.[92] Clark has chosen on many occasions to play the role of witness, traveling to innumerable regions of the planet for this purpose. But he did not do so to enable himself to personally feel the suffering; rather, he traveled in search of a better understanding of the circumstances of the suffering, skeptical of the portrayals offered by the U.S. government and the mainstream media.

Generally, in terms of why Clark ties himself to what appear to be evil regimes—Iran, Libya, Iraq, Syria—it seems that he gravitates toward turmoil or unrest, particularly when America has a hand in it. In his own words, "I go where the violence is, and where the problems are."[93]

As with other rationales, this one sounds overly simplistic and it does not address why Clark almost inevitably identifies with reputedly evil dictators. He invariably goes to great lengths to humanize such leaders and to suggest that their image is little more than manufactured demonization by the U.S. government. Clark has attempted to humanize President Assad by describing him as a man with the "values of a person who was trained in saving life, not taking life," because he is a medical doctor.[94] This myopic statement fails to acknowledge that Assad's regime seems to be the very antithesis of what one would expect from someone who purportedly values the saving of lives. It also tellingly reflects Clark's prophet-like approach to identified evildoers—he avoids making judgments and is willing to offer forgiveness and the benefit of the doubt to those subjected to persecution, even when the vilification is arguably warranted. In his words, lawyers should never "accept assumptions about who's good and who's evil when the life or liberty of a human being is at risk."[95]

CHAPTER TWELVE

COLD PIZZA

"Fear will be the enemy, as it is of every human act that defies
cultural norms. . . . 'We must not be afraid to be free.'"
Ramsey Clark[1]

RAMSEY CLARK IS WITHOUT PRETENTION and has never been driven
by a desire for wealth. Upon meeting him, no one would guess that he has
made headlines around the world for traveling to North Vietnam to visit
America's enemy during the height of the Vietnam War or that he voluntarily
served as counsel to an eye-popping assortment of international villains,
including Iraq's Saddam Hussein and Syria's Bashar al-Assad. And this has
always been the case—not just now that he is a kindly, gentle 91-year-old
grandfather. From his younger days, he has naturally maintained a sort of
sophisticated, Forrest Gump-like persona. And this unassuming demeanor
matched perfectly with his equally down-to-earth wife Georgia.

Victor Navasky wrote a piece for the *Saturday Evening Post* about Clark
in connection with his elevation to attorney general.[2] In writing that piece,
he spent some time at the Clark home and was immediately struck by Georgia's manner. He recalls that she was nothing like what one would expect
of an attorney general's wife. She was more like an itinerant folksinger or a
1960s flower child.[3] During his first visit to the couple's home in Virginia
in late 1967, Navasky remembers that Georgia casually walked about the
house in her bare feet.[4] While this may have seemed cool to Navasky, J.
Edgar Hoover's reaction to Mrs. Clark's apparent penchant for going shoe-
less was quite the opposite. On a visit to the Clarks' home, the FBI director was appalled to see Georgia unshod in the kitchen of all places, causing
him to rhetorically ponder to a reporter, "What kind of person is *that*?"[5]

Almost everyone else who has expressed an opinion about Ramsey and Georgia, however, viewed the two as a perfect couple, the love of each other's lives. Navasky described them to me as an exceptional couple.[6] Lois Akner, a close friend and former staffer on Clark's senatorial campaigns, called them a true pair.[7] Larry Temple, President Johnson's special counsel, said that Georgia and Ramsey were totally on the same page about everything. They were definitely soulmates.[8] And Stephen Pollak, Clark's assistant attorney general for the Civil Rights Division, maintained that the couple had a very good marriage. He surmised that this had to be the case in order for their relationship to endure the grueling workload that Clark had while with the DOJ.[9]

Philosophically and intellectually, Ramsey and Georgia were in sync. To quote Forrest Gump, the two of them went "together like peas and carrots."[10] Georgia supported Ramsey in all that he did. Without her, he could not have accomplished so much. She cared for their family and made it possible for Ramsey to spend his life tilting at windmills throughout the world. Georgia's simple obituary perhaps best captured her husband's assessment and appreciation of his wife: "Her beauty, wisdom and limitless love inspire all who knew her. Her steadfast support and love-filled labors for her daughter Ronda . . . and for her husband Ramsey, in pursuit of his ideals, made the lives they have lived possible."[11]

It is important to stress, however, that Georgia did not merely play a supporting role; she was a force to be reckoned with in her own right. She handled all of the family finances, as well as those of Ramsey's law practice. Georgia also managed various administrative aspects of her husband's legal work and otherwise contributed substantially to many of his extralegal endeavors, including the writing of his bestselling book *Crime in America*. As her niece Pia Welch recounted to me, Georgia had a "superb brain," with a memory that even surpassed her husband's.[12] While Ramsey was getting his J.D. and master's in history from the University of Chicago, Georgia was completing her master's in political science alongside him.

Their time together in Chicago leads me to one of the most vivid and revealing examples of Ramsey Clark's humility and nonchalance. Specifically, I'm referring to the circumstances surrounding an endowed lecture that the former attorney general delivered at Loyola University Chicago

School of Law, at the invitation of his law school classmate and friend Professor George Anastaplo. First, it is important to know a little bit about Anastaplo himself. He was a fascinating man in his own right, with a life story that rivals his dear friend's.

The son of Greek immigrants, Anastaplo was hardworking and industrious from an early age. At 17, during the height of World War II, he desperately wanted to enlist in the Army Air Corps, but he was too scrawny and unhealthy to be accepted. Unwilling to take no for an answer, he diligently persevered, gaining weight and incessantly pestering the corps. Eventually, his persistence paid off, and he became a bomber pilot, flying in every major theater of the war, though never actually engaging in battle.[13]

After his military service, Anastaplo would go on to breeze through his undergraduate education at the University of Chicago in a single year and then proceed to the university's prestigious law school. There he would graduate at the top of his class, along with notable classmates Ramsey Clark and future Congresswoman Patsy Mink, as well as Abner Mikva, who would later serve as a congressman, federal appeals court judge, and chief counsel to President Bill Clinton.[14] Unlike his distinguished classmates, however, the brilliant Anastaplo would become known for what at the time was a singularly ignoble reason.

After passing the Illinois bar exam in fall 1950, during the height of U.S. paranoia about communism, Anastaplo was denied admission because of his principled refusal to answer questions about his possible association with the Communist Party. What is typically a routine, perfunctory inquiry into an applicant's character and fitness turned into a multi-year odyssey for Anastaplo that ended before the U.S. Supreme Court.[15] He was not a member of the Communist Party and had a sterling, ethically upstanding academic and professional record.[16] He was an ideal candidate for bar membership, and he could have easily skated through the admission process if he simply truthfully answered the communist-related questions posed by the Illinois Bar's Character and Fitness Committee. That, however, would go against all that the upright intellectual believed. Not only did he refuse to answer questions about his ties to communist organizations, but he indicated that he saw nothing wrong with admitting an applicant who was a member of the Communist Party or with firmly supporting the people's right to forcefully revolt to overthrow the government in the event that it becomes unsatisfactory.[17]

Neither Anastaplo's unblemished record nor his glowing personal recommendations could overcome the perception that he was somehow un-American and unfit to practice law. Though the ostensible basis for his denial was his refusal to answer what were deemed to be questions rationally connected to law practice, the transcripts of his various hearings clearly reflect an anticommunist sentiment.[18]

Justice Hugo Black, in a powerful dissent from the U.S. Supreme Court's 5–4 affirmance of the Illinois Bar's rejection of Anastaplo, made it clear that he viewed the case as hinging on the concept of freedom.[19] Black believed that Anastaplo had a clear First Amendment right to refuse to answer the committee's questions about his organizational affiliations, and he ominously voiced concern about government intimidation of citizens in order to force them to conform to a certain way of thinking. What could be more un-American and contrary to the very founding principles of this nation—principles actually contained in the Declaration of Independence, which Anastaplo, by the way, relied upon in explaining his views regarding the right of the people to revolt.[20] Black concluded his dissent with a moving passage, befitting both Anastaplo and his equally principled classmate and friend Ramsey Clark:

> Too many men are being driven to become government-fearing and time-serving because the Government is being permitted to strike out at those who are fearless enough to think as they please and say what they think. This trend must be halted if we are to keep faith with the Founders of our Nation and pass on to future generations of Americans the great heritage of freedom which they sacrificed so much to leave to us. The choice is clear to me. If we are to pass on that great heritage of freedom, we must return to the original language of the Bill of Rights. We must not be afraid to be free.[21]

Anastaplo felt somewhat vindicated by Justice Black's assessment and proceeded to press forward with his life, dropping his bar admission battle.[22] Unfortunately, he was thereafter blackballed and encountered great difficulty finding a job in academia, which is what he desired following completion of a Ph.D. from the University of Chicago's Committee on Social Thought.[23] His alma mater would not touch him, nor would any other school, for that matter—and especially not law schools because, after all, he was not admitted to the bar.

Eventually he got hired by Dominican University when a friend became the school's president, and in 1981 he finally broke into the legal arena, joining the law faculty at Loyola University Chicago, where he blossomed into a prolific scholar and beloved teacher until his death in 2014.[24]

In 2009, I spent an afternoon with Anastaplo. He was warm and hospitable, much like his well-known friend. After he showed me around the University of Chicago campus, we had apple pastries with his wife Sara at their home. They had very fond memories of Ramsey and Georgia Clark, but the most revealing story they shared involved a 1984 lecture, referenced earlier, that the former attorney general delivered at Loyola.

The lecture was apparently a really big deal, the culmination of a series with lots of important people involved and in attendance. Clark would arrive on the day before the scheduled event, spend the night, and then deliver his address the following afternoon. Anastaplo offered to secure suitable accommodations for the guest of honor for the first evening, but Clark declined, choosing instead to sleep on his host's studio couch. Rather than having a fancy dinner as might be expected in association with a prestigious endowed lecture, Clark opted for carry-out pizza in the Anastaplo home with George and Sara.[25]

When Ramsey awoke the next morning, George had already left for campus to teach a class. Sara remained at the house and planned to prepare a nice breakfast. However, in response to her inquiry about what Ramsey wanted to eat, he asked if there was any pizza left from the previous evening. There was and Sara offered to heat it up for him. Nope, he just wanted it cold, straight out of the refrigerator.

As the distinguished guest dined on his cold pizza, he asked Sara if she knew what he was supposed to talk about during his lecture later that day. One might think this was a way for him to make conversation with Sara. "Guess what I am going to talk about today?" She would ask what, and then he would tell her. That, however, was not at all the intent behind Ramsey's question. Shockingly, he actually did not recall his assigned topic. Sara had no idea either. So she called her husband at work, and he then reminded Ramsey about the parameters for his talk. The featured speaker casually responded, "Oh yeah, now I remember."[26]

As I listened to the Anastaplos tell this tale, I was partly charmed by Clark's utter lack of pretention, but, at the same time, somewhat confused by his seemingly slack approach to such a significant event. He slept on a couch, ate cold pizza for breakfast, and could not even remember the subject for his speech. The description to this point sounded more like a frat boy stoner than a revered legal titan.

Although I was cringing inside at the thought of how bad Clark's address must have been—especially since I had personally witnessed a couple of his snoozers myself—I figured that the Anastaplos probably would not be sharing the story with me unless it had a good ending. Sure enough, they reported that the lecture was a resounding success. Despite having virtually no time to prepare between when he relearned what his topic was and delivered his remarks, according to George, Clark, without any notes, gave an inspiring and emotional lecture about a lawyer's duty of loyalty.[27]

I have since read the speech, and while there are definitely gems of wisdom scattered throughout, it was, in truth, kind of a mess, at least until the poignant conclusion when he paid tribute to his close friend. In speaking of the danger posed by fear and the importance of freedom of thought in securing justice for all, Clark ended with an "admonition from a glorious case we should all remember, *In re Anastaplo*: 'We must not be afraid to be free.'"[28]

Clark's Loyola visit provides a vivid snapshot of his personality and character. He really is that laid-back and unassuming, while simultaneously being brilliant enough to deliver a lengthy, extemporaneous speech peppered with insightful quotes from sources ranging from German philosopher Hegel to all manner of Supreme Court jurisprudence. More importantly, those last few words that he spoke revealed volumes about what motivates him. He believes that fear is the real enemy, and that our government wants citizens to be afraid in order to exert control over them and to limit their ability to be free. Clark views justice as a means to freedom, and freedom as an ideal to which all people are entitled, no matter what their skin color.

Interesting, too, is the fact that Ramsey's father, Supreme Court Justice Tom Clark, sided with the majority in affirming the Illinois bar's denial of Anastaplo's admission. Rather than pointing out this fact and highlighting his personal disagreement with his dad, Ramsey simply indicated his full embrace of the sentiment expressed in the dissent. It could be viewed as Ramsey's tacit apology for how his father had voted.

On a purely selfish level, I was extremely thankful for learning about this story because I had invited Ramsey Clark to be the keynote speaker at a legal ethics symposium my law school was hosting later in 2009 in Athens, Georgia. The insight that I gained from George Anastaplo about Clark's apparent proclivity to "wing it" put me on notice that I really needed to hammer home the topic for his speech in order to ensure that he would be prepared.

Notwithstanding detailed phone calls, followed up with confirming correspondence, on the day of his scheduled lecture Clark turned to me and asked what exactly I wanted him to talk about. I wanted to say, "Dude, you have got to be kidding me!" but it was kind of what I had expected, so I wasn't upset. The topic for the symposium was "Drawing the Ethical Line: Controversial Cases, Zealous Advocacy, and the Public Good." It was something that he probably could have extemporized about in his sleep. Hence, it all worked out in the end.

However, his visit was not without controversy. Some alums were dismayed by the invitation and suggested that we were providing Clark with a platform to spew unpatriotic and anti-Semitic venom. This made me nervous. I did not know Clark very well at the time, and I was a little worried that he might go off on some rant once he seized the podium. Maybe all of the negative stuff I had read about him online was true. I am now ashamed that I ever doubted him, even for a moment. He was my guest, and he was going to adhere to the scope of the invitation, even if he couldn't remember what that was until reminded. Moreover, Clark underscored his personal integrity by refusing to accept the generous honorarium that we tried to pay him. He simply said, "You're a public institution. I am sure there are better things that you can use that money for."

Ramsey Clark is seemingly innately averse to wealth. Material things like clothes have never been important to him.[29] He wore in the 2000s the same suits and other clothing he had worn during the 1960s and 70s. I actually have a picture of him from the 2009 ethics symposium in Athens seemingly wearing the same tie and jacket that he wore in a famous 1977 photo with Bruce Beyer, whom he represented in connection with Beyer's efforts to obtain amnesty after the Vietnam War.[30] Though complex on many levels, at his core Clark is a simple and forthright man.

Larry Temple admiringly described Clark to me as the "purest human being that he has ever met" and observed that "Ramsey believes in everything he does."[31] Although he acknowledged his lack of agreement with much of that, Temple insisted that he has never questioned the former attorney general's motives "simply because I am satisfied that he fully believes that he is doing the right thing with all these actions he pursues."[32]

Temple confirmed that Clark's motives have never been monetary in nature.[33] He certainly could have been a very wealthy man if that had been his objective, but it clearly was not. In most of the cases that he took on, his fee was not even part of the consideration, and more often than not, he received no remuneration whatsoever. His commitment was to the cause, not to the dollar. That was largely why his tenure at New York mega-firm Paul Weiss was short-lived and his partnership with Melvin Wulf and Alan Levine failed—Clark kept taking on too many pro bono clients. Money simply meant nothing to him.

Clark's beloved friend and recurring co-counsel Abdeen Jabara likewise attests to Clark's disinterest in lining his pockets. When Jabara approached him in 1980 to ask for his assistance in representing Palestinian dissident Ziyad Abu Eain, Clark readily agreed without even discussing the possibility of a fee.[34] Jabara vividly recalls that even though Clark devoted significant time and energy to the matter, he never asked to be compensated. I asked him whether this was always the case with Clark's representations because I suspected that it could not be so. After all, in many instances he was representing individuals and entities who seemed well equipped to pay him, like Saddam Hussein and the PLO to name but two. Jabara indicated that Clark did receive payment for some of his representations; for those that involved extensive foreign travel, at a minimum his expenses were usually covered.[35] My own review of some of Clark's billing information suggests that he may have gotten paid for various of his big-ticket, ongoing attorney–client relationships, such as those with the PLO and Syria. However, even with these, he seemed indifferent about actually collecting on amounts owed.

It is almost as if Clark felt like there was something impure about getting paid for providing legal services that were based on a cause, and for him every matter was, in some respect, about securing justice and fairness. He has frequently spoken with disdain about those who covet wealth, expressing dismay over why anyone would want to amass a personal fortune when there are people suffering all over the world: "Would any moral person accumulate a billion dollars when there are 10 million infants dying of starvation every year?"[36]

Clark has similarly denounced his country's general infatuation with affluence, often characterizing our form of government as a plutocracy rather than a democracy.[37] Wealth rules. Without money, one cannot get elected to office, and multinational corporations control those in power once they are elected. This is Clark's take on things, and his lack of concern for worldly possessions could be a rebellion of sorts against the perceived status quo. It also could be a further reflection of his commitment to integrity and principle. He has to put his money, or lack thereof, where his mouth is. It would be highly hypocritical for him to prosecute greed while simultaneously raking in large fees.

Larry Temple recalled a story that Ramsey's son Thomas told him about asking his father if he could borrow $100 on one occasion. According to Temple's retelling, Ramsey said, "Son, if I had $100 it would be yours. I would give it to you, I wouldn't loan it to you. But I'm sorry, son. I don't have $100."[38] While it seems that Thomas told Temple the story in order to highlight what a wonderfully generous person his father was, Temple could not help but note with some incredulity that a former attorney general of the United States was in such a financial condition that he could not loan his son $100. How could that be?[39]

Although the story was meant to demonstrate Thomas's high regard for his father, I came away with a possible alternative take on this. First, it saddened me to think that Ramsey Clark was ever in so dire a financial state. However, I also could not help but look at this situation through the eyes of Thomas. If I were him, I believe I might have resentfully wondered how my father could give so much of himself to so many, but have nothing to give to me when I was in need. Is there something askew about trying to save the world, when doing so has adverse effects at home?

I don't know exactly how Thomas felt at the time. According to Temple, the tenor of Thomas's story seemed complimentary. Nevertheless, if on some level he was angry with his father for seemingly putting the interests of others above him, I would have completely understood. As the saying goes, generosity starts at home, right? Even so, it is admittedly difficult to come down too hard on Ramsey for his tireless devotion to the oppressed. If Thomas harbored any possible resentment toward him, it paled in comparison to the admiration and pride that he felt for his father and for all the good that he has done on behalf of so many. And Thomas surely knew that there was absolutely nothing that Ramsey would not do for him, if he could. I think that was the real point of the story.

Indeed, Ramsey Clark's generosity and concern for others, particularly those of different races, is ever on display. At first, it might simply seem that he is a polite southerner, offering to pay for things or assist someone because that is what Texas-style etiquette dictates. However, this sort of superficial kindness has its limits and likewise can carry an air of phoniness. As a lifelong citizen of the South, I have witnessed this on many occasions. Clark's warmth feels genuine. One example of his magnanimity and empathy played out in an amazingly serendipitous manner with the hiring of a gentleman named Ben Chaney as his office assistant.

During the summer of 1964, when Ben was just a young boy, his brother James Chaney was participating in an organized effort throughout the South to educate and register black voters. Known as the Freedom Summer initiative, it was spearheaded by the Congress of Racial Equality (CORE), of which Chaney was a member, along with two men named Andrew Goodman and Michael Schwerner.[40] On June 21, 1964, these three men were tragically murdered by white racists—one of whom was apparently a deputy sheriff—in Philadelphia, Mississippi, while en route to investigate the destruction of a local church.[41] The murders were a major turning point for the civil rights movement, garnering national attention and outraging many, including influential figures in Washington, DC. Indeed, this tragedy ironically assisted President Johnson in securing passage of the Civil Rights Act of 1964.[42]

Not surprisingly, the murders had a profound impact on Ramsey Clark and further solidified his commitment to aiding black citizens in their quest for equality and justice. At the time, Clark had no idea that he would be able to help James Chaney's little brother one day. Following James's death, Ben slowly gravitated toward the black nationalist movement, a more confrontational brand of civil rights activism that took hold during the late 1960s. At the age of 18, Ben accompanied a friend on a trip to Florida, the purpose of which turned out to be retrieving a shipment of guns to later transport to a black militant group in Ohio. The trip did not end well. At one point a gun battle ensued that ultimately led to Ben being convicted of murdering a white insurance salesman and two college students. He was sentenced to life in prison.[43]

Ben served thirteen years of his sentence before Ramsey Clark intervened in 1983 and persuaded the parole board to release him.[44] Ben immediately moved to New York City and later was hired by Clark as his office assistant. Ben did all of the typing for Clark and his partner Larry Schilling, and he handled communications and general office organization. He was actually more of a paralegal than an office assistant.[45] Clark described him as an incredibly smart and talented guy. He clearly felt that Ben's tragic life circumstances put him in a bad place personally. All he needed was a helping hand, someone who believed in him, and an opportunity to flourish. Ramsey Clark gave Ben all of these. The two men worked together for many years and remained very loyal to each other.

I called Ben Chaney years ago in an effort to speak with him about his relationship with Clark. I was struck by how suspicious he was of me. It was clear that he had great love for Clark, and he did not want to do anything that might harm his friend. He told me that he would have to check with Clark first to make sure it was okay to talk with me. Unfortunately, for a number of reasons, we never had a substantive conversation. That one brief exchange, however, told me an awful lot about the power and effect of Ramsey Clark.

Clark's generosity and empathy for others is complemented and highlighted by his sincere humility and complete lack of concern for worldly possessions. A case in point is his "Cabinet chair." Apparently, all U.S. attorneys general have a Cabinet chair with their title engraved on the back, presumably so they would know where to sit during Cabinet meetings. This important, historical vestige of Clark's time in the Department of Justice is positioned in his living room, with the engraving facing the wall where no one can see it. I sat in this chair on several occasions before he told me its story.[46] My guess is that most former attorneys general probably have their chairs placed in some prominent location either in their offices or homes. For Ramsey Clark, it is just another piece of furniture, occupying a less auspicious space than the family sofa.

Similarly, Clark's bedroom is unsurprising insofar as it is entirely consistent with everything else about him. The decor is sparse and shambolic. I got my first glimpse of his sleeping quarters during one visit when he was trying to locate the Adolf Hitler bust to show me. As we approached Clark's bedroom, though, I completely lost interest in finding the fürher's head. I was mesmerized by an enormous set of built-in bookshelves that lined the wall, completely filled with an unbelievable assortment of books. As we continued into his bedroom, he told me to excuse the mess, but he really didn't seem to be at all concerned. And it was really, really messy—I mean, lazy-teenager messy. His bed was only partially made and appeared to simply be on top of box springs, with no frame or headboard. There were also boxes of stuff everywhere, piles of papers, and a stationary exercise bike. Directly across from the bed was another gigantic, pristine set of built-in bookshelves, likewise filled. I had never seen so many books, other than in a library or a bookstore. It was dumbfounding. And these are in addition to the stacks of books that are scattered in various places throughout the apartment.

I asked him if he had read all of the books, thinking that the answer would most assuredly be "No, I just accumulated them over the years" or something like that. These were big, fat hardback books: biographies, histories, learned texts and treatises, and everything else imaginable. No one could possibly read all of these, especially when they have a full-time, demanding law practice that takes them all over the world. In response to my question, he sheepishly laughed and said he could lie and say that he had read all of them, but instead, he simply understated that he had read "a good many."[47] To me, that was a humble way of saying that he had read most of the books, which is insane. But what is even crazier is that he remembers an inordinate amount of what he has read, to the point of being able to quote lengthy passages from memory. This either means that he has, or had, a photographic memory or else he has read many of the books multiple times. Either one is impressive, and I suspect that there is probably a little bit of both involved.

You no doubt noticed that I intimated that his photographic memory, if it ever existed, is no longer present. Sadly, Ramsey Clark's short-term ability to recall events or even conversations has diminished dramatically in recent years. During visits and conversations with him in 2016 and 2017, I noticed that he repeated himself a great deal. He would tell me a story, and then we would move on to another topic, only to later return to the exact same story. The details were inevitably intricate, and with each retelling nothing changed. Although he had no idea that he had just told me the same story a short while earlier, he could remember meticulous nuances that most would have long ago forgotten. Some of these tales were from the 1940s.

Notwithstanding his failing memory, Clark still has a knack for endearingly remembering personal tidbits about others that demonstrate what an attentive listener he is. He has met my wife Kim on a single occasion over dinner in Athens, Georgia. That was in 2009. During virtually every subsequent conversation that we have had since then, he has asked about her by name and often alluded to aspects of their conversation that evening. We literally have not ended a single phone call without him saying "Give my love to Kim and the girls [my two daughters]." His short-term memory may be failing, but his warm heart remains firmly intact.

Speaking of his heart, not too long after Clark's visit to Athens in late 2009, his wife was diagnosed with lung cancer and passed away rather quickly following that discovery. When I learned of her passing, I called him and was somewhat surprised that he sounded relatively normal, like his usual kind self. I definitely detected a melancholy, lost character to his voice, but he did not come across nearly as grief-stricken as I had expected. He gave a clinical overview of what caused Georgia's death—non-small cell cancer, apparently originating in her lungs. While this form of cancer typically does not spread quickly, by the time it was detected, it had already reached many of Georgia's vital organs. There was nothing that could be done, and she died very soon after the initial diagnosis. Clark told me he was there when she took her last breath and that it was very hard to believe that she was gone, reminding me that they had been together for sixty-one years.[48]

Although I had a lump in my throat and a tear in my eye, Clark sounded sad but not the least bit choked up. While he had gone a little bit deeper than customary in discussing Georgia's death, he was still relatively superficial, maybe just for my benefit. And he rather quickly changed the subject, turning our conversation to my family and me, wanting to know how everyone was doing. Even during what was surely the saddest time of his life, Ramsey Clark's altruistic concern for others remained on display. It may have just been a deflection, a way of avoiding the pain that he was feeling; or perhaps it was a subtle message to me that he really didn't want to talk about it anymore. At some point, I had planned to delve more acutely into the nature of their relationship, but now I sort of felt like that was off limits. I regretted that I had never felt comfortable enough to ask more questions when I had the opportunity.

Over the ensuing years, he would occasionally volunteer tidbits about him and Georgia. I never pried, out of respect; I just listened, hoping that I would learn some enlightening details. That was wishful thinking. He usually treaded lightly at the surface, casually reminiscing when the urge hit him. Mostly, he spoke of how much he loved her and how difficult it was to be away from her over the years. Once he told me that she was a dancer—tap dancing and ballet, according her niece Pia—and fondly remembered the time they got to see the Russian Ballet at the Kremlin. I was intrigued that Georgia was a dancer, but I must admit that the Kremlin part probably fascinated me more. Why on earth were they at the Kremlin? I did not press him on this because it seemed like an aside, albeit a mind-boggling one, but at this point there was little that could really shock me about Ramsey Clark. I think he had a certain affection for Russia because of the time he spent there during World War II. I also suspect that his leftist ideology tends toward the communist way of life, at least in its purest sense. But back to Georgia.

During a fairly recent conversation, Ramsey described her to me as a "water bug" because of her love of the water. While in Washington, DC, they lived in Falls Church, Virginia, on Lake Barcroft. He characterized it as idyllic and a great place to raise a family. Some of his friends moved there as well for that very reason, including Thurgood Marshall, Ernie Friesen, and Harold Barefoot Sanders.[49]

Ramsey and Georgia, however, loved their Dallas home the most. The couple designed and built it together. Ramsey called it their dream home, small but wonderful. Interestingly, he indicated that everything in the house was divisible by seven in terms of measurements—seven is his lucky number. Besides the structurally vested interest that he and Georgia had in the house, it also seems that it was particularly special because it was the first home for his two children, and it represented a time when they were all together as a family, before Ramsey set off to change the world.[50] I sensed a hint of regret. Perhaps that is where he should have stayed. It was impossible to replicate the same thing in the Washington area, even on a beautiful, serene lake. The tumult of the life path that he chose would never subside for long enough to allow for a peaceful family existence. This seems especially hard to reconcile with his obvious immense love for his family and the unique challenges presented by his firstborn, Ronda.

I desperately wanted to know as much as possible about Ronda, but I was even more reluctant to pry there than I was with regard to Georgia. I knew that she was their eldest child and that she was born with a serious mental disability; she was also deaf and unable to speak. I could not help but speculate that there was something about life with Ronda that had profoundly affected her dad. Maybe she was the inspiration behind all of the things that he has done, the one who made him love the poor, oppressed, and ostracized of the world. I felt that not gaining a better understanding of Ronda and Ramsey's relationship would leave a significant hole in my effort to tell his story.

Just when I was about to resign myself to the fact that, as with Georgia, I might simply be forced to proceed with the superficial knowledge that I had, fate intervened. On January 16, 2016, I got the chance to meet Ronda in person and actually spend the entire evening with father and daughter. It proved to be an entertaining and enlightening experience.

I was in New York for a conference and had arranged to spend some time with Ramsey while I was there. He suggested that I come over to his apartment, and then we could go out to dinner together. That sounded great. Then he added that Ronda would have to join us because there was not anyone who could stay with her during the time that we would be meeting. Although I responded with excitement at the opportunity to meet her, in reality I was apprehensive, mainly because I envisioned Ronda as wheelchair-bound with limited mobility. I was worried about how we would get to and from dinner, as well as what other logistical impediments might be presented by her accompanying us.

When I arrived at Clark's apartment, he met me at the door with his characteristic greeting, telling me that it was good to see me and that I looked good. I responded by telling him how good he looked, but I could not help but notice how much he had aged in terms of his ability to get around. He still had a face that belied his 88 years, but his hunched posture and painfully slow, shuffling gate evidenced the wear and tear of a long life's journey. I also observed that he was very thin, particularly around the waist—it appeared that he could barely keep his pants up.

Notwithstanding his frailty, Clark was still the consummate host, offering me a glass of wine almost immediately. While he retrieved the wine from his kitchen, I finally got the chance to meet his then 64-year-old daughter Ronda. I was surprised to see her seated at a table working with some index cards. She stood up, shook my hand, and then proceeded to frisk me and have me empty my pockets. I naively interpreted this as an expression of concern for her father's safety, and I obliged. When she got to my cell phone, she took it from me and positioned it upright on her table and then walked away. I had no idea what was going on, but I surmised that I should probably grab my phone back while I had the chance. When Ramsey returned with my wine, he asked if Ronda had taken anything from me. I told him about the phone seizure and then learned that his daughter has a habit of doing that. It wasn't just me. Ronda loves photographs. Pia Welch shared with me that when Ronda was young, she had a Polaroid camera, and at family gatherings she would tell everyone where to sit and take photos. Pia speculates that Ronda's affinity for pictures may be why she is so enamored with cell phones—they contain photos.[51]

Although Ramsey had described Ronda to me on previous occasions as being "severely mentally challenged," that is not at all how I perceived her. She is definitely very ritualistic. If things are not how she wants them, Ronda is as stubborn as her father about persevering until everything is suitable to her. When she put on her coat to leave for dinner, her hood had to be tightly fastened on in just the right way or she wasn't going any-where. Her father patiently assisted her for what seemed like an inordinate amount of time. In addition, during dinner, Ronda pulled the hood of her light-blue sweat jacket snuggly around her face, concealing about half of her forehead. Ramsey tried repeatedly to get her to take it off, but she did not do so until she was good and ready. I got the distinct impression that she gets pretty much anything that she wants from Dad.

Our walk to dinner was excruciatingly slow, not quite a snail's pace but about as close as one could get to that. Although Clark now uses a walker to help him get around after having broken a hip, at the time of my visit he simply shuffled his feet in kind of an off-balanced manner, barely lifting them off the ground. He sweetly held Ronda's hand for the entire, plod-ding walk, which I found to be quite touching.

As we made our way toward the French Roast, Clark's favorite restau-rant, it occurred to me what a spectacle we must have been—an elderly white man, hunched over and shuffling along, affectionately grasping his senior-citizen daughter's hand, accompanied by me, a middle-aged black man who was strangely walking just as slow as father and daughter. Even by New York standards, we were quite a sight, garnering as many stares as the topless women in Times Square. To add to the oddity of our excur-sion, the French Roast was a trendy, bustling Greenwich Village bistro that played loud, hip music throughout our meal. During the walk and especially at the restaurant, I could distinctly feel many eyes on us. But Ramsey Clark clearly could not—or, if he could, he plainly could not have cared less. His observable love for and patience with Ronda, and his utter lack of self-consciousness under the circumstances, revealed so much about his heart and soul.

Everything that I learned about Ronda and her father on that visit, however, came from sheer observation. Ramsey did not really volunteer much, other than a few comments every now and then. When he ordered steak frites for Ronda, he told me that was her go-to dish. He also shared with me that Ronda loves to write notes and open the mail. Nothing really deep was shared, though, until a later visit in June of the same year when Ramsey uncharacteristically opened up.

We were seated together in his living room as Ronda wandered busily around the apartment. Watching her seemed to stir something within him, and he began to reflect upon his firstborn, recalling what a beautiful baby she had been. It was not until she was almost 2 years old that he and Georgia realized something was not quite right with their daughter. Then came a battery of tests in an effort to determine what exactly was wrong. Ramsey could not stand for Ronda to endure this without him knowing what she would be experiencing. As a result, he insisted that the tests be performed on him as well. One test that he recounted involved the dinging of a bell followed by the administration of a shock. After a few rounds of this, one would normally get the hang of the routine and invariably react at the sound of the bell in preparation for the shock that was to follow. Ronda, I surmised, never reacted in this fashion, because she could not hear the bell. As a result of her health issues, Ramsey conceded that he and Georgia doted on Ronda to the extreme, and he conjectured that this probably made his son Thomas somewhat jealous.[52]

While Ramsey spoke with me, Ronda kept demanding that he write notes with her. Ramsey's eldest granddaughter Whitney volunteered to serve as his stand-in so that he could continue talking with me. About this time, not long after Ramsey had been waxing eloquently about his daughter, Ronda got up from the couch, walked between us, and unceremoniously belched.[53] It struck me as particularly funny because I realized that Ronda was unaware of her volume or that she might be interrupting a serious conversation.

I know this may seem like an unnecessary aside, but it is not. In that brief, humorous moment, I comprehended how free Ronda was. She has no reason to care what anyone thinks. She may be entirely oblivious to the concept of others judging her; however, if they happen to be judging, she is unconcerned. It occurred to me that her father has a very similar disposition, which may have been inspired or cultivated, in part, by his relationship with Ronda. How else could he endure the unbelievably harsh criticism that has been hurled at him over the years? How else could he do all of the difficult, controversial things that he has done? Ramsey Clark truly does not care what other people think of him. He knows that he can't control that. As long as he is true to himself and his principles, he is at peace. Like Ronda, he is free. Others who conform, hate, demonize, or attack are the ones in bondage.

Many undoubtedly do not consider Ramsey Clark as free based on the image of him often portrayed by his detractors. Those who don't know him personally could objectively conclude that he is aloof, selfish, and power hungry, willing to undertake fringe causes out of some narcissistic desire for personal acclaim and attention. But that is not why he does what he does. If that were the case, he would not still be living the almost monastic life that he has always led. He has never wanted power or glory. He only wanted to be a part of making things better in this country and beyond.

The reason he left Dallas was because of the hope for a brighter America that he saw possible under the Kennedy administration. Ramsey's law practice there was not making a difference in society. He needed more. Was that superficially selfish and potentially detrimental to his home life? Perhaps to some extent.

But remember this is the example with which he had grown up. Tom Clark peripatetically pursued his ambitions all the way to the highest reaches of government notwithstanding the toll that it must have taken on his home life. But, at the same time, Tom unquestionably cared very deeply for his wife and children. Experiencing this family life, maybe Ramsey came to believe that this was just how it was done. To be sure, Ramsey flipped the script in terms of the content of his ambitions, taking on matters and advocating for positions that his father would never have entertained. In many other respects, though, the apple certainly did not fall far from the tree.

CHAPTER THIRTEEN

LIKE FATHER, LIKE SON

"He labors because he believes an individual can make a difference.
He saw in the collective energies of all people the main chance for
freedom and equality and justice. He believes we can overcome.
. . . He might say with the poet, 'Mourn not the dead, but rather
mourn the apathetic throng, the frightened and the weak who see
the world's great anguish and its wrong yet dare not speak.'"

Ramsey Clark[1]

ALTHOUGH THERE HAVE BEEN several fathers and sons who have held
our nation's highest office, Tom and Ramsey Clark are the only such team
to serve as attorney general. As a boy, Ramsey wandered the halls of the
Department of Justice and rubbed elbows with Cabinet members, seemingly
preordaining his destiny. Based on the outward politics and personalities
of the two Clark men, few would have predicted that Ramsey would follow so closely in his father's footsteps. While he replicated aspects of Tom's
prominent career, much of Ramsey's professional life and public views could
not have been more different, and the imprint that the younger Clark has
made upon American history is truly unique.

The most obvious difference between the two men was their respective political philosophies. As evidence of how diametrically opposed they
were politically, Ramsey's future good friend and 1974 Senate campaign
manager Victor Navasky contrasted father and son at the time of Ramsey's
ascension to attorney general by observing that it was "Tom Clark who
inaugurated the Attorney General's list of subversive organizations," while
his offspring firmly "believes that in a free society, free thought must get
maximum protection."[2]

Another interesting point of philosophical diversion is in the area of criminal justice. Tom Clark was a dissenter in the landmark U.S. Supreme Court decision in *Miranda v. Arizona,* which required that police officers inform arrestees of their various rights, including the right to counsel. Ramsey's view of the case at the time that he was attorney general was positive, believing that it helped rather than hindered law enforcement. When confronted with the fact that his father did not agree with him, Ramsey joked, "Then don't tell him what I said."[3]

As a Supreme Court justice, Tom was considered a conservative, but he was by no means on the far right of that spectrum like later justices such as Antonin Scalia and Clarence Thomas. Like them, some would have characterized Justice Clark as a strict constructionist of the Constitution. However, he personally took issue with that categorization, pointing out that he was not unyieldingly wedded to the text of the Constitution or the language of a statute. He was willing to consider legislative history and to engage in interpretation when there was ambiguity.[4] By the end of his eighteen-year stint on the Court, Tom was no longer viewed as a conservative; he could more accurately be described as "a moderate at the ideological center of [the] Court."[5]

Despite the divergence in their politics, it seems that father and son respected each other's views. Neither criticized nor tried to influence the other. Ramsey maintains that he and his father never talked about their work or got into heated policy debates.[6] Though difficult to believe, especially given Ramsey's unbridled liberalism, friends and family corroborate the portrayal. A former law partner described Tom and Ramsey as being like "fellow fishermen."[7] They enjoyed being together and thought highly of their respective skills and accomplishments, but as Victor Navasky wrote in 1969, "when it [came] to the things that matter[ed], a great deal seem[ed] to be understood rather than spoken. Too much talk [might] scare the fish."[8]

Ramsey confirms this, acknowledging that they likely disagreed a lot on various issues, but it never came between them because they just did not talk about it.[9] Given their dramatically different views on important topics, one could speculate that their verbal reticence represented an intentional effort to maintain family peace. But holding one's tongue can create tension and frustration. Ramsey's cryptic appraisal of his relationship with Tom may hint at this: "Most questions in life have simple answers except a few, and one of them is a man's relation with his father."[10]

The existence of possible friction or perhaps even rivalry is supported by the very nature of Ramsey's life journey. Though it mirrored that of his father in many respects, Ramsey did things in his own fashion, maybe— consciously or unconsciously—to distinguish himself from Tom. One early, fairly innocuous but revealing example can be found in Ramsey's fraternity experience during college. Like Tom, he joined Delta Tau Delta fraternity. But young Ramsey was really a brother in name only, spending very little time on fraternity activities. He had met his future wife Georgia and was far more interested in "courting her" than engaging in the Greek-life scene.[11] Tom, on the other hand, had been very active, to the point of serving as chapter president while in college and in his later years as international president. It appears as though Ramsey may have felt almost required to join because of his dad's commitment to the organization.

Notwithstanding any unspoken tension or tacit acts of rebellion, by most accounts, father and son had a very powerful bond. Tom's former Supreme Court law clerk Larry Temple, who also served as President Johnson's special counsel, is of the view that the two men had a terrific relationship. They had great respect and affection for each other, and despite the many positions and legal representations over which Tom and Ramsey undoubtedly disagreed, Temple maintains that he never once heard Tom utter a negative word about his son.[12] He recalls one lunch meeting at which he was present with Ramsey and President Johnson in which the president was unhappy with something that his independent-minded attorney general was doing or failing to do, and he extolled the virtues of Tom when he was President Truman's attorney general. Johnson went on and on about how loyal and supportive Tom was to Truman and then got right into Ramsey's face, in that inimitable close-talking LBJ way, and said: "I wish you could be more like your daddy." Without flinching, Ramsey simply responded, "Oh Mr. President, a lot of people have said that to me."[13]

One common thread among Ramsey, Tom, and the president was their intense work drive. All three men were inveterate workaholics. It seems that they enjoyed their work, which makes it easier to exhibit such all-consuming devotion, but they also each appeared to be motivated by other forces. Johnson was undoubtedly preoccupied with his legacy. He wanted to be remembered as a revered leader and was fanatical in his futile efforts to avoid being saddled with the stigma of the Vietnam War. Tom seemed inspired by both ambition and a desire to prove his worth. Ramsey, to be sure, was influenced by both his father's and the president's hard-driving examples. But unlike those two men, Ramsey seemed to be impelled by a more personal desire to make things better in the country and the world. He did not seek government positions for the prestige, power, or accolades, but rather to make a difference, optimistically believing that this was possible with tireless hard work and dedication. His assiduous post-DOJ life evinced the same work ethic. If anything, Ramsey may have been even more driven then, perhaps recognizing, as a former government insider, how difficult it is to bring about meaningful change.

While impressive and admirable, the three men's excessive diligence must have affected their families. At one time or another, they each openly touted the closeness of their families, but is it possible to devote exorbitant numbers of hours to work, week in and week out, and still maintain a happy, well-adjusted home life? Recently, in describing President Johnson's work habits, Ramsey may have subconsciously revealed some insight into his own life. He observed that Johnson worked seven days a week and close to sixteen or seventeen hours a day; he acknowledged that it may have made a difference, but "it wasn't good for family, perhaps, although what you find is that you make a lot better use of the time together when you don't have much time together. So [President Johnson] and the girls and Ladybird were a very tight little family."[14]

Tom put in countless hours in connection with his various government positions. This is a characteristic of Tom that Ramsey highlighted in a eulogy delivered at a memorial service for his father. "He was a doer. He was driven—a driven human being." In discussing the lessons that he learned from his famous father, Ramsey's recollections are also noticeably work related. He does not recall Tom ever dispensing wisdom from on high. Rather, whatever Ramsey absorbed from him came through observation:

The lessons were not from what he said but from what he did: his inner drive to get things accomplished, his long and tireless hours, his sacrifices to the bar and the bench, his craftsmanship.[15]

On another occasion, Ramsey came across as a bit regretful in discussing his father's absence around the house during his teenage years: "[F]rom the time I was twelve until I was seventeen, my father had become, you know, a fairly important person in the Department of Justice. . . . [H]e just wasn't home very much. As a practical matter, he wasn't home at all hardly."[16] At age 17, Ramsey left home himself to join the military and began his own independent journey. One might reasonably predict that the example of his father's absence and the effect it may have had on Ramsey might have inspired a different approach in the younger Clark. That did not prove to be the case.

Ramsey's personal and work life suggest that he viewed his father and President Johnson's examples as ones to be emulated. He never took a single vacation during his eight years in the Justice Department, and, by all accounts, it seems as though he has taken few, if any, since then. Although he has glowingly characterized the closeness of his family relationships, was there really enough time in the day for this idyllic perception to be a reality? Ramsey's love for his family was and is unquestionably deep and profound, but his commitment to the law and the public good seemed to pull him away at least as much as did the work habits of his father.

Indeed, Ramsey became somewhat obsessed with the need to be engaged with his various causes, seemingly out of a fear that if he allowed for any distance, he might become numb to the suffering around him, which in turn would blunt his passion. He once described this as the need for so-called revitalization: "Whether it's urban poverty or whatever it is, if I don't re-experience it fairly regularly, the pain subsides."[17] This compulsive need for "revitalization" appears to be why he eschewed vacations and kept up such a frenetic work and travel schedule well into his later years. If he let up, he might give up. But what was the cost to his personal life? Up until the untimely deaths of his wife and son, Ramsey was still tilting at windmills, here and around the globe.

In thinking about Tom and Ramsey, Harry Chapin's classic "Cat's in the Cradle" comes to mind. The song tells the story of a busy father who never quite has time for his son, always promising that at some later point in the future, there will be time, "and you know we'll have a good time then." Observing his father's commitment, the son admiringly thinks that someday he's going to be just like his dad. By the end of the ballad, the roles are predictably reversed. The son has grown up, moved away, and is too busy to find the time for his now-available dad. And the father realizes that "[m]y boy was just like me."[18] Of course this is not an uncommon dynamic for many families, but there is a decidedly profound parallel between it and the Clark men. In many respects, Ramsey turned out just like his dad, even though they could not have been more different in a number of ways. At their core, Tom and Ramsey were unquestionably on the same page. Love of family, loyal devotion to each other, and social consciousness, not to mention a herculean work ethic, were defining qualities for both men.

It may come as a surprise that father and son were actually fundamentally similar in their views on two of the most critical issues of their respective times—crime and civil rights. As attorney general, Tom recognized that there was a growing crime problem in America after the end of World War II. His reaction was not the typical conservative call for more law and order. Rather, he sought creatively to address the causes of crime, not the after effects, and he saw those causes as being fundamentally linked to the social conditions of individuals, namely, employment. In a memo to President Truman, Tom maintained: "We can meet [the threat of more crime], first of all, by concerted effort toward the achievement of prosperity and a high standard of living for all our people. Honest and well-paid employment must be made available to all."[19]

He also recognized the importance of rehabilitation as a tool for combatting crime, especially with regard to juvenile first offenders. According to Tom, "The erring youngster from 18 to early 20s must be given every opportunity for rehabilitation so that he may take his place with our useful citizens of tomorrow."[20] While he has been criticized for his maintenance of the Attorney General's List of Subversive Organizations and for prosecuting reputed communists,[21] Tom was also labeled a "softie" by some for his refusal to charge certain alleged communist spies, despite intense political pressure for him to do so. Like his son would later maintain under very similar circumstances in resisting passionate calls for charges to be brought against Black Power activist Stokely Carmichael, Tom contended that there was no case to be brought. As he put it, "those were not violations of the law."[22]

Ramsey is well known for his views on the causes and remedies for crime, extensively recounted in his bestselling book *Crime in America*. Like his father, he firmly believed that the social conditions played a significant role in the fostering of criminal behavior. Ramsey observed that the "fountainheads of crime" were

> the dehumanizing effect on the individual of slums, racism, ignorance and violence, of corruption and impotence to fulfill rights, of poverty and unemployment and idleness, of generations of malnutrition, of congenital brain damage and prenatal neglect, of sickness and disease, of pollution, of decrepit, dirty, ugly, unsafe, overcrowded housing, of alcoholism and narcotics addiction, of avarice, anxiety, fear, hatred, hopelessness and injustice.[23]

In Ramsey's view, addressing these harsh realities, particularly through the equalization of employment and educational opportunities for all people, was the key to reducing the crime problem.

In terms of punishment, he would go even further than Tom with regard to his belief in the importance of rehabilitation. Ramsey would not just concentrate on juveniles, as his father did; he believed that rehabilitation had to be the focus for all convicted individuals—whether youth or adult.

Moreover, to incentivize rehabilitation, Ramsey favored indeterminate sentencing. Under this model, instead of imposing sentences of definite duration, imprisonment would be based on a range. Individuals who make sufficient progress toward rehabilitation would be eligible for conditional or unconditional release.[24] Without this, Ramsey thought that prison was a hopeless place for most that only served to create more crime. For these types of views—as well as his perceived delicate treatment of black militants, rioters, and in late 1968, antiwar protesters—Ramsey was considered "soft on crime" or, more derisively, labeled a "cream puff." When asked about the legitimacy of the label in a 1970 interview on *Meet the Press*, Ramsey bristled:

> I am probably not the best person to judge that. I would let others.
> . . . My view on crime control is very clear. We have to professional-
> ize police. We have got to increase vastly the salaries of police. We
> can't go on like this. Courts have to be modernized. We have got to
> rehabilitate persons convicted of crime. . . . We have got to increase
> immensely our effort in prison reforms. If that is being a "cream puff,"
> so be it.[25]

The one area of crime control and enforcement where the Clarks diverged dramatically was in their respective relationships with FBI Director J. Edgar Hoover. Whereas Tom diplomatically appeased Hoover and stroked his massive ego in order to maintain a conducive working rapport, Ramsey had no qualms about squarely butting heads with the powerful director.[26] Not surprisingly, Hoover loved Tom but hated Ramsey. Perhaps the most significant point of contention between Hoover and Ramsey was the director's cherished investigative tool, wiretapping. While Ramsey routinely thwarted Hoover's efforts to spy on the likes of Martin Luther King, Jr. and Stokely Carmichael, Tom was somewhat of a pliant rubber stamp.[27] Hoover clearly preferred the latter approach.

The two men's respective relationship with Hoover seems to reflect a rather intense difference between father and son. Tom was more politically savvy, less dogmatic, and more willing to compromise. Though surely principled, he was much less likely than his son to obstinately dig in his heels in the belief that he was right and everyone else was wrong. Ramsey, would stand on principle no matter what the cost or damage to him personally or to those around him, including the president. Even when any reasonable person would compromise, he would remain unmoved. This is the quality that led President Johnson to fantasize aloud to Ramsey, "I wish you could be more like your daddy."[28]

On the Court, Tom was certainly viewed as tough on crime and a proponent of enhanced law enforcement. In fact, Ramsey warned the president
that his father stepping down in order to clear the way for his son to be
attorney general would adversely affect Johnson's already precarious reputation on crime. He had recently vetoed a stringent DC crime bill around
the time of Ramsey's proposed elevation, and the future attorney general
cautioned him about the dangers of losing Tom on the Court.[29]

Ironically, despite his public soft-on-crime image, Ramsey was as tough
or tougher than any attorney general preceding him, especially with regard
to organized crime. Fred M. Vinson, Jr., Johnson's assistant attorney general for the Criminal Division, described Ramsey as having "been the most
effective organized-crime buster in history."[30] He was also a big supporter
of law enforcement, but his view regarding the necessity of establishing a
community-oriented, professionalized police force and his compassion for
those historically subjected to police abuse made him an easy target for those
who wanted to convey a distorted image of his bona fides on crime.

On the civil rights front, Tom's views were markedly more progressive
than one would expect from a conservative. He firmly believed in equal rights
for all, and from his early days, he harbored a soft spot for African American
citizens. It is unclear exactly where this came from, but as a governmental
official and as a Supreme Court justice, Tom invariably advocated positions
that were beneficial to blacks. Tom's stint as attorney general came at a time
when the nation was making strides with regard to addressing racial discrimination. President Truman had a strong interest in civil rights, and he and
his attorney general dealt with racial issues in a manner that would not be
matched until President Johnson embarked on his Great Society initiatives
with the committed assistance of Tom's son.[31]

President Truman made it clear that he would not tolerate unlawful violence directed toward black citizens. One noteworthy example of this was his
reaction to the brutal beating and blinding of a young black military sergeant
by police in Batesburg, South Carolina. Upon learning of the incident, he
informed Tom Clark, who in turn promptly brought federal charges against
the local chief of police. Although an all-white jury acquitted the police chief,
that Tom even pursued such a matter in 1946 was amazing.[32]

Eerily, twenty years later, Ramsey would find himself in a very similar position in Orangeburg, South Carolina, when he mounted an uphill battle seeking the conviction of local police officers for civil rights violations stemming from the shooting deaths of three black South Carolina State College students who were part of a large group protesting outside of a segregated bowling alley.[33] Like the Batesburg prosecution, this one ended with a defense verdict. Nevertheless, in both instances, although it appears that father and son could have foreseen the outcomes of their respective cases, winning was not the point. The act of pursuing the cases, in and of itself, sent an important message, and at the time, that was the best that Tom and Ramsey could do.

Tom Clark would again flex his civil rights muscles in the aftermath of a gruesome act of racial violence in Monroe, Georgia. A large gathering of white men lynched two African American men and their wives, filled them with bullets, and then threw their bodies into some bushes. One of the victims was a veteran, which particularly angered Truman, who ordered his attorney general to conduct a sifting investigation into the incident. Tom readily did so, expanding the reach of his inquiry by enlisting the FBI and examining Ku Klux Klan activities in seven states. He also made it clear to all U.S. attorneys that protecting the civil rights of minorities was to be a priority for the Justice Department.[34] In a letter, Tom stated:

> The civil rights of minorities in this country were never in greater danger than at this time. It is my purpose to protect human rights and civil liberties, whenever they are infringed, to the full extent and intent of the Constitution and of statutory provisions.[35]

Although the Monroe investigation did not end in an indictment, that was not for lack of trying. Rather, it stemmed from the intransigence of the local officials, who seemed to have obstructed the federal authorities' ability to obtain the evidence necessary to establish probable cause.[36]

It is noteworthy that civil rights icon Thurgood Marshall—who replaced Tom on the Court after his resignation in anticipation of Ramsey's appointment as attorney general—expressed praise for his predecessor's progressiveness during his tenure as attorney general. In reflecting upon Tom following his sudden death, Marshall observed that he would be "remembered as the first Attorney General of the United States to file a brief amicus curiae in a civil rights case," which was actually the first brief of any kind ever filed by an attorney general in support of such a case.[37]

Apart from his case-specific activities in the area of civil rights, Tom Clark was instrumental in President Truman's significant legislative efforts in this regard. Most notably, Truman pressed for passage of the Civil Rights Act of 1949, which, if enacted, would have implemented a number of groundbreaking initiatives concerning civil rights for black citizens, including, among many other things, the guaranteeing of voting rights in all elections. Tom played a major role in the development and promotion of this legislation.

Although it was a laudable undertaking, the country was not yet ready for such monumental advances, and the bill ultimately failed.[38] However, what President Truman and his attorney general started, ironically, President Johnson and Ramsey finished, achieving landmark victories in Congress with the passage of the Civil Rights Acts of 1964 and 1968, as well as the Voting Rights Act of 1965. Ramsey's role in connection with these historic legislative enactments was even more substantial than his father's previous unsuccessful attempt with Truman. As discussed in an earlier chapter, Ramsey was largely the impetus behind the 1964 act (maybe inspired by his father's earlier effort) and participated in formulating, drafting, and lobbying for the other two acts. The parallels between father and son in terms of commitment to civil rights are striking, and the differences in outcome seem to be mostly a product of timing, though Ramsey's intense drive and President Johnson's persuasive personality and legendary legislative skills surely played major roles.

It is not difficult to discern that Ramsey's sincere dedication to the civil rights cause of black Americans must have been shaped and influenced by his father; however, as with other similarities, Ramsey's penchant in this direction has been more pronounced. Civil rights has not simply been one area among many that he has embraced; it has consistently been the single most important issue for him, broadening in later years to encompass the concept of international human rights—beginning with his work in the South during the 1960s to ensure compliance with desegregation and his handling of the various racial riots, and continuing through to his more contemporary humanitarian advocacy on behalf of people in foreign lands. The examples of Ramsey coming to the aid or defense of black Americans are legion, and it is safe to speculate that these associations cultivated in him an attraction to the oppressed, whatever their complexion, that naturally led him down the path to his many controversial causes and representations.

On the nuclear family front, there also appear to be striking similarities in terms of composition and interactive dynamic. Though often absent, Tom's love for his family was ever-present and on display, a quality that his son clearly learned or inherited. Both men likewise married the loves of their lives, each of whom just happened to be the daughter of a judge. Tom and Ramsey both had a daughter and a son. Tom technically had two sons, but his namesake died tragically at the tender age of 6. Ramsey was then a few years younger, and his mother later gave birth to his sister Mimi. In Ramsey's family Ronda, his daughter, was the eldest by two years over her brother who was named after his grandfather—Thomas Campbell Clark II. It has never been clear to me exactly what Tom II was called growing up. My guess is that it may have been something other than Tom because that was Grandpa's moniker. I have not come across any nicknames, however; in our conversations, sometimes he referred to his son as Thomas, and I even heard Tommy a few times, which I believe is what Ramsey's older brother was called.[39] I refer to him as Thomas to distinguish grandson from grandfather. Whatever he was called, it is clear to me that Ramsey loved him every bit as deeply as Tom loved Ramsey.

As with his grandfather and father, Thomas ended up in the Department of Justice, ironically in the same division in which Ramsey had gotten his start. Then it was known as the Lands Division, but by the time Thomas arrived on the scene, it was the Environment and Natural Resources Division. Unlike Ramsey and Tom, Thomas was a career lawyer rather than a political appointee, working in the Environmental Enforcement Section of the Division. He graduated from Duke and later from

Golden Gate University Law School.[40] His path to the law was not a straight one. It took him a little longer than his father to figure out that this was what he wanted to do. I can't help but suspect that the lofty legal legacies of Ramsey and his grandfather may have made him reluctant to venture in their footsteps.

Based on everything that I have been able to uncover, Ramsey and Thomas had a very good relationship. Despite this, it's difficult to imagine that father and son's rapport was not without some tension, particularly in light of Ramsey's intense devotion to external causes throughout his life. Like his dad, Ramsey was literally absent for significant chunks of time, and when present, he still had to deal with stressful work-related demands.

I pressed Ramsey's niece Julie Gronlund on this point, and her response was that although it's hard to believe, the Clark family life was amazingly positive and happy, including Ramsey's relationship with Thomas. She said they were very close, describing their bond as "pretty perfect." Julie acknowledged that Ramsey and Thomas undoubtedly had some typical father–son clashes, but those were rare and fleeting.[41] It is possible that Julie may be too close to be objective, or perhaps she was reluctant to speak freely with a stranger who was writing a book. But my sense is that her account was heartfelt, and no one I asked—even nonrelatives—ever had anything negative to say about Clark's relationship with his family. Given such positive assessments, three thoughts come to mind to explain this loving family dynamic.

First, that is just how it was; Georgia and Ramsey were loving, amazing parents, and they simply made a great home for their family. Second, if you don't know any better, then you can't expect any better. In other words, things may not have been so perfect, with Ramsey working constantly, but that is all that the family ever knew. This is just how things were. That is how it was for Ramsey and Mimi growing up: Like father, like son. Third, Ramsey is such a prodigiously kind and warmhearted person that his children and family cannot help but love him unconditionally and give him a pass on things that others might resent. I actually think the reality may be a combination of the three, but the third explanation seems to carry the most weight. Whether or not Ramsey was an ideal parent, it's hard to refute that he is a pretty ideal person, as sincere and thoughtful as they come. To know him is to love him. I have heard that from others, and I have experienced it personally.

On one visit to New York, I got the chance to meet Ramsey's granddaughter Whitney, the eldest daughter of Thomas and his wife Cheryl. She struck me as independent and engaging, with a confident, easygoing manner. Like her grandfather, Whitney refreshingly seemed entirely comfortable in her own skin, unconcerned about what others may think. I even noticed a couple of tattoos, which did not surprise me in the least. My presence would have disrupted the natural flow of things in many households, but it did not seem to bother Whitney one bit.

I was really happy that Whitney was there because I thought this would give me a chance to observe the Clark family dynamic firsthand. Perhaps I would detect some edginess between her and Ramsey that would reveal the tension that no one else had been willing to articulate. Nothing even remotely close to this ever surfaced. Whitney obviously adores her grandfather. She recounted the time that he came to Virginia Tech to speak while she was a student there, indicating how cool all of her friends thought he was. She had also recently arranged a Reddit interview of Ramsey and told me that it was really fascinating.[42] No surprise there. Throughout the evening, I noticed that she referred to him as Gramsey, clearly a play on Grandpa and Ramsey. Pretty sweet. She said he told her to call him that.[43] Whitney's loving and playful interaction with her grandfather was pure and unaffected, and it reinforced for me how difficult it is not to love Ramsey Clark if you truly know him.

Tension and disdain would have surely permeated the household if Clark had been a narcissistic, power-hungry workaholic. Those are the type of men about whom tortured, seething memoirs are written. That, however, is not Ramsey Clark. His intense work ethic was born out of a sense of altruism, not egotism. He gave everything that he had to others, not for personal acclaim or praise, but because he cared to make a difference in the lives of the ignored and mistreated. His actions and positions certainly have not always been right, but their genesis has always been untainted.

And no matter what his views were, those who opposed Clark often found it virtually impossible to dislike him personally. Marie Hagen—former senior trial counsel in the DOJ who represented the government in Ramsey Clark's suit on behalf of the Branch Davidians—contacted me on her own accord to convey what a wonderful person she thought he was. She had read a law review article that I had written about Ramsey's representation of Saddam Hussein, and it spurred her to reach out to me. Hagen indicated that he was a consummate gentleman, always kind, considerate, and professional. Although she disagreed with his legal positions in the case, Hagen nevertheless found his advocacy to be sincere.[44] He wasn't out to extort a settlement in order to line his own pockets. To him, the Branch Davidians had suffered an egregious wrong for which they deserved to be compensated. Earlier, he had felt the same way about innocent Libyans who were injured and killed as a result of U.S. bombing, and he therefore filed a similarly unmeritorious lawsuit against President Reagan and British Prime Minister Margaret Thatcher.

Another adversary, David Strachman, who has frequently represented plaintiffs in tort actions against the PLO and Syria, expressed respect for Clark, though he admittedly is a bit baffled by the positions that Clark has taken in many of these matters over the years. He suspects that Clark may have been parroting some rash views that were being fed to him by others, but he still likes Clark as a person and does not doubt the sincerity of his commitment; Strachman just questions the commitment itself.[45]

If you Google "Ramsey Clark," you will be hit with scads of vitriol suggesting that he must be one of the evilest, most hated individuals on earth. The authors of these diatribes, however, do not know Clark; they only think they do. As both Hagen and Strachman would likely attest, it is hard to imagine that one could truly know him and still view him with personal disdain. His son Thomas clearly knew him better than these two attorneys, and I can only imagine that the love and respect that he had for his father was profound and immense. Unfortunately, I did not have an opportunity to interview Thomas before he passed away in 2013 from cancer. I did run across one quote that demonstrated the depth of Thomas's understanding of his father's character and the obvious pride with which he viewed Ramsey:

> He has always had a core set of beliefs—in the rule of law, in civil rights. . . . He is not willing to alter his beliefs to win a vote or gain a client or earn a fee. He's going to give it to you straight and he's not going to sugarcoat it. People find it hard to believe, but it's genuine.[46]

Ramsey and I had several conversations about his son, mostly center-ing around Thomas's illness. We spoke in August 2011, and our exchange quickly turned to the subject of Thomas, who was scheduled to undergo surgery related to his cancer later that month. Referring to him as Tom, Ramsey clinically schooled me on the nature of his son's procedure, calling it "heavy surgery" and observing that it would be followed by more sur-gery in about a month and a half.[47] He commented on the danger posed by surgery and regretfully noted that if everything went well, it would mean that Thomas would have about ten more years to live, but he would never be his once-strong and physically active self.[48]

We spoke again in early September, and he shared a glum update on Thomas's health status, indicating that the doctors had to "open him up again" because of a lung infection. He told me that a large portion of his son's esophagus and stomach had to be removed, which was going to inhibit his ability to eat and make it difficult for him to talk. The healing process would be slow and arduous.[49]

While I sensed that Ramsey must have been deeply troubled by his son's condition, that had nothing to do with the tone of our conversa-tion. I was amazed and somewhat confounded by the detached sterility of his narrative of Thomas's condition and what lay ahead for him. I could not detect any semblance of sadness or remorse in his voice, although I know those feelings were beneath the surface. In assessing Ramsey's emotional equilibrium, one of his friends told me that he was a snorkeler rather than a scuba diver—he prefers to stay near the surface instead of going deep. That image seemed particular apt, and also captured how he behaved with me after Georgia's death. But the question that lingered was why. What causes a man with such a warm and loving heart to sup-press his emotions?

My exposure to him suggests that he does not like a lot of attention, nor does he care to burden others with his troubles. In our numerous con-versations, whenever we ventured into an emotional area, I found that he would not-so-subtly change the topic, usually by asking me about my wife or daughters. Even when we discussed his beloved wife's death, I got the sense that he was more concerned with comforting me than he was with receiving my condolences. I remember that he sounded lost and somewhat broken, but that was only detectable through the tone of his voice, not the substance of our exchange. He would not allow himself to descend into the painful depths of grief.

Perhaps this is the only way that a man who has seen so much tragedy and suffering throughout his life can persevere for over nine decades. Up close and personally, he lived through the violent deaths of John F. Kennedy, Martin Luther King, Jr., and Bobby Kennedy. He was with his dear friend and civil rights leader Whitney Young when he drowned in Lagos, Nigeria, fruitlessly performing mouth-to-mouth resuscitation in an effort to revive him.[50] More broadly, he has witnessed wholesale death and devastation in North Vietnam, Libya, Grenada, Panama, and Iraq, to name but a few. And he endured the sudden, tragic loss of his beloved father, who died of a heart attack at Ramsey and Georgia's New York apartment while the couple was away. Diving deep when faced with such enormous, recurrent bereavement could take a toll on one's body and soul, but so can circumventing the grieving process altogether. Since the deaths of his wife and son, I have watched Ramsey decline, both physically and mentally.

He has recounted on a number of occasions that in the aftermath of Bobby Kennedy's assassination, he instructed Chief U.S. Marshal Jim McShane to keep an eye on Kennedy's wife Ethel and the rest of her family. Two weeks later, Ethel called Ramsey to let him know that although they loved Jim, he had to get out of their house. Ramsey could not believe that he was still there; he thought McShane would have gone home the next day. According to Ramsey, "[h]e stayed because he was devoted to [Bobby] and was so crushed by his death. Jim died later that year. People die of broken hearts, you know."[51] That may be true, but the death is not always a physical one. Ramsey Clark carried on after the loss of Georgia and Thomas; however, that warm heart of his may have been hopelessly damaged. He could not possibly be the same person after that, no matter how close to the surface he swam.

"CARRY ON . . . AND KICK UP SOME DUST"

"We cannot be forced by our leaders to choose between justice
and our country. We must make our country just."

Ramsey Clark[1]

MY FINAL VISIT with Ramsey Clark in connection with this book took place on December 16, 2017, when I had the pleasure of attending, along with many of his family members and friends, a birthday celebration in honor of his impending 90th birthday. Although Ramsey was the man of the hour, he was as unassuming as ever. He had fallen and broken his hip earlier in the year. In my experience with elderly relatives, an injury of this nature often signals a precipitous decline. That's what crossed my mind at the time I learned of his condition, and I was worried. Upon seeing him on December 16, it was quite obvious that my concerns were unwarranted. He looked great and was getting around pretty well with the aid of a walker. When I shared my rosy assessment of his condition with him, he deadpanned, "I haven't won any races lately, but of course, I haven't run any."

I did not want to monopolize his time at the party because there were so many other people there who clearly wanted to visit with him, but we ended up talking for quite a while. He seemed unconcerned about others who were waiting their turn. Ramsey was focused on our conversation. Even with a failing memory and physical discomfort, he was an attentive listener. When we finished chatting, I watched him accord the same level of mental presence to everyone else who spoke with him.

Observing him at this point in his life, it is hard to believe that he is the same person who spent the vast majority of his adult years working at a frenetic pace, tirelessly waging battles for those he considered to be oppressed or suffering. The vivid stories of bygone escapades seem almost fictional. How could anyone have been a part of so many historically significant episodes, let alone this warm, gentle soon-to-be 90-year-old? That he was—and that so few people, generally, are aware of it—is even more astonishing.

Besides attending Ramsey's birthday celebration, I was also in New York to attend a screening of a documentary about his life, produced and directed by Joseph C. Stillman, aptly titled *Citizen Clark . . . A Life of Principle*.[2] The screening was to take place almost directly across the street from Clark's Greenwich Village apartment later that evening at The New School, and I asked him if he was going to be there. He said that he was, even though his niece Julie had told me that he would not be attending, which made sense because it would have meant leaving his family and friends to celebrate his birthday without the guest of honor. I was curious about how this would play out, as well as about how many people would be at the screening. From my perspective, a movie about his life should attract a standing-room only crowd in a large auditorium. But my experience suggested that this would almost surely not be the case, as there are so many who either don't know anything about Ramsey Clark or else have an unfavorable picture of him. I expected to find a very small audience.

To my surprise, when I arrived at the auditorium for the screening, there was a pretty sizable and diverse assortment of viewers. It was not packed, but I would guess that it was about two-thirds full, between 150 and 200 people. I quickly ascertained that my fellow moviegoers were mostly diehard Ramsey Clark fans, many of whom were obviously long-time acquaintances. For the most part, they already knew a great deal about his story. These were simply admirers, there to pay tribute to Clark's remarkable legacy.

At the conclusion of the screening, a panel comprised of Stillman, Frank Serpico, Victor Navasky, and International Action Center Director Sara Flounders discussed the film and Ramsey's life. Although the moderator endeavored to push the panelists to delve into the more controversial aspects of Clark's journey and to acknowledge the legitimacy of some of the criticism that he has received throughout the years, no one seemed willing to do so. Navasky came as close as anyone by admitting that he disagreed with his friend's prosecution of the Boston Five, but then he went on to state that once he heard Ramsey's explanation he understood the principle upon which that case was based and no longer harbored the same misgivings.[3] What about Saddam Hussein and Slobodan Milosevic? None of the panelists appeared interested in even entertaining the notion that perhaps the former attorney general was wrong to have taken on such matters or that his motivations may have been anti-American on some level.

I think that an overly rosy depiction of such a complicated and polarizing figure is unfortunate. Although there is no question that Ramsey Clark is a miraculous human being who has positively influenced our nation's history in innumerable ways that are grossly underappreciated, he is not infallible. To many he is divisive and maybe even infuriating. Others consider him to be so far off the deep end as to be a nonentity. His willingness to side with and defend the demons of the world has resulted in his being demonized and vilified himself. Ignoring or giving short shrift to this reality does a disservice to him and to history.

Trying to explain Ramsey Clark's life journey is a hopelessly complex undertaking. But isn't that the case with any truly pivotal, transformative figure? The quest to understand him and to communicate that understanding is what enriches his life story. I have tried very hard not to be an apologist for him in this book. But I must concede how difficult that has been at times. While I am somewhat critical of the fawning nature of the panel discussion, I certainly get it. He is a very special man—to know him is to love him. And it's challenging to be critical of someone whom you love. Even when there are major character flaws, the tendency may be to overlook or rationalize those shortcomings, or else to simply focus on the positive. I think that this is what many of Clark's close friends and associates do.

It is important for them and for others to remember Ramsey Clark's perception of love as it pertains to his relationship with America. Although he has been derided as anti-American and unpatriotic, he has always maintained that he loves America very deeply and that is why he is such a staunch critic of its leaders—and their policies and actions.[4] If he were to sit back and only look for the positive in his country, ignoring the flaws and areas of weakness, what good would that do? His has been a tough love, similar to the kind that a stern parent shows a child in order to make them a better person in the long run.

I certainly don't want to convey the impression that I have somehow solved the puzzle of Ramsey Clark. Having taken a detailed journey through his incredible life, I am still left with more questions than answers. And after reading this book, I suspect that you are as well. Many times over the past eleven years I naively thought I had a firm handle on who Ramsey Clark is and why he did what he did. Early iterations of some chapters were written as if I had it all figured out. Clearly, I did not. It was foolish for me to think that there was some straightforward conceptualization of someone who has lived such a complex and enigmatic life. That complexity is what makes him so fascinating. The widely disparate theories offered to explain the arc of his eclectic professional path add to the allure of his persona.

Some view Clark as decidedly disloyal, bordering on treasonous in his antipathy toward his own country.[5] Why else, they speculate, would he be willing, almost unfailingly, to defend the enemies of the United States? Others suggest that Ramsey's disenchantment with our government is what has driven him to the enemy's side. John Seigenthaler, for one, expressed the belief that "the purchasing of the American government by special interests (or the perception that this is what has occurred) very probably offended Ramsey."[6] Consistent with this, Clark has long maintained that America is a plutocracy rather than a democracy, which has undeniably disturbed him very deeply, particularly when considered against the hypocritical backdrop of the government's purported quest to spread democracy around the world.[7] Maybe this is what has animated and motivated him.

On the other hand, there are many who view Ramsey Clark simply as a legal hero, the very epitome of the quintessential lawyer–statesman. He is willing to undertake any cause, no matter how controversial or antagonistic to U.S. interests, in order to ensure that the system has integrity and that justice is served for all.

Everyone is of course entitled to his or her opinion. I am confident that this is Ramsey Clark's position, and I am equally certain that he cares very little about what that opinion may be, whether positive or negative. He has never been propelled by concerns over what others might think of him. His journey has not been influenced by a desire to be loved or admired, though for many that has been the end result. Throughout his life, Ramsey has merely sought to do what he believed to be right, irrespective of the political or personal consequences.[8] Undeniably, the correctness of his views concerning what happens to be "right" is subject to debate, but the purity of his motivation and commitment is difficult to question. Nicholas Katzenbach, his predecessor as attorney general, once said that "Ramsey doesn't always show great judgment, but he's always shown great courage" and went on to describe him as a man of "absolute decency, total honesty, and sincerity."[9]

Whether right or wrong, Ramsey Clark's lifelong quest has been a search for the truth, wherever it may rest and whatever it may be. If the truth is that America has indiscriminately killed scores of civilians through bombing in Vietnam, Grenada, or Libya, then that reality must be made known. There will always be another side to the story. But Ramsey's objective was to get the entire story out in the open to allow the people to make informed decisions concerning their views on a given issue. This has been his approach as a government insider and as a dedicated, concerned citizen on the outside. He has incessantly sought to ensure the exposure of truth and the attainment of justice for the voiceless and the powerless of his country and of the world.

True to this theme, one common thread that Ramsey Clark personally contends is present throughout all that he has done is his dedication to peace, nonviolence, and justice.[10] He maintains that there is nothing in which he has been involved that is contrary to these principles. Objectively, that might seem like a stretch, but I firmly believe that in Ramsey's mind and heart he has always been committed to these ideals. Although representing brutal dictators or alleged terrorists may seem like an abandonment of these principles, Ramsey's dedication to the integrity of the rule of law and to the preservation of human dignity, no matter the nature of the reputed wrongful act, has been his foremost motivation. Though he shuns accolades, his commitment to promoting peace and justice throughout the world was deservingly noted through his selection as a recipient of the 2008 United Nations Human Rights Prize.

Nevertheless, many are still inclined to only conduct a superficial appraisal of Ramsey Clark and to reflexively characterize him as somehow evil because of his inveterate association with the vilified.[11] A deeper analysis can just as easily lead to the conclusion that he is innately good. He loves and helps those who are ostracized, loathed, and persecuted, those whom some might call the sinners of the world. Various religious men and women throughout history can be described as having done the same thing. And like Ramsey Clark, many of these people were often viewed in their times as crazy or evil. They were themselves condemned and persecuted for the positions they espoused or the causes they championed. With the passage of time and the wisdom of hindsight, they are often recast in a positive light. In death, they are able to achieve a level of credibility and reverence that escaped them while alive. Whether this too will be the fate of Ramsey's broader legacy is yet to be seen. History will have to be the judge.

During my first interview with him, I asked Ramsey what was the most exciting thing that had occurred during his lifetime. I thought that was a great question. He had seen and done so much. To get him to single out the most exciting event would be revelatory. Would it be one of his controversial representations? Or maybe his involvement with the march from Selma to Montgomery? Or perhaps the apprehension of Dr. King's assassin James Earl Ray? It was none of these. And although upon reflection his answer makes complete sense, it took me by surprise, mainly because of the plethora of things from which he had to choose.

His answer was the election of President Obama, which had just occurred a few days before my interview. This response spoke volumes. A white man, who had literally been associated with innumerable monumental events throughout his long life, placed the election of America's first African American president at the top of his list. Why was this election so significant to him? It was because of what he thought Obama could accomplish, which was a function of what the newly minted president knew and understood.

Bobby Kennedy exposed himself to America's poverty, especially in the black community, as did Ramsey Clark. He and Bobby, therefore "got it" in a way that few white people did. However, Ramsey recognized that Obama "got it" on a whole different level. As a black man who had witnessed Third

World poverty firsthand, he predicted that Obama would be a different kind of president—he knew more about the real world than any of his predecessors. Ramsey was very optimistic about Obama's administration, though he was also concerned. He had entertained similar high hopes in connection with John F. Kennedy and Bobby Kennedy, only to watch their promise for a brighter tomorrow broken by assassins' bullets. He worried that the immense possibilities for America presented by President Obama's election might be destined for the same tragic ending. This fear of assassination was certainly understandable in light of Ramsey's proximity to the murders of the Kennedys and Martin Luther King. During his lifetime, that seemed to be the fate of those who offered the most hope. Fortunately, his worries never came to fruition.

Along similar presidential lines, in late 2016 I asked Ramsey Clark what he thought of then–President Elect Donald Trump. I expected him to unleash a harsh critique, the very antithesis of his appraisal of President Obama. But he surprised me again, offering a cerebral analysis—pretty much his approach to any question, though. He described Trump as a "willful" person who "doesn't listen or learn easily."[12] He is smart, Ramsey acknowledged, but in his opinion, does not appear to be morally grounded.[13] This was a perceptive but by no means caustic evaluation.

He then proceeded to observe, somewhat despondently, that "wars make great leaders." He maintained that history would not remember a president as truly great unless there was some sort of significant military challenge that he had successfully endured.[14] As a man of peace, Ramsey surely finds this to be a troubling reality, a sad commentary on what our nation values. He has stated that our country has made war a way of life, a vehicle for dominating others, and lamented that America has been at war in one form or another for his entire life. This fixation on war translates into making it the highest budgetary priority, which is tragic as that money could be used to solve so many other problems in our society and the world. Ramsey has unswervingly maintained that until the American government cuts its military budget by 90 percent, neither the United States nor the rest of the world can be safe.[15]

Though ever the optimist throughout his life, Ramsey Clark has come to recognize that he is unlikely to be successful in changing the views of those in power, most of whom have simply tuned him out. As a result, he has instead sought to free those whom the powers that be have scorned and demonized, the so-called public enemies. And this is what he has done, from his early days in the Department of Justice protecting subjugated black citizens to his representations of anti–Vietnam War activists, capital defendants, prison inmates, alleged terrorists, and reputed brutal dictators. To him, securing human dignity for all is the paramount objective, and he knows that without true freedom, such a laudable goal can never be a reality. This is why he so loves Justice Black's quote from *In re Anastaplo*: "We must not be afraid to be free."[16] He is the very embodiment of that simple sentence.

I harbor misgivings about a number of the positions and causes that Ramsey Clark has undertaken during the course of his life journey, and I would not have been comfortable representing many of his clients. Notwithstanding this, his powerful example has inspired me to ask questions and to think critically about the legitimacy of what's transpiring around me, especially within the justice system. As Ramsey has stated, "truth is hard to find. You don't really know, you have to search for it—you have to inquire diligently, be very skeptical."[17] Through his probing outspokenness and legal representation of the public's putative enemies, he has sought to compel reconsideration of our preconceived notions of what is true and, more importantly, draw needed attention to the human face that is always a part of any conflict or controversy. His example provides a lesson for all, especially those within the legal profession.

As the attorney general for the United States, Ramsey Clark frequently emphasized the importance of integrity within our legal system, both in fact and in perception. In his later role as a citizen of the world, an internationalist, he has consistently adhered to that mantra, striving to ensure that the system indeed has integrity. For him, if it lacks this critical element, justice will forever be in doubt. Determinations of liability, guilt, or innocence will be viewed with skepticism, fomenting fear and distrust, the very feelings that were rampant in the black community during Ramsey's tenure in the Kennedy and Johnson administrations. While the attainment of absolute integrity and the elimination of all doubt are likely unachievable aspirations, he has played an indispensable role, by reminding us through his controversial undertakings of the significance of persevering in pursuit of these objectives, no matter how difficult and no matter the cost. Revealingly, while reflecting on his friend Muhammad Ali, Ramsey once said, "You know, the joy of life is that you have to persevere and do what you can to make this a better world."[18] Clearly, these are words that the former attorney general himself lived by.

At the conclusion of the December 16 documentary screening, Ramsey Clark made a short videotaped cameo appearance. Apparently his family had won out, not allowing him to leave his own party. Frank Serpico joked that he could report to the audience that Ramsey was being held against his will. I think Serpico was probably right. In the video, Ramsey made a few self-deprecating remarks, including that it was actually Beethoven's birthday—his favorite composer—rather than his own, and ended with a simple but poignant entreaty to the viewers. He looked warmly into the camera, with a slight smile and said, "Carry on . . . and kick up some dust."

It struck me that this was really the essence of what Ramsey Clark has done throughout his life. Whatever the challenge, he has carried on, leaving quite a mound of dust in his wake, and in doing so he demonstrated unwavering courage, commitment to principle, and love for all of humanity. Whether you agree or disagree with him, love him or hate him, if you are not inspired by his cosmic journey, you must not have been paying attention.

ACKNOWLEDGMENTS

Writing this book has been the experience of a lifetime, but it has also been the most difficult professional undertaking that I could imagine. When I first decided to write a book about Ramsey Clark, I had absolutely no idea what I was doing or what I was getting myself into. The more I learned about him, the more inadequate I felt to the task of telling his story in a manner that would do him justice. His life was too complex, too overwhelming, too controversial.

To avoid what I viewed as inevitable failure, on numerous occasions over the past eleven years I actively pursued excuses that would relieve me of the responsibility of finishing this enormous project. But every time I sought to divert myself, someone or something intervened to get me back on track to do what I am now convinced I was meant to do.

Ramsey Clark's story, in many ways, embodies and exposes much about political culture, the legal profession, human nature, and most importantly from my perspective, race relations. In studying him, I have gained new insights into American and international history, but I have learned even more about myself and about the person that I want to be, about the legacy that I hope to leave behind. I am not the same person who began working on this book in 2008, which is a good thing, and it is all due to Ramsey Clark. His life has enriched mine, and I hope that my account does the same for others. I owe a debt of gratitude to a host of people who made this experience possible.

First and foremost, I thank Ramsey Clark. Throughout the evolution of this book, he has been open and cooperative, completely unconcerned with what I might write about him. Either he trusted me or simply didn't care what I or anyone else said about him. I like to think that he trusted me, but in reality, it was probably a combination of both. Ramsey Clark does not waste time dwelling on the critiques of his detractors. Indeed, at times, he seemed most worried about the effect of my association with him *on me*. He often joked that I was going to ruin my reputation fooling around with him. Initially, this caused me some anxiety, but eventually it just made me more determined to tell his tale. Thank you, Ramsey Clark, for allowing me to flirt with reputational disaster. I assure you that it was well worth the risk.

Next, I must thank Professor Stephen Gillers of New York University School of Law. Without his early encouragement, I am not sure that I would have ever reached out directly to Ramsey Clark, which was obviously essential. In addition, I am indebted to many other fellow law professors who read drafts of chapters and related articles, or were simply there for me when I needed some encouragement or reassurance. Thank you to Professors Carlos Ball, Ben Barton, Alfred Brophy, Dan Coenen, Russell Gabriel, Bruce Green, Erica Hashimoto, Ellen Podgor, Brad Wendel, and David Wilkins. I also owe a special thank you to Roger Newman, who provided me with guidance on the biography-writing process and pushed me to examine the complexity of Ramsey Clark's life.

Ramsey Clark's family, friends, and even some former adversaries were enormously helpful to me. Thank you for making yourselves available and sharing your impressions of Ramsey. I am most appreciative of the assistance and cooperation of Beda Acharya, Lois Akner, Karima Al-Amin, George Anastaplo, Cheryl Clark, Whitney Clark, Julie Gronlund, Marie Hagen, Abdeen Jabara, Nicholas Katzenbach, Victor Navasky, Stephen Pollak, Jack Rosenthal, Bob Schwartz, John Seigenthaler, David Strachman, Larry Temple, Pia Welch, and Roger Wilkins.

The University of Georgia School of Law has been a faithful and patient supporter. I am grateful for the law school's financial support of my research, and especially to Dean Emerita Rebecca White for standing by me in the face of some controversy. I also must thank our incredible library staff—Sharon Bradley, Anne Burnett, Maureen Cahill, T.J. Striepe, Amy Taylor, and Jason Tubinis—who scoured my manuscript for citation accuracy and tracked down innumerable obscure resources for me. T.J., in particular, was ever attentive and helpful throughout this process. I cannot thank him enough.

Many a research assistant has had a hand in the development of this book, each bringing unique talents and insights to bear. I must first single out two for special recognition. Joe Reynolds and Ben Thorpe were more than research assistants to me; they became partners and dear friends. They immersed themselves in the book, so much so that they enhanced my excitement. Their interest was infectious, and the time, energy, and enthusiasm that they poured into helping me were invaluable. My other highly capable and dedicated research assistants were Pam Brannon, Joseph Crumbley, Kate Hicks, Kerrie Howze, Brooks Land, Merritt McAlister, Austin McClanahan, Gary McGinty, Thomas Moore, Will Owens, Marshall Sims, and Rob Snyder. Thank you all for your quality work and dedication.

One of the biggest challenges for me was navigating the unfamiliar world of archival research. Thankfully, I had the able assistance of Allen Fisher, archivist at the LBJ Library in Austin, Texas, to shepherd me through my review of Ramsey Clark's Personal Papers, as well as those of other important figures during the Johnson era. I am also grateful to Margaret Harman, audiovisual archivist, for helping me locate and use some wonderful images of Ramsey Clark that appear in the book. In addition, my research benefited greatly from my access to Ramsey Clark's post–Department of Justice Personal Papers that were made available to me by the University of Texas–Austin's Dolph Briscoe Center for American History.

A number of special friends and family members lent helping hands, expressed belief in me, and endured long conversations about my favorite subject, Ramsey Clark. Their loving support was greatly appreciated and necessary. Thank you to John Burgess, Dr. Randy Dishaw, Andy Friedlander, Barbara and Tom Frieling, and Bruce Gelb. My in-laws Hank and Kathy Rose and the rest of the extended Rose family took a deep and abiding interest in this project from the very beginning, reading law review articles, preliminary reviews, and providing support and encouragement at every stage. This meant more to me than you will ever know.

All the work in the world would have been for naught without someone to publish the book. Fortunately, the Stanford University Press decided to take a chance on an untested author thanks to the guidance and persuasive powers of my terrific editor Michelle Lipinski. Michelle believed in me when all I had was a rough book proposal and a couple of related law review articles. Thanks for your faith, creativity, efficiency, and commitment. I am forever in your debt. I also owe special thanks to my copyeditor Jennifer Gordon and my production editor Emily Smith.

Last, but far from least, I thank my wonderful family—my wife Kim and daughters Sophie and Olivia. Olivia and Sophie have pretty much grown up hearing their father talk ceaselessly about Ramsey Clark. When I began this work in earnest, they were 6 and 7, and now they are 17 and 18. Thank you both for patiently listening and for your prideful interest in my work. I know it was a lot to endure at times, but you never made me feel that way.

Although I certainly could not have finished this book without Ramsey Clark, my wife is a very close second. She had a hand in every aspect of my work, reading law review articles and draft chapters, serving as a sounding board for all of my ideas, listening to me complain, comforting me when I was stressed or distraught, and above all, believing in me no matter what the circumstance. Thank you for putting up with me during this extended odyssey. You are my muse, my love, and my most cherished friend.

NOTES

PROLOGUE

1. Lonnie T. Brown, Jr., "Representing Saddam Hussein: The Importance of Being Ramsey Clark," *Georgia Law Review* 42, no. 1 (2007), 47–129.

2. Ramsey Clark, telephone interview by the author (August 8, 2008) (on file with the author).

3. Alexander Wohl later did so in 2013, with the publication of his dual biography of Ramsey Clark and his father Tom C. Clark. Alexander Wohl, *Father, Son, and Constitution: How Justice Tom Clark and Attorney General Ramsey Clark Shaped American Democracy* (Lawrence: University Press of Kansas, 2013).

INTRODUCTION

1. Thomas Hauser, *Muhammad Ali: His Life and Times* (New York: Simon & Schuster, 1991), 175 (quoting Ramsey Clark).

2. See Dr. Martin Luther King, Jr., "Beyond Vietnam" (address delivered to the Clergy and Laymen Concerned About Vietnam), Riverside Church, New York (April 4, 1967); John H. Richardson, "How the Attorney General of the United States Became Saddam Hussein's Lawyer," *Esquire* (February 1, 2007), https://archive.esquire.com/article/2007/2/1/how -the-attorney-general-of-the-united-states-became-saddam-husseins-lawyer

3. Lukas I. Alpert, "Former U.S. Attorney General Ramsey Clark Has Made a Career of Defending the Hated," *Free Republic* (November 23, 2001).

4. Josh Getlin, "For a Politician, Former U.S. Attorney General Ramsey Clark Took a Road Less Traveled—a Hard Left into the Hotbed of Human Rights Causes: Loner of the Left," *Los Angeles Times* (February 18, 1990), http://articles.latimes.com/1990-02-18/ news/vw-1604_1_ramsey-clark

5. See David Margolick, "The Long and Lonely Journey of Ramsey Clark," *New York Times* (June 14, 1991), https://www.nytimes.com/1991/06/14/washington/the-long -and-lonely-journey-of-ramsey-clark.html

6. Robert Little, "Fitting Defender for Hussein: Former U.S. Official Ramsey Clark Has Taken Many Reviled Clients," *Baltimore Sun* (December 6, 2005), http://articles. baltimoresun.com/2005-12-06/news/0512060166_1_ramsey-clark-hussein-trial-lawyer

7. Lizzy Ratner, "Ramsey Clark: Why I'm Taking Saddam's Case," *New York Observer* (January 9, 2005), http://observer.com/2005/01/ramsey-clark-why-im -taking-saddams-case

8. Getlin, "For a Politician, Former U.S. Attorney General Ramsey Clark Took a Road Less Traveled" (quoting Ramsey Clark).

9. Ramsey Clark, "125th Anniversary Issue: Patriotism," *The Nation* (July 15, 1991), 81.

10. Claudia Dreifus, "The Progressive Interview: Ramsey Clark," *Progressive* 55, no. 4 (April 1991), 32.

11. Andrew Maykuth, "Standing Alone," *Philadelphia Inquirer Sunday Magazine* (July 7, 1991), http://www.maykuth.com/Projects/clark91.htm (quoting Ramsey Clark).

12. Ibid.

13. Josh Saunders, "Ramsey Clark's Prosecution Complex," *Legal Affairs* (November–December 2003).

14. Fred P. Graham, "Clark: Target on the Law and Order Issue," *New York Times* (October 20, 1968), https://www.nytimes.com/1968/10/20/archives/law-clark-target-on-the-law-and-order-issue.html

15. Michelle Alexander, *The New Jim Crow: Mass Incarceration in the Age of Colorblindness* (New York: New Press, revised edition 2012), 46; John B. Judis, "The Strange Case of Ramsey Clark," *New Republic* 204, no. 16 (April 22, 1991), 27–28.

16. Michael Flamm, *Law and Order: Street Crime, Civil Unrest, and the Crisis of Liberalism in the 1960s* (New York: Columbia University Press, 2005), 172.

17. See Robert Sherrill, "A Talk with Ramsey Clark: Justice in a Torn Nation," *The Nation* (December 7, 1970), 591.

18. Margolick, "The Long and Lonely Journey of Ramsey Clark" (quoting Ramsey Clark).

19. Ibid. Clark maintains that he has viewed as his life's duty Albert Camus's famous wish that "I should love to be able to love my country and love justice."

20. Ibid.

21. Ibid.

22. Maykuth, "Standing Alone" (quoting Melvin Wulf).

23. Getlin, "For a Politician, Former U.S. Attorney General Ramsey Clark Took a Road Less Traveled"(quoting Warren Christopher).

24. Judis, "The Strange Case of Ramsey Clark," 29.

25. Getlin, "For a Politician, Former U.S. Attorney General Ramsey Clark Took a Road Less Traveled" (quoting Victor Navasky).

26. Ibid. (quoting Ramsey Clark).

27. Monroe H. Freedman, "Henry Lord Brougham and Zeal," *Hofstra Law Review* 34, no. 4 (2006), 1322 (quoting *Trial of Queen Caroline 2* (1821)).

28. Rebecca R. Ruiz, "Attorney General Orders Tougher Sentences, Rolling Back Obama Policy," *New York Times* (May 12, 2017), https://www.nytimes.com/2017/05/12/us/politics/attorney-general-jeff-sessions-drug-offenses-penalties.html

29. David Strachman, telephone interview by the author (April 11, 2011) (on file with the author).

30. See Richardson, "How the Attorney General of the United States Became Saddam Hussein's Lawyer."

31. *I Am Not Your Negro*, directed by Raoul Peck (New York: Magnolia Pictures, 2016).

CHAPTER ONE

1. Mimi Clark Gronlund, *Supreme Court Justice Tom C. Clark: A Life of Service* (Foreword by Ramsey Clark) (Austin: University of Texas Press, 2010), vii.

2. Robert M. Langran, "Tom C. Clark," in *The Supreme Court Justices Illustrated*

Biographies 1789–1995, edited by Clare Cushman (Washington, DC: Congressional Quarterly, 1995), 427.

3. Gronlund, *Supreme Court Justice Tom C. Clark*, 13.

4. Richard Kluger, *Simple Justice: The History of Brown v. Board of Education and Black America's Struggle for Equality* (New York: Vintage Books, 1975), 250.

5. Gronlund, *Supreme Court Justice Tom C. Clark*, 32.

6. See Alexander Wohl, *Father, Son, and Constitution: How Justice Tom Clark and Attorney General Ramsey Clark Shaped American Democracy* (Lawrence: University Press of Kansas, 2013), 184.

7. Gronlund, *Supreme Court Justice Tom C. Clark*, 35–36.

8. Ramsey Clark, interview by the author, New York, NY (January 6, 2016) (on file with the author).

9. Ramsey Clark, telephone interview by the author (July 16, 2010) (on file with the author).

10. Gronlund, *Supreme Court Justice Tom C. Clark*, 50.

11. Ibid., 51.

12. Ibid., 58.

13. Miles Corwin, "Ex-Chancellor Convicted of Embezzlement at UCSB," *Los Angeles Times* (July 16, 1988), http://articles.latimes.com/1988-07-16/news/mn-6030_1_uc -santa-barbara-professors

14. Ramsey Clark, interview by the author, New York, NY (June 7, 2016) (on file with the author). It should be noted that in a different account of a similar story, Clark is reported to have stated that his DC classmate, future Senator Joseph Tydings, was wearing knickers when they first met. See Wohl, *Father, Son, and Constitution,* 186.

15. Gronlund, *Supreme Court Justice Tom C. Clark*, 62.

16. Ibid., 74.

17. Ibid., 14.

18. Larry Temple Oral History Interview V (August 11, 1970), by Joe B. Frantz, LBJ Presidential Library, https://www.discoverlbj.org/item/oh-templel-19700811 -5-72-33-e; Larry Temple, interview by the author, Austin, TX (March 24, 2011) (on file with the author). See also Bruce Allen Murphy, *Fortas: The Rise and Ruin of a Supreme Court Justice* (New York: William Morrow, 1988), 295 (observing that Ramsey Clark "may have been one of the few men who could say no to Lyndon Johnson").

19. Ramsey Clark, interview by the author, New York, NY (November 8, 2008) (on file with the author).

20. "Ramsey Clark About the History of the Hitler Bust," in Ramsey Clark Papers, Dolph Briscoe Center for American History, University of Texas–Austin, Box 2016-086/10.

21. Deborah Hastings, "The Life and Times of Ramsey Clark," *Free Republic* (April 29, 2006), http://www.freerepublic.com/focus/f-news/1623980/posts (quoting Ramsey Clark: "I was appalled at what I saw. I couldn't hardly stand it").

22. Ramsey Clark, interview by the author, New York, NY (November 8, 2008) (on file with the author).

23. "Ramsey Clark About the History of the Hitler Bust"; Ramsey Clark, interview by the author, New York, NY (June 10, 2016) (on file with the author).

24. Ibid.

25. Ramsey Clark, letter to the author (August 19, 2008) (on file with the author); "Nomination of Ramsey Clark to Be Deputy Attorney General of the United States: Hearing

Before the Committee on the Judiciary," U.S. Senate, 89th Congress (February 8, 1965).

26. Ramsey Clark, letter to the author (August 19, 2008) (on file with the author).

27. During the summer of 1948, he worked on a tramp steamer traveling throughout China, an experience that further broadened his cultural perspective and exposed him to aspects of human suffering that he had never before witnessed. He saw people starving to death on the streets. Ramsey Clark, interview by the author, New York, NY (November 8, 2008) (on file with the author); Ramsey Clark, interview by the author, New York, NY (January 7, 2016) (on file with the author).

28. Ramsey Clark, interview by the author, New York, NY (November 8, 2008) (on file with the author).

29. Claudia Dreifus, "The Progressive Interview: Ramsey Clark," *Progressive* 55, no. 4 (April 1991), 32.

30. Wohl, *Father, Son, and Constitution*, 193.

31. "Robert Bork, Jurist and Scholar, 1927–2012," *UChicago News* (December 19, 2012), https://news.uchicago.edu/story/robert-bork-jurist-and-scholar-1927-2012

32. Ramsey Clark, interview by the author, New York, NY (November 8, 2008) (on file with the author).

33. Ibid.

34. Ibid.

35. Ramsey Clark Oral History Interview (January 9, 2003), https://www.c-span .org/video/?317441-1/ramsey-clark-oral-history-interivew (referring to Thomas as Tommy and Tom interchangeably in recounting the youngster's interaction with then–Vice President Johnson).

36. John H. Richardson, "How the Attorney General of the United States Became Saddam Hussein's Lawyer," *Esquire* (February 1, 2007), https://archive .esquire.com/article/2007/2/1/how-the-attorney-general-of-the-united-states -became-saddam-husseins-lawyer

CHAPTER TWO

1. "An Interview with Ramsey Clark," *ADA World Magazine* (May–June 1971), 5.

2. Tom Wicker, "Ramsey Clark: A Candid Conversation with the Civil-Libertarian Ex-Attorney General," *Playboy Magazine* (August 1969), 74.

3. Ramsey Clark, interview by the author, New York, NY (November 8, 2008) (on file with the author); Tom Clark Oral History Interview I (October 7, 1969), by Joe B. Frantz, LBJ Presidential Library, http://www.lbjlibrary.net/assets /documents/archives/oral_histories/clark_t/Clark-T.PDF

4. See Ramsey Clark, interview by the author, New York, NY (June 10, 2016) (on file with the author).

5. Ramsey Clark Oral History Interview I (October 30, 1968), by Harri Baker, LBJ Presidential Library, http://www.lbjlibrary.net/collections/oral-histories /clark-ramsey.html

6. Ibid.

7. Larry Temple Oral History Interview I (June 11, 1970), by Joe B. Frantz, LBJ Presidential Library, https://www.discoverlbj.org/item/oh-templel-19700611 -1-72-33-a

8. See Bruce Allen Murphy, *Fortas: The Rise and Ruin of a Supreme Court Justice* (New York: William Morrow, 1988), 295.

9. Tom Clark Oral History Interview I (October 7, 1969).

10. Ibid.

11. Ramsey Clark, interview by the author, New York, NY (November 8, 2008) (on file with the author).

12. Ibid.

13. Victor S. Navasky, "Wrong Guy for the Wrong Post at the Wrong Time?" *Saturday Evening Post* (December 16, 1967), 74–77.

14. Tom Clark Oral History Interview I (October 7, 1969) (noting that Ramsey "pulled it out of the graveyard").

15. Ramsey Clark, interview by the author, New York, NY (November 8, 2008) (on file with the author).

16. Ibid.

17. "Ramsey Clark, Assistant Attorney General-Designate: Hearing Before the Committee on the Judiciary," U.S. Senate, 87th Congress (February 27, 1961).

18. Alexander Wohl, *Father, Son, and Constitution: How Justice Tom Clark and Attorney General Ramsey Clark Shaped American Democracy* (Lawrence: University Press of Kansas, 2013), 203–205.

19. Ibid., 204–205.

20. Ramsey Clark, interview by the author, New York, NY (November 8, 2008) (on file with the author).

21. Navasky, "Wrong Guy for the Wrong Post at the Wrong Time?" See also Tom Clark Oral History Interview I (October 7, 1969).

22. Richard L. Schott and Dagmar S. Hamilton, *People, Positions, and Power: The Political Appointments of Lyndon Johnson* (Chicago: University of Chicago Press, 1983), 89.

23. *Brown v. Board of Education*, 347 U.S. 483 (1954).

24. Victor S. Navasky, *Kennedy Justice* (New York: Atheneum, 1970), 97 (observing that while there was passion in the DOJ with regard to the plight of blacks in the South, "civil rights" was not an early priority of the Kennedy administration).

25. Schott and Hamilton, *People, Positions, and Power*, 89; Ramsey Clark Oral History Interview II (February 11, 1969), by Harri Baker, LBJ Presidential Library, http://www.lbjlibrary.net/assets/documents/archives/oral_histories/clark_r/clark-r2.pdf

26. Ramsey Clark, interview by the author, New York, NY (November 8, 2008) (on file with the author).

27. Ibid.

28. Navasky, *Kennedy Justice*, 184.

29. Ramsey Clark Oral History Interview II (February 11, 1969).

30. Andrew Maykuth, "Standing Alone," *Philadelphia Inquirer Sunday Magazine* (July 7, 1991), http://www.maykuth.com/Projects/clark91.htm (quoting Ed Guthman).

31. John Seigenthaler, telephone interview by the author (July 7, 2011) (on file with the author).

32. Murphy, *Fortas*, 295–296.

33. Ibid., 296.

34. Larry Temple Oral History Interview V (August 11, 1970), by Joe B. Frantz, LBJ Presidential Library, https://www.discoverlbj.org/item/oh-templel-19700811-5-72-33-e

35. Peter Carlson, "The Crusader," *Washington Post* (December 15, 2002), https://www.washingtonpost.com/archive/lifestyle/2002/12/15/the-crusader/9de49dd7

-43fd-45e0-a4ef-3df4475cb4a0/?noredirect=on&utm_term=.463341d9223d

36. Ramsey Clark, interview by the author, New York, NY (January 6, 2016) (on file with the author).

37. Nicholas deB. Katzenbach, *Some of It Was Fun: Working with RFK and LBJ* (New York: Norton, 2008), 134, 145.

38. Ibid., 146.

39. Ibid., 150, 158–159.

40. Schott and Hamilton, *People, Positions, and Power,* 89.

41. Navasky, "Wrong Guy for the Wrong Post at the Wrong Time?"

42. John Seigenthaler, telephone interview by the author (July 7, 2011) (on file with the author).

43. Katzenbach, *Some of It Was Fun,* 161; Nicholas deB. Katzenbach, telephone interview by the author (June 15, 2011) (on file with the author).

44. Letter from Tom C. Clark to President Johnson (July 22, [1964]), Presidential Papers, "White House Famous Names, Clark, Tom C.," LBJ Presidential Library.

45. "Nomination of Ramsey Clark to Be Deputy Attorney General of the United States: Hearing Before the Committee on the Judiciary," U.S. Senate, 89th Congress (February 8, 1965).

CHAPTER THREE

1. Tom Wicker, "Ramsey Clark: A Candid Conversation with the Civil-Libertarian Ex-Attorney General," *Playboy Magazine* (August 1969), 56.

2. Jean Stein, *American Journey: The Times of Robert Kennedy,* edited by George Plimpton (New York: Harcourt Brace Jovanovich, 1970), 94 (quoting Ramsey Clark: "The action tended to begin with the Freedom Riders early that summer of 1961").

3. David Halberstam, *The Children* (New York: Random House, 1998), 255.

4. See *Boynton v. Virginia,* 364 U.S. 454 (1960).

5. Victor S. Navasky, *Kennedy Justice* (New York: Atheneum, 1971), 20.

6. Halberstam, *The Children,* 260–264. The Freedom Riders also visited Birmingham, Alabama, on the same day, and there too were met by a horrifically violent white mob. Ibid., 264–265.

7. Ibid., 254.

8. Ibid., 283–284.

9. Ibid., 284.

10. Ibid., 286–287.

11. Ibid., 300–304.

12. Ibid., 309–313.

13. Ibid., 316–317; Nicholas deB. Katzenbach, *Some of It Was Fun: Working with RFK and LBJ* (New York: Norton, 2008), 45.

14. Halberstam, *The Children,* 318.

15. Ibid.

16. Ramsey Clark Oral History Interview II (February 11, 1969), by Harri Baker, LBJ Presidential Library, http://www.lbjlibrary.net/assets/documents/archives/oral_histories/clark_r/clark-r2.pdf

17. Ramsey Clark, interview by the author, New York, NY (November 8, 2008) (on file with the author); Ramsey Clark Oral History Interview II (February 11, 1969).

18. Ramsey Clark Oral History Interview II (February 11, 1969).

19. Ibid.

20. James T. Patterson, *The Eve of Destruction: How 1965 Transformed America* (New York: Basic Books, 2012), 71–73.

21. See Andrew Glass, "Civil Rights March Ends as 'Bloody Sunday,' March 7, 1965," *Politico* (March 7, 2018), https://www.politico.com/story/2018/03/07/this-day-in-politics-march-7-1965-437394

22. Taylor Branch, *At Canaan's Edge: America in the King Years—1965–68* (New York: Simon & Schuster, 2006), 38–39.

23. Halberstam, *The Children*, 511–515.

24. Branch, *At Canaan's Edge*, 68.

25. Halberstam, *The Children*, 515.

26. Branch, *At Canaan's Edge*, 76–77.

27. Halberstam, *The Children*, 516; Branch, *At Canaan's Edge*, 123.

28. Branch, *At Canaan's Edge*, 113–114 (quoting President Johnson) (emphasis added).

29. Ibid., 122.

30. Ibid., 125–128.

31. Ibid., 84.

32. Jack Rosenthal, telephone interview by the author (July 20, 2016) (on file with the author).

33. Ramsey Clark Oral History Interview II (February 11, 1969).

34. Alexander Wohl, *Father, Son, and Constitution: How Justice Tom Clark and Attorney General Ramsey Clark Shaped American Democracy* (Lawrence: University Press of Kansas, 2013), 254.

35. Stephen Pollak Oral History Interview II (January 29, 1969), by Harri Baker, LBJ Presidential Library, https://www.discoverlbj.org/item/oh-pollaks-19690129-2-84-15 (Pollak stating that "the final day when 25,000 people came to Montgomery was one of the most memorable days of [his] life"); Branch, *At Canaan's Edge*, 161.

36. Ramsey Clark Oral History Interview II (February 11, 1969).

37. Branch, *At Canaan's Edge*, 172–174.

38. Ramsey Clark Oral History Interview II (February 11, 1969).

39. Branch, *At Canaan's Edge*, 175–183.

40. Ramsey Clark Oral History Interview II (February 11, 1969).

41. Ibid.

42. Martin Luther King, Jr., "Letter from a Birmingham Jail" (April 14, 1963) https://www.africa.upenn.edu/Articles_Gen/Letter_Birmingham.html (quoting a "white brother in Texas").

43. Ibid.

44. Ibid.

45. Ibid.

46. Ralph Ellison, *Invisible Man* (New York: Random House, 1952), 3.

47. Peniel E. Joseph, *Waiting 'Til the Midnight Hour: A Narrative History of Black Power in America* (New York: Henry Holt, 2006), 141–142; Michael T. Kaufman, "Stokely Carmichael, Rights Leader Who Coined 'Black Power,' Dies at 57," *New York Times* (November 16, 1998), https://www.nytimes.com/1998/11/16/us/stokely-carmichael-rights-leader-who-coined-black-power-dies-at-57.html

48. Branch, *At Canaan's Edge,* 468.

49. See King, "Letter from a Birmingham Jail."

50. "MLK: A Riot Is the Language of the Unheard," *CBS News* (August 25, 2013), http://www.cbsnews.com/news/mlk-a-riot-is-the-language-of-the-unheard/

51. Tom Wicker, "Ramsey Clark: A Candid Conversation with the Civil-Libertarian Ex-Attorney General," *Playboy Magazine* (August 1969), 55.

52. See *Report of the National Advisory Commission on Civil Disorders*, New York Times Edition (New York: Dutton, 1968), 219 (observing that rage over the alleged stoning and drowning of a black youth led to a deadly clash between black and white citizens on the South Side of Chicago).

53. See generally Alfred L. Brophy, *Reconstructing the Dreamland: The Tulsa Riot of 1921: Race, Reparation, and Reconciliation* (New York: Oxford University Press, 2002). The white-fueled unrest in Tulsa resulted in the devastation of one of the most affluent black areas in the country at that time.

54. Riots also took place in parts of Florida, New Jersey, Ohio, and Illinois. See *Report of the National Advisory Commission on Civil Disorders*, 35–36. See also David C. Carter, *The Music Has Gone Out of the Movement: Civil Rights and the Johnson Administration, 1965–1968* (Chapel Hill: University of North Carolina Press, 2009), 25, 58; Patterson, *The Eve of Destruction*, 5.

55. See Lonnie T. Brown, Jr., "Different Lyrics, Same Song: Watts, Ferguson, and the Stagnating Effect of the Politics of Law and Order," *Harvard Civil Rights–Civil Liberties Law Review* 52, no. 2 (2017), 305, 313–316. Some content of the current chapter, as well as Chapter 5, was excerpted or derived from portions of this article.

56. Jerry Cohen and William S. Murphy, *Burn, Baby, Burn!: The Los Angeles Race Riots of August 1965* (New York: Dutton, 1966), 317–318.

57. Ibid., 68.

58. Ibid., 69.

59. Ibid., 280–281.

60. Ibid., 281 (quoting Mayor Yorty).

61. Ramsey Clark, Andrew F. Brimmer, and Jack T. Conway, "Report of the President's Task Force on the Los Angeles Riots, August, 1965" (September 17, 1965), 23.

62. Michael Flamm, *Law and Order: Street Crime, Civil Unrest, and the Crisis of Liberalism in the 1960s* (New York: Columbia University Press, 2005), 63. See also Michelle Alexander, *The New Jim Crow: Mass Incarceration in the Age of Colorblindness* (New York: New Press, revised edition 2012), 40–41.

63. 89 Cong. Rec. H20792 (daily edition) (August 17, 1965) (statement of Rep. Watson).

64. 89 Cong. Rec. S20626 (daily edition) (August 17, 1965) (statement of Sen. Mondale).

CHAPTER FOUR

1. Tom Wicker, "Ramsey Clark: A Candid Conversation with the Civil-Libertarian Ex-Attorney General," *Playboy Magazine* (August 1969), 56.

2. See David C. Carter, *The Music Has Gone Out of the Movement: Civil Rights and the Johnson Administration, 1965–1968* (Chapel Hill: University of North Carolina Press, 2009), 57, 170–171 (noting that "Johnson felt betrayed after 'all that [he] had done' for black Americans"). See also Robert Dallek, *Flawed Giant: Lyndon Johnson and His Times 1961–1973* (New York: Oxford University Press, 1998), 223.

3. President Lyndon B. Johnson, "Commencement Address at Howard University: 'To Fulfill These Rights'" Washington, DC (June 4, 1965), http://teachingamericanhistory.org/library/document/commencement-address-at-howard-university-to-fulfill-these-rights/ archived at https://perma.cc/9N3K-S67Y

4. James T. Patterson, *The Eve of Destruction: How 1965 Transformed America* (New York: Basic Books, 2012), 182.

5. Nicholas deB. Katzenbach, *Some of It Was Fun: Working with RFK and LBJ* (New York: Norton, 2008), 175–176.

6. Ibid.

7. Carter, *The Music Has Gone Out of the Movement*, 60–61 (quoting President Johnson).

8. Ramsey Clark, Andrew F. Brimmer, and Jack T. Conway, "Report of the President's Task Force on the Los Angeles Riots, August, 1965" (September 17, 1965), 1–2.

9. Roger Wilkins, *A Man's Life: An Autobiography* (New York: Simon & Schuster, 1982), 171–172 (recounting his initial impression that Clark would conduct a superficial investigation and his temptation to dismiss him as just a lackey for the federal government).

10. Clark, Brimmer, and Conway, "Report of the President's Task Force on the Los Angeles Riots," 61.

11. Carter, *The Music Has Gone Out of the Movement*, 172 (observing that Clark "listened" and "took copious notes while those in attendance, their indignation often coming out, shared accounts of all the problems—most notably police brutality—they faced in Watts").

12. Wilkins, *A Man's Life*, 172–173.

13. Ibid.

14. Clark, Brimmer, and Conway, "Report of the President's Task Force on the Los Angeles Riots," 27.

15. Ibid.

16. Ibid.

17. Ibid., 24.

18. Ibid., 3.

19. Ibid., 31.

20. Ibid., 57–58.

21. See "Final Report of the President's Task Force on 21st Century Policing" (2015), http://elearning-courses.net/iacp/html/webinarResources/170926/FinalReport21stCenturyPolicing.pdf

22. See Clark, Brimmer, and Conway, "Report of the President's Task Force on the Los Angeles Riots," 51, 59–60.

23. Ibid., 42–43.

24. Ibid.

25. Ibid., 43 (noting that black citizens' frustration seems to have emanated from the "belief that they [were] not included in the making of decisions which affect[ed] their own future").

26. Ibid.

27. Ibid., 61.

28. Ibid., 56.

29. Carter, *The Music Has Gone Out of the Movement*, 172–173.

30. Memo, Califano to President Johnson, "Ramsey Clark Report," Office Files of Joseph Califano, Box 47, LBJ Presidential Library.

31. Carter, *The Music Has Gone Out of the Movement*, 173.

32. Richard L. Schott and Dagmar S. Hamilton, *People, Positions, and Power: The Political Appointments of Lyndon Johnson* (Chicago: University of Chicago Press, 1983), 90; Ramsey Clark, telephone interview by the author (July 26, 2010) (on file with the author).

33. Schott and Hamilton, *People, Positions, and Power*, 91.

34. Ibid. (quoting John Macy).

35. Katzenbach, *Some of It Was Fun*, 212.

36. Ibid., 212–213.

37. Schott and Hamilton, *People, Positions, and Power*, 88. See also Harry McPherson Oral History Interview V (April 9, 1969), by T. H. Baker, LBJ Presidential Library, http://www.lbjlibrary.net/assets/documents/archives/oral _histories/mcpherson/mcpher05.pdf (stating that Johnson was also concerned about Clark's youth, inexperience in dealing with Congress, and probably his "mustang independence").

38. Lucas A. Powe, Jr., *The Warren Court and American Politics* (Cambridge, MA: Belknap Press, 2001), 291; David Alistair Yalof, *Pursuit of Justices: Presidential Politics and the Selection of Supreme Court Nominees* (Chicago: University of Chicago Press, 1999), 88–89.

39. Bruce Allen Murphy, *Fortas: The Rise and Ruin of a Supreme Court Justice* (New York: William Morrow, 1988), 295.

40. Schott and Hamilton, *People, Positions, and Power*, 92–93.

41. See "Nomination of Ramsey Clark to Be Attorney General of the United States: Hearing Before the Committee on the Judiciary," U.S. Senate, 90th Congress (March 2, 1967).

42. Letter from Ramsey Clark to President Lyndon B. Johnson, "R. Clark, Personal, Miscellaneous Correspondence, 1961–67," in Personal Papers of Ramsey Clark, Box 121, LBJ Presidential Library.

43. Carter, *The Music Has Gone Out of the Movement*, 201–208.

44. Sidney Fine, *Violence in the Model City: The Cavanaugh Administration, Race Relations, and the Detroit Riot of 1967* (Ann Arbor: University of Michigan Press, 1989), 195.

45. Ibid., 244 (noting that Ramsey Clark assured "priority handling" in prosecuting cases against offending police officers).

46. Ibid., 244–246.

47. Ibid., 271–281.

48. Ibid., 289; "4 in Motel Trial Freed in Michigan," *New York Times* (February 26, 1970), https://www.nytimes.com/1970/02/26/archives/4-in-motel-trial-freed-in-michigan -police-and-a-guard-cleared-in-67.html

49. Fine, *Violence in the Model City*, 290.

50. *Report of the National Advisory Commission on Civil Disorders*, New York Times Edition (New York: Dutton, 1968), 1.

51. Ibid.

52. Ibid., 10.

53. Ibid.

54. Ibid., 1.

55. Ibid., 2.

56. Carter, *The Music Has Gone Out of the Movement*, 227–231.

57. Ibid., 232.

58. Ibid., 62.

59. See Steven J. Gold, *The Store in the Hood: A Century of Ethnic Business and Conflict*

(Lanham, MD: Rowman & Littlefield, 2010), 107 (acknowledging theories that "the rioters were disaffected and marginal youth or criminals" and that "looting was opportunistic").

60. Carter, *The Music Has Gone Out of the Movement*, 216; Michael Flamm, *Law and Order: Street Crime, Civil Unrest, and the Crisis of Liberalism in the 1960s* (New York: Columbia University Press, 2005), 96–97.

61. Michael Flamm, "The 'Long Hot Summer' and the Politics of Law and Order," in *Looking Back at LBJ: White House Politics in a New Light*, edited by Mitchell B. Lerner (Lawrence: University Press of Kansas, 2005), 128, 136–137 (noting that one scholar's view that Johnson "became convinced a conspiracy existed, perhaps fostered by communists").

62. Ramsey Clark, *Crime in America: Observations on Its Nature, Causes, Prevention and Control* (New York: Simon & Schuster, 1970), 168–169.

63. Giovanni Russonello, "Fascination and Fear: Covering the Black Panthers," *New York Times* (October 15, 2016), https://www.nytimes.com/2016/10/16/us/black-panthers-50-years.html

64. Wicker, "Ramsey Clark: A Candid Conversation with the Civil-Libertarian Ex-Attorney General," 60.

65. Ramsey Clark, telephone interview by the author (July 27, 2010) (on file with the author).

66. John H. Richardson, "How the Attorney General of the United States Became Saddam Hussein's Lawyer," *Esquire* (February 1, 2007), https://archive.esquire.com/article/2007/2/1/how-the-attorney-general-of-the-united-states-became-saddam-husseins-lawyer (quoting Ramsey Clark, *Crime in America*).

67. Ramsey Clark, telephone interview by the author (September 11, 2015) (on file with the author).

CHAPTER FIVE

1. Tom Wicker, "Ramsey Clark: A Candid Conversation with the Civil-Libertarian Ex-Attorney General," *Playboy Magazine* (August 1969), 56.

2. Ramsey Clark Oral History Interview IV (April 16, 1969), by Harri Baker, LBJ Presidential Library, http://www.lbjlibrary.net/assets/documents/archives/oral_histories/clark_r/clark-r4.pdf

3. Gerold Frank, *An American Death: The True Story of the Assassination of Dr. Martin Luther King, Jr. and the Greatest Manhunt of Our Time* (London: Hamish Hamilton, 1972), 119.

4. Ramsey Clark, "Dr. King, Non-Violence, and U.S. Policy Today," *Executive Intelligence Review* (January 23, 2015), 21.

5. Ibid., 22; Hampton Sides, *Hellhound on His Trail: The Stalking of Martin Luther King, Jr. and the International Hunt for His Assassin* (New York: Doubleday, 2010), 55 (quoting Ramsey Clark: "Here we all were biting our nails, and he was just sleeping like a baby").

6. *Citizen Clark . . . A Life of Principle*, directed by Joseph C. Stillman (Oneonta, NY: La Paloma Films, 2018), https://alifeofprinciple.com

7. H. Rap Brown, "Speech to Cambridge, Maryland, Crowd," Cambridge, MD (July 24, 1967).

8. Taylor Branch, *At Canaan's Edge: America in the King Years—1965–68* (New York: Simon & Schuster, 2006), 296–297.

9. Sides, *Hellhound on His Trail*, 23.

10. Martin Luther King, Jr., "Beyond Vietnam" (address delivered to the Clergy and Laymen Concerned About Vietnam), Riverside Church, New York, NY (April 4, 1967).

11. Steven F. Lawson, "Civil Rights," in *Exploring the Johnson Years*, edited by Robert A. Divine (Austin: University of Texas Press, 1981), 109; Sides, *Hellhound on His Trail*, 23.

12. Sides, *Hellhound on His Trail*, 21.

13. Ibid., 22.

14. Ibid., 21.

15. Ibid., 68 (quoting Coretta Scott King).

16. Ibid., 75.

17. Ibid., 76–77.

18. Ibid., 76.

19. Ibid., 81.

20. Ibid., 245 (quoting Ramsey Clark).

21. Ibid., 89–90.

22. Ibid., 92–94.

23. Ibid., 102–103.

24. Ibid., 105; Branch, *At Canaan's Edge*, 731–733.

25. Sides, *Hellhound on His Trail*, 105–106.

26. Ibid., 109 (quoting Martin Luther King, Jr.).

27. Ibid., 116–117.

28. Ibid., 121.

29. Ibid., 199.

30. Ibid., 55.

31. Ramsey Clark Oral History Interview IV (April 16, 1969).

32. Victor S. Navasky, *Kennedy Justice* (New York: Atheneum, 1971), 139; Curt Gentry, *J. Edgar Hoover: The Man and His Secrets* (New York: Norton, 1991), 598, 601; Ramsey Clark Oral History Interview IV (April 16, 1969). See also Sides, *Hellhound on His Trail*, 56, 58–59.

33. Burton Hersh, *Bobby and J. Edgar: The Historic Face-Off Between the Kennedys and J. Edgar Hoover That Transformed America* (New York: Carroll & Graf, 2007), 486.

34. Michael Friedly and David Gallen, *Martin Luther King, Jr.: The FBI File* (New York: Carroll & Graf, 1993), 621.

35. Sides, *Hellhound on His Trail*, 56.

36. Ibid., 199–200.

37. Ibid., 201.

38. Ramsey Clark Oral History Interview IV (April 16, 1969).

39. Sides, *Hellhound on His Trail*, 207, 214.

40. Ibid., 208 (quoting Stokely Carmichael).

41. John T. Elliff, *Crime, Dissent, and the Attorney General: The Justice Department in the 1960's* (Beverly Hills: Sage Publications, 1971), 112; Frank, *An American Death*, 120–121; Sides, *Hellhound on His Trail*, 260.

42. Sides, *Hellhound on His Trail*, 253 (quoting President Johnson).

43. See Clay Risen, "The Legacy of the 1968 Riots," *The Guardian* (April 4, 2008), https://www. theguardian.com/commentisfree/2008/apr/04/thelegacyofthe1968riots

44. Sides, *Hellhound on His Trail*, 248 (quoting Ramsey Clark).

45. Ibid., 245.

46. Richard Harris, *Justice: The Crisis of Law, Order, and Freedom in America* (New York: Dutton, 1970), 13; Risen, "The Legacy of the 1968 Riots."

47. Harris, *Justice*, 14 (quoting Richard Nixon).

48. Michael Flamm, *Law and Order: Street Crime, Civil Unrest, and the Crisis of Liberalism in the 1960s* (New York: Columbia University Press, 2005), 155.

49. Ramsey Clark, "'How Can You Represent That Man?' Ethics, the Rule of Law, and Defending the Indefensible," *Georgia Law Review* 44, no. 4 (2010), 921, 926.

50. Constituent Letter to President Johnson (undated), "Letters Re: Riots and Shooting of Looters," in Personal Papers of Ramsey Clark, Box 68, LBJ Presidential Library.

51. Constituent Letter to Ramsey Clark (April 30, 1968), "Letters Re: Riots and Shooting of Looters," in Personal Papers of Ramsey Clark, Box 69, LBJ Presidential Library.

52. John G. Tower, "Speech About the Riots" (?1968), Senator John G. Tower Collection, Southwestern University, https://texashistory.unt.edu/ark:/67531/metapth612156/ (emphasis in original).

53. Hampton Sides's riveting and suspenseful account of the investigation in *Hellhound on His Trail: The Stalking of Martin Luther King, Jr. and the International Hunt for His Assassin* is a must read for anyone interested in the details surrounding Dr. King's death and the fascinating story of his killer, James Earl Ray. Sides, *Hellhound on His Trail*.

54. Ibid., 380–382; Anthony Burton, "James Earl Ray Pleads Guilty for the Assassination of Martin Luther King Jr.," *New York Daily News* (March 11, 1969), http://www. nydailynews.com/news/crime/james-earl-ray-pleads-guilty-murder-mlk-1969-article-1.2559939

55. Ramsey Clark Oral History Interview IV (April 16, 1969) (Clark conceding that he did not "think all question of a conspiracy [had] been removed" but maintaining that "the overwhelming preponderance of the evidence today is that he acted alone"). Though there are potential holes in the lone-gunman hypothesis, Hampton Sides offers compelling evidence that contradicts the conspiracy theories. See Sides, *Hellhound on His Trail*.

56. Sides, *Hellhound on His Trail*, 218, 333–334.

57. Ibid., 267–270.

58. Ibid., 333–334.

59. Ibid., 334.

60. Ibid., 112.

61. Ramsey Clark Oral History Interview V (June 3, 1969), by Harri Baker, LBJ Presidential Library, http://www.lbjlibrary.net/assets/documents/archives/oral_histories/clark_r/clark-r5.pdf

62. Ibid.

63. Ibid.

64. Ibid.

65. Sides, *Hellhound on His Trail*, 348.

66. Ibid., 348–349.

67. Harris, *Justice*, 62.

68. John H. Richardson, "How the Attorney General of the United States Became Saddam Hussein's Lawyer," *Esquire* (February 1, 2007, https://archive.esquire.com/article/2007/2/1/how-the-attorney-general-of-the-united-states-became-saddam-husseins-lawyer; see also Harris, *Justice*, 18.

69. Harris, *Justice*, 18.

70. Ibid. See also Richardson, "How the Attorney General of the United States Became Saddam Hussein's Lawyer."

71. Harris, *Justice*, 18.

72. See Richardson, "How the Attorney General of the United States Became Saddam Hussein's Lawyer."

73. See Jean Stein, *American Journey: The Times of Robert Kennedy*, edited by George Plimpton (New York: Harcourt Brace Jovanovich 1970), 348 (quoting Roger Wilkins: "I remember thinking that we had lost one of the few men in the country who had the capacity to gather the dreams of an awful lot of Americans").

74. Wicker, "Ramsey Clark: A Candid Conversation with the Civil-Libertarian Ex-Attorney General," 60 (quoting Ramsey Clark).

75. Dennis J. Bernstein, "Respecting a Courageous American," *Consortium News* (May 11, 2017), https://consortiumnews.com/2017/05/11/respecting-a-courageous-american/; Clark, "Dr. King, Non-Violence, and U.S. Policy Today," 24.

76. Wicker, "Ramsey Clark: A Candid Conversation with the Civil-Libertarian Ex-Attorney General," 60 (Clark observing that "[f]rightened, you want to shoot looters, to arrest without cause, to hold without bail, to force confessions").

77. King, "Beyond Vietnam."

78. See Clark, "Dr. King, Non-Violence, and U.S. Policy Today," 21.

79. Richardson, "How the Attorney General of the United States Became Saddam Hussein's Lawyer."

CHAPTER SIX

1. Derrick Jensen, "Neighborhood Bully: Ramsey Clark on American Militarism," *The Sun Magazine* (August 2001), https://www.thesunmagazine.org/issues/308/neighborhood-bully

2. See Mark K. Updegrove, "Lyndon Johnson's Vietnam," *New York Times* (February 24, 2017), https://www.nytimes.com/2017/02/24/opinion/lyndon-johnsons-vietnam.html

3. See Viet Thanh Nguyen and Richard Hughes, "The Forgotten Victims of Agent Orange, *New York Times* (September 15, 2017), https://www.nytimes.com/2017/09/15/opinion/agent-orange-vietnam-effects.html

4. See *The Vietnam War* (Episode 2: "Riding the Tiger" 1961–1963), directed by Ken Burns and Lynn Novick (PBS Documentary, 2017).

5. Robert Dallek, *Flawed Giant: Lyndon Johnson and His Times 1961–1973* (New York: Oxford University Press, 1998), 258.

6. Ibid., 284.

7. Ibid., 451.

8. Steven F. Lawson, "Civil Rights," in *Exploring the Johnson Years*, edited by Robert A. Divine (Austin: University of Texas Press, 1981), 109; Hampton Sides, *Hellhound on His Trail: The Stalking of Martin Luther King, Jr. and the International Hunt for His Assassin* (New York: Doubleday, 2010), 23.

9. 50 U.S.C.A. app. § 462 (West 1968).

10. David Maraniss, *They Marched into Sunlight: War and Peace, Vietnam and America, October 1967* (New York: Simon & Schuster, 2004), 314, 455; Taylor Branch, *At Canaan's Edge: America in the King Years 1965–68* (New York: Simon & Schuster, 2006), 451.

11. Ramsey Clark Oral History Interview, *C-SPAN* (January 9, 2003), https://www.c-span.org/video/?317441-1/ramsey-clark-oral-history-interivew; Ramsey Clark Oral History Interview V (April 16, 1969), by Harri Baker, LBJ Presidential Library, http://www.lbjlibrary.net/assets/documents/archives/oral_histories/clark_r/clark-r5.pdf

12. Richard Harris, *Justice: The Crisis of Law, Order, and Freedom in America* (New York: Dutton, 1970), 62–63.

13. See generally Lonnie T. Brown, Jr., "A Tale of Prosecutorial Indiscretion: Ramsey Clark and the Selective Non-Prosecution of Stokely Carmichael," *South Carolina Law Review* 62, no. 1 (2010), 1–39. Some content of the current chapter was excerpted or derived from portions of this article.

14. Stokely Carmichael, "The Dialectics of Liberation" (July 18, 1967), in *Stokely Speaks: Black Power Back to Pan-Africanism*, edited by Ethel N. Minor (New York: Random House, 1971), 77, 95.

15. See Branch, *At Canaan's Edge*, 486.

16. Peniel E. Joseph, *Waiting 'Til the Midnight Hour: A Narrative History of Black Power in America* (New York: Henry Holt, 2006), 180–181 (quoting Stokely Carmichael).

17. See the photograph caption of Carmichael speaking to students in Hampton, Virginia, in Stokely Carmichael with Michael Thelwell, *Ready for Revolution: The Life and Struggles of Stokely Carmichael (Kwame Ture)* (New York: Scribner, 2003), following p. 500.

18. Stokely Carmichael, "Berkeley Speech" (October 1966), in *Stokely Speaks: Black Power Back to Pan-Africanism*, 53.

19. Branch, *At Canaan's Edge*, 608.

20. See Lawson, "Civil Rights," 93, 108.

21. Roger Wilkins, *A Man's Life: An Autobiography* (New York: Simon & Schuster, 1982), 205–207.

22. Joseph, *Waiting 'Til the Midnight Hour*, 161–162, 166.

23. Ibid., 166.

24. Michael Flamm, "The 'Long Hot Summer' and the Politics of Law and Order," in *Looking Back at LBJ*, edited by Mitchell B. Lerner (Lawrence: University Press of Kansas, 2005), 128, 136.

25. Minutes of President Johnson's Cabinet Meeting (August 2, 1967), 3 (internal quotation marks omitted).

26. Ibid. (internal quotation marks omitted).

27. Ibid., 5 (internal quotation marks omitted).

28. Ibid.

29. Harry McPherson, *A Political Education* (Boston: Little, Brown, 1972), 362–363; Harry McPherson Oral History Interview V (April 9, 1969), by T. H. Baker, LBJ Presidential Library, http://www.lbjlibrary.net/assets/documents/archives/oral_histories/mcpherson/mcpher05.pdf

30. Minutes of President Johnson's Cabinet Meeting (August 2, 1967), 5 (internal quotation marks omitted).

31. Ramsey Clark Oral History Interview V (April 16, 1969).

32. Josh Saunders, "Ramsey Clark's Prosecution Complex: How Did Lyndon Johnson's Attorney General Come to Defend Dictators, War Criminals, and Terrorists?" *Legal Affairs* (November–December 2003), 43, 44.

33. See generally Jessica Mitford, *The Trial of Dr. Spock, the Rev. William Sloane Coffin, Jr., Michael Ferber, Mitchell Goodman, and Marcus Raskin* (New York: Knopf, 1969); Brown, "A Tale of Prosecutorial Indiscretion," 1, 25–27.

34. Benjamin Spock, *The Common Sense Book of Baby and Child Care* (New York: Duell, Sloan, and Pearce, 1945); Russell Ash, *The Top Ten of Everything* (London, New

York: DK Publishing, 1994), 124 (ranking Dr. Spock's book seventh on the list of all-time bestselling books).

35. Mitford, *The Trial of Dr. Spock, the Rev. William Sloane Coffin, Jr., Michael Ferber, Mitchell Goodman, and Marcus Raskin*, 39–40.

36. Ibid., 33.

37. Ibid., 107–108.

38. Ibid., 41.

39. Ibid.

40. Ibid., 45; Saunders, "Ramsey Clark's Prosecution Complex," 43, 45.

41. Michael S. Foley, *Confronting the War Machine: Draft Resistance During the Vietnam War* (Chapel Hill: University of North Carolina Press, 2003), 154–155, 228; Mitford, *The Trial of Dr. Spock, The Rev. William Sloane Coffin, Jr., Michael Ferber, Mitchell Goodman, and Marcus Raskin*, 5.

42. "Texts of Letter and Memo on the Draft," *New York Times* (November 9, 1967); George Q. Flynn, *The Draft, 1940–1973* (Lawrence: University Press of Kansas, 1993), 215–216.

43. See Mitford, *The Trial of Dr. Spock, the Rev. William Sloane Coffin, Jr., Michael Ferber, Mitchell Goodman, and Marcus Raskin*, 55. See also Foley, *Confronting the War Machine*, 154–155, 230.

44. Mitford, *The Trial of Dr. Spock, the Rev. William Sloane Coffin, Jr., Michael Ferber, Mitchell Goodman, and Marcus Raskin*, 56.

45. Foley, *Confronting the War Machine*, 230.

46. Ramsey Clark Oral History Interview V (April 16, 1969).

47. Ibid.

48. Ibid.

49. Foley, *Confronting the War Machine*, 232 ("A draft resistance test case . . . would 'ventilate the issues, escalate them where they can be seen, [and] provide vigorous defense' for the defendants. . . . ") (alteration in original).

50. Saunders, "Ramsey Clark's Prosecution Complex," 43, 45.

51. Ramsey Clark, "'How Can You Represent That Man?': Ethics, the Rule of Law, and Defending the Indefensible," *Georgia Law Review* 44, no. 4 (2010), 921, 925 (indicating that "[b]efore sentencing in the Spock case, [Clark] personally wrote the judge" and noting that Clark "thought any penalty would be improper"); Harris, *Justice*, 64.

52. Ramsey Clark, telephone interview by the author (August 4, 2008) (on file with the author).

53. Harris, *Justice*, 63.

54. Ramsey Clark, telephone interview by the author (August 4, 2008) (on file with the author).

55. Harris, *Justice*, 62; Ramsey Clark, telephone interview by the author (July 26, 2010) (on file with the author).

56. Stokely Carmichael, "Free Huey" (February 17, 1968), in *Stokely Speaks: Black Power Back to Pan-Africanism*, 111.

57. Branch, *At Canaan's Edge*, 605.

58. Ramsey Clark, interview by the author, Athens, GA (October 17, 2009) (on file with the author).

59. See Joseph O'Meara, "'No Man Is Above the Law,'" *A.B.A. Journal* 53 (December 1967), 1107, 1109–1110 (the dean of Notre Dame Law School strongly advocating for the prosecution of Carmichael for his antiwar activities).

60. Letter from Fred M. Vinson, Jr., Assistant Attorney General, to James O. Eastland, U.S. Senator (November 2, 1966), "Anti-Riot Plans 1968," in Personal Papers of Ramsey Clark, Box 61, LBJ Presidential Library.

61. Ramsey Clark, interview by the author, Athens, GA (October 17, 2009) (on file with the author).

62. Ramsey Clark, telephone interview by the author (July 26, 2010) (on file with the author).

63. Ibid.

64. See Ramsey Clark, telephone interview by the author (July 27, 2010) (on file with the author).

65. Ibid.

66. Dave Zirin, "Don't Remember Muhammad Ali as a Sanctified Sports Hero. He Was a Powerful, Dangerous Political Force," *Los Angeles Times* (June 4, 2016), http://www.latimes.com/opinion/op-ed/la-oe-zirin-muhammad-ali-legacy-20160603-snap-story.html

67. Hampton Dellinger, "When Muhammad Ali Took on America," *Slate* (June 6, 2016), http://www.slate.com/articles/news_and_politics/jurisprudence/2016/06/what_muhammad_ali_won_in_his_supreme_court_fight_over_the_vietnam_war_and.html

68. Ramsey Clark, telephone interview by the author, (July 27, 2010) (on file with the author).

69. *When We Were Kings*, directed by Leon Gast (Los Angeles: PolyGram Filmed Entertainment, 1996).

70. Ramsey Clark, telephone interview by the author (July 27, 2010) (on file with the author).

71. Ramsey Clark, interview by the author, New York, NY (June 7, 2016) (on file with the author).

72. Ramsey Clark, interview by the author, New York, NY (June 10, 2016) (on file with the author).

73. See David Lamb, "'60s Radical Draws Life in Killing of Deputy," *Los Angeles Times* (March 14, 2002), http://articles.latimes.com/2002/mar/14/news/mn-32824; see also Obaid H. Siddiqui, "Rap Sheet: H. Rap Brown, Civil Rights Revolutionary—Cop Killer or FBI Target?" *Illume* (September 13, 2012).

74. Karima Al-Amin, interview by the author, Clarkston, GA (September 22, 2016) (on file with the author).

75. Ramsey Clark, telephone interview by the author (August 8, 2008) (on file with the author).

76. Roger Wilkins, interview by the author, Washington, DC (July 28, 2009) (on file with the author).

77. Nicholas deB. Katzenbach, telephone interview by the author (June 15, 2011) (on file with the author).

78. Lizzy Ratner, "Ramsey Clark: Why I'm Taking Saddam's Case," *New York Observer* (January 9, 2005), http://observer.com/2005/01/ramsey-clark-why-im-taking-saddams-case/ (quoting Melvin Wulf).

CHAPTER SEVEN

1. Richard Harris, *Justice: The Crisis of Law, Order, and Freedom in America* (New York: Dutton, 1970), 16.

2. Bruce Allen Murphy, *Fortas: The Rise and Ruin of a Supreme Court Justice* (New York: William Morrow, 1988), 296.

3. Ramsey Clark Oral History Interview V (June 3, 1969), by Harri Baker, LBJ Presidential Library, http://www.lbjlibrary.net/assets/documents/archives/oral_histories/clark_r/clark-r5.pdf

4. Murphy, *Fortas,* 336.

5. Ibid., 336.

6. Ibid., 336–337, 338.

7. See, for example, Philip Rucker and Robert Barnes, "As Obama's Nominees Languish in GOP Senate, Trump to Inherit More Than 100 Court Vacancies," *Chicago Tribune* (December 25, 2016), http://www.chicagotribune.com/news/nationworld/politics/ct-trump-court-vacancies-20161225-story.html

8. Murphy, *Fortas*, 337–338.

9. Ibid., 338.

10. Ibid., 338–339.

11. Ibid., 339.

12. Ibid., 339–340.

13. Ibid., 340–341.

14. Ibid., 341.

15. Ibid.

16. Ibid., 342–343.

17. Ibid., 346.

18. Ibid., 349–350; Robert Dallek, *Flawed Giant: Lyndon Johnson and His Times 1961–1973* (New York: Oxford University Press, 1998), 560–561; Larry Temple, interview by the author, Austin, TX (March 24, 2011) (on file with the author).

19. Murphy, *Fortas*, 349.

20. Ibid., 352.

21. Ibid., 356.

22. Ibid., 356, 358.

23. Dallek, *Flawed Giant*, 560–561.

24. Michael Flamm, *Law and Order: Street Crime, Civil Unrest, and the Crisis of Liberalism in the 1960s* (New York: Columbia University Press, 2005), 155.

25. Harris, *Justice*, 16.

26. Ibid., 17 (quoting Ramsey Clark).

27. W. Marvin Watson with Sherwin Markman, *Chief of Staff: Lyndon Johnson and His Presidency* (New York: Thomas Dunne Books, 2004), 296.

28. Ibid.

29. Ibid., 297.

30. Ibid. (quoting Mayor Daley).

31. Ibid.; Bruce A. Ragsdale, *The Chicago Seven: 1960s Radicalism in the Federal Courts* (Federal Judicial Center, 2008), 2, https://www.fjc.gov/sites/default/files/trials/chicago7.pdf

32. Ragsdale, *The Chicago Seven*.

33. David J. Langum, *William M. Kunstler: The Most Hated Lawyer in America* (New York: New York University Press, 1999), 102.

34. Ibid., 2–3.

35. Ibid.

36. Flamm, 157 (quoting Norman Mailer).

37. Ragsdale, *The Chicago Seven.*

38. Harris, *Justice,* 69.

39. Langum, *William M. Kunstler,* 103.

40. Harris, *Justice,* 69.

41. Ramsey Clark, telephone interview by the author (July 27, 2010) (on file with the author).

42. Harris, *Justice,* 69.

43. Ragsdale, *The Chicago Seven.*

44. Langum, *William M. Kunstler,* 101–103.

45. Harris, *Justice,* 65.

46. Langum, *William M. Kunstler,* 103.

47. Ramsey Clark, telephone interview by the author (July 27, 2010) (on file with the author); Langum, *William M. Kunstler,* 102.

48. Langum, *William M. Kunstler,* 104.

49. Ibid., 100, 108.

50. Ibid., 106–109.

51. Ibid., 106–107, 111–112.

52. Ibid., 112.

53. Ibid., 114.

54. Ibid.

55. Ibid., 114–115.

56. "Too Prominent to Be Relevant," *Time Magazine* (February 9, 1970), 42.

57. Langum, *William M. Kunstler,* 118–120.

58. Ramsey Clark, telephone interview by the author (July 27, 2010) (on file with the author).

59. Ibid.

60. "Clark Hits 'Deadly Force,'" *Akron Beacon Journal* (April 18, 1968).

61. See, for example, Ramsey Clark, *Crime in America: Observations on Its Nature, Causes, Prevention and Control* (New York: Simon & Schuster, 1970), 188.

62. Ramsey Clark Oral History Interview V (June 3, 1969).

63. Ibid.

64. Jack Bass and Jack Nelson, *The Orangeburg Massacre* (New York: World Press, 1970), 65–77; Clark, *Crime in America,* 176.

65. Clark, *Crime in America,* 176; Bass and Nelson, *Orangeburg Massacre,* 76–137.

66. Bass and Nelson, *The Orangeburg Massacre,* 180.

67. Ibid., 101, 180.

68. Ibid., 226 (quoting Ramsey Clark).

69. George Edwards, *The Police on the Urban Frontier* (foreword by Ramsey Clark) (New York: Institute of Human Relations, 1968), viii.

70. Tom Wicker, "Ramsey Clark: A Candid Conversation with the Civil-Libertarian Ex-Attorney General," *Playboy Magazine* (August 1969), 62 (quoting Ramsey Clark).

71. Ramsey Clark Oral History Interview V (June 3, 1969).

72. Wicker, "Ramsey Clark: A Candid Conversation with the Civil-Libertarian Ex-Attorney General," 53 (quoting Baltimore's police commissioner).

73. "The Challenge of Crime in a Free Society," a report by the President's Commission on Law Enforcement and Administration of Justice (1967), https://assets.documentcloud.org/documents/3932081/Crimecommishreport.pdf

74. Larry Temple, interview by the author, Austin, TX (March 24, 2011) (on file with the author).

75. Harris, *Justice*, 128.

76. Larry Temple, interview by the author, Austin, TX (March 24, 2011) (on file with the author).

77. Ramsey Clark Oral History Interview V (June 3, 1969).

78. Ibid.; Harry McPherson Oral History Interview V (April 9, 1969), by T. H. Baker, LBJ Presidential Library, http://www.lbjlibrary.net/assets/documents/archives/oral_histories/mcpherson/mcpher05.pdf

79. Jack Rosenthal, telephone interview by the author (July 20, 2016) (on file with the author).

80. Ibid.

CHAPTER EIGHT

1. Ramsey Clark, "We Have Become Soft on Truth," *Britannica Roundtable* 2, no. 3 (1973), 6.

2. Richard Harris, *Justice: The Crisis of Law, Order, and Freedom in America* (New York: Dutton, 1970), 16.

3. Alexander Wohl, *Father, Son, and Constitution: How Justice Tom Clark and Attorney General Ramsey Clark Shaped American Democracy* (Lawrence: University Press of Kansas, 2013), 374–375.

4. Ramsey Clark, *Crime in America: Observations on Its Nature, Causes, Prevention and Control* (New York: Simon & Schuster, 1970); Josh Getlin, "For a Politician, Former U.S. Attorney General Ramsey Clark Took a Road Less Traveled—a Hard Left into the Hotbed of Human Rights Causes: Loner of the Left," *Los Angeles Times* (February 18, 1990), http://articles.latimes.com/1990-02-18/news/vw-1604_1_ramsey-clark

5. Clark, *Crime in America*, 94–97, 222.

6. Josh Saunders, "Ramsey Clark's Prosecution Complex: How Did Lyndon Johnson's Attorney General Come to Defend Dictators, War Criminals, and Terrorists?" *Legal Affairs* (November–December 2003), 46.

7. Ibid. (noting that fellow antiwar activist David McReynolds and former law partner Melvin Wulf both believe that "Clark may have felt guilty enough about the prosecution [of the Boston Five] that he decided to spend his career doing penance").

8. Transcript of *Face the Nation* (May 23, 1971), *CBS*, 5, in "Face the Nation Transcript," in Personal Papers of Ramsey Clark, Box 313, LBJ Presidential Library.

9. "An Interview with Ramsey Clark," *ADA World Magazine* (May–June 1971), 3.

10. Ramsey Clark, interview by the author, New York, NY (November 8, 2008) (on file with the author).

11. James W. Clinton, *The Loyal Opposition: Americans in North Vietnam, 1965–1972* (Niwot: University Press of Colorado, 1995), 255 (quoting Ramsey Clark).

12. Ibid., 257.

13. Ramsey Clark, "Ramsey Clark on the Impact of Bombing," *Washington Post*, in Personal Papers of Ramsey Clark, Box 249, LBJ Presidential Library.

14. Ibid.

15. Ramsey Clark, *American Report* (October 25, 1971), 4, in Personal Papers of Ramsey Clark, Box 171, LBJ Presidential Library.

16. "The War as a Campaign Issue," *Washington Post* (August 16, 1972). See also "Messenger from Hanoi," *The Evening Star and the Washington Daily News* (August 15, 1972).

17. "Clark, in Hanoi, Is Said to Find U.S. Prisoners in Good Health," *New York Times* (August 13, 1972).

18. Ibid.

19. "Clark Describes 'Good' POW Camp," *The Evening Star and the Washington Daily News* (August 15, 1972).

20. See Clinton, *The Loyal Opposition*, 256–259.

21. Ramsey Clark, interview by the author, New York, NY (November 8, 2008) (on file with the author).

22. Clinton, *The Loyal Opposition*, 256.

23. "Repudiate Clark, McGovern Told," UPI (undated), in Personal Papers of Ramsey Clark, Box 249, LBJ Presidential Library.

24. Tim O'Brien, "Ramsey Clark Airings Called 'Contemptible,'" *Washington Post* (August 12, 1972).

25. Sanford J. Ungar, "U.S. Sees No Law Violation by Clark, Salinger Overseas," *Washington Post* (August 23, 1972).

26. Letter from Mrs. Marie Taylor to Ramsey Clark (August 15, 1972), in Personal Papers of Ramsey Clark, Box 170, LBJ Presidential Library.

27. Letter from Mrs. Barbara Olson to Ramsey Clark (undated), in Personal Papers of Ramsey Clark, Box 248, LBJ Presidential Library.

28. Note (unsigned, undated), in Personal Papers of Ramsey Clark, Box 248, LBJ Presidential Library.

29. Ibid.

30. Letter from Lt. Col. Edison W. Miller, U.S.M.C., to Ramsey Clark (May 8, 1973), in Personal Papers of Ramsey Clark, Box 248, LBJ Presidential Library.

31. "Wife of POW Praises Clark for N. Viet Visit," *Los Angeles Times* (August 17, 1972).

32. Note from Jane Fonda to Ramsey Clark (undated), in Personal Papers of Ramsey Clark, Box 248, LBJ Presidential Library.

33. Deb Kiner, "Harrisburg 7 Conspiracy Verdict Came 45 Years Ago Today," *Pennlive* (April 5, 2017), http://www.pennlive.com/life/2017/04/harrisburg_7_conspiracy_verdic.html

34. "A Justice Department Official Named to Prosecute Berrigan," *New York Times* (March 10, 1971), https://www.nytimes.com/1971/03/10/archives/a-justice-department-official-named-to-prosecute-berrigan.html

35. Ramsey Clark, telephone interview by the author (July 26, 2010) (on file with the author).

36. Ibid.

37. Wohl, *Father, Son, and Constitution*, 383.

38. Homer Bigart, "Berrigan Defense Calls No Witnesses and Rests Its Case," *New York Times* (March 25, 1972), https://www.nytimes.com/1972/03/25/archives/berrigan-defense-calls-no-witnesses-and-rests-its-case-defense.html

39. "Jury Deadlocked on Harrisburg 7," *Cornell Daily Sun* (April 6, 1972), http://cdsun.library.cornell.edu/?a=d&d=CDS19720406&

40. "'My God! They're Killing Us': Newsweek's 1970 Coverage of the Kent State Shooting," *Newsweek* (May 4, 2015), https://www.newsweek.com/my-god-theyre-killing-us-our-1970-coverage-kent-state-328108; John Kifner, "4 Kent State Students Killed by Troops," *New York Times* (May 5, 1970), http://movies2.nytimes.com/learning/general/onthisday/big/0504.html

41. Kifner, "4 Kent State Students Killed by Troops."

42. Ibid.

43. "'My God! They're Killing Us.'"

44. Agis Salpukas, "Judge Acquits Guardsmen in Slayings at Kent State," *New York Times* (November 9, 1974), https://www.nytimes.com/1974/11/09/archives/judge-acquits-guardsmen-in-slayings-at-kent-state-judge-acquits.html

45. David J. Langum, *William M. Kunstler: The Most Hated Lawyer in America* (New York: New York University Press, 1999), 224.

46. "The Selective Service System: Its Operation, Practices, and Procedures: Hearings Before the Subcommittee on Administrative Practice and Procedure of the Committee on the Judiciary," U.S. Senate, 91st Congress (November 3, 1969), 139.

47. Ibid., 142–143.

48. Ibid., 149.

49. Ibid., 144.

50. William F. Buckley, Jr., "Amnesty, with Ramsey Clark," *Firing Line* (June 3, 1974), Hoover Institution Video Library, Stanford University, https://youtu.be/u2CCBPSvKFg

51. Ibid.

52. Ibid.

53. See Ramsey Clark, "Libya, Grenada and Reagan," *The Nation* (May 3, 1986), 604, https://www.thefreelibrary.com/Libya%2C+Grenada+and+Reagan.-a04838994

54. Peter Carlson, "The Crusader," *Washington Post* (December 15, 2002), https://www.washingtonpost.com/archive/lifestyle/2002/12/15/the-crusader/9de49dd7-43fd-45e0-a4ef-3df4475cb4a0/?noredirect=on&utm_term=.463341d9223d

55. Bob Schwartz, telephone interview by the author, (September 8, 2016) (on file with the author).

56. Carlson, "The Crusader."

57. Ibid.

58. Tom Wicker, "Ramsey Clark: A Candid Conversation with the Civil-Libertarian Ex-Attorney General," *Playboy Magazine* (August 1969), 58.

59. Claudia Dreifus, "The Progressive Interview: Ramsey Clark," *Progressive* 55, no. 4 (April 1991), 32.

60. Derrick Jensen, "Neighborhood Bully: Ramsey Clark on American Militarism," *The Sun Magazine* (August 2001), https://www.thesunmagazine.org/issues/308/neighborhood-bully

61. See Reports by UN Food and Agricultural Organization, Ramsey Clark, and World Leaders, *The Impact of Sanctions on Iraq: The Children Are Dying* (International Action Center, 2nd edition 1998), 6–8.

62. Ibid., 1.

63. Mary C. Schneidau, "Former AG Defends Hussein Work: Revered for Principle, Reviled for Clients, Clark Says Fair Trial Is a Right," *Dallas Morning News* (December 24, 2005).

64. Wohl, *Father, Son, and Constitution*, 380–381.

65. Mark Green, *Bright, Infinite Future: A Generational Memoir on the Progressive Rise*

(New York: St. Martin's Press, 2016), 133.

66. Lois Akner, telephone interview by the author (July 11, 2016) (on file with the author).

67. Green, *Bright, Infinite Future*, 133.

68. Victor Navasky, telephone interview by the author (April 26, 2016) (on file with the author).

69. Victor Navasky, interview by the author, New York, NY (June 7, 2016) (on file with the author).

70. Ibid.

71. Lois Akner, telephone interview by the author (July 11, 2016) (on file with the author).

72. Green, *Bright, Infinite Future*, 134.

73. Victor Navasky, interview by the author, New York, NY (June 7, 2016) (on file with the author).

74. Victor Navasky, telephone interview by the author (April 26, 2016) (on file with the author).

75. Green, *Bright, Infinite Future*, 134.

76. Victor Navasky, interview by the author, New York, NY (June 7, 2016) (on file with the author).

77. John Corry, "Serpico Returns and Nominates Clark for the Senate," *New York Times* (June 15, 1974), https://www.nytimes.com/1974/06/15/archives/serpico-returns-and-nominates-clark-for-senate-serpico-explains.html

78. Ramsey Clark, interview by the author, New York, NY (June 10, 2016) (on file with the author).

79. Ibid.; Minyvonne Burke, "Former NYPD Detective Frank Serpico Reflects on Knapp Commission, Exposing Police Corruption and Today's Issues," *New York Daily News* (May 20, 2017), http://www.nydailynews.com/news/national/frank-serpico-reflects-knapp-commission-exposing-corruption-article-1.3179229

80. Although Clark hunted some as a child, he had grown to detest guns, which he viewed as being at the center of violence in society. Indeed, even as attorney general, he was an ardent proponent of gun control measures, testifying on various occasions before Congress in support of such legislation. See, for example, "The Proposed Federal Gun Registration and Licensing Act of 1968: Hearing Before the Subcommittee to Investigate Juvenile Delinquency of the Senate Judiciary Committee," U.S. Senate, 90th Congress, 2nd session (1968) (statement of Attorney General Ramsey Clark: "Guns have scarred our national character, marking many of the most terrible moments of our history. Destroyer of life, causer of crime, guns threaten our future").

81. Heather Ann Thompson, *Blood in the Water: The Attica Prison Uprising of 1971 and Its Legacy* (New York: Pantheon, 2016), 6, 13–14.

82. Ibid., 30–35, 38–40, 45–48.

83. Ibid., 50–63.

84. Ibid., 69.

85. Ibid., 74, 102–103.

86. Langum, *William M. Kunstler*, 188 (noting that the Attica commission's official report found that "racism, oppression, and injustice were the chief factors underlying the uprising").

87. Thompson, *Blood in the Water*, 78.

88. Langum, *William M. Kunstler*, 205.

89. Ibid., 210, 214.

90. Ibid., 211.

91. Thompson, *Blood in the Water*, 340.

92. Ibid., 342.

93. Ibid., 343–358; Michael T. Kaufman, "Attica Jury Convicts One of Murder, 2d of Assault," *New York Times* (April 6, 1975), https://www.nytimes.com/1975/04/06/archives/attica-jury-convicts-one-of-murder-2d-of-assault-attica-jury-finds.html

94. Langum, *William M. Kunstler*, 214; Kaufman, "Attica Jury Convicts One of Murder, 2d of Assault."

95. Green, *Bright, Infinite Future*, 134.

96. "Remarks by Ramsey Clark, Alumni Reunion to Celebrate the 1974 Ramsey Clark for U.S. Senate Campaign" (November 1, 2012) (video by Lois Akner) (copy on file with the author); Corry, "Serpico Returns and Nominates Clark for the Senate."

97. "Remarks by Ramsey Clark, Alumni Reunion."

98. Ibid.

99. Linda Greenhouse, "Two Democratic Insurgents File Petitions for U.S. Senate Race," *New York Times* (July 16, 1974), https://www.nytimes.com/1974/07/16/archives/two-democratic-insurgents-file-petitions-for-us-senate-race-20000.html

100. Robert Sam Anson, "The Anti-Politician," *New Times* (November 1, 1974), 18.

101. Wohl, *Father, Son, and Constitution*, 391; Rowland Evans and Robert Novak, "Ramsey Clark Threatens Javits' Senate Seat," *St. Petersburg Times* (October 28, 1972).

102. Green, *Bright, Infinite Future*, 135.

103. Ibid., 136–140.

104. Carlson, "The Crusader."

CHAPTER NINE

1. Ramsey Clark, *Crime in America: Observations on Its Nature, Causes, Prevention and Control* (New York: Simon & Schuster, 1970), 341.

2. Magee's story is fascinating and complex, worthy of book-length treatment itself in Clark's estimation; but here I will only cover the most salient details related to the backdrop for his involvement.

3. See Nina Strochlic, "Locked Up in Louisiana: Inside America's Bloodiest Prison," *The Daily Beast* (July 28, 2015), https://www.thedailybeast.com/locked-up-in-louisiana-inside-americas-bloodiest-prison

4. Alexandra Close, "Ruchell Magee: The Defense Never Rests," *Ramparts* (June 1973), 21, 22.

5. Ibid., 22.

6. Ibid., 22–23.

7. Ibid., 23.

8. Sol Stern, "The Campaign to Free Angela Davis and Ruchell Magee," *New York Times* (June 27, 1971), https://www.nytimes.com/1971/06/27/archives/the-campaign-to-free-angela-davis-and-ruchell-magee-the-campaign-to.html

9. Ramsey Clark, telephone interview by the author (June 14, 2011) (on file with the author).

10. Ibid.

11. See also Ramsey Clark, "'How Can You Represent That Man?': Ethics, the Rule of Law, and Defending the Indefensible," *Georgia Law Review* 44, no. 4 (2010), 921, 929–930.

12. Stern, "The Campaign to Free Angela Davis and Ruchell Magee."

13. Ibid.

14. Close, "Ruchell Magee: The Defense Never Rests," 22, 24, 62.

15. "Clark Argues for Magee," *News Sentinel* (March 24, 1973).

16. Ibid.; Close, "Ruchell Magee: The Defense Never Rests," 22.

17. Lacey Fosburgh, "Ruchell Magee, Once Angela Davis' Co-Defendant, Gets Life for Kidnapping," *New York Times* (January 24, 1975), https://www.nytimes.com/1975/01/24/archives/ruchell-magee-once-angela-davis-codefendant-gets-life-for.html

18. Ibid.

19. Close, "Ruchell Magee: The Defense Never Rests," 24; see also Clark, "'How Can You Represent that Man?'" 930; Clark, telephone interview by the author (June 14, 2011) (on file with the author).

20. Ramsey Clark, interview by the author, New York, NY (December 16, 2017) (on file with the author); Ramsey Clark, interview by the author, New York, NY (June 7, 2016) (on file with the author).

21. Fosburgh, "Ruchell Magee, Once Angela Davis' Co-Defendant, Gets Life for Kidnapping."

22. "Magee Enters Guilty Plea to Marin Co. Shooting," *Afro-American* (May 14–18, 1974); Fosburgh, "Ruchell Magee, Once Angela Davis' Co-Defendant, Gets Life for Kidnapping"; Ramsey Clark, interview by the author, New York, NY (December 16, 2017) (on file with the author); Ramsey Clark, telephone interview by the author (June 14, 2011) (on file with the author).

23. Ramsey Clark, interview by the author, New York, NY (December 16, 2017) (on file with the author); Ramsey Clark, interview by the author, New York, NY (June 7, 2016) (on file with the author).

24. Fosburgh, "Ruchell Magee, Once Angela Davis' Co-Defendant, Gets Life for Kidnapping."

25. Ramsey Clark, telephone interview by the author (June 14, 2011) (on file with the author).

26. Ibid.

27. See, for example, Jeffrey Mayer, "Ramsey Clark Calls for New Humanism," *Yale News* (March 5, 1971), in Personal Papers of Ramsey Clark, Box 167, LBJ Presidential Library.

28. See also Clark, "'How Can You Represent That Man?'" 927.

29. See Giovanni Russonello, "Fascination and Fear: Covering the Black Panthers, "*New York Times* (October 15, 2016), https://www.nytimes.com/2016/10/16/us/black-panthers-50-years.html; Jeff Cohen and Jeff Gottlieb, "Was Fred Hampton Executed?" *The Nation* (December 25, 1976), https://www.thenation.com/article/was-fred-hampton-executed/

30. See Colbert I. King, "Government Snooping Is a Bipartisan Thing," *Washington Post* (June 15, 2002), https://www.washingtonpost.com/archive/opinions/2002/06/15/government-snooping-is-a-bipartisan-thing/6a672d37-d705-415a-a6a6-3a6d73ae229a/. See also Peniel E. Joseph, *Waiting 'Til the Midnight Hour: A Narrative History of Black Power in America* (New York: Henry Holt, 2006), 187.

31. Russonello, "Fascination and Fear: Covering the Black Panthers."

32. Ibid.

33. Cohen and Gottlieb, "Was Fred Hampton Executed?"

34. Roy Wilkins and Ramsey Clark, *Search and Destroy: A Report by the Commission*

of Inquiry into the Black Panthers and the Police (New York: Metropolitan Applied Research Center, 1973), 4.

35. Ibid.

36. Cohen and Gottlieb, "Was Fred Hampton Executed?"

37. See, for example, Wilkins and Clark, *Search and Destroy*, 12.

38. Cohen and Gottlieb, "Was Fred Hampton Executed?"

39. Memorandum from Herbert O. Reid to Steering Committee, Commission of Inquiry (June 8, 1970), "Commission of Inquiry into Black Panthers," in Personal Papers of Ramsey Clark, Box 171, LBJ Presidential Library.

40. Wilkins and Clark, *Search and Destroy*, 241.

41. Ibid., 35–36, 38.

42. Ibid., 242.

43. Ibid., 240 (refusing to adjudge guilt as such a finding could only be properly rendered by a jury).

44. See Cohen and Gottlieb, "Was Fred Hampton Executed?"

45. See Richard Harris, *Justice: The Crisis of Law, Order, and Freedom in America* (New York: Dutton, 1970), 250.

46. Wilkins and Clark, *Search and Destroy*, 247.

47. Ramsey Clark, telephone interview by the author (July 16, 2010) (on file with the author).

48. Ramsey Clark, interview by the author, New York, NY (June 7, 2016) (on file with the author).

49. Ramsey Clark, interview by the author, New York, NY (December 16, 2017) (on file with the author).

50. "Remarks by Ramsey Clark, Alumni Reunion to Celebrate the 1974 Ramsey Clark for U.S. Senate Campaign" (November 1, 2012) (video by Lois Akner) (copy on file with the author).

CHAPTER TEN

1. Timna Rosenheimer, "'This War Is Genocide'—An Interview with Former US Attorney General Ramsey Clark," *Common Dreams News Center* (January 3, 2003), https://archive.commondreams.org/headlines03/0103-08.htm

2. David Margolick, "The Long and Lonely Journey of Ramsey Clark," *New York Times* (June 14, 1991), https://www.nytimes.com/1991/06/14/washington/the-long-and-lonely-journey-of-ramsey-clark.html (quoting Norman Podhoretz). See also Andrew Maykuth, "Standing Alone," *Philadelphia Inquirer Sunday Magazine* (July 7, 1991), http://www.maykuth.com/Projects/clark91.htm; Ian Williams, "Ramsey Clark, the War Criminal's Best Friend," *Salon* (July 7, 1999), https://www.salon.com/1999/06/21/clark/

3. See, for example, Lizzy Ratner, "Ramsey Clark: Why I'm Taking Saddam's Case," *New York Observer* (January 9, 2005), http://observer.com/2005/01/ramsey-clark-why-im-taking-saddams-case/ (quoting Beth Stevens: "I support many of the causes he supports, but I also vehemently disagree with some of the choices he's made, because I perceive him as thinking that any enemy of the United States is a friend of his, and I think that leads him in to representing people he should not").

4. See Maurice Carroll, "Javits Wins a 4th Term, Defeating Ramsey Clark," *New York Times* (November 4, 1974), https://www.nytimes.com/1974/11/06/archives/javits-wins-a-4th-term-defeating-ramsey-clark-javits-is-victor-in.html

5. Rosenheimer, "'This War Is Genocide.'"

6. Jonathan S. Tobin, "Ramsey Clark Embraces Hamas: Whose Reputation Is Damaged?" *Commentary* (January 5, 2011), https://www.commentarymagazine. com/american-society/ramsey-clark-embraces-hamas-whose-reputation-is-damaged/; "Former US Attorney-General Visits Hamas in Gaza," *Jerusalem Post* (January 5, 2011), https://www.jpost.com/Middle-East/Former-US-attorney-general-visits -Hamas-leader-in-Gaza

7. Margolick, "The Long and Lonely Journey of Ramsey Clark" (quoting Ramsey Clark).

8. *United States v. Linnas*, 527 F. Supp. 426, 430, 434 (E.D.N.Y. 1981); *Linnas v. INS*, 790 F.2d 1024, 1026–1027 (2d Cir. 1986).

9. *Linnas v. INS*, 790 F.2d 1024, 1026–1027 (2d Cir. 1986); John B. Judis, "The Strange Case of Ramsey Clark," *New Republic* (April 22, 1991), 23, 29.

10. *United States v. Linnas*, 527 F. Supp. 426, 435–436 (E.D.N.Y. 1981).

11. Ibid., 438.

12. Ibid., 437.

13. Ibid., 437–438.

14. Ibid., 428.

15. *Linnas v. INS*, 790 F.2d 1024, 1027 (2d Cir. 1986).

16. Ibid., 1027–1028; Petition for Writ of Certiorari at *6, *30–31, *Linnas v. INS*, No. 86-336, 1986 WL 766707 (U.S. August 29, 1986).

17. Petition for Writ of Certiorari at *i, *Linnas v. INS*, No. 86-336, 1986 WL 766707 (U.S. August 29, 1986).

18. *Linnas v. INS*, 790 F.2d 1024, 1028, 1032 (2d Cir. 1986).

19. Petition for Writ of Certiorari at *1, *Linnas v. INS*, No. 86-336, 1986 WL 766707 (U.S. August 29, 1986).

20. Ibid., *27.

21. Ibid., *30–31.

22. John F. Burns, "In Defending Hussein, an American Contrarian Seeks to Set the Historical Record Straight," *New York Times* (December 6, 2005), https:// www.nytimes.com/2005/12/06/world/middleeast/in-defending-hussein-an -american-contrarian-seeks-to-set.html

23. Petition for Writ of Certiorari at *i–ii, 37–39, 41, *Linnas v. INS*, No. 86-336, 1986 WL 766707 (U.S. August 29, 1986).

24. Ibid., *41.

25. Ibid., *36–38.

26. Ibid., *30–31.

27. Ibid., *43–44.

28. Josh Getlin, "For a Politician, Former U.S. Attorney General Ramsey Clark Took a Road Less Traveled—a Hard Left into the Hotbed of Human Rights Causes: Loner of the Left," *Los Angeles Times* (February 18, 1990), http://articles .latimes.com/1990-02-18/news/vw-1604_1_ramsey-clark

29. Margolick, "The Long and Lonely Journey of Ramsey Clark"; Jared Israel and Nico Varkevisser, "How Ramsey Clark Championed Baltic Nazi War Criminals . . . and He's Still Doing It," *Emperor's Clothes* (June 19, 2003), tenc.net/ramsey/ramsey4.htm

30. Howell Raines, "The Birmingham Bombing," *New York Time* (July 24, 1983), https://www.nytimes.com/1983/07/24/magazine/the-birmingham -bombing.html

31. *U.S. v. Reimer*, 356 F.3d 456 (2d Cir. 2004); Benjamin Weiser, "Reporter's Notebook: Former Attorney General Defending a Brooklyn Man in Nazi War Crimes," *New York Times* (August 9, 1998), https://www.nytimes.com/1998/08/09/nyregion/reporter-s-notebook-former-attorney-general-defending-brooklyn-man-nazi-war.html

32. "Suspected Terrorist Surrenders," *New York Times* (August 23, 1979), https://www.nytimes.com/1979/08/23/archives/suspected-terrorist-surrenders.html; "Arab Extradited from U.S. Indicted as Terrorist in Israel," *New York Times* (December 14, 1981), https://www.nytimes.com/1981/12/14/world/arab-extradited-from-us-indicted-as-terrorist-in-israel.html

33. "Arab Extradited from U.S. Indicted as Terrorist in Israel."

34. Abdeen Jabara, interview by the author, New York, NY (June 11, 2016) (on file with the author).

35. Deirdre Sinnott, "Ramsey Clark: A Life of Action," *Ramsey Clark 85 International Action Center 20 Gala* (January 11, 2013), 7, http://www.deirdresinnott.com/Clark_85th_Birthday_Gala-Bio.pdf

36. Abdeen Jabara, interview by the author, New York, NY (June 11, 2016) (on file with the author).

37. Ibid.

38. *Eain v. Wilkes*, 641 F.2d 504, 518 (1981).

39. Ibid.

40. Ibid., 520.

41. Ibid., 521.

42. Lucia Muoat, "One Man's Struggle to Avoid Extradition by US to Israel," *Christian Science Monitor* (March 5, 1981), https://www.csmonitor.com/1981/0305/030545.html

43. Abdeen Jabara, interview by the author, New York, NY (June 11, 2016) (on file with the author).

44. Abdeen Jabara, interview by the author, New York, NY (December 16, 2017) (on file with the author).

45. Maykuth, "Standing Alone" (noting that some thought Clark sympathized with "virulent anti-Semitic positions" of those he chose to defend).

46. Kenneth Reich, "Clark Fires Back at Jewish Group: He Says L.A. Federation Is 'Politicizing Human Rights,'" *Los Angeles Times* (March 26, 1987), http://articles.latimes.com/1987-03-26/news/mn-427_1_human-rights

47. Emanuel Perlmutter, "Javits Scores U.N. Role for Palestine Group," *New York Times* (October 16, 1974), https://www.nytimes.com/1974/10/16/archives/javits-scores-u-n-role-for-palestine-group-clark-is-applauded.html

48. John Corcoran, "Ramsey Clark Speaks on Middle East Issues," *Philadelphia Inquirer* (March 30, 1989) (copy on file with the author).

49. Getlin, "For a Politician, Former U.S. Attorney General Ramsey Clark Took a Road Less Traveled" (quoting Ramsey Clark).

50. *Klinghoffer v. Achille Lauro*, 937 F.2d 44, 47 (2d Cir. 1991).

51. Ibid.

52. Anti-Terrorism Act of 1987, Pub. L. No. 100-204, Title X, 101 Stat. 1406–1407 (codified at 22 U.S.C.A. §§ 5201–5203 (West Supp. 1987)).

53. See, for example, *Estate of Ungar v. PLO and Palestinian Authority*, C.A. No. 00-105L (D.R.I.); *Sokolow v. Palestinian Authority and PLO*, No. 04-CV-397 (GBD) (S.D.N.Y.); *Gilmore v. Palestinian Authority and PLO*, 01-CV-0853GK (D.D.C.).

54. Letter from Rafiq Husseini, Chief of Staff, Office of the President, Palestinian National Authority, to Ramsey Clark (May 17, 2007), in Ramsey Clark Papers, Dolph Briscoe Center for American History, University of Texas–Austin, Box 2016-086/142.

55. Judis, "The Strange Case of Ramsey Clark," 23, 26, 29.

56. Joseph P. Fried, "The Terror Conspiracy: The Overview; Sheik and 9 Followers Guilty of a Conspiracy of Terrorism, *New York Times* (October 2, 1995), https://www.nytimes.com/1995/10/02/nyregion/terror-conspiracy-overview-sheik-9-followers-guilty-conspiracy-terrorism.html

57. Josh Saunders, "Ramsey Clark's Prosecution Complex: How Did Lyndon Johnson's Attorney General Come to Defend Dictators, War Criminals, and Terrorists?" *Legal Affairs* (November–December 2003), 43.

58. *Andrade v. Chojnacki*, 65 F. Supp. 2d 431, 441 (W.D. Tex. 1999).

59. Ibid., 442

60. Ibid., 441.

61. Ibid., 441–442.

62. Ibid., 442.

63. Ibid., 442–443.

64. Ibid., 443–444.

65. Ibid., 445.

66. Ibid., 445–446.

67. Ibid., 446.

68. Ross E. Milloy, "Jury Finds for U.S. in Deaths at Waco," *New York Times* (July 15, 2000), https://www.nytimes.com/2000/07/15/us/jury-finds-for-us-in-deaths-at-waco.html

69. *Andrade v. Chojnacki* (W.D. Tex.), trial transcript (July 14, 2000), 3193.

70. Ibid., 3193–3194.

71. "Supreme Court Turns Down Waco Case," *NBC News* (March 22, 2004), http://www.nbcnews.com/id/4579805/ns/us_news/t/supreme-court-turns-down-waco-case/

72. Milloy, "Jury Finds for U.S. in Deaths at Waco" (quoting Ramsey Clark).

73. Bob Schwartz, telephone interview by the author (September 8, 2016) (on file with the author).

74. Victor Navasky, telephone interview by the author (April 16, 2016) (on file with the author).

75. Margolick, "The Long and Lonely Journey of Ramsey Clark"; Stephen Pollak, telephone interview by the author (August 3, 2011) (on file with the author).

76. Margolick, "The Long and Lonely Journey of Ramsey Clark."

77. Stephen Pollak, telephone interview by the author (August 3, 2011) (on file with the author).

78. Kenneth Reich, "Jewish Group Cancels Talk by Ramsey Clark," *Los Angeles Times* (March 25, 1987), http://articles.latimes.com/1987-03-25/news/mn-268_1_ramsey-clark

79. Reich, "Clark Fires Back at Jewish Group" (quoting Ramsey Clark).

80. Ibid.

81. Ibid.

CHAPTER ELEVEN

1. *Today Show*, Interview of Ramsey Clark by Katie Couric, NBC (December 2005).

2. Erica Goode, "Stalin to Saddam: So Much for the Madman Theory," *New York Times* (May 4, 2003), https://www.nytimes.com/2003/05/04/weekinreview/the-world-stalin-to-saddam-so-much-for-the-madman-theory.html

3. "List of Saddam's Crimes Is Long," *ABC News* (December 30, 2006), https://abcnews.go.com/WNT/IraqCoverage/story?id=2761722&page=1

4. See generally Lonnie T. Brown, Jr., "Representing Saddam Hussein: The Importance of Being Ramsey Clark," *Georgia Law Review* 42, no. 1 (2007), 47–129. Some content of the current chapter was excerpted or derived from portions of this article.

5. Michael Rubin, "Relearning the Iran Crisis' Lessons," *Commentary* (November 4, 2016), https://www.commentarymagazine.com/foreign-policy/middle-east/iran/relearning-iran-crisis-lessons/

6. Stuart Auerbach, "Iran's Anti-U.S. Conference Call for Peaceful End to Crisis," *Washington Post* (June 6, 1980), https://www.washingtonpost.com/archive/politics/1980/06/06/irans-anti-us-conference-calls-for-peaceful-end-to-crisis/209f9a7a-d56f-4647-a76f-a8f8bc4b5df2/?utm_term=.ee599c81d255; John H. Richardson, "How the Attorney General of the United States Became Saddam Hussein's Lawyer," *Esquire* (February 1, 2007), https://archive.esquire.com/article/2007/2/1/how-the-attorney-general-of-the-united-states-became-saddam-husseins-lawyer

7. Ramsey Clark, "'How Can You Represent That Man?' Ethics, the Rule of Law, and Defending the Indefensible," *Georgia Law Review* 44, no. 4 (2010), 921, 931.

8. "Iranian Political Factions Dispute Clark's Trip and Trials for Hostages," *Washington Post* (June 7, 1980), https://www.washingtonpost.com/archive/politics/1980/06/07/iranian-political-factions-dispute-clarks-trip-and-trials-for-hostages/b8003baa-25fc-4de4-a379-2f3aa472d0d5/?utm_term=.013c5d746e1e

9. Robert Pear, "Clark Is Not Facing U.S. Criminal Action," *New York Times* (January 8, 1981), https://www.nytimes.com/1981/01/08/world/clark-is-not-facing-us-criminal-action.html; Richardson, "How the Attorney General of the United States Became Saddam Hussein's Lawyer."

10. See Kevin Drum, "Flashback: Why Ronald Reagan Invaded Grenada," *Mother Jones* (March 6, 2014), https://www.motherjones.com/kevin-drum/2014/03/flashback-why-ronald-reagan-invaded-grenada/

11. Rick Atkinson, "Estimates of Casualties in Grenada Are Raised," *Washington Post* (November 9, 1983), https://www.washingtonpost.com/archive/politics/1983/11/09/estimates-of-casualties-in-grenada-are-raised/9fedcefc-0ead-437c-84f5-170bac27d9c4/?noredirect=on&utm_term=.7d10c3bb6506; "Brother of Grenadian Says Contact Is Denied," *New York Times* (November 15, 1983), https://www.nytimes.com/1983/11/15/world/brother-of-grenadian-says-contact-is-denied.html; Anthony Lewis, "Abroad at Home: The American Way," *New York Times* (November 17, 1983), https://www.nytimes.com/1983/11/17/opinion/abroad-at-home-the-american-way.html

12. Lewis, "Abroad at Home: The American Way."

13. Ramsey Clark, "Libya, Grenada and Reagan," *The Nation* (May 3, 1986), https://www.thefreelibrary.com/Libya%2C+Grenada+and+Reagan.-a04838994

14. See Linda Straker, "7 Convicted of Killing Grenada Leader Released," *San*

Diego Union Tribune (September 5, 2009), http://www.sandiegouniontribune
.com/sdut-cb-grenada-coup-prisoners-090509-2009sep05-story.html

15. Ramsey Clark, "Libyan Epilogue," *The Nation* (July 12, 1986), https://www.
thenation.com/article/libyan-epilogue/; Anthony D'Amato, "Comment: The Imposition
of Attorney Sanctions for Claims Arising from the U.S. Air Raid on Libya," *American
Journal of International Law* 84, no. 3 (1990), 705.

16. Judis, "The Strange Case of Ramsey Clark," 28.

17. See generally Clark, "Libyan Epilogue," 5.

18. *Saltany v. Reagan*, 702 F. Supp. 319 (D.D.C. 1988), *aff'd in part, rev'd in part*,
886 F.2d 438 (D.C. Cir. 1989); "U.S. Compensation for Libya Raid Sought," *Los Angeles
Times* (April 16, 1987), http://articles.latimes.com/1987-04-16/news/mn-734_1_libya-
raid-compensation

19. *Saltany v. Reagan*, 702 F. Supp. 319, 320 (D.D.C. 1988), *aff'd in part, rev'd in
part*, 886 F.2d 438 (D.C. Cir. 1989).

20. Ibid., 322.

21. Ibid.

22. *Saltany v. Reagan*, 886 F.2d 438, 440 (D.C. Cir. 1989).

23. Ibid.

24. Glenn Kessler, "Libya's Final Payment to Victim's Fund Clears
Way for Normal U.S. Ties," *Washington Post* (November 1, 2008), http://www
.washingtonpost.com/wp-dyn/content/article/2008/10/31/AR2008103103616
.html. Libya paid $1.5 billion of a $1.8-billion fund that was used to settle claims of U.S.
victims of terrorism, as well as those of the Libyan victims of the 1986 U.S. attack. The
Libyan victims received $300 million, contributed from U.S. sources, though not individual
taxpayers. Ibid. See also Clark, "'How Can You Represent That Man?'" 932.

25. Clark, "Libya, Grenada and Reagan," 605.

26. Ibid.

27. John T. Elliff, *Crime, Dissent, and the Attorney General: The Justice Department in
the 1960's* (Beverly Hills: Sage Publications, 1971), 237.

28. Martin Luther King, Jr., "Beyond Vietnam" (address delivered to the Clergy and
Laymen Concerned About Vietnam), Riverside Church, New York, NY (April 4, 1967).

29. Giovanni Russonello, "Fascination and Fear: Covering the Black Panthers," *New
York Times* (October 15, 2016), https://www.nytimes.com/2016/10/16/us/black-panthers-
50-years.html

30. Lizzy Ratner, "Ramsey Clark: Why I'm Taking Saddam's Case," *New York
Observer* (January 9, 2005), http://observer.com/2005/01/ramsey-clark-why-im
-taking-saddams-case/ (quoting Ramsey Clark).

31. Ramsey Clark, "Shedding Light on Ray: Need to Investigate James Earl Ray's Role
in the Assassination of Martin Luther King, Jr.," *The Nation* (March 10, 1997), 5.

32. Andrew Maykuth, "The Tutsis' Faith in a Man of God Proves Fatal," *Andrew
Maykuth Online* (September 9, 1998), www.maykuth.com/projects/rwan4.htm

33. Ibid.; Marlise Simons, "Rwandan Pastor and His Son Are Convicted of Genocide,"
New York Times (February 20, 2003), https://www.nytimes.com/2003/02/20/world/
rwandan-pastor-and-his-son-are-convicted-of-genocide.html

34. Maykuth, "The Tutsis' Faith in a Man of God Proves Fatal."

35. *Ntakirutimana v. Reno*, 184 F.3d 419, 431 (5th Cir. 1999) (Parker, J., concurring)
(emphasis added).

36. Josh Saunders, "Ramsey Clark's Prosecution Complex: How Did Lyndon Johnson's Attorney General Come to Defend Dictators, War Criminals, and Terrorists?" *Legal Affairs* (November–December 2003), 46.

37. Simons, "Rwandan Pastor and His Son Are Convicted of Genocide."

38. John Darnton, "Does the World Still Recognize a Holocaust?" *New York Times* (April 17, 1993), https://www.nytimes.com/1993/04/25/weekinreview/does-the-world-still-recognize-a-holocaust.html

39. David Hearst, Martin Walker, and Richard Norton-Taylor, "Milosevic Indicted for War Crimes, *The Guardian* (May 27, 1999), https://www.theguardian .com/world/1999/may/27/warcrimes.davidhearst

40. Darnton, "Does the World Still Recognize a Holocaust?"

41. Carol J. Williams, "World Leaders Hail Milosevic Arrest as End of Turbulent Era," *Los Angeles Times* (April 2, 2001), http://articles.latimes.com/2001/apr/02/news/mn-45859

42. "American Lawyer to Advise Milosevic," *Los Angeles Times* (November 18, 2001), http://articles.latimes.com/2001/nov/18/news/mn-5621; Ian Black, "Moment of Truth," *The Guardian*, (February 7, 2002), https://www.theguardian.com/world/2002/feb/08/ warcrimes.milosevictrial

43. Peter Carlson, "The Crusader," *Washington Post* (December 15, 2002), https:// www.washingtonpost.com/archive/lifestyle/2002/12/15/the-crusader/9de49dd7 -43fd-45e0-a4ef-3df4475cb4a0/?noredirect=on&utm_term=.463341d9223d (emphasis added).

44. Molly Moore and David Williams, "Milosevic Found Dead in Prison," *Washington Post* (March 12, 2006), http://www.washingtonpost.com/wp-dyn/content/article/2006/03/11/ AR2006031100525.html

45. See Letter from Ramsey Clark to UN Secretary General Kofi Annan in Reference to "The Trial of Slobodan Milosevic, Former President of the Federal Republic of Yugoslavia Before the International Criminal Tribunal for the Former Yugoslavia" (February 12, 2004), http://milosevic.co/icdsm/more/rclarkUN1 .htm; Moore and Williams, "Milosevic Found Dead in Prison."

46. Sean Alfano, "Milosevic Remains Returned Home," *CBS News* (March 18, 2006), http://www.cbsnews.com/news/milosevics-remains-returned-home/

47. Letter from Ramsey Clark to UN Secretary General Kofi Annan in Reference to "The Trial of Slobodan Milosevic."

48. Ibid.

49. Abdeen Jabara, interview by the author, New York, NY (June 11, 2016) (on file with the author).

50. Mary C. Schneidau, "Former AG Defends Hussein Work: Revered for Principle, Reviled for Clients, Clark Says Fair Trial Is a Right," *Dallas Morning News* (December 24, 2004); Richardson, "How the Attorney General of the United States Became Saddam Hussein's Lawyer."

51. Claudia Dreifus, "The Progressive Interview: Ramsey Clark," *Progressive* 55, no. 4 (April 1991), 32.

52. Schneidau, "Former AG Defends Hussein Work"; Clark, "'How Can You Represent That Man?'" 935–936.

53. See generally Ramsey Clark, *The Fire This Time: U.S. War Crimes in the Gulf* (New York: International Action Center, 3rd reprint edition 2002).

54. Andrew Maykuth, "Standing Alone," *Philadelphia Inquirer Sunday Magazine* (July 7, 1991), http://www.maykuth.com/Projects/clark91.htm

55. Clark, *The Fire This Time*, 37, 151.

56. Maykuth, "Standing Alone."

57. Clark, *The Fire This Time*, 61.

58. Ibid.

59. Ramsey Clark, "A Report on U.S. War Crimes Against Iraq to the Commission of Inquiry for International War Crimes Tribunal" (May 1, 1991), https://jacobsm.com/deoxy/deoxy.org/wc/warcrime.htm

60. See Clark, "'How Can You Represent That Man?'" 935.

61. Ratner, "Ramsey Clark: Why I'm Taking Saddam's Case."

62. Letter from ISNAD President Ziyad al-Khasawneh to Ramsey Clark (undated), in Ramsey Clark Papers, Dolph Briscoe Center for American History, University of Texas–Austin, Box 2016-086/28; William Langewiesche, "Ziad for the Defense," *The Atlantic* (June 2005), https://www.theatlantic.com/magazine/archive/2005/06/ziad-for-the-defense/303960/ (observing that Ziad al-Khasawneh "calls the [defense] committee ISNAD, an acronym that reflects some descriptive words, means 'support,' and has a useful religious significance").

63. Letter from Ramsey Clark to President George W. Bush (January 31, 2005), in Ramsey Clark Papers, Dolph Briscoe Center for American History, University of Texas–Austin, Box 2016-086/27.

64. Ibid.

65. Letter from Charles A. Allen, Deputy General Counsel in the Department of Defense, to Ramsey Clark (February 3, 2005), in Ramsey Clark Papers, Dolph Briscoe Center for American History, University of Texas–Austin, Box 2016-086/27.

66. Formation of the Emergency Committee of Iraq (June 15, 2005), in Ramsey Clark Papers, Dolph Briscoe Center for American History, University of Texas–Austin, Box 2016-086/27.

67. Letter from Ramsey Clark to Raghad Saddam Hussein (September 11, 2005), in Ramsey Clark Papers, Dolph Briscoe Center for American History, University of Texas–Austin, Box 2016-086/27.

68. Letter from Raghad Saddam Hussein to Ramsey Clark (May 6, 2005), in Ramsey Clark Papers, Dolph Briscoe Center for American History, University of Texas–Austin, Box 2016-086/27.

69. Letter from Raghad Saddam Hussein to Ramsey Clark (June 13, 2005), in Ramsey Clark Papers, Dolph Briscoe Center for American History, University of Texas–Austin, Box 2016-086/27.

70. Letter from Ramsey Clark to Raghad Saddam Hussein (September 11, 2005), in Ramsey Clark Papers, Dolph Briscoe Center for American History, University of Texas–Austin, Box 2016-086/27.

71. Letter from Ramsey Clark to Raghad Saddam Hussein (December 30, 2006), in Ramsey Clark Papers, Dolph Briscoe Center for American History, University of Texas–Austin, Box 2016-086/28.

72. Letter from Dr. Abdul-Haq Al-Ani to Ramsey Clark (September 10, 2005), in Ramsey Clark Papers, Dolph Briscoe Center for American History, University of Texas–Austin, Box 2016-086/28.

73. "Int'l Saddam Defence Committee Soon," News from Bangladesh, *Daily News Monitoring Service* (June 15, 2005), in Ramsey Clark Papers, Dolph Briscoe Center for American History, University of Texas–Austin, Box 2016-086/27.

74. Statement of Ramsey Clark (June 20, 2005), in Ramsey Clark Papers, Dolph Briscoe

Center for American History, University of Texas–Austin, Box 2016-086/28.

75. Letter from Ramsey Clark to the Honorable Kofi Annan (May 5, 2006), in Ramsey Clark Papers, Dolph Briscoe Center for American History, University of Texas–Austin, Box 2016-086/28. It should be noted that ISNAD disagreed with the approach taken by Hussein's defense team, believing that it would be better to simply boycott the trial in light of the illegitimate nature of the tribunal and Saddam's inevitable *fait accompli*. See Letter from Matthias to Mr. Dolami (February 14, 2006), in Ramsey Clark Papers, Dolph Briscoe Center for American History, University of Texas–Austin, Box 2016-086/28.

76. Letter from Saddam Hussein to the American People (July 7, 2006), in Ramsey Clark Papers, Dolph Briscoe Center for American History, University of Texas–Austin, Box 2016-086/28.

77. Ibid., 6.

78. Ibid., 8.

79. See John F. Burns, "In Defending Hussein, an American Contrarian Seeks to Set the Record Straight," *New York Times* (December 6, 2005), https://www.nytimes.com/2005/12/06/world/middleeast/in-defending-hussein-an-american-contrarian-seeks-to-set.html

80. Letter from Ramsey Clark to Raghad Saddam Hussein (December 30, 2006), in Ramsey Clark Papers, Dolph Briscoe Center for American History, University of Texas–Austin, Box 2016-086/28.

81. "Ramsey Clark: Impossible to Prepare a Defense for Hussein," *CNN* (June 27, 2006), http://www.cnn.com/2006/WORLD/meast/06/27/cnna.clark/index.html

82. Ibid.

83. Ibid.

84. See, for example, Ratner, "Ramsey Clark: Why I'm Taking Saddam's Case"; Letter from Ramsey Clark to the Honorable Kofi Annan (May 5, 2006); Memorandum with Exhibits from Ramsey Clark to UN Ambassador Al-Hussein of the Hashemite Kingdom of Jordan (October 10, 2006), in Ramsey Clark Papers, Dolph Briscoe Center for American History, University of Texas–Austin, Box 2016-086/27.

85. Larry Temple, interview by the author, Austin, TX (March 24, 2011) (on file with the author).

86. For example, television commentator Joe Scarborough rhetorically asked: "Would Saddam Hussein have ever hired Ramsey Clark to defend him if he didn't believe that Ramsey Clark hated America?" *Scarborough Country, MSNBC* (November 28, 2005), http://www.nbcnews.com/id/10254914/ns/msnbc-morning_joe/t/scarborough-country-november/#.Wz56bMInaM8. See also David Margolick, "The Long and Lonely Journey of Ramsey Clark," *New York Times* (June 14, 1991), https://www.nytimes.com/1991/06/14/washington/the-long-and-lonely-journey-of-ramsey-clark.html

87. Ratner, "Ramsey Clark: Why I'm Taking Saddam's Case."

88. Gamal Nkrumah, "Ramsey Clark: A Voice of Reason," *Al-Ahram Weekly* (February 12, 2003), http://weekly.ahram.org.eg/archive/2003/624/profile.htm

89. Russell Goldman, "Assad's History of Chemical Attacks, and Other Atrocities," *New York Times* (April 5, 2017), https://www.nytimes.com/2017/04/05/world/middleeast/syria-bashar-al-assad-atrocities-civilian-deaths-gas-attack.html

90. See also Clark, "'How Can You Represent That Man?'"

91. Richardson, "How the Attorney General of the United States Became Saddam Hussein's Lawyer."

92. See, for example, Timna Rosenheimer, "'This War Is Genocide'—An Interview with Former US Attorney General Ramsey Clark," *Common Dreams News Center* (January 3, 2003), https://archive.commondreams.org/headlines03/0103-08.htm

93. "I Am Ramsey Clark: Lawyer, Activist, and Former Public Official. Ask Me Anything," *Reddit* (March 27, 2015), https://www.reddit.com/r/IAmA/comments/30iozw/i_am_ramsey_clark_lawyer_activist_and_former/

94. Ibid.

95. See also Clark, "'How Can You Represent That Man?'" 937.

CHAPTER TWELVE

1. Ramsey Clark, "The Lawyer's Duty of Loyalty: To the Client or to the Institution?" *Loyola University Law Journal* 16, no. 3 (1985), 469 (quoting *In re Anastaplo*, 366 U.S. 82, 116 (1961) (Black, J., dissenting)).

2. Victor S. Navasky, "Wrong Guy for the Wrong Post at the Wrong Time?" *Saturday Evening Post* (December 16, 1967), 74.

3. Ibid., 75.

4. Victor Navasky, telephone interview by the author (April 26, 2016) (on file with the author).

5. Hampton Sides, *Hellhound on His Trail: The Stalking of Martin Luther King, Jr. and the International Hunt for His Assassin* (New York: Doubleday, 2010), 55 (quoting J. Edgar Hoover, emphasis in original).

6. Victor Navasky, telephone interview by the author (April 26, 2016) (on file with the author).

7. Lois Akner, telephone interview by the author (June 20, 2017) (on file with the author).

8. Larry Temple, interview by the author, Austin, TX (March 24, 2011) (on file with the author).

9. Stephen Pollak, telephone interview by the author (August 3, 2011) (on file with the author).

10. *Forrest Gump*, directed by Robert Zemeckis (Los Angeles: Paramount Pictures, 1994).

11. "Obituary of Georgia Welch Clark," *New York Times* (July 6, 2010), http://query.nytimes.com/gst/fullpage.html?res=9D04E2D8123AF935A35754C0A9669D8B63

12. Pia Welch, telephone interview by the author (September 18, 2017) (on file with the author).

13. Cornelia Grumman, "Wrong Question," *Chicago Tribune Magazine* (November 26, 2000), 14, 24; Ephraim S. London, "Heresy and the Illinois Bar: The Application of George Anastaplo for Admission," *Lawyers Guild Review* 12, no. 4 (Fall 1952).

14. Grumman, "Wrong Question," 16.

15. London, "Heresy and the Illinois Bar"; *In re Anastaplo*, 366 U.S. 82 (1961).

16. Grumman, "Wrong Question"; London, "Heresy and the Illinois Bar."

17. London, "Heresy and the Illinois Bar."

18. See generally ibid.

19. *In re Anastaplo*, 366 U.S. 82 (1961).

20. Grumman, "Wrong Question."

21. *In re Anastaplo*, 366 U.S. 82, 116 (1961) (Black, J., dissenting).

22. Grumman, "Wrong Question," 14, 22.

23. Ibid., 20–22.

24. Ibid., 22.

25. George Anastaplo, interview by the author, Chicago, IL (May 29, 2009) (on file with the author).

26. Ibid.

27. George Anastaplo, interview by the author, Chicago, IL (May 29, 2009) (on file with the author); Clark, "The Lawyer's Duty of Loyalty," 459.

28. Clark, "The Lawyer's Duty of Loyalty," 469 (quoting *In re Anastaplo*, 366 U.S. 82, 116 (1961) (Black, J., dissenting)).

29. Ibid.

30. A copy of the photo of Clark and Beyer may be viewed at http://www .vietnamfulldisclosure.org/bruce-beyer-reflects-d-c-october-20th-1967-1977/

31. Larry Temple, interview by the author, Austin, TX (March 24, 2011) (on file with the author).

32. Ibid.

33. Ibid.

34. Abdeen Jabara, interview by the author, New York, NY (June 11, 2016) (on file with the author).

35. Ibid.

36. Derrick Jensen, "Neighborhood Bully: Ramsey Clark on American Militarism," *The Sun Magazine* (August 2001), https://www.thesunmagazine .org/issues/308/neighborhood-bully

37. See Claudia Dreifus, "The Progressive Interview: Ramsey Clark," *Progressive* 55, no. 4 (April 1991), 32.

38. Larry Temple, interview by the author, Austin, TX (March 24, 2011) (on file with the author).

39. Ibid.

40. John Lewis, with Michael D'Orso, *Walking with the Wind: Memoir of the Movement* (New York: Simon & Schuster, 1998), 256, 261.

41. Ibid., 256–257, 261, 269; Camila Domonoske, "Officials Close Investigation into 1964 'Mississippi Burning' Killings," *NPR* (June 21, 2016), https://www.npr .org/sections/thetwo-way/2016/06/21/482914440/officials-close-investigation -into-1964-mississippi-burning-killings

42. Lewis with D'Orso, *Walking with the Wind*, 265–266.

43. John Blake, "'Mississippi Burning' Murders Still Smolder for One Brother," *CNN* (June 28, 2014), http://www.cnn.com/2014/06/28/us/mississippi -murders/index.html

44. Ibid.

45. Ramsey Clark, interview by the author, New York, NY (November 8, 2010) (on file with the author).

46. Ramsey Clark, interview by the author, New York, NY (January 7, 2016) (on file with the author).

47. Ibid.

48. Ramsey Clark, telephone interview by the author (July 16, 2010) (on file with the author).

49. Ramsey Clark, telephone interview by the author (March 15, 2016) (on file with the author).

50. Ibid.

51. Pia Welch, e-mail message to the author (July 9, 2018) (on file with the author).

52. Ramsey Clark, interview by the author, New York, NY (June 10, 2016) (on file with the author).

53. Ibid.

CHAPTER THIRTEEN

1. "Tributes to Tom C. Clark," *A.B.A. Journal* 63 (August 1977), 1105 (Ramsey Clark loosely quoting "Mourn Not the Dead" by Ralph Chaplin).

2. Victor S. Navasky, "Wrong Guy for the Wrong Post at the Wrong Time?" *Saturday Evening Post* (December 16, 1967), 74, 75. See also Alexander Wohl, *Father, Son, and Constitution: How Justice Tom Clark and Attorney General Ramsey Clark Shaped American Democracy* (Lawrence: University Press of Kansas, 2013), 113–119.

3. Navasky, "Wrong Guy for the Wrong Post at the Wrong Time?" 75.

4. Transcript of *Meet the Press*, NBC (April 19, 1970), 8, in Personal Papers of Ramsey Clark, Box 171, LBJ Presidential Library.

5. Wohl, *Father, Son, and Constitution*, 404.

6. Ramsey Clark, interview by the author, New York, NY (November 8, 2008) (on file with the author).

7. Navasky, "Wrong Guy for the Wrong Post at the Wrong Time?" 77.

8. Ibid.

9. Claudia Dreifus, "The Progressive Interview: Ramsey Clark," *Progressive* 55, no. 4 (April 1991), 32; "I Am Ramsey Clark: Lawyer, Activist, and Former Public Official. Ask Me Anything." *Reddit* (March 27, 2015), https://www.reddit.com/r/IAmA/comments/30iozw/i_am_ramsey_clark_lawyer_activist_and_former/

10. Josh Getlin, "For a Politician, Former U.S. Attorney General Ramsey Clark Took a Road Less Traveled—a Hard Left into the Hotbed of Human Rights Causes: Loner of the Left," *Los Angeles Times* (February 18, 1990), http://articles.latimes.com/1990-02-18/news/vw-1604_1_ramsey-clark

11. Ramsey Clark, telephone interview by the author (March 18, 2011) (on file with the author).

12. Larry Temple, interview by the author, Austin, TX (March 24, 2011) (on file with the author).

13. Ibid.

14. "I Am Ramsey Clark."

15. Tom Wicker, "Ramsey Clark: A Candid Conversation with the Civil-Libertarian Ex-Attorney General," *Playboy Magazine* (August 1969), 74.

16. Ramsey Clark Oral History Interview V (June 3, 1969), by Harri Baker, LBJ Presidential Library, http://www.lbjlibrary.net/assets/documents/archives/oral_histories/clark_r/clark-r5.pdf

17. James W. Clinton, *The Loyal Opposition: Americans in North Vietnam, 1965–1972* (Niwot: University Press of Colorado, 1995), 262.

18. Harry Chapin, "Cat's in the Cradle" (Elektra, 1974).

19. Mimi Clark Gronlund, *Supreme Court Justice Tom C. Clark: A Life of Service* (Austin: University of Texas Press, 2010), 97.

20. Ibid., 98.

21. Wohl, *Father, Son, and Constitution*, 113–124.

22. Transcript of *Meet the Press*, 6–7.

23. Ramsey Clark, *Crime in America: Observations on Its Nature, Causes, Prevention and Control* (New York: Simon & Schuster, 1970), 17.

24. Ibid., 222.

25. Transcript of *Meet the Press*, 4.

26. Wohl, *Father, Son, and Constitution*, 90, 106.

27. Ibid., 90, 106, 122.

28. Larry Temple, interview by the author, Austin, TX (March 24, 2011) (on file with the author).

29. Robert Dallek, *Flawed Giant: Lyndon Johnson and His Times 1961–1973* (New York: Oxford University Press, 1998), 406.

30. Richard Harris, *Justice: The Crisis of Law, Order, and Freedom in America* (New York: Dutton, 1970), 35.

31. Gronlund, *Supreme Court Justice Tom C. Clark*, 106. See also Wohl, *Father, Son, and Constitution*, 82–93.

32. Gronlund, *Supreme Court Justice Tom C. Clark*, 107; Wohl, *Father, Son, and Constitution*, 86.

33. Jack Bass and Jack Nelson, *The Orangeburg Massacre* (New York: World Press, 1970), 65–67, 143–157.

34. Gronlund, *Supreme Court Justice Tom C. Clark*, 107–108; Wohl, *Father, Son, and Constitution*, 85–88.

35. Gronlund, *Supreme Court Justice Tom C. Clark*, 108 (quoting Tom C. Clark).

36. Ibid.

37. "Tom C. Clark, Former Justice, Dies; On the Supreme Court for 18 Years," *New York Times* (June 14, 1977), https://www.nytimes.com/1977/06/14/archives/tom-c-clark-former-justice-dies-on-the-supreme-court-for-18-years.html; Gronlund, *Supreme Court Justice Tom C. Clark*, 111–112; Wohl, *Father, Son, and Constitution*, 87.

38. Gronlund, *Supreme Court Justice Tom C. Clark*, 109–111; Wohl, *Father, Son, and Constitution*, 88–92.

39. See Ramsey Clark Oral History Interview, *C-SPAN* (January 9, 2003), https://www.c-span.org/video/?317441-1/ramsey-clark-oral-history-interivew (referring to Thomas as Tommy and Tom interchangeably in recounting the youngster's interaction with then–Vice President Johnson).

40. Bart Barnes, "Tom C. Clark II, Environmental Lawyer, Dies at 59," *Washington Post* (December 23, 2013), https://www.washingtonpost.com/local/obituaries/tom-c-clark-ii-environmental-lawyer-dies-at-59/2013/12/23/8f84f506-6c03-11e3-b405-7e360f7e9fd2_story.html?utm_term=.f9483f55e190

41. Julie Gronlund, telephone interview by the author (August 26, 2016) (on file with the author).

42. "I Am Ramsey Clark."

43. Ramsey and Whitney Clark, interview by the author, New York, NY (June 10, 2016) (on file with the author).

44. Marie Hagen, telephone interview by the author (October 17, 2008) (on file with the author).

45. David Strachman, telephone interview by the author (April 11, 2011) (on file with the author).

46. Peter Carlson, "The Crusader," *Washington Post* (December 15, 2002), https://www.washingtonpost.com/archive/lifestyle/2002/12/15/the-crusader/9de49dd7-43fd-45e0-a4ef-3df4475cb4a0/?noredirect=on&utm_term=.463341d9223d (quoting Thomas C. Clark, emphasis added).

47. Ramsey Clark, telephone interview by the author (August 19, 2011) (on file with the author).

48. Ibid.

49. Ramsey Clark, telephone interview by the author (September 6, 2011) (on file with the author).

50. Statement of Ramsey Clark (March 11, 1971), "South Africa Trip May 1971," in Personal Papers of Ramsey Clark, Box 245, LBJ Presidential Library; Ramsey Clark, interview by the author, New York, NY (June 7, 2016) (on file with the author).

51. Lester David and Irene David, *Bobby Kennedy: The Making of a Folk Hero* (New York: Dodd, Mead, 1986), 318; Ramsey Clark, interview by the author, New York, NY (June 7, 2016) (on file with the author); Ramsey Clark, interview by the author, New York, NY (June 7, 2016) (on file with the author).

CONCLUSION

1. Ramsey Clark, "Ramsey Clark on the Impact of Bombing," *Washington Post* (August 1972), in Personal Papers of Ramsey Clark, Box 249, LBJ Presidential Library.

2. *Citizen Clark . . . A Life of Principle*, directed by Joseph C. Stillman (Oneonta, NY: La Paloma Films, 2018), https://alifeofprinciple.com

3. Panel discussion following the screening of *Citizen Clark . . . A Life of Principle*, The New School, New York, NY (December 16, 2017), https://www.youtube.com/watch?v=dNAzq3y7wdo

4. David Margolick, "The Long and Lonely Journey of Ramsey Clark," *New York Times* (June 14, 1991), https://www.nytimes.com/1991/06/14/washington/the-long-and-lonely-journey-of-ramsey-clark.html

5. Deborah Hastings, "The Life and Times of Ramsey Clark," *Free Republic* (April 29, 2006), http://www.freerepublic.com/focus/f-news/1623980/posts (observing that Clark "has been called misguided, a traitor, a Communist and a fool"); Adam Sparks, "Ramsey Clark: An American Traitor," *News Max* (March 4, 2003), http://www.freerepublic.com/focus/news/860295/posts; Ian Williams, "Ramsey Clark, the War Criminal's Best Friend," *Salon* (July 7, 1999), https://www.salon.com/1999/06/21/clark/

6. John Seigenthaler, telephone interview by the author (July 7, 2011) (on file with the author).

7. Claudia Dreifus, "The Progressive Interview: Ramsey Clark," *Progressive* 55, no. 4 (April 1991), 32; Derrick Jensen, "Neighborhood Bully: Ramsey Clark on American Militarism," *The Sun Magazine* (August 2001), https://www.thesunmagazine.org/issues/308/neighborhood-bully

8. See Josh Getlin, "For a Politician, Former U.S. Attorney General Ramsey Clark Took a Road Less Traveled—a Hard Left into the Hotbed of Human Rights Causes: Loner of the Left," *Los Angeles Times* (February 18, 1990), http://articles.latimes.com/1990-02-18/news/vw-1604_1_ramsey-clark

9. Margolick, "The Long and Lonely Journey of Ramsey Clark" (quoting Nicholas deB. Katzenbach).

10. Ramsey Clark, telephone interview by the author (March 18, 2011) (on file with the author).

11. John H. Richardson, "How the Attorney General of the United States Became Saddam Hussein's Lawyer," *Esquire* (February 1, 2007), https://archive .esquire.com/article/2007/2/1/how-the-attorney-general-of-the-united-states -became-saddam-husseins-lawyer (observing that "[j]udging from the raw spew of the Internet, [Clark] could be the single most hated man in America").

12. Ramsey Clark, telephone interview by the author (December 18, 2016) (on file with the author).

13. Ibid.

14. Ibid.

15. See Ramsey Clark, "Address at the United National Antiwar Committee Rally," New York, NY (April 9, 2011), https://www.youtube.com/watch?v=lubd9ZRX5to

16. *In re Anastaplo*, 366 U.S. 82, 116 (1961) (Black, J., dissenting).

17. Lizzy Ratner, "Ramsey Clark: Why I'm Taking Saddam's Case," *New York Observer* (January 9, 2005), http://observer.com/2005/01/ramsey-clark -why-im-taking-saddams-case

18. Thomas Hauser, *Muhammad Ali: His Life and Times* (New York: Simon & Schuster, 1991), 514 (quoting Ramsey Clark).

SELECTED BIBLIOGRAPHY

BOOKS AND CHAPTERS

Alexander, Michelle. *The New Jim Crow: Mass Incarceration in the Age of Colorblindness.* New York: New Press, revised edition 2012.

Ash, Russell. *The Top Ten of Everything.* London, New York: DK Publishing, 1994.

Bass, Jack, and Jack Nelson. *The Orangeburg Massacre.* New York: World Press, 1970.

Branch, Taylor. *At Canaan's Edge: America in the King Years—1965–68.* New York: Simon & Schuster, 2006.

Brophy, Alfred L. *Reconstructing the Dreamland: The Tulsa Riot of 1921: Race, Reparation, and Reconciliation.* New York: Oxford University Press, 2002.

Carmichael, Stokely. "Berkeley Speech" (October 1966). In *Stokely Speaks: Black Power Back to Pan-Africanism,* edited by Ethel N. Minor. New York: Random House, 1971.

Carmichael, Stokely. "The Dialectics of Liberation" (July 18, 1967). In *Stokely Speaks: Black Power Back to Pan-Africanism,* edited by Ethel N. Minor. New York: Random House, 1971.

Carmichael, Stokely. "Free Huey" (February 17, 1968). In *Stokely Speaks: Black Power Back to Pan-Africanism,* edited by Ethel N. Minor. New York: Random House, 1971.

Carmichael, Stokely, with Michael Thelwell. *Ready for Revolution: The Life and Struggles of Stokely Carmichael (Kwame Ture).* New York: Scribner, 2003.

Carter, David C. *The Music Has Gone Out of the Movement: Civil Rights and the Johnson Administration, 1965–1968.* Chapel Hill: University of North Carolina Press, 2009.

Clark, Ramsey. *Crime in America: Observations on Its Nature, Causes, Prevention and Control.* New York: Simon & Schuster, 1970.

Clark, Ramsey. *The Fire This Time: U.S. War Crimes in the Gulf.* New York: International Action Center, 3rd reprint edition 2002.

Clinton, James W. *The Loyal Opposition: Americans in North Vietnam, 1965–1972.* Niwot: University Press of Colorado, 1995.

Cohen, Jerry, and William S. Murphy. *Burn, Baby, Burn!: The Los Angeles Race Riots of August 1965.* New York: Dutton, 1966.

Dallek, Robert. *Flawed Giant: Lyndon Johnson and His Times 1961–1973*. New York: Oxford University Press, 1998.

David, Lester, and Irene David. *Bobby Kennedy: The Making of a Folk Hero*. New York: Dodd, Mead, 1986.

Edwards, George. *The Police on the Urban Frontier*. New York: Institute of Human Relations, 1968.

Elliff, John T. *Crime, Dissent, and the Attorney General: The Justice Department in the 1960's*. Beverly Hills: Sage Publications, 1971.

Ellison, Ralph. *Invisible Man*. New York: Random House, 1952.

Fine, Sidney. *Violence in the Model City: The Cavanaugh Administration, Race Relations, and the Detroit Riot of 1967*. Ann Arbor: University of Michigan Press, 1989.

Flamm, Michael. *Law and Order: Street Crime, Civil Unrest, and the Crisis of Liberalism in the 1960s*. New York: Columbia University Press, 2005.

Flamm, Michael. "The 'Long Hot Summer' and the Politics of Law and Order." In *Looking Back at LBJ: White House Politics in a New Light*, edited by Mitchell B. Lerner. Lawrence: University Press of Kansas, 2005.

Flynn, George Q. *The Draft, 1940–1973*. Lawrence: University Press of Kansas, 1993.

Foley, Michael S. *Confronting the War Machine: Draft Resistance During the Vietnam War*. Chapel Hill: University of North Carolina Press, 2003.

Frank, Gerold. *An American Death: The True Story of the Assassination of Dr. Martin Luther King, Jr. and the Greatest Manhunt of Our Time*. London: Hamish Hamilton, 1972.

Friedly, Michael, and David Gallen. *Martin Luther King, Jr.: The FBI File*. New York: Carroll & Graf, 1993.

Gentry, Curt. *J. Edgar Hoover: The Man and His Secrets*. New York: Norton, 1991.

Gold, Steven J. *The Store in the Hood: A Century of Ethnic Business and Conflict*. Lanham, MD: Rowman & Littlefield, 2010.

Green, Mark. *Bright, Infinite Future: A Generational Memoir on the Progressive Rise*. New York: St. Martin's Press, 2016.

Gronlund, Mimi Clark. *Supreme Court Justice Tom C. Clark: A Life of Service*. Austin: University of Texas Press, 2010.

Halberstam, David. *The Children*. New York: Random House, 1998.

Harris, Richard, *Justice: The Crisis of Law, Order, and Freedom in America*. New York: Dutton, 1970.

Hauser, Thomas. *Muhammad Ali: His Life and Times*. New York: Simon & Schuster, 1991.

Hersh, Burton. *Bobby and J. Edgar: The Historic Face-Off Between the Kennedys and J. Edgar Hoover That Transformed America*. New York: Carroll & Graf, 2007.

Joseph, Peniel E. *Waiting 'Til the Midnight Hour: A Narrative History of Black Power in America*. New York: Henry Holt, 2006.

Katzenbach, Nicholas deB. *Some of It Was Fun: Working with RFK and LBJ*. New York: Norton, 2008.

Kluger, Richard. *Simple Justice: The History of Brown v. Board of Education and Black America's Struggle for Equality*. New York: Vintage Books, 1975.

Langran, Robert M. "Tom C. Clark." In *The Supreme Court Justices Illustrated Biographies 1789–1995*, edited by Clare Cushman. Washington, DC: Congressional Quarterly, 1995.

Langum, David J. *William M. Kunstler: The Most Hated Lawyer in America*. New York: New York University Press, 1999.

Lawson, Steven F. "Civil Rights." In *Exploring the Johnson Years*, edited by Robert A. Divine. Austin: University of Texas Press, 1981.

Lewis, John, with Michael D'Orso. *Walking with the Wind: Memoir of the Movement*. New York: Simon & Schuster, 1998.

Maraniss, David. *They Marched into Sunlight: War and Peace, Vietnam and America, October 1967*. New York: Simon & Schuster, 2004.

McPherson, Harry. *A Political Education*. Boston: Little, Brown, 1972.

Mitford, Jessica. *The Trial of Dr. Spock, the Rev. William Sloane Coffin, Jr., Michael Ferber, Mitchell Goodman, and Marcus Raskin*. New York: Knopf, 1969.

Murphy, Bruce Allen. *Fortas: The Rise and Ruin of a Supreme Court Justice*. New York: William Morrow, 1988.

Navasky, Victor S. *Kennedy Justice*. New York: Atheneum, 1970.

Patterson, James T. *The Eve of Destruction: How 1965 Transformed America*. New York: Basic Books, 2012.

Powe, Jr., Lucas A. *The Warren Court and American Politics*. Cambridge, MA: Belknap Press, 2001.

Report of the National Advisory Commission on Civil Disorders. New York Times Edition. New York: Dutton, 1968.

Schott, Richard L., and Dagmar S. Hamilton. *People, Positions, and Power: The Political Appointments of Lyndon Johnson*. Chicago: University of Chicago Press, 1983.

Sides, Hampton. *Hellhound on His Trail: The Stalking of Dr. Martin Luther King, Jr. and the International Hunt for His Assassin*. New York: Doubleday, 2010.

Spock, Benjamin. *The Common Sense Book of Baby and Child Care*. New York: Duell, Sloan, and Pearce, 1945.

Stein, Jean. *American Journey: The Times of Robert Kennedy*, edited by George Plimpton. New York: Harcourt Brace Jovanovich, 1970.

Thompson, Heather Ann. *Blood in the Water: The Attica Prison Uprising of 1971 and Its Legacy*. New York: Pantheon, 2016.

Watson, W. Marvin, with Sherwin Markman. *Chief of Staff: Lyndon Johnson and His Presidency*. New York: Thomas Dunne Books, 2004.

Wilkins, Roger. *A Man's Life: An Autobiography*. New York: Simon & Schuster, 1982.

Wilkins, Roy, and Ramsey Clark. *Search and Destroy: A Report by the Commission of Inquiry into the Black Panthers and the Police*. New York: Metropolitan Applied Research Center, 1973.

Wohl, Alexander. *Father, Son, and Constitution: How Justice Tom Clark and Attorney General Ramsey Clark Shaped American Democracy*. Lawrence: University Press of Kansas, 2013.

Yalof, David Alistair. *Pursuit of Justice: Presidential Politics and the Selection of Supreme Court Nominees*. Chicago: University of Chicago Press, 1999.

ARTICLES, ESSAYS, AND LETTERS

Alfano, Sean. "Milosevic Remains Returned Home." *CBS News* (March 18, 2006). http://www.cbsnews.com/news/milosevics-remains-returned-home/

Alpert, Lukas I. "Former U.S. Attorney General Ramsey Clark Has Made a Career of Defending the Hated." *Free Republic* (November 23, 2001).

"American Lawyer to Advise Milosevic." *Los Angeles Times* (November 18, 2001). http://articles.latimes.com/2001/nov/18/news/mn-5621

Anson, Robert Sam. "The Anti-Politician." *New Times* (November 1, 1974), 18.

"Arab Extradited from U.S. Indicted as Terrorist in Israel." *New York Times* (December 14, 1981). https://www.nytimes.com/1981/12/14/world/arab-extradited-from-us-indicted-as-terrorist-in-israel.html

Atkinson, Rick. "Estimates of Casualties in Grenada Are Raised." *Washington Post* (November 9, 1983). https://www.washingtonpost.com/archive/politics/1983/11/09/estimates-of-casualties-in-grenada-are-raised/9fedcefc-0ead-437c-84f5-170bac27d9c4/?noredirect=on&utm_term=.7d10c3bb6506

Auerbach, Stuart. "Iran's Anti-U.S. Conference Call for Peaceful End to Crisis." *Washington Post* (June 6, 1980). https://www.washingtonpost.com/archive/politics/1980/06/06/irans-anti-us-conference-calls-for-peaceful-end-to-crisis/209f9a7a-d56f-4647-a76f-a8f8bc4b5df2/?utm_term=.b3f4932a6f6f

Barnes, Bart. "Tom C. Clark II, Environmental Lawyer, Dies at 59." *Washington Post* (December 23, 2013). https://www.washingtonpost.com/local/obituaries/tom-c-clark-ii-environmental-lawyer-dies-at-59/2013/12/23/8f84f506-6c03-11e3-b405-7e360f7e9fd2_story.html?utm_term=.f9483f55e190

Bernstein, Dennis J. "Respecting a Courageous American." *Consortium News* (May 11, 2017). https://consortiumnews.com/2017/05/11/respecting-a-courageous-american/

Bigart, Homer. "Berrigan Defense Calls No Witnesses and Rests Its Case." *New York Times* (March 25, 1972). https://www.nytimes.com/1972/03/25/archives/berrigan-defense-calls-no-witnesses-and-rests-its-case-defense.html

Black, Ian. "Moment of Truth." *The Guardian* (February 7, 2002). https://www.theguardian.com/world/2002/feb/08/warcrimes.milosevictrial

Blake, John. "'Mississippi Burning' Murders Still Smolder for One Brother." *CNN* (June 28, 2014). http://www.cnn.com/2014/06/28/us/mississippi-murders/index.html

"Brother of Grenadian Says Contact Is Denied." *New York Times* (November 15, 1983). https://www.nytimes.com/1983/11/15/world/brother-of-grenadian-says-contact-is-denied.html

Brown, Jr., Lonnie T. "Different Lyrics, Same Song: Watts, Ferguson, and the Stagnating Effect of the Politics of Law and Order." *Harvard Civil Rights–Civil Liberties Law Review* 52, no. 2 (2017), 305–356.

Brown, Jr., Lonnie T. "Representing Saddam Hussein: The Importance of Being Ramsey Clark." *Georgia Law Review* 42, no. 1 (2007), 47–129.

Brown, Jr., Lonnie T. "A Tale of Prosecutorial Indiscretion: Ramsey Clark and the Selective Non-Prosecution of Stokely Carmichael." *South Carolina Law Review* 62, no. 1 (2010), 1–39.

Burke, Minyvonne. "Former NYPD Detective Frank Serpico Reflects on Knapp Commission, Exposing Police Corruption and Today's Issues." *New York Daily News* (May 20, 2017). http://www.nydailynews.com/news/national/frank-serpico-reflects-knapp-commission-exposing-corruption-article-1.3179229

Burns, John F. "In Defending Hussein, an American Contrarian Seeks to Set the Record Straight." *New York Times* (December 6, 2005). https://www.nytimes.com/2005/12/06/world/middleeast/in-defending-hussein-an-american-contrarian-seeks-to-set.html

Burton, Anthony. "James Earl Ray Pleads Guilty for the Assassination of Martin Luther King Jr." *New York Daily News* (March 11, 1969). http://www.nydailynews.com/news/crime/james-earl-ray-pleads-guilty-murder-mlk-1969-article-1.2559939

Carlson, Peter. "The Crusader." *Washington Post* (December 15, 2002). https://www
.washingtonpost.com/archive/lifestyle/2002/12/15/the-crusader/9de49dd7-43fd-4
5e0-a4ef-3df4475cb4a0/?noredirect=on&utm_term=.463341d9223d

Carroll, Maurice. "Javits Wins a 4th Term, Defeating Ramsey Clark." *New York Times*
(November 4, 1974). https://www.nytimes.com/1974/11/06/archives/javits-wins-
a-4th-term-defeating-ramsey-clark-javits-is-victor-in.html

"Clark Argues for Magee." *News Sentinel* (March 24, 1973).

"Clark Describes 'Good' POW Camp." *The Evening Star and the Washington Daily News*
(August 15, 1972).

"Clark, in Hanoi, Is Said to Find U.S. Prisoners in Good Health." *New York Times* (August
13, 1972).

"Clark Hits 'Deadly Force.'" *Akron Beacon Journal* (April 18, 1968).

Clark, Ramsey. "125th Anniversary Issue: Patriotism." *The Nation* (July 15, 1991).

Clark, Ramsey. "Dr. King, Non-Violence, and U.S. Policy Today." *Executive Intelligence Review* (January 23, 2015). https://larouchepub.com/other/2015/4204rclark_ny_sch
_conf.html

Clark, Ramsey. "'How Can You Represent That Man?' Ethics, the Rule of Law, and Defending the Indefensible." *Georgia Law Review* 44, no. 4 (2010), 921–937.

Clark, Ramsey. "The Lawyer's Duty of Loyalty: To the Client or to the Institution?" *Loyola
University Law Journal* 16, no. 3 (1985), 459–469.

Clark, Ramsey. Letter to UN Secretary General Kofi Annan in Reference to "The Trial of
Slobodan Milosevic, Former President of the Federal Republic of Yugoslavia Before
the International Criminal Tribunal for the Former Yugoslavia" (February 12, 2004).
http://milosevic.co/icdsm/more/rclarkUN1.htm

Clark, Ramsey. "Libya, Grenada and Reagan." *The Nation* (May 3, 1986). https://www
.thefreelibrary.com/Libya%2C+Grenada+and+Reagan.-a04838994

Clark, Ramsey. "Libyan Epilogue." *The Nation* (July 12, 1986). https://www.thenation
.com/article/libyan-epilogue/

Clark, Ramsey. "A Report on U.S. War Crimes Against Iraq to the Commission of Inquiry
for International War Crimes Tribunal" (May 1, 1991). https://jacobsm.com/deoxy
/deoxy.org/wc/warcrime.htm

Clark, Ramsey. "Shedding Light on Ray: Need to Investigate James Earl Ray's Role in the
Assassination of Martin Luther King, Jr." *The Nation* (March 10, 1997).

Clark, Ramsey. "We Have Become Soft on Truth." *Britannica Roundtable* 2, no. 3 (1973),
6.

Close, Alexandra. "Ruchell Magee: The Defense Never Rests." *Ramparts* (June 1973), 21–
24, 60–62.

Cohen, Jeff, and Jeff Gottlieb. "Was Fred Hampton Executed?" *The Nation* (December 25,
1976). https://www.thenation.com/article/was-fred-hampton-executed/

Corcoran, John. "Ramsey Clark Speaks on Middle East Issues." *Philadelphia Inquirer*
(March 30, 1989) (copy on file with the author).

Corry, John. "Serpico Returns and Nominates Clark for the Senate." *New York Times* (June
15, 1974). https://www.nytimes.com/1974/06/15/archives/serpico-returns-and
-nominates-clark-for-senate-serpico-explains.html

Corwin, Miles. "Ex-Chancellor Convicted of Embezzlement at UCSB." *Los Angeles Times*
(July 16, 1988). http://articles.latimes.com/1988-07-16/news/mn-6030_1_uc
-santa-barbara-professors

D'Amato, Anthony. "Comment: The Imposition of Attorney Sanctions for Claims Arising from the U.S. Air Raid on Libya." *American Journal of International Law* 84, no. 3 (1990), 705–711.

Darnton, John. "Does the World Still Recognize a Holocaust?" *New York Times* (April 17, 1993). https://www.nytimes.com/1993/04/25/weekinreview/does-the-world-still-recognize-a-holocaust.html

Dellinger, Hampton. "When Muhammad Ali Took on America." *Slate* (June 6, 2016). http://www.slate.com/articles/news_and_politics/jurisprudence/2016/06/what_muhammad_ali_won_in_his_supreme_court_fight_over_the_vietnam_war_and.html

Domonoske, Camila. "Officials Close Investigation into 1964 'Mississippi Burning' Killings." *NPR* (June 21, 2016). https://www.npr.org/sections/thetwo-way/2016/06/21/482914440/officials-close-investigation-into-1964-mississippi-burning-killings

Dreifus, Claudia. "The Progressive Interview: Ramsey Clark." *Progressive* 55, no. 4 (April 1991), 32.

Drum, Kevin. "Flashback: Why Ronald Reagan Invaded Grenada." *Mother Jones* (March 6, 2014). https://www.motherjones.com/kevin-drum/2014/03/flashback-why-ronald-reagan-invaded-grenada/

Evans, Rowland, and Robert Novak. "Ramsey Clark Threatens Javits' Senate Seat." *St. Petersburg Times* (October 28, 1972).

"Former US Attorney-General Visits Hamas in Gaza." *Jerusalem Post* (January 5, 2011). https://www.jpost.com/Middle-East/Former-US-attorney-general-visits-Hamas-leader-in-Gaza

Fosburgh, Lacey. "Ruchell Magee, Once Angela Davis' Co-Defendant, Gets Life for Kidnapping." *New York Times* (January 24, 1975). https://www.nytimes.com/1975/01/24/archives/ruchell-magee-once-angela-davis-codefendant-gets-life-for.html

"4 in Motel Trial Freed in Michigan." *New York Times* (February 26, 1970). https://www.nytimes.com/1970/02/26/archives/4-in-motel-trial-freed-in-michigan-police-and-a-guard-cleared-in-67.html

Freedman, Monroe H. "Henry Lord Brougham and Zeal." *Hofstra Law Review* 34, no. 4 (2006), 1319–1324.

Fried, Joseph P. "The Terror Conspiracy: The Overview; Sheik and 9 Followers Guilty of a Conspiracy of Terrorism." *New York Times* (October 2, 1995). https://www.nytimes.com/1995/10/02/nyregion/terror-conspiracy-overview-sheik-9-followers-guilty-conspiracy-terrorism.html

Getlin, Josh. "For a Politician, Former U.S. Attorney General Ramsey Clark Took a Road Less Traveled—a Hard Left into the Hotbed of Human Rights Causes: Loner of the Left." *Los Angeles Times* (February 18, 1990). http://articles.latimes.com/1990-02-18/news/vw-1604_1_ramsey-clark

Glass, Andrew. "Civil Rights March Ends as 'Bloody Sunday,' March 7, 1965." *Politico* (March 7, 2018). https://www.politico.com/story/2018/03/07/this-day-in-politics-march-7-1965-437394

Goode, Erica. "The World: Stalin to Saddam: So Much for the Madman Theory." *New York Times* (May 4, 2003). https://www.nytimes.com/2003/05/04/weekinreview/the-world-stalin-to-saddam-so-much-for-the-madman-theory.html

Graham, Fred P. "Clark: Target on the Law and Order Issue." *New York Times* (October

20, 1968). https://www.nytimes.com/1968/10/20/archives/law-clark-target-on-the
-law-and-order-issue.html

Greenhouse, Linda. "Two Democratic Insurgents File Petitions for U.S. Senate Race." *New York Times* (July 16, 1974). https://www.nytimes.com/1974/07/16/archives/two
-democratic-insurgents-file-petitions-for-us-senate-race-20000.html

Grumman, Cornelia. "Wrong Question." *Chicago Tribune Magazine* (November 26, 2000), 14–24.

Goldman, Russell. "Assad's History of Chemical Attacks, and Other Atrocities." *New York Times* (April 5, 2017). https://www.nytimes.com/2017/04/05/world/middleeast/
syria-bashar-al-assad-atrocities-civilian-deaths-gas-attack.html

Hastings, Deborah. "The Life and Times of Ramsey Clark." *Free Republic* (April 29, 2006). http://www.freerepublic.com/focus/f-news/1623980/posts

Hearst, David, Martin Walker, and Richard Norton-Taylor. "Milosevic Indicted for War Crimes." *The Guardian* (May 27, 1999). https://www.theguardian.com/world/1999/
may/27/warcrimes.davidhearst

"An Interview with Ramsey Clark." *ADA World Magazine* (May–June 1971).

"Int'l Saddam Defence Committee Soon." News from Bangladesh. *Daily News Monitoring Service* (June 15, 2005).

"Iranian Political Factions Dispute Clark's Trip and Trials for Hostages." *Washington Post* (June 7, 1980). https://www.washingtonpost.com/archive/politics/1980/06/07/
iranian-political-factions-dispute-clarks-trip-and-trials-for-hostages/b8003baa-25fc
-4de4-a379-2f3aa472d0d5/?utm_term=.013c5d746e1e

Israel, Jared, and Nico Varkevisser. "How Ramsey Clark Championed Baltic Nazi War Criminals . . . and He's Still Doing It." *Emperor's Clothes* (June 19, 2003). http://emperors
-clothes.com/ramsey/ramsey4.htm

Jensen, Derrick. "Neighborhood Bully: Ramsey Clark on American Militarism." *The Sun Magazine* (August 2001). https://www.thesunmagazine.org/issues/308/neighbo
rhood-bully

Judis, John B. "The Strange Case of Ramsey Clark." *New Republic* 204, no. 16 (April 22, 1991).

"Jury Deadlocked on Harrisburg 7." *Cornell Daily Sun* (April 6, 1972). http://cdsun.library.
cornell.edu/?a=d&d=CDS19720406&

"A Justice Department Official Named to Prosecute Berrigan." *New York Times* (March 10, 1971). https://www.nytimes.com/1971/03/10/archives/a-justice-department
-official-named-to-prosecute-berrigan.html

Kaufman, Michael T. "Attica Jury Convicts One of Murder, 2d of Assault." *New York Times* (April 6, 1975). https://www.nytimes.com/1975/04/06/archives/attica-jury
-convicts-one-of-murder-2d-of-assault-attica-jury-finds.html

Kaufman, Michael T. "Stokely Carmichael, Rights Leader Who Coined 'Black Power,' Dies at 57." *New York Times* (November 16, 1998). https://www.nytimes.com/1998/11/16/
us/stokely-carmichael-rights-leader-who-coined-black-power-dies-at-57.html

Kessler, Glenn. "Libya's Final Payment to Victims Fund Clears Way for Normal U.S. Ties." *Washington Post* (November 1, 2008). http://www.washingtonpost.com/wp-dyn/
content/article/2008/10/31/AR2008103103616.html

Kifner, John. "4 Kent State Students Killed by Troops." *New York Times* (May 4, 1970). http://movies2.nytimes.com/learning/general/onthisday/big/0504.html

Kiner, Deb. "Harrisburg 7 Conspiracy Verdict Came 45 Years Ago Today." *Pennlive* (April 5, 2017). http://www.pennlive.com/life/2017/04/harrisburg_7_conspiracy_verdic.html

King, Colbert I. "Government Snooping Is a Bipartisan Thing." *Washington Post* (June 15, 2002). https://www.washingtonpost.com/archive/opinions/2002/06/15/government -snooping-is-a-bipartisan-thing/6a672d37-d705-415a-a6a6-3a6d73ae229a/

King, Jr., Martin Luther. "Letter from a Birmingham Jail" (April 14, 1963). https://www .africa.upenn.edu/Articles_Gen/Letter_Birmingham.html

Langewiesche, William. "Ziad for the Defense." *The Atlantic* (June 2005). https://www .theatlantic.com/magazine/archive/2005/06/ziad-for-the-defense/303960/

Lamb, David. "'60s Radical Draws Life in Killing of Deputy." *Los Angeles Times* (March 14, 2002). http://articles.latimes.com/2002/mar/14/news/mn-32824

Lewis, Anthony. "Abroad at Home: The American Way." *New York Times* (November 17, 1983). https://www.nytimes.com/1983/11/17/opinion/abroad-at-home-the -american-way.html

Little, Robert. "Fitting Defender for Saddam Hussein." *Baltimore Sun* (December 6, 2005). http://articles.baltimoresun.com/2005-12-06/news/0512060166_1_ramsey-clark -hussein-trial-lawyer

"List of Saddam's Crimes Is Long." *ABC News* (December 30, 2006). https://abcnews .go.com/WNT/IraqCoverage/story?id=2761722&page=1

London, Ephraim S. "Heresy and the Illinois Bar: The Application of George Anastaplo for Admission." *Lawyers Guild Review* 12, no. 4 (Fall 1952).

"Magee Enters Guilty Plea to Marin Co. Shooting." *Afro-American* (May 14–18, 1974).

Margolick, David. "The Long and Lonely Journey of Ramsey Clark." *New York Times* (June 14, 1991). https://www.nytimes.com/1991/06/14/washington/the-long-and -lonely-journey-of-ramsey-clark.html

Maykuth, Andrew. "Standing Alone." *Philadelphia Inquirer Sunday Magazine* (July 7, 1991). http://www.maykuth.com/Projects/clark91.htm

Maykuth, Andrew. "The Tutsis' Faith in a Man of God Proves Fatal." *Andrew Maykuth Online* (September 9, 1998). www.maykuth.com/projects/rwan4.htm

"Messenger from Hanoi." *The Evening Star and the Washington Daily News* (August 15, 1972).

Milloy, Ross, E. "Jury Finds for U.S. Deaths in Waco." *New York Times* (July 15, 2000). https://www.nytimes.com/2000/07/15/us/jury-finds-for-us-in-deaths-at-waco.html

"MLK: A Riot Is the Language of the Unheard." *CBS News* (August 25, 2013). http://www .cbsnews.com/news/mlk-a-riot-is-the-language-of-the-unheard/

Moore, Molly, and Daniel Williams. "Milosevic Found Dead in Prison." *Washington Post* (March 12, 2006). http://www.washingtonpost.com/wp-dyn/content/article /2006/03/11/AR2006031100525.html

Muoat, Lucia. "One Man's Struggle to Avoid Extradition by US to Israel." *Christian Science Monitor* (March 5, 1981). https://www.csmonitor.com/1981/0305/030545.html

"My God! They're Killing Us": Newsweek's 1970 Coverage of the Kent State Shooting." *Newsweek* (May 4, 2015). https://www.newsweek.com/my-god-theyre-killing-us-our -1970-coverage-kent-state-328108

Navasky, Victor S. "Wrong Guy for the Wrong Post at the Wrong Time?" *Saturday Evening Post* (December 16, 1967), 74–77.

Nguyen, Viet Thanh, and Richard Hughes. "The Forgotten Victims of Agent Orange." *New York Times* (September 15, 2017). https://www.nytimes.com/2017/09/15/opinion/agent-orange-vietnam-effects.html

Nkrumah, Gamal. "Ramsey Clark: A Voice of Reason." *Al-Ahram Weekly* (February 12, 2003). http://weekly.ahram.org.eg/archive/2003/624/profile.htm

"Obituary of Georgia Welch Clark." *New York Times* (July 6, 2010). http://query.nytimes.com/gst/fullpage.html?res=9D04E2D8123AF935A35754C0A9669D8B63

O'Brien, Tim. "Ramsey Clark Airings Called 'Contemptible.'" *Washington Post* (August 12, 1972).

O'Meara, Joseph. "'No Man Is Above the Law.'" *A.B.A. Journal* 53 (December 1967), 1107–1110.

Pear, Robert. "Clark Is Not Facing U.S. Criminal Action." *New York Times* (January 8, 1981). https://www.nytimes.com/1981/01/08/world/clark-is-not-facing-us-criminal-action.html

Perlmutter, Emanuel. "Javits Scores U.N. Role for Palestine Group." *New York Times* (October 16, 1974). https://www.nytimes.com/1974/10/16/archives/javits-scores-u-n-role-for-palestine-group-clark-is-applauded.html

Raines, Howell. "The Birmingham Bombing." *New York Times Magazine* (July 24, 1983). https://www.nytimes.com/1983/07/24/magazine/the-birmingham-bombing.html

"Ramsey Clark: Impossible to Prepare a Defense for Hussein." *CNN* (June 27, 2006). http://www.cnn.com/2006/WORLD/meast/06/27/cnna.clark/index.html

Ratner, Lizzy. "Ramsey Clark: Why I'm Taking Saddam's Case." *New York Observer* (January 9, 2005). http://observer.com/2005/01/ramsey-clark-why-im-taking-saddams-case/

Reich, Kenneth. "Clark Fires Back at Jewish Group: He Says L.A. Federation Is 'Politicizing Human Rights.'" *Los Angeles Times* (March 26, 1987). http://articles.latimes.com/1987-03-26/news/mn-427_1_human-rights

Reich, Kenneth. "Jewish Group Cancels Talk by Ramsey Clark." *Los Angeles Times* (March 25, 1987). http://articles.latimes.com/1987-03-25/news/mn-268_1_ramsey-clark

Richardson, John H. "How the Attorney General of the United States Became Saddam Hussein's Lawyer." *Esquire* (February 1, 2007). https://archive.esquire.com/article/2007/2/1/how-the-attorney-general-of-the-united-states-became-saddam-husseins-lawyer

Risen, Clay. "The Legacy of the 1968 Riots." *The Guardian* (April 4, 2008). https://www.theguardian.com/commentisfree/2008/apr/04/thelegacyofthe1968riots

"Robert Bork, Jurist and Scholar, 1927–2012," *UChicago News* (December 19, 2012), https://news.uchicago.edu/story/robert-bork-jurist-and-scholar-1927-2012

Rosenheimer, Timna. "'This War Is Genocide'—An Interview with Former US Attorney General Ramsey Clark." *Common Dreams News Center* (January 3, 2003). https://archive.commondreams.org/headlines03/0103-08.htm

Rubin, Michael. "Relearning the Iran Crisis' Lessons." *Commentary* (November 4, 2016). https://www.commentarymagazine.com/foreign-policy/middle-east/iran/relearning-iran-crisis-lessons/

Rucker, Philip, and Robert Barnes. "As Obama's Nominees Languish in GOP Senate, Trump to Inherit More Than 100 Court Vacancies." *Chicago Tribune* (December 25, 2016). http://www.chicagotribune.com/news/nationworld/politics/ct-trump-court-vacancies-20161225-story.html

Ruiz, Rebecca R. "Attorney General Orders Tougher Sentences, Rolling Back Obama Policy." *New York Times* (May 12, 2017). https://www.nytimes.com/2017/05/12/us/politics/attorney-general-jeff-sessions-drug-offenses-penalties.html

Russonello, Giovanni. "Fascination and Fear: Covering the Black Panthers." *New York Times* (October 15, 2016). https://www.nytimes.com/2016/10/16/us/black-panthers-50-years.html

Salpukas, Agis. "Judge Acquits Guardsmen in Slayings at Kent State." *New York Times* (November 9, 1974). https://www.nytimes.com/1974/11/09/archives/judge-acquits-guardsmen-in-slayings-at-kent-state-judge-acquits.html

Saunders, Josh. "Ramsey Clark's Prosecution Complex: How Did Lyndon Johnson's Attorney General Come to Defend Dictators, War Criminals, and Terrorists?" *Legal Affairs* (November–December 2003). http://www.legalaffairs.org/issues/November-December-2003/feature_saunders_novdec03.msp

Schneidau, Mary C. "Former AG Defends Hussein Work: Revered for Principle, Reviled for Clients, Clark Says Fair Trial Is a Right." *Dallas Morning News* (December 24, 2005).

Sherrill, Robert. "A Talk with Ramsey Clark: Justice in a Torn Nation." *The Nation* (December 7, 1970).

Siddiqui, Obaid H. "Rap Sheet: H. Rap Brown, Civil Rights Revolutionary—Cop Killer or FBI Target?" *Illume* (September 13, 2012).

Simons, Marlise. "Rwandan Pastor and His Son Are Convicted of Genocide." *New York Times* (February 20, 2003). https://www.nytimes.com/2003/02/20/world/rwandan-pastor-and-his-son-are-convicted-of-genocide.html

Sinnott, Deirdre. "Ramsey Clark: A Life of Action." *Ramsey Clark 85 International Action Center 20 Gala* (January 11, 2013). http://www.deirdresinnott.com/Clark_85th_Birthday_Gala-Bio.pdf

Sparks, Adam. "Ramsey Clark: An American Traitor." *News Max* (March 4, 2003). http://www.freerepublic.com/focus/news/860295/posts

Stern, Sol. "The Campaign to Free Angela Davis and Ruchell Magee." *New York Times* (June 27, 1971). https://www.nytimes.com/1971/06/27/archives/the-campaign-to-free-angela-davis-and-ruchell-magee-the-campaign-to.html

Straker, Linda. "7 Convicted of Killing Grenada Leader Released." *San Diego Union Tribune* (September 5, 2009). http://www.sandiegouniontribune.com/sdut-cb-grenada-coup-prisoners-090509-2009sep05-story.html

Strochlic, Nina. "Locked Up in Louisiana: Inside America's Bloodiest Prison." *The Daily Beast* (July 28, 2015). https://www.thedailybeast.com/locked-up-in-louisiana-inside-americas-bloodiest-prison

"Supreme Court Turns Down Waco Case." *NBC News* (March 22, 2004). http://www.nbcnews.com/id/4579805/ns/us_news/t/supreme-court-turns-down-waco-case/

"Suspected Terrorist Surrenders." *New York Times* (August 23, 1979). https://www.nytimes.com/1979/08/23/archives/suspected-terrorist-surrenders.html

"Texts of Letter and Memo on the Draft." *New York Times* (November 9, 1967). https://www.nytimes.com/1967/11/09/archives/texts-of-letter-and-memo-on-the-draft.html

Tobin, Jonathan S. "Ramsey Clark Embraces Hamas: Whose Reputation Is Damaged?" *Commentary* (January 5, 2011). https://www.commentarymagazine.com/american-society/ramsey-clark-embraces-hamas-whose-reputation-is-damaged/

"Tom C. Clark, Former Justice, Dies; On the Supreme Court for 18 Years." *New York Times*

(June 14, 1977). https://www.nytimes.com/1977/06/14/archives/tom-c-clark -former-justice-dies-on-the-supreme-court-for-18-years.html

"Too Prominent to Be Relevant." *Time Magazine* (February 9, 1970), 42.

"Tributes to Tom C. Clark." *A.B.A. Journal* 63 (August 1977), 1105.

Ungar, Sanford J. "U.S. Sees No Law Violation by Clark, Salinger Overseas." *Washington Post* (August 23, 1972).

Updegrove, Mark K. "Lyndon Johnson's Vietnam." *New York Times* (February 24, 2017). https://www.nytimes.com/2017/02/24/opinion/lyndon-johnsons-vietnam.html

"U.S. Compensation for Libya Raid Sought." *Los Angeles Times* (April 16, 1987). http://articles.latimes.com/1987-04-16/news/mn-734_1_libya-raid-compensation

"The War as a Campaign Issue." *Washington Post* (August 16, 1972).

Weiser, Benjamin. "Reporter's Notebook: Former Attorney General Defending a Brooklyn Man in Nazi War Crimes." *New York Times* (August 9, 1998). https://www.nytimes .com/1998/08/09/nyregion/reporter-s-notebook-former-attorney-general-defending -brooklyn-man-nazi-war.html

Wicker, Tom. "Ramsey Clark: A Candid Conversation with the Civil-Libertarian Ex-Attorney General." *Playboy Magazine* (August 1969), 53–74.

"Wife of POW Praises Clark for N. Viet Visit." *Los Angeles Times* (August 17, 1972).

Williams, Carol J. "World Leaders Hail Milosevic Arrest as End of Turbulent Era." *Los Angeles Times* (April 2, 2001). http://articles.latimes.com/2001/apr/02/news/mn-45859

Williams, Ian. "Ramsey Clark, the War Criminal's Best Friend." *Salon* (July 7, 1999). https://www.salon.com/1999/06/21/clark/

Zirin, Dave. "Don't Remember Muhammad Ali as a Sanctified Sports Hero. He Was a Powerful, Dangerous Political Force." *Los Angeles Times* (June 4, 2016). http://www.latimes .com/opinion/op-ed/la-oe-zirin-muhammad-ali-legacy-20160603-snap-story.html

ORAL HISTORIES

Clark, Ramsey. Oral History Interview I (October 30, 1968), by Harri Baker. LBJ Presidential Library. http://www.lbjlibrary.net/collections/oral-histories/clark-ramsey.html

Clark, Ramsey. Oral History Interview II (February 11, 1969), by Harri Baker. LBJ Presidential Library. http://www.lbjlibrary.net/assets/documents/archives/oral_histories /clark_r/clark-r2.pdf

Clark, Ramsey. Oral History Interview IV (April 16, 1969), by Harri Baker. LBJ Presidential Library. http://www.lbjlibrary.net/assets/documents/archives/oral_histories/clark_r /clark-r4.pdf

Clark, Ramsey. Oral History Interview V (June 3, 1969), by Harri Baker. LBJ Presidential Library. http://www.lbjlibrary.net/assets/documents/archives/oral_histories/clark_r /clark-r5.pdf

Clark, Ramsey. Oral History Interview. *C-SPAN* (January 9, 2003). https://www.c-span .org/video/?317441-1/ramsey-clark-oral-history-interivew

Clark, Tom. Oral History Interview I (October 7, 1969), by Joe B. Frantz. LBJ Presidential Library. http://www.lbjlibrary.net/assets/documents/archives/oral_histories/clark_t /Clark-T.PDF

McPherson, Harry. Oral History Interview V (April 9, 1969), by T. H. Baker. LBJ Presidential Library. http://www.lbjlibrary.net/assets/documents/archives/oral_histories/ mcpherson/mcpher05.pdf

Pollak, Stephen J. Oral History Interview II (January 29, 1969), by Harri Baker. LBJ Presidential Library. https://www.discoverlbj.org/item/oh-pollaks-19690129-2-84-15

Temple, Larry. Oral History Interview I (June 11, 1970), by Joe B. Frantz. LBJ Presidential Library. https://www.discoverlbj.org/item/oh-templel-19700611-1-72-33-a

Temple, Larry. Oral History Interview V (August 11, 1970), by Joe B. Frantz. LBJ Presidential Library. https://www.discoverlbj.org/item/oh-templel-19700811-5-72-33-e

GOVERNMENT AND PERSONAL PAPERS

Office Files of Joseph Califano. LBJ Presidential Library.

Personal Papers of Ramsey Clark. LBJ Presidential Library.

Presidential Papers, LBJ Presidential Library.

Ramsey Clark Papers. Dolph Briscoe Center for American History, University of Texas–Austin.

PUBLIC ADDRESSES

Brown, H. Rap. "Speech to Cambridge, Maryland, Crowd." Cambridge, MD (July 24, 1967).

Clark, Ramsey. "Address at the United National Antiwar Committee Rally." New York, NY (April 9, 2011). https://www.youtube.com/watch?v=lubd9ZRX5to

Johnson, Lyndon B. "Commencement Address at Howard University: 'To Fulfill These Rights.'" Washington, DC (June 4, 1965). http://teachingamericanhistory.org/library/document/commencement-address-at-howard-university-to-fulfill-these-rights/, archived at https://perma.cc/9N3K-S67Y

King, Jr., Martin Luther. "Beyond Vietnam" (address delivered to the Clergy and Laymen Concerned About Vietnam). Riverside Church, New York, NY (April 4, 1967).

Tower, John G. "Speech About the Riots" (?1968). Senator John G. Tower Collection, Southwestern University. https://texashistory.unt.edu/ark:/67531/metapth612156/

GOVERNMENT MATERIALS

89 Cong. Rec. H20792. Daily edition (August 17, 1965) (statement of Rep. Watson).

89 Cong. Rec. S20626. Daily edition (August 17, 1965) (statement of Sen. Mondale).

Anti-Terrorism Act of 1987. Pub. L. No. 100-204, Title X, 101 Stat. 1406–1407. Codified at 22 U.S.C.A. 5201–5203 (West Supp. 1987).

"The Challenge of Crime in a Free Society." A report by the President's Commission on Law Enforcement and Administration of Justice (1967). https://assets.documentcloud.org/documents/3932081/Crimecommishreport.pdf

Clark, Ramsey, Andrew F. Brimmer, and Jack T. Conway. "Report of the President's Task Force on the Los Angeles Riots, August, 1965" (September 17, 1965).

"Final Report of the President's Task Force on 21st Century Policing" (2015). http://elearning-courses.net/iacp/html/webinarResources/170926/FinalReport21stCentury Policing.pdf

Military Selective Service Act. 50 U.S.C. app. § 462 (West 1968).

Minutes of President Johnson's Cabinet Meeting (August 2, 1967).

"Nomination of Ramsey Clark to Be Deputy Attorney General of the United States: Hearing Before the Committee on the Judiciary." U.S. Senate, 89th Congress (February 8, 1965).

"Nomination of Ramsey Clark to Be Attorney General of the United States: Hearing Before the Committee on the Judiciary." U.S. Senate, 90th Congress (March 2, 1967).

Ragsdale, Bruce A. *The Chicago Seven: 1960s Radicalism in the Federal Courts.* Federal Judicial Center, 2008. https://www.fjc.gov/sites/default/files/trials/chicago7.pdf

"Ramsey Clark, Assistant Attorney General-Designate: Hearing Before the Committee on the Judiciary." U.S. Senate, 87th Congress (February 27, 1961).

Report of the National Advisory Commission on Civil Disorders. New York Times Edition. New York: Dutton, 1968.

Reports by UN Food and Agricultural Organization, Ramsey Clark, and World Leaders, *The Impact of Sanctions on Iraq: The Children Are Dying.* International Action Center, 2nd edition 1998.

"The Selective Service System: Its Operation, Practices, and Procedures: Hearings Before the Subcommittee on Administrative Practice and Procedure of the Committee on the Judiciary." U.S. Senate, 91st Congress (November 3, 1969).

"The Proposed Federal Gun Registration and Licensing Act of 1968: Hearing Before the Subcommittee to Investigate Juvenile Delinquency of the Senate Judiciary Committee." U.S. Senate, 90th Congress, 2nd session (1968).

OTHER MEDIA

Buckley, Jr., William F. "Amnesty, with Ramsey Clark." *Firing Line* (June 3, 1974). Hoover Institution Video Library, Stanford University. https://youtu.be/u2CCBPSvKFg

Chapin, Harry. "Cat's in the Cradle." Elektra, 1974.

Citizen Clark . . . A Life of Principle. Directed by Joseph C. Stillman. Oneonta, NY: La Paloma Films, 2018. https://alifeofprinciple.com

Forrest Gump. Directed by Robert Zemeckis. Los Angeles: Paramount Pictures, 1994, DVD.

I Am Not Your Negro. Directed by Raoul Peck. New York: Magnolia Pictures, 2016, DVD.

"I Am Ramsey Clark: Lawyer, Activist, and Former Public Official. Ask Me Anything." *Reddit* (March 27, 2015). https://www.reddit.com/r/IAmA/comments/30iozw/i_am _ramsey_clark_lawyer_activist_and_former/

Panel discussion of *Citizen Clark . . . A Life of Principle.* Directed by Joseph C. Stillman (La Paloma Films). The New School, New York, NY (December 16, 2017). https://www.youtube.com/watch?v=dNAzq3y7wdo

"Remarks by Ramsey Clark, Alumni Reunion to Celebrate the 1974 Ramsey Clark for U.S. Senate Campaign" (November 1, 2012) (video by Lois Akner).

Scarborough Country. MSNBC (November 28, 2005). http://www.nbcnews.com/id/10254914/ns/msnbc-morning_joe/t/scarborough-country-november/#.Wz56bMInaM8

Today Show. Interview of Ramsey Clark by Katie Couric. NBC, December 2005.

The Vietnam War. Directed by Ken Burns and Lynn Novick. PBS Documentary, 2017.

When We Were Kings. Directed by Leon Gast. Los Angeles: PolyGram Filmed Entertainment, 1996, DVD.

INTERVIEWS AND OTHER COMMUNICATIONS

Akner, Lois. Telephone interview by the author (June 20, 2017).

Al-Amin, Karima. Interview by the author. Clarkston, GA (September 22, 2016).

Anastaplo, George. Interview by the author. Chicago, IL (May 29, 2009).

Clark, Ramsey. Telephone interview by the author (August 8, 2008).

Clark, Ramsey. Letter to the author (August 19, 2008).

Clark, Ramsey. Interview by the author. New York, NY (November 8, 2008).

Clark, Ramsey. Interview by the author. Athens, GA (October 17, 2009).

Clark, Ramsey. Telephone interview by the author (July 16, 2010).

Clark, Ramsey. Telephone interview by the author (July 26, 2010).

Clark, Ramsey. Telephone interview by the author (July 27, 2010).

Clark, Ramsey. Telephone interview by the author (August 4, 2010).

Clark, Ramsey. Telephone interview by the author (March 18, 2011).

Clark, Ramsey. Telephone interview by the author (June 14, 2011).

Clark, Ramsey. Telephone interview by the author (August 19, 2011).

Clark, Ramsey. Telephone interview by the author (September 6, 2011).

Clark, Ramsey. Telephone interview by the author (September 11, 2015).

Clark, Ramsey. Interview by the author. New York, NY (January 6, 2016).

Clark, Ramsey. Interview by the author. New York, NY (January 7, 2016).

Clark, Ramsey. Telephone interview by the author (March 15, 2016).

Clark, Ramsey. Interview by the author. New York, NY (June 7, 2016).

Clark, Ramsey. Interview by the author. New York, NY (June 10, 2016).

Clark, Ramsey, with Whitney Clark. Interview by the author. New York, NY (June 10, 2016).

Clark, Ramsey. Telephone interview by the author (December 18, 2016).

Clark, Ramsey. Interview by the author. New York, NY (December 16, 2017).

Gronlund, Julie. Telephone interview by the author (August 26, 2016).

Hagen, Marie. Telephone interview by the author (October 17, 2008).

Jabara, Abdeen. Interview by the author. New York, NY (June 11, 2016).

Jabara, Abdeen. Interview by the author. New York, NY (December 16, 2017).

Katzenbach, Nicholas deB. Telephone interview by the author (June 15, 2011).

Navasky, Victor. Telephone interview by the author (April 26, 2016).

Navasky, Victor. Interview by the author. New York, NY (June 7, 2016).

Pollak, Stephen. Telephone interview by the author (August 3, 2011).

Rosenthal, Jack. Telephone interview by the author (July 20, 2016).

Schwartz, Bob. Telephone interview by the author (September 8, 2016).

Seigenthaler, John. Telephone interview by the author (July 7, 2011).

Strachman, David. Telephone interview by the author (April 11, 2011).

Temple, Larry. Interview by the author. Austin, TX (March 24, 2011).

Welch, Pia. Telephone interview by the author (September 18, 2017).

Welch, Pia. E-mail message to the author (July 9, 2018).

Wilkins, Roger. Interview by the author. Washington, DC (July 28, 2009).

CASES AND RELATED DOCUMENTS

Andrade v. Chojnacki, 65 F. Supp. 2d 431 (W.D. Tex. 1999).

Boynton v. Virginia, 364 U.S. 454 (1960).

Brown v. Board of Education, 347 U.S. 483 (1954).

Eain v. Wilkes, 641 F. 2d 504 (7th Cir. 1981).

Estate of Ungar v. PLO and Palestinian Authority, C.A. No. 00-105L (D.R.I.).

Gilmore v. Palestinian Authority and PLO, 01-CV-0853GK (D.D.C.).

In re Anastaplo, 366 U.S. 82 (1961).

Klinghoffer v. Achille Lauro, 937 F.2d 44 (2d Cir. 1991).

Linnas v. INS, 790 F.2d 1024 (2d Cir. 1986).

Ntakirutimana v. Reno, 184 F.3d 419 (5th Cir. 1999).

Petition for Writ of Certiorari, Linnas v. INS, No. 86-336, 1986 WL 766707 (U.S. Aug. 29, 1986).

Saltany v. Reagan, 702 F. Supp. 319 (D.D.C. 1988), *aff'd in part, rev'd in part*, 886 F.2d 438 (D.C. Cir. 1989).

Saltany v. Reagan, 886 F. 2d 438 (D.C. Cir. 1989).

Sokolow v. Palestinian Authority and PLO, No. 04-CV-397 (S.D.N.Y.).

United States v. Linnas, 527 F. Supp. 426 (E.D.N.Y. 1981).

United States v. Reimer, 356 F. 3d 456 (2d Cir. 2004).

INDEX

Note: Page numbers in italic type indicate photographs. "RC" refers to Ramsey Clark. "MLK" refers to Martin Luther King, Jr.